e the Learning Resources
Centre

RING OF SEASONS

RING OF SEASONS

Iceland – Its Culture and History

Text and Photos
Terry G. Lacy

Ann Arbor
THE UNIVERSITY OF MICHIGAN PRESS

The characters in this book constituting the "family"
are fictional and not to be identified with any real per-
sons, living or dead.

Cover picture: *Gaia* at Reykjavík (by Terry G. Lacy)

Copyright © by Terry G. Lacy 1998
All rights reserved
Published in the United States of America by
The University of Michigan Press
Manufactured in the United States of America
∞ Printed on acid-free paper

2001   2000   1999   1998   4   3   2   1

A CIP catalog record for this book is available from the British Library.

Library of Congress Cataloging-in Publication Data

Lacy, Terry G.
  Ring of seasons : Iceland, its culture and history / text and
photos, Terry G. Lacy.
    p. cm.
Includes bibliographical references and index.
ISBN: 0-472-10926-X (alk. paper)
  1. Iceland—Civilization. 2. Iceland—Social life and customs.
3. Iceland— I. Title.
DL326.L33 1998
949.12—dc21
                                                                97-48294
                                                                CIP

For Marji...

...then and forever

Acknowledgements

No book of such scope could be written without the help and support of a large number of people. I am indebted to all those who have encouraged me, answered questions and suggested reading material, though their names are too numerous to list. Very special thanks go to those who have had the patience to read through the entire manuscript: Barbara Kathe, Haraldur Ólafsson, Dick Ringler, and Mikael Karlsson. I am deeply grateful to those who have criticized chapters in their special fields, above all Bergsteinn Jónsson, who painstakingly went over the history chapters with a fine–toothed comb, as well as Diana Whaley, Eyþór Einarsson, Gísli Már Gíslason, Gudrún Björk Guðsteinsdóttir, Hallgerður Gísladóttir, Jacob Hautaluoma, Kristín Bjarnadóttir, Terry Gunnell, Laufey Steingrímsdóttir, Páll Einarsson, Páll Bergþórsson, and Þór Whitehead. I have acted on all their criticisms. However, they bear no responsibility for any lingering misconceptions or opinions they may not share. In addition, I would like to thank the staff of the National and University Library of Iceland for their courtesy and assistance, and especially Barbara Nelson, director of Interlibrary Loan.

Very special thanks are due the hundreds of Icelanders I have known, taught, sung with, and worked with, for their welcome and acceptance of me as a part of Icelandic life.

Above all, I want to thank Haraldur Ólafsson and Hólmfridur Gunnarsdóttir and their children for their warm friendship. They are my real foster family in Iceland and, though they nowhere appear in these pages, the times we have spent together and the insight they have helped me gain inform the events recounted in this book.

Reykjavík, 1997

Contents

Contents

List of Illustrations

A Note on the Icelandic Alphabet

There are thirty–two letters in the Icelandic alphabet, most of them the same as in English. However, because of the inclusion of three letters used in Old English but lost to Modern English, Icelandic looks very foreign to English speakers.

Letter	Name	Mod. Eng. equivalent	Transliteration in this book
Ð, ð	eth	*th* as in *thy*	d
Þ, þ	thorn	*th* as in *thigh*	th
Æ, œ	"eye"	*y* as in *sky*	ae

In this book, words and names containing the above three letters—except on maps, when in italics, and in the bibliography and notes—have been respelled as shown. For instance, the god *Þór* becomes Thór, the man's name *Guðmundur* becomes Gudmundur, and the Norse gods or *Æsir* become the Aesir. Note that in this book all names are given in the nominative form and not shortened to the stem or accusative form: Gudmundur rather than Gudmund, Ódinn rather than Odin.

Understanding Icelanders

There have been important reasons for writing this book. When I first visited Iceland as a tourist the starkly beautiful landscape and the evident hospitality of the people drew me like a magnet. I wanted to find out more about the Icelandic people and their culture. Then there were all the comments that had no meaning until I learned more. Who was Jón Sigurdsson? was Aegir man or beast? and who or what are the Hidden People? This book has been written to answer these and other questions by presenting a picture of Icelanders at home, showing something of how they think and act and what is important to them.

Despite my training in sociology and anthropology and the fact that I had already lived in more than one country, in the beginning adjusting to Icelandic culture was a bit like passing through Alice's looking glass. Teaching Icelanders was definitely not the same as teaching Americans. I found I had a roomful of jack–in–the–boxes who, at university level, still had something of the exuberance of nine–year–olds but who, unlike American students, were extraordinarily shy about volunteering an opinion. Nor, I might add, did Icelanders always know what to think of me. I set about learning about the country and in time the hundreds of Icelanders I have drunk coffee with, taught, sung and played music with and worked for have given me a deep understanding of what it means to be an Icelander.

I soon came to realize that genealogy and language are the two factors, more than any others, that have defined Icelandic ethnicity and nationhood from the earliest years of the settlement. Partly because of the small size of the population, the relative isolation of the farms, and the difficulty during some periods of merely surviving, the family was and remains the focal point of social organization. Brothers and sisters and their children typically celebrate holidays and birthdays together, keeping family ties alive. The emphasis on genealogy defines the interrelationships, and the literary inheritance and the continuing deep interest in the language forge common and continuing bonds, defining and maintaining the distinction between Icelanders and all others. The emphasis on upholding family ties is so great that relatives who live in other countries, however distantly related, are enthusiastically welcomed when they visit. In short, there is no understanding modern Icelanders without an understanding of the family, as well as the importance of the language. After a presentation of background information on Iceland and the Icelandic character, including the natural history that has often forged the outcome of events over the centuries, this book is therefore organized around the life of a typical family through the year as they gather together to celebrate holidays and the family's special events.

In order to provide the reader with necessary information on the cultural background, two other threads parallel the course of the family through the year: Norse myths and the history of Iceland. The conversion to Christianity in the year 1000 did not completely eradicate all aspects of the old Norse religion; the myths and, for many, a fatalistic acceptance of events and belief in the lesser spirits remain. As the myths continue to be very much a part of the common cultural heritage, they are sketched here in broad outline. Clearly, also, an acquaintance with Icelandic history is necessary in order not only to understand references but also to appreciate the magnitude of the Icelandic economic achievement. Therefore, as the family moves through the year from spring beginnings to the New Year's eve celebration, the book presents Norse mythology from the creation myth to Ragnarok and the history of Iceland from the settlement to the present day, tracing the foundation and collapse of the Commonwealth, the effects of the harsher climate that ensued, the survival of natural disasters and foreign domination that occurred before the country gained independence in the twentieth century and attained a standard of living on a par with other western nations.

This is a book for anyone who is curious about Iceland, the armchair traveller or the person who has actually walked over the landscape. The book is organized either for browsing or more serious reading. Each of the three parallel threads of family, history and myths can be followed separately, or any chapter can be read for itself. Taken together, the book presents a very informative view of Icelandic culture.

All the Icelanders I have talked to have wanted me to write this book; as they have said, "You can say it so that other people will understand." Most have added, "You're an Icelander now but you see the other side, too." Here in this book, then, Icelanders can speak to you as they have spoken to me, both through the yearly round of activities that Icelanders thrive on and the heritage that they all share—the history, attitudes and ideas that constitute the basis of Icelandic culture and achievements.

The tourist who visits a place once has a static picture of what he or she has seen. Yet the key factor for those who live in Iceland is the constant change. The equipment we use, the clothes we wear, the country's relations with the rest of the world are all in flux, and therefore the very root, the Icelandic language itself, must also change and accommodate to these new inputs. "I feel like I am watching history," a Norwegian friend commented, referring to all the changes that have unfolded in Iceland since the early 1970s. My own adjustments here are an example of this change. Though I have taught both social psychology and anthropology at the University of Iceland, the increasing emphasis on English as the medium for relating to the rest of the world led me to build on the experience I already had in teaching technical journalism at an American university. I have been an instructor in English ever since, principally at the University of Iceland, as well as author and translator.

In this book I have dealt less with the things that change most rapidly, such as economic statistics, because they are so quickly outdated, and have emphasized what is relatively enduring and what continues to characterize Icelanders and life in Iceland.

Iceland and Icelanders

What Is an Icelander?

The first time I flew over Iceland the cloud cover stretched beneath the plane in a solid gray floor east from Greenland, with no glimpse of the sea. Then suddenly the clouds broke and Iceland lay under the wing, green and black and ringed with blue–gray sea. Since then I have seen Iceland from the air many times, usually partly covered by cloud. The most notable time, however, was once when I was returning from the continent of Europe and the whole land was white with snow; the only gray, seemingly stormy area was a patch in the far north that was actually a volcanic eruption in process.

Those who visit Iceland today enjoy the hospitality of a small nation with a high standard of living, replete with all the computers, cars and gadgets that characterize modern living. Furthermore, most of the rise in the standard of living to equality with the other western countries occurred after Iceland gained full independence in 1944. What are the people like who have accomplished this economic success story?

To a great extent modern Icelanders are not unlike their ancestors. Icelanders have been known for their hospitality, for example, from the time of the settlement, as the great English scientist Sir Joseph Banks discovered on his visit in 1772. He found the people clean and tidy, courteous and hospitable, shorter than the English of the day, honest, curious but not overly bright, and rather cold.[1] The men, he said, were polite to the women but the women did the hard work like processing the fish. Sir Henry Holland, in 1812, wrote that morally and intellectually Icelanders were the equals of the most civilized of Europeans.[2] And in 1856, Lord Dufferin, who later, as governor general of Canada, saw to it that the Icelandic immigrants were given land, found the same "frank energetic cordiality" that is common today and quickly came to realize that hospitality, then as now, entailed consuming "several cups of coffee."[3]

Today Icelanders are still clean and tidy and hospitable and the women still process the fish but, with improved living conditions, the people are no longer shorter than the English.

Individualism, Equality, and the Importance of Personal Contact

Icelandic society is characterized by a strong emphasis on individualism, even rampant individualism, though the high valuation on individual freedom is paired with a belief in equality.[4] In a 1990 Gallup poll, 51% rated equality and 45% individual freedom as their top values, with those on the political left emphasizing the importance of equality and those on the right freedom.[5] Both values have a long history in Iceland, dating to the time of the settlement, when people had to be self–reliant but also had to stand together to make survival possible. Individual freedom and equality have therefore been practical values to uphold. Of the 23 countries surveyed in the Gallup polls, more Icelanders than others felt they had freedom on the job and freedom generally.

Icelandic individualism and equality are expressed in different ways. For instance, Icelanders are far less prone to play roles than are other Europeans and westerners in general. Whomever you talk to—clerk, repairman, physician, tour guide—you are talking to an individual, a "full person," and not just to someone performing a job. From an economic standpoint there are, of course, class differences, but those differences are small compared to those in most other countries and the fact of being an Icelander transcends class differences. The president of Iceland is respected as such, but every Icelander is basically his or her equal. Those hired in businesses perform their jobs, but there is still a feeling of personality and less emphasis on deference to the executives than is common elsewhere. The students in my university classroom, for instance, are not students so much as full personalities, each with his own genealogy. Like young children, they express their personalities and their thoughts of the moment, if they aren't too reserved to speak up. They never wholly play the role of student as it is understood in many other countries. By the same token, as their instructor I am a source of information, but, like them, an individual with my own personality—though as a foreigner, they discount my genealogy. Teaching them is a rewarding experience, though sometimes quite a challenge, like teaching a roomful of jack–in–the–boxes.

Icelanders do not want their freedom curtailed, neither theirs personally nor the nation's. There can be no understanding of either official policy or public support of an issue without understanding that fact. Discussions and decisions about major topics such as the NATO base, fishing limits, whether to hunt whales, and whether to join the EC revolve around maintaining freedom.

Maintaining individuality also means taking responsibility. Icelanders will take orders on the job but they want to know that the orders make sense. In the 1984 Gallup poll 76% felt it was important to see the results of one's work.[6] They also want to know how their work fits into the total job to be done; foreign engineers working at Krafla in the north have been impressed that Icelanders wanted to know "how it works" and not just "what do I do?"

Individualism and freedom of choice apply to religion as well: Icelanders have faith but each chooses what that faith shall be. In the 1984 survey, 78% of Icelanders professed belief in God, but only about 1% attend church weekly, though Christmas and Easter services are usually packed. The God that Icelanders typically believe in is not a "personal God" but rather "a kind of universal spirit or life force." Seventy–four percent of Icelanders say they derive comfort and strength from religious beliefs (of the 23 countries surveyed, only Ireland had a higher percentage).[7] Often spiritual healing and the actions of ghosts and the Hidden People are part of the belief system. Though the 64% of Icelanders who have had a supernatural experience[8] is comparable to the percentage in other countries, the difference in Iceland is that these beliefs and presences are open, often talked about, and only sometimes doubted.

Of course all these individualists are going to hold varying opinions about politics as well. Usually a wry joke puts the political scene into perspective. One variant on the exercise of free speech was provided by the meteorologist giving the weather report on state television one day in November 1992: "I want to say that for myself I don't really believe the prediction for Monday and Tuesday."

Coalition governments have provided a way of establishing a working political relationship among all the blatant individuals and differing opinions. What surprises foreign diplomats is that the cabinet ministers, including those from the same political party, not only do not agree with each other privately but freely air their differences through the mass media. Winter is always spiced with cabinet minister disagreements.

From the earliest times the values of self–reliance and individualism were coupled with an emphasis on working together. Icelanders express a high level of caring and invest a great deal of energy in helping others. In the 1984 Gallup poll 21% said they belong to a charitable institution (the comparable figures for Denmark and Norway were 5% and 13%, respectively). These associations include rescue groups, Scouts, the Cancer Society, and other medical support and youth groups. In a small country the contribution from each person is important and family and friendship ties are strong. Icelanders are quick to give emotional support in the case of a death or sickness or other difficulty. In the same Gallup poll 41% of Icelanders said it was worth risking one's own life to save another's; this was the highest response level of all the countries tested.

The emphasis on personal contact is as much a part of Icelandic life as is individualism. At work the personal is accentuated: in the 1984 Gallup poll 78% said they felt comfortable working relationships mattered a great deal. Importantly, Icelanders want face–to–face contact or to telephone, rather than to write. A visiting American professor was impressed with how meaningful personal contact with Icelanders can be, even leading rather quickly to lifelong friendships. In talking, Icelanders really look at the other person and maintain eye contact. In class Icelandic students have a long attention span and most of the time look directly at the teacher. This trait has been remarked as well by opera coaches who have come from New York to help with a performance. In a television news interview Icelanders face the questioner rather than the camera.

The small size of the country of course facilitates knowing a significant proportion of the population. The former American ambassador Charles Cobb commented that it gave him the opportunity to form personal ties with the nation's leaders.[9] He also remarked on the personal basis of politics and the speed with which decisions could be carried out, even overnight. Though Iceland has bureaucracies, both government offices and various firms, there are never more than a few levels of command and decisions can be carried out quickly.

Work, Happiness, and Relaxation

Icelanders are well taught from an early age to work hard. They are also taught to be self–reliant and to try to take care of a problem themselves before turning to others for help.

It is impossible to be in Iceland for long without hearing about being *duglegur* (working hard) a characteristic that is stressed for children and expected in adults. Young people usually work in the summer, as they had to in the old days when almost everyone was on the farm. The person who misses work because of sickness often explains "I had a *fever*," stressing the word *fever* to justify the absence. On the other hand, alcoholism sometimes excuses a person from working hard.

The emphasis on working hard is coupled with a strong desire for progress.[10] Though progress includes materialistic gain, this has been a realistic goal, given the relatively low level of the standard of living in Iceland in the early twentieth century. Icelanders want only quality equipment and the latest fashions in clothes. On the other hand, Icelanders themselves have criticized the fact that, along with their feelings of warmth for others and solidarity with the nation, they are so often envious of those who have acquired more.[11]

Iceland has a very high standard of living but emphasis on materialism continues. For one thing, Icelanders simply like gadgets. They also like to be amused. As soon as computers became available with Icelandic keyboards, Icelanders rushed to acquire them. At one point Icelanders owned more VCRs per capita than anybody else. In 1990 they owned more copies of the game Trivial Pursuit than any other country.[12] The use of computers and VCRs is lasting, but the latest gadget becomes everyone's Christmas present and then quickly goes out of fashion. One year it was soda streams, the gismo that puts fizz in your drink. Another year it was whirlpool footbaths. The year after the footbath craze a notice appeared in the newspaper: a family was looking to buy a secondhand one. The ad was meant to be a joke but the people who ran it were deluged with phone calls for several days!

Icelanders are eager to return to work after a vacation. In fact, only 10% answering the 1984 Gallup poll said they felt it was important to have a lot of vacation time. To make ends meet Icelanders work long hours, in 1991 five to ten hours more per week than the usual in other western countries, but they accept the long hours as a means toward what counts: family life, hobbies and increased ownership of consumer goods.[13] Overtime plus second jobs not necessarily reported to the tax authorities have raised the level of income. In the 1984 survey 93% of Icelanders said an increased emphasis on family life would be good, and 64% said they would spend more time with family and friends if the workweek were shortened.

In the Gallup polls of 1984 and 1990 Iceland emerged as the happiest nation in the world. Icelanders were happy with life in general though, realistically, they were nowhere near as satisfied with their financial standing. The long workweek and difficulties in maintaining the buying power of the krona have affected nearly everyone. Happiness, according to the 1984 survey, is being married (rated 1.48 on a scale of 1–10, where 1 equals very happy). Living together was rated almost as highly as being married.

How is this state of happiness achieved? The roots go back to the time of the settlement, when Icelanders were characterized by a certain tenacity and a fatalistic acceptance and belief that everything would work out. *Það reddast* (it will work out) is a common comment and, in fact, things usually do. This is an attitude that applies equally to the farmer who is faced with no hay crop whatsoever because of the weather ("this farm has always made out") and a chorus when it has not really practiced enough for a concert. The farmer does find a way, and the chorus pulls itself together and sings beautifully.

Icelanders believe in staying positive and cheerful and maintaining at least an outward calmness. The person who is always in a good mood is admired. Icelanders tend to find a bright side to a problem. In the face of a difficulty they typically instantly point out a positive point: *lán í óláni*, "good luck in the midst of bad." Emotions tend to be held in. Though there is a great deal of discussion about the depressing effect of the winter darkness, research shows that, in fact, Icelanders suffer less depression in the dark than do other peoples, evidently the result of genetic selection to cope with Icelandic winters.[14] Faces reflect a quiet, fatalistic acceptance of good and bad. This attitude helps to make Icelanders unusually competent in handling an emergency without panicking. During the 1973 eruption of the volcano in the Westman Islands, for instance, every one of the more than 5000 inhabitants was evacuated to the mainland without a single casualty.

One way that Icelanders cope with the pressures of work is to have a relaxed sense of time. Foreigners often have some trouble in adjusting to this sense of time and may feel that Icelanders are not hardworking at all. There are no clocks on classroom walls, for instance. Because of the unpredictability of the weather, the personal approach to getting things done, and the small number of people involved, decisions are often made and carried out with a short time lag. Typically a concert or play is advertised only a few days before the performance. Promptness has its own definition. On the state television the evening news begins promptly at 8:00, but the programs that follow usually begin later than scheduled because something intervened ("Sorry, pause" flashes on the screen) or more TV advertising time was sold than expected or the people interviewed were simply allowed to talk longer. Even children's bedtimes can be very variable. Promptness, in other words, really means "comfortably prompt."

Hard work is tempered by having a wonderful time at a party. The winter months, especially, are full of parties, the theatre, operas, annual banquets. Despite the lack of any tradition of opera in Iceland, an average of 10,000 people went to see each of the Icelandic Opera Company's productions from 1979–1992, a truly impressive attendance for a country of not many more than a quarter of a million inhabitants. One custom, especially on Sundays, is to go to one of the numerous art shows and stop for refreshment in the gallery coffee shop.

At a party, Icelanders put themselves wholeheartedly into a party mode. A visiting professor was impressed with the high level of energy and amount of conversation at these parties. Icelanders relax, forget cares, and typically stay well into the wee hours. A person can always sleep some other time.

Often one drink calls for another and an opened bottle demands to be finished. I had some students over one night and watched as they carefully nursed half a fifth. Then, sure enough, as they began to say things about leaving, they downed the other half in record time. Though there are many Icelanders who never touch a drop and many more who drink moderately, for others a Saturday night party is like a seaman returned to shore: drink and enjoy it!

The negative side of drinking, of course, is alcoholism. Thirty–two percent replied in the 1984 survey that alcohol had at some time caused family problems. There is medical and group support for those who cannot control their drinking, and interestingly a considerable number of Icelanders go to Freeport, Long Island in the States to dry out and redirect their lives. On the other hand, 16% never drink at all. The important point is that Icelanders "seldom drink but usually a great deal at each time."[15] Despite police vigilance, accidents are frequently caused by drunk drivers.

Growing up Icelandic

In Iceland boys and girls are raised in virtually the same way. The strong differences in upbringing found in so many other countries don't exist in Iceland. Perhaps that's why Iceland has so many strong, capable, warm women.

Icelanders are also typically patient with children, realizing that the child will grow up if helped and given a chance. The Icelandic child is virtually never corrected in front of anyone other than the immediate family and is almost never spanked. This attitude has old roots; at the time of the Commonwealth children were cherished and never strongly disciplined.[16] Of course there are "no's" to save the two year old from disaster, and "come along now" so the child isn't left behind, but independence is encouraged. I've seen more than one young child decide its own bedtime, for instance. Like their parents, Icelandic children go to bed later than is usual in other western countries; the average bedtime for eleven year olds, for instance, is about 11:30 p.m.[17]

Much has been said and written about promiscuity in Iceland, but the results of the Gallup polls do not support any such conclusion. Though the first birth usually occurs out of wedlock, often the parents are living together and later marry. In the 1990 survey, 94% replied that marriage is not an outmoded institution, though 84% felt it was perfectly all right to be a single mother. Seventy–eight percent felt both parents should be in the home for the child's sake, and 80% recognized that the bonds between a child and its working mother are just as warm and strong as those between a child and a mother who stays home.

For the child to be encouraged to learn independence when a member of the family is nearby is one thing, but the latter part of the twentieth century saw a less promising development. With both parents working in order to cope with the rising cost of living, and the father, especially, gone most of the time, many children, even young ones, are not supervised for much of the day. Grandmothers and nursery schools take care of a great many children, but not all. The results are that the rate of children's accidents requiring medical attention has been the highest in Europe, and self–discipline, in the old days learned automatically on the farm, is all too often lacking.

Though discipline may be lacking, most Icelandic children have learned to be practical, realistic, and independent, and to work with others. Most have earned money at a fairly young age. Other teachers have also remarked on what I have seen: Icelandic school students are more mature than their age mates in many other countries.

Meeting People and Relations with the Outside World

Icelanders' greatest interest is in Iceland. The results of the 1990 Gallup poll showed that Icelanders are much prouder of their country than are other Europeans. They will gladly tell you what Icelanders do and are, but typically have less interest in learning about other countries. Proud of having survived the exigencies of weather and history, they like to define themselves as different. The mass media often gloat over any international achievement by an Icelander: an author, a chess champion, a beauty queen, a handball or soccer team.

In addition to individual differences, the level or point where people either open up and are friendly or close down and seem cold varies with the culture. I've known Americans to complain that Icelanders walking by on the street don't smile. If you are no part of their lives, Icelanders will more or less ignore you. A visiting German actor who dressed up like the devil and walked the streets of Reykjavík to promote his one–man show said in an interview that Icelanders showed the least response of any people he had been among.

"Coldness" may have another basis as well. An Icelandic fortune teller, on returning from Europe, has commented that it's harder to tell Icelanders' fortunes as facial expressions and body movements give less away. Jazz players have said Icelanders don't loosen up as much at a jazz concert—though I am sure Icelanders feel they are letting go. Nor do they laugh out loud as readily when listening to a talk, even though they find a comment funny. There is almost no gesturing. On the other hand, they are attuned to catching small changes in facial expression. And if there becomes a real reason to know you, especially if you seem to be accepting of the Icelandic way of doing things, then the door to their homes is open and warmth flows forth.

Decisions are practical, tied to a specific case or event. In the 1984 survey 85% opted for situational ethics, choosing right and wrong based on the attendant circumstances.[18] Though situational ethics can be satisfying and productive, the scenarios can be theoretical as well as actual. Icelandic students typically deal with the actual but founder on the theoretical. The typical Icelandic university student is bright, often superior, partly because he or she has internalized well the habit of working and thinking for him– or herself, but university teaching can sometimes be difficult because of the Icelandic "tendency to favor empiricism or the analysis of the immediate appearance of things rather than abstraction and the discovery of hidden structures."[19]

On the other hand, reacting to the immediate has a positive side. Icelanders are opportunistic. They organized the Reagan–Gorbachev summit meeting in 1986 with only 10 days advance notice. Foreign officials with the 1995 World Handball Championship, involving 24 teams, commented afterwards that the event had been the best organized up to that time, a surprising feat for such a small country.

To a large extent it is the use of "negative pressure" that encourages people everywhere to conform to a society and to fit in. In the days of the Icelandic Commonwealth the driving force, at least for the elite, was to maintain *drengskapur* (honor); the loss of honor meant being shamed. Though modern Icelanders of course often suffer from pangs of guilt, an Icelandic psychiatrist has agreed with me that the greater driving "negative" force in modern Icelandic life is still shame rather than guilt.[20]

The fear of being shamed by making a mistake, coupled with practicality and Icelandic reserve, may mean that Icelanders will not respond as fast as foreigners expect in discussing a controversial subject or in asking a politician or speaker questions. With further acquaintance, the reserve disappears to be replaced by warmth and acceptance. Icelanders often display a fine tolerance of others, having, for example, greatly respected the Austrian Jew they appointed as head of Lutheran church music after World War II.

The flip side of pride in being an independent nation is the need, because of the small population, to prove equality with the rest of the world. The we–have–it–too syndrome sometimes leads Icelanders down rather ridiculous paths; I've actually been told with some pride, "We have lots of junk mail, too"! Some visiting foreigners have discovered a we–already–know–it–all approach, but on further acquaintance such reactions generally disappear from a conversation.

The late twentieth century has seen increasing contacts with the rest of the world and a greatly increased desire to make Iceland known to other peoples. The majority of Icelanders have lived, studied or travelled abroad and a growing swarm of tourists enjoy Icelandic hospitality. With increased contacts naiveté is giving way to a greater cosmopolitanism than before.

What does all this add up to? The "legalistically minded, non–violent, egalitarian, cooperative [and] individualistic" traits of the nineteenth century Icelander still apply.[21] Icelanders remain warm, hardworking, cooperative, and surprisingly artistic and musical. They are also individualists who nevertheless strive to look alike. The row houses are all painted the same color and Icelanders are slaves to the latest fashion: when black leather jackets were in they became de rigueur for virtually everyone, our uniform of the time. Some have even asked, when donating clothes to the Red Cross for the destitute in Africa: "Is it all right? I mean, they're out of fashion."

Icelanders are few in number but amazingly productive. Not surprisingly, family ties are important in jobs and politics as well as for emotional support. And Icelanders are eager to keep up with the times, wanting the new and not the old, overnight inveterate users of the information highway.

They are a nation that will tell you that the language is difficult and their country isolated, yet learning Icelandic is no harder for outsiders than their learning English, and ships, planes, and tourists arrive daily, hardly evidence of isolation. As with people everywhere, it's just difficult not to keep repeating old beliefs.

Above all else, Icelanders remain rampant individualists.

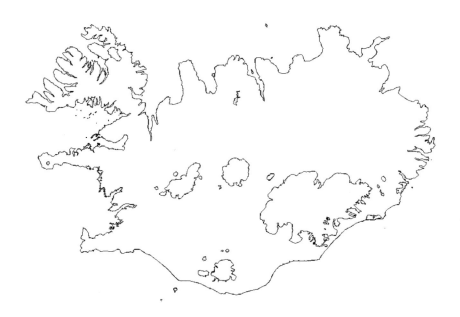

The Formation of the Land

At 2:00 a.m. on the night of January 23, 1973, a two–kilometer long fissure began to open on the island of Heimaey in the Westman Islands. First gas, and then cinders and lava erupted from the earth. Phone calls alerted relatives and rescue groups on the mainland, though one man, when called, actually thought it was a joke and hung up! Just how serious the situation was, however, soon became evident.[1]

Fortunately the night was calm and the people began to board the hundred fishing boats in the harbor in order to flee their homes. There were fear and uncertainty about the future; would there be anything left of their town to come back to? But the people remained outwardly calm and by the end of the morning, with no accidents or casualties, all had been transported to the mainland by ship or plane. Of the total population of 5237, only those necessary for rescue work remained on the island. The islanders found shelter on the mainland with friends and relatives, many eventually going to live in pre-fabricated houses imported from abroad. All the cars and sheep and a great deal of furniture and other belongings were ferried to the mainland.

In the days that followed, as the eruption continued and the world watched on television, the column of volcanic ejecta, gas, and steam towered into the air and a new volcanic cone was built, Eldfell or Fire Mountain. Cinders rained down onto the town, burying some houses and collapsing others.

The lava dwarfed the buildings it overrode, glowing red with blocks of black, cooler lava carried along on the current. Its seemingly inexorable path threatened to close off the harbor, which was vital to the islanders' fishing economy. Following directions by the Icelandic geologist Thorbjörn Sigurgeirsson, seawater was pumped onto the hot lava to retard the flow. The attack was effective: one kilogram (2.2 lbs.) of seawater cooled 1.7 kg (3.7 lbs.) of lava from 1100^0C. down to 100^0C (the boiling point of water). With constant pumping, the chilled layer on the surface of the lava thickened and forward movement slowed.

On July 3 the eruption came to an end. Four hundred buildings or 40% of the town had been destroyed, but the town had acquired a source of geothermal heat and the harbor was actually far better sheltered from ocean waves than before.[2] However, the eruption had inevitably changed the inhabitants' lives. Though many returned, others did not, and new inhabitants came to the island to live. The former tighter, more isolated community became more open, with more frequent travel to and from the mainland. In 1993, twenty years after the eruption, there were fewer inhabitants but more houses and a second primary school, though there had been a drop in the number of younger people and a rise in the number of people aged 30–60.[3]

Birth in Fire

At the beginning of the Tertiary period about 100 million years ago, the Laurasian landmass in the northern hemisphere began to split apart; this was the beginning of the present Mid–Atlantic Ridge and the separation of North America from Europe. A hot spot formed at a point along the north–south axis which, coupled with the spreading action along the rift, eventually gave birth to the island of Iceland.[4]

Though geologists are not in complete agreement as to the nature of hot spots, they are basically large areas of hot rock beneath the Earth's crust with a cap that may be 2000 km in diameter and which may thicken the crust as well as providing the source of surface lava and ejecta.[5] To this day Iceland remains centered over the intersection of the hot spot with the rifting Mid–Atlantic Ridge. This rift or active volcanic zone runs through Iceland from south to north in an area that is roughly the shape of an upside–down Y. Although Iceland is splitting apart in this zone the void is continuously filled by molten rock from below.[6]

The constant rifting has pushed the older rocks outward to the east and west. The oldest rocks are the Tertiary flood basalts. In some areas these Tertiary beds include lignite, a low–grade coal that formed from the alder and birch and other plant growth that flourished in the relatively warm and humid climate of the time.[7] During the Ice Age, starting about 3 million years ago, volcanism produced hyaloclastites (volcanic tuff or *móberg*) that now lie as belts on either side of the active volcanic zone. After the end of the Ice Age about 10,000 years ago, volcanism again produced lava flows, originating from about 30 active volcanic systems.[8]

Iceland, then, is built up of volcanoes and lava flows, interspersed with a few layers of sedimentary rock. Though much of the south coast is composed of extensive black sand beaches, the south also has the highest mountains, with a peak elevation of 2119 m (6950 ft.). Eleven percent of the land is covered by postglacial lava, and an equal percentage is still glaciated.[9]

Various types of volcanic forms can be found in Iceland, including crater rows that can be up to 100 km (62 mi.) long.[10] However, many volcanoes erupt from a central vent and may produce either lava (which flows like a river) or gas and tephra (pyroclastic ejecta, including ash, cinders and volcanic bombs), or both. Snaefellsjökull, visible from Reykjavík in clear weather, is a beautiful example of a stratovolcano built up of mixed tephra and lava flows. Skjaldbreidur, which can be seen well from Thingvellir, is a shield volcano built up symmetrically by fluid lava flows. The small Kerid in the south is a collapsed crater with a lake in the bottom. Iceland's deepest lake, however, is found in Askja, a caldera or collapsed volcano in the north. Boreholes in the Krafla caldera in the north have produced geothermal water for the generation of electricity. Mt. Hverfjall by Lake Mývatn is an impressive explosion crater, a large tephra ring that formed in a single eruption.

Some lava will solidify on the outside while the molten center continues to flow, leaving behind tubes or caves; the largest lava cavern in the world is in the Bláfjöll Mountains near Reykjavík, over 150,000 m³ in volume. In cooling, basalt often forms hexagonal columns that can be seen at many places in

Iceland; the exterior trim of the tower of Hallgríms Church in Reykjavík is based on the shape of columnar basalt.

The tephra or solid airborne fragments spewed forth in an eruption range in size from dust to large blocks of lava. Tephra deposits are generally more destructive than lava flows as wind can deposit the finer particles over a huge area, even spanning continents. The largest tephra fall in Iceland in historic times was produced in the Öraefajökull eruption of 1362 and laid waste a large part of the south.[11]

Volcanism can result in other geographic features as well. Carbonated springs (*ölkeldur*), such as the one on Snaefells Peninsula, produce naturally carbonated water. Sometimes craters are produced not by an eruption but by lava flowing over wet ground; the resulting steam causes explosions that produce a swarm of small pseudocraters, as at Skútustadir by Lake Mývatn.

Earthquakes and Rifting

Iceland sits on both the North American and Eurasian plates. As these plates are pushed apart, tension builds until the rock breaks under the strain and the plates diverge at an average of about 2 cm or not quite one inch per year. The two main seismic zones are the belt of land between the two parts of the active volcanic zone in the south and a much larger area along the north coast.

Most earth tremors are so mild that it takes a seismograph to register them, though some are strong enough to destroy buildings. Earth tremors can also alter the activity in geothermal areas, causing geysers to start or stop erupting.

The minister at Thingvellir recorded that on June 10, 1789, earthquakes woke the people and continued for ten days without even an hour's respite. Farm buildings were largely destroyed and, even more importantly, the land dropped so that Lake Thingvallavatn flooded part of the land where the parliament had traditionally met.[12]

The two worst earthquake periods were in 1784 and 1896, estimated at having reached magnitude 7.0 on the Richter scale.[13] The quake in 1896 threw people to the ground and flattened the buildings on 161 farms.

Eruptions in Historical Times

Icelanders have managed to survive, living on a powder keg that erupts at unpredictable times. Since the time of the settlement 1040 km^2 (ca. 400 sq. mi.) or 1% of the land has been covered by lava flows. Far worse is the damage from tephra falls. Farms have not generally been abandoned if the tephra has been less than 8–10 cm (ca. 3 in.) thick. A 15–25 cm layer (6–10 in.) means farm abandonment for 1–5 years, and a 20–40 cm layer (up to 16 in.) means the land has been unusable for a decade or longer.[14]

In earlier times Hekla was thought to be literally the Gate to Hell. The damage caused by the 1104 eruption was so extensive that the Thjórsá River valley was not resettled for eight and a half centuries.[15]

The worst was the Laki eruption (or Skaftá Fires) of 1783–1785.[16] An esti-

15

After eruption, Westman Islands, 1974

mated 14.7 km³ (3.5 cu. mi.) of lava poured from the Laki crater row for eight months, the largest lava flow on earth in historical times. The eruptive column reached as high as 15 km (9 1/2 mi.) and could be seen all over Iceland. The air was polluted with a haze composed of gases and aerosols that persisted into 1786 and was responsible for the fluorine that killed up to 70% and more of the livestock and lowered temperatures in the northern hemisphere by as much as 1°–2° C (3.5° F). Though water and food were not dangerously contaminated, the severe winters coupled with smallpox and other diseases resulted in the death of 22% of the population. Carried by wind currents, the haze reached Europe, Asia, and north Africa, and even North America. In Venice, Italy, the fallout was so rich in iron particles that it could be collected with a magnet.

The Askja eruption of 1875, in the northeast, was the third largest tephra eruption in historical times. Carried by the wind, the tephra covered an area of 10,000 km² in Iceland and a total area of 650,000 km² (250,000 sq. mi.). The hardships that ensued drove many farmers from the northeast, especially, to emigrate to North America.[17]

Recent eruptions have become media events, including the eruption in 1963–1967 that created the new island of Surtsey off the south coast. Though shielded to some extent by lava and hyaloclastite rock, the island is subject to erosion by the sea.[18] More recently a series of earthquakes and eruptions from 1975–1984 took place in the Lake Mývatn area; though there were spectacular lava fountains, much of the magma emptied out of the magma chamber laterally below the surface.[19] In 1977, glowing lava actually spurted from a steam well which had been drilled to produce power for the nearby diatomite plant.[20]

Glaciation

Ice cores drilled from the Greenland ice cap have shown that the climate during the Ice Age oscillated between rather mild and considerably colder periods.[21] In Iceland, there were multiple stages of glaciation separated by warmer periods. Almost the entire country was covered by ice at some point during the cold spells from 120,000 years ago until the end of the Ice Age about 10,000 years ago, with the exception of a few ice–free peaks and some northern and western areas.[22] With so much water locked into glacial ice, by the end of glaciation, sea level, in Iceland and worldwide, was considerably lower than today. Glaciation was greatest in the south of Iceland, where, as today, both the elevation of the land and the precipitation rate were higher. The ice cap ranged from 500 m to as much as 1500 m (330 ft.–500 ft.) in thickness and reached as far as some of the islands off the present coast.[23]

Meanwhile, the effect of the underlying hot spot and the rifting continued. The table mountains, such as Herdubreid, were formed under the ice in the late Pleistocene. They have pillow lavas on their steep lower sides and, where they were high enough to break through the ice, gently sloping lava flows on the top. With the melting of the glaciers, sea level rose, but fell again when the land rebounded as the weight of the glaciers was removed.

After the Ice Age the plants that had survived spread and other flora and fauna were added, brought by sea, wind, and birds. From about 9000 to 7000 years ago, during the Early Birch Period, the climate was warm and dry, with birch forests growing widely over the lowlands.[24] In the ensuing Early Bog Period the climate turned wetter and sphagnum moss grew widely. The Late Birch Period followed, when the climate again became warmer and dryer, vegetation covered about three–fourths of the land, and glaciers had disappeared from all but the highest mountains.

Another major climate change occurred about 2500 years ago, ushering in the Late Bog Period. The climate was again colder and wetter and the Vatnajökull ice cap formed. This is the period, with its cyclical variations in climate, in which we still live.

In historical times, glacier expanse and thickness changed with climate changes. In colder periods the interior was less accessible; some glacier tongues advanced in the first part of the eighteenth century, for example, destroying several farms.[25] In the twentieth century most glaciers have retreated, but the glaciers that remain are still impressive. The Vatnajökull ice cap covers an area of 8400 km² (3240 sq. mi.) and is up to 900 meters (3000 ft.) in thickness.

Glacier bursts occur when subterranean heat or a volcanic eruption melts the ice or when a lagoon breaks through an ice blockade. The ensuing floods can be catastrophic. Glacial bursts and more gradual glacial melting have produced extensive outwash plains along the southern coast. Glacier tongues also sometimes surge forward at incredible speeds when normal water channels under the glacier collapse under the weight of the ice and the water, instead of escaping, "greases" the bottom. In 1994, for example, the huge mass of Sídujökull in the south surged for several months. The ice was 500 m thick, 50 km long and 10 km wide (1640 ft. x 164 ft. x 33 ft.), covering an area of 350 km² (135 sq. mi.), yet surged forward as rapidly as 100 meters (330 ft.) in 24 hours. As the glacier tongue progressed the ice broke, forming huge crevasses, each large enough to contain a multi–story office building.[26] The glacier burst that followed the eruption under the Vatnajökull Glacier in 1996 produced a maximum flow of 45,000 m³ per second (over 1.5 million cu. ft.).

Erosion

Despite the fact that volcanism continually adds to the area of Iceland the land is easy prey to the forces of erosion. Glaciers, wind, water and ocean waves take their toll. Glaciers scour the stream–cut V–shaped valleys into broad U–shaped ones. Iceland's fjords are glacier–scoured valleys filled by the sea. The strong winds in Iceland often denude large areas and make it harder for plants to regain a foothold after overgrazing or being buried under volcanic ash and cinders.

The volcanoes themselves are subject to erosion. The sea usually reduces the volcanic islands to stacks and skerries and continues to erode them until they may disappear beneath the waves. Kolbeinsey in the north, which has helped define Iceland's 200 mile fishing limit, has almost disappeared into the sea.

The rate of erosion was clearly intensified after the settlement and the advent of grazing mammals and cutting down of the forests. From the point of view of loss of life, however, avalanches are even more destructive. The worst was in Seydisfjördur in 1885 when 24 were killed and many injured. In 1995 the avalanche at Súdavík destroyed a third of the town and killed 14, and the same year another avalanche at Flateyri killed 20 individuals.[27]

Research and Utilization of Resources

The shallow seas around Iceland have given the country one of the world's richest fishing banks. The shallowness of the seas and the fact that so much of the active volcanic and rifting zone is exposed on the surface have also facilitated geophysical and volcanological research. This research has taken different directions, including the use of the new island of Surtsey as a carefully protected laboratory to study colonization by plants and animals.

Though Iceland is not rich in minerals, there are a few of economic importance. In earlier times bog iron supplied much of the domestic need.[28] Later, the thin layers of sulphur crusted on the surface in geothermal areas, as at Námafjall (Mine Mountain) near Lake Mývatn in the north, were dug and exported for use in making gunpowder. Large crystals of Iceland spar, a variety of calcite, were exported up until World War I, and are still valuable. More importantly today, Iceland has ample sand and gravel for road and building construction, and man-

Strokkur

ufactures sufficient cement, using shells for limestone. The diatomaceous earth excavated from the bottom of a part of Lake Mývatn is exported for industrial use as fine filters; however, the dredging has caused considerable controversy because of its effect on the biology of the lake. A processing plant for obtaining sea salt and magnesium from the geothermal brine that has penetrated the lava is in operation on the Reykjanes Peninsula. Rock wool is manufactured from volcanic sinter.

Iceland's abundant supply of clean, freshwater is vital for the economy, with a large volume used in processing fish. Freshwater is also used to generate electricity and to process bauxite at the aluminum smelter at Straumsvík. Beginning in the late twentieth century, bottled freshwater has been successfully exported.

In areas where the underlying magma has brought hot temperatures close to the surface, the heat can be tapped by pumping the water up through a borehole. Iceland has about one thousand such geothermal localities. There are also geothermal areas on the sea floor, as at Gardskagi at the end of the Reykjanes Peninsula, where the smell of sulphur is always evident.

Geothermal water has been used for washing since the time of the settlement. Today there is a much wider range of uses, including fish farming and warming greenhouses. Geothermal heat is now widely tapped, principally for space heating; by 1990, in fact, 31% of energy needs were supplied by geothermal heat and 37% by hydropower.[29] Though the first borehole for Reykjavík was drilled in 1928, it was not until the 1940s that large–scale use was made of the potential for geothermal heating. By 1972, virtually all the inhabitants of Reykjavík had geothermal heat. With the growth of the city and rising demand, the Nesjavellir area near Lake Thingvallavatn has been developed. The large, domed structure called the Pearl, which is atop Öskjuhlíd Hill in Reykjavík, is actually several hot water storage tanks arranged to provide an attractive covered exhibition area between the tanks.

The Land

At Svartsengi on the Reykjanes Peninsula geothermal water is used to heat freshwater pumped from the ground, which is then distributed to the region's municipalities. The salty effluent from this plant forms a Blue Lagoon in the surrounding lava field that has become famous as the sulphur–rich water has been found to be beneficial for psoriasis patients and others.

Last but not least, Iceland's geology makes the country a prime tourist attraction. Built up by volcanism and sculpted by ice, Iceland is an awesome, rugged land, barren in places where ashfalls or the wind have denuded the land of vegetation, characterized by steep cliffs and fissures and rough flows of lava, but also by deeply indented fjords, lakes, pastureland, and sweeping views.

Living with the Weather

On the 4th of January, 1983, I was dressed to go out when the wind began screaming past my windows, driving the snow in horizontal bands of large, white flakes. The wind was relentless, giving me a view of the houses across the street through a moving curtain of shaggy white lines. I abandoned all idea of leaving home. The shrieking of the wind and the horizontal blizzard continued unabated for six hours as the air streaked obliquely from a high pressure area to fill an unusually deep low.

Suddenly, at about 4:00 in the afternoon, the screaming dance stopped. The snow no longer flew past in horizontal lines but dropped quietly to the ground. Stillness followed. Later, as several people made it home from work on foot, I could hear them shouting like children with the novelty of negotiating the drifts.

Iceland is an island in the north Atlantic, 102,950 km² in area with adjacent islands accounting for an additional 150 km², in other words about the size of the U.S. state of Kentucky or slightly larger than Scotland and Wales combined. The country is subarctic, with the northernmost point of the mainland lying just south of the Arctic Circle and the highest area a massif in the south covered by the Vatnajökull Glacier. The climate and therefore living conditions are influenced by the fact that the land lies at the conjunction of warm and cold air masses and warm and cold ocean currents that circle the land clockwise. The cold East Greenland polar current runs south along the east coast, whereas the warmer water of a branch of the Gulf Stream (the Irminger Current or the North Atlantic drift) warms the south and west coasts, bringing with it relatively warm air.[1]

Watching the daily weather forecast on television means following a series of lows from North America as they make their way towards us, often deepening as they cross the ocean, especially in winter, to form the "Icelandic low." "The next low on the agenda," as one woman meteorologist put it, is the one that will affect us in the next few hours or days. The frequent highs over Greenland are often squeezed north, especially in winter, and the depressions pass over Iceland in succession, bringing precipitation first, and foremost, to the southwest. In summer the wind patterns change sufficiently to allow Iceland a share in the high pressure areas. Winter and summer, even in a rainstorm, the air typically has a startling clarity.

Mediated by the surrounding ocean, Iceland's climate is milder and with less change between winter and summer than on a continent at the same latitude. The average yearly temperature in Reykjavík, for instance, is 5° C (41° F), or 11° C (52° F) warmer than the average for this northern latitude. Average monthly temperatures in Reykjavík in the winter oscillate only about 2° C above and below freezing, and the average temperature in July is about 11° C (52° F). Thus the average winter temperatures are not low and the difference

21

between winter and summer is not great. The relative humidity averages 85%. It feels much warmer in summer than the average midday temperature of 12°–15° C (54°–59° F) for the country as a whole would suggest, as the clear air and absence of real darkness give prolonged brightness and effective warmth.

Though some aspects of the climate are the same for the country as a whole—for example, the spring months are driest—Iceland is large enough and varied enough in topography to have more than one climate. Reykjavík in the southwest has an average precipitation of 805 mm (ca. 31 1/2 in.) per year, most of which, even in winter, falls as rain or sleet rather than snow. Akureyri in the north more often has a real winter and the summer sun is brighter due to the more northern latitude. Temperature fluctuations are greater inland than on the coasts—the lowest measured was –37.9° C (–36° F) at Grímstadir in January, 1918, but the average January temperature in the highlands is usually only –4° to –8° C (25°–18° F). In the rain shadow north of the Vatnajökull Glacier there is little precipitation, only 400 mm (just under 16 in.) per year, and sandstorms are common. The east is often hot and sunny in summer and the Mývatn area in the north usually makes a fine place to visit, with more hours of sunshine than in the south.

Despite the relatively small change between winter and summer, the differences from year to year can still be marked and the daily weather is so variable that it is often unpredictable from moment to moment. On rare occasions it may shift between snow, rain, and sunshine in a matter of minutes; "We don't have weather," Icelanders say, "only samples." In some years the ground can be white with snow in early May, whereas in other years May can be mild and wet, sometimes followed by weeks of sunshine and drought. In late June 1992, most of the country was under a blanket of snow, the coldest Midsummer's Day in thirty years. Though the farmers rounded up a good number of the sheep and lambs that were already on summer pasture, many sheep did not survive as they could not get through the snow to find grass.

It is usually windy in Reykjavík but even stronger winds typically blow over the Westman Islands off the south coast. In September 1973 the winds gusted to 120 knots (61.8 m/sec). On February 3, 1991, the winds averaged 110 knots (56.6 m/sec) with gusts that certainly exceeded 120 knots (the upper limit of the anemometers used), the strongest winds ever recorded in Iceland. Despite the winds, however, the Westman Islands average slightly over 69 days of fog per year.

The weather in Iceland is dependent, then, on ocean and air currents and the northerly latitude. It is also dependent on the proximity of sea ice and the lay of the land. There is snow year–round at the highest altitudes, with glaciers covering 11,800 km^2 (4555 sq. mi.) or 11.5% of the country. The largest of these glaciers are in the southern part of the country, where the land is highest and precipitation greatest, as much as 5000–6000 mm a year (for reference, 1 in. is about 25 mm). Summer skiing in the Kerlingafjöll Mountains is so popular that accommodations have to be reserved well in advance.

Ring of Seasons

The changes in daylight, of course, are "built in," occasioned by the northern latitude. This far north, the sun appears to circle around the sky, never rising really far above the horizon. Thus in Icelandic the 24–hour day is called *sólarhringurinn*, the sun's ring. In Reykjavík the sun is above the horizon for 21 hours on the summer solstice, and in Akureyri, in the north, for 23 1/2 hours. Since the sun barely dips beneath the horizon in the summer, we have, in effect, one day lasting about three months when it never gets really dark. In winter, of course, the sun does not rise very far above the horizon so that from mid– or late November on we have about two months of rather dreary darkness. However, since Iceland lies south of the Arctic Circle, on the shortest day we still have just over 4 hours when the sun is above the horizon in Reykjavík and 3 hours in the north, plus another hour or so of twilight at sunrise and sunset.

But the darkness is not the whole story. In Reykjavík the thermometer rarely drops to −18° C (about 0° F), but the wind–chill factor may at times make the effective temperature bitingly cold. "It's the wind," is a favorite Icelandic comment. Quite a few winters, on the other hand, are very mild, so much so that I've had pansies still blooming on my balcony in December, people have played golf in Reykjavík and in Akureyri in the north, and others have waterskied in Nordfjördur.

The Climate in Historical Times

Direct measurements of temperature were begun in Stykkishólmur in 1845. However, it is possible to extend our knowledge of the climate even further back. The old annals, in which the clerics recorded anything of note, give the extent of sea ice and also other information such as the years of poor harvests, from which the temperature can be inferred. Analyses of soil changes and ice cores from glaciers in Iceland and in Greenland[2] yield information on the thickness of depositional layers, oxygen isotope comparisons, and deuterium content which can be used to infer the climatic conditions of the past.

It is clear that the climate at the time of the settlement of Iceland in the latter part of the ninth century was relatively warm and remained so until the middle of the twelfth century. The author of the thirteenth century *Book of Settlements* described the land as having been "wooded from mountain to shore." It is estimated that vegetation covered 40,000 km² (15440 sq. mi.), an area since cut in half by erosion and other factors.[3]

After the middle of the twelfth century the climate turned colder, with the coldest period the century from 1250–1350. Glaciers began to form where they had not been before, on the Ok and Gláma mountains, and the interior of Iceland became less accessible. Grain cultivation was curtailed, though in the south and southwest not before the mid–sixteenth century.

Evidently in response to the colder climate, the average height of males decreased from 172 cm (ca. 5 ft. 9 in.) in 1000 A.D. to 167 cm (5 ft. 5 1/2 in.) in the mid–eighteenth century. [With a warmer climate and improved living conditions, the average rose to 177 cm in the 1940s and in the late twentieth century to 181 cm (over 5 ft. 11 in.) for 30–year–old males].[4] The highlands, where outlaws real and imaginary fled, would have been colder still. The trees were cut down to provide fuel. The wood yielded warmth, but the destruction of the forests and the protective root systems has meant the loss of 1 m^2 (ca. 11 sq. ft.) of vegetative cover per person per day since the time of the settlement, a horrendous rate of erosion. Some years were so hard they were given names, for example, the Great Glacier Winter of 1233, the Wet Summer of 1312 and for 1313, the Winter the Horses Died.

Though the climate was probably somewhat warmer from the fourteenth century to about 1600, the Little Ice Age continued until the sharp change that occurred about 1920, with a rapid warming to temperature levels similar to the temperatures at the time of the settlement. Sea ice was virtually absent from Icelandic shores from 1919–1964, though in some years since then sea ice has encroached upon the land. In 1989, for instance, when the pack ice froze against the coast of the West Fjords the inhabitants reported it was "strange" that they could walk out onto the ice and could no longer tell where the land ended and the sea began; there was an "eerie silence."

Living with the Climate

Though the Icelandic climate is mild for the northern latitude, it has not been the easiest environment to survive in for a people dependent for a livelihood first on farming and then largely on fishing. A colder or wetter than normal summer, especially after a winter of more than average snowfall, can mean a poor hay crop or a meager harvest of potatoes. When the climate worsened, beginning in the twelfth century, there were serious famines, and vitamin C deficiency in the colder months continued into the twentieth century. The climate affects the temperature of the sea, and hence the fish species available for utilization, the plants on land that are both food and a check to erosion, and the bird life that, even now to some extent, continues to provide meat and eggs.

The wind can play games with us. In February 1991, it lifted the 140–year–old wooden church in Árnes right off its foundation and moved it over a few feet, though nothing inside was damaged! More than once long sections of asphalt have been lifted off the main highway near the south coast. One bus driver reported on the evening news that "the asphalt rose up and disappeared like a huge black wall." After a particularly bad windstorm in the south, one young man interviewed on television was obviously in shock after his new prefab had been blown to pieces and even his washing machine had been blown off the site.

To help cope with the more difficult aspects of the climate, warnings of impassable road conditions and icy streets are publicized through the mass media and weather reports for the fishing trawlers are broadcast throughout the day. Over half of the nation lives and works in buildings made cosy with geothermal heat and virtually all have double–glazed windows. We live indoors more than some nations and the ambience in our homes may therefore matter more, but many people swim outdoors all year in the geothermal swimming pools.

There are always wry comments about the weather mixed with the serious ones. The sand on one construction site blew away, "probably back to where it came from"; more sand was therefore needed: "So the building firm is selling the same sand over again!" And a greenhouse grower said, "We're all optimistic people here. There's no point in giving up. Sure, the tomatoes will be late. We'll miss the best market in May and June." Then, wryly, "Maybe Christmas tomatoes, who knows."

It would be a mistake, however, to think that Iceland has only rough weather. Round–the–clock daylight in the summer, with stunning sunlit days and no or little wind, means that sheep thrive and vacationers can comfortably bike and tent. The light at midnight in summer has its own beauty, as does the aurora borealis on still winter nights. But no matter what the weather, it is a frequent topic of conversation.

The Icelandic Language

She wheeled up to me suddenly on her tricycle just as I was stepping out of my car. She was adorable, with red hair and blue eyes, all of three years old.

"Ertu útlenskt?" she asked. ("Are you foreign?")

"En ég er kona. Útlensk," I said, smiling and pointing out the obvious, that since I am a woman the adjective for foreign ought to be in the feminine form. At three she could hardly be expected to have learned all the different endings, but she was certain she was right and had no patience with me.

"ÚtlenS – K – T!" She spat out the final sounds and then wheeled off, her back straight, her red hair gleaming.

She had neutered me!

Language and genealogy have defined Icelandic identity down through the ages. The original ninth century settlers spoke Old Norse (or Old Icelandic). With little immigration after the settlement period and frequent contacts among themselves, Icelanders kept their language alive, developing only a minimum of regional and pronunciation differences, a situation unlike that of other European languages. The summer meeting of the Althing or legislative assembly; the literary heritage, both oral and written, including early translation of the Bible; the frequent travelling of fishermen, farm hands and others around the country; the schools that were established; and the deep interest in the language all combined to promote and sustain the use of a single language rather than fractionating into dialects, and to maintain that language with remarkably little change down to the present time.[1]

The language of the settlers included a very few loan words from Old Irish (such as the names *Njáll* and *Kjartan*). The acceptance of Christianity as the national religion in the year 1000 necessitated the borrowing of a number of words from Latin and Greek: *kirkja* (church), *skóli* (school), *prestur* (priest/minister). The clergymen who arrived from England brought other words: *synd* (sin), *guðspjall* (God's word/gospel). A few words came from Old French through the knights' tales (*kurteis*, courteous), and still others from Low German and Danish through commerce, but these loan words were relatively few in number and, in general, Icelandic vocabulary remained intact.[2] In fact, changes were taking place much more rapidly elsewhere in Scandinavia, distancing the languages there from Icelandic, with the result that the *First Grammatical Treatise* written in the twelfth century could refer to Icelandic as "our language" as distinct from Norwegian.[3] By 1400 the language spoken in Norway had diverged so much that Norwegians no longer found Icelandic readily intelligible.

After the Reformation in 1550 commerce with the Danes and schooling in Denmark increased the influence of Danish vocabulary and syntax on Icelandic. Though the eighteenth century saw a very real attempt to deal with new concepts by constructing new words from native roots, the language spoken in Reykjavík in the mid–nineteenth century was described as a "laughable" mixture of Danish and Icelandic.[4] The Romantic and nationalistic movements of the nineteenth century encouraged linguistic "purism" and admiration of the speech of the common people as the "purest."[5] Those Icelanders who led the nineteenth century struggle for independence from Denmark were also deeply concerned with the integrity of the language as one aspect of Icelandic independence; they made a point of publishing articles and poems in Icelandic. The need for new words continued, however, and most of these were coined from traditional roots and preserved the declensional and conjugational systems. In the late twentieth century, the number of necessary new words rose exponentially, though most have been made to fit the structural and phonetic systems. In fact, it is still relatively easy, by keeping a few spelling changes in mind, for a modern Icelander to read the oldest works.

Icelandic belongs to the North Germanic branch of the Indo–European family of languages. Old Norse is the name given to the ancestral language which, modified through time, gave rise to modern Danish, Icelandic, Swedish and Norwegian. Modern Icelandic, unlike the other Scandinavian languages, retains the grammatical structure of Old Norse, maintaining the highly inflected noun and adjectival declensions that indicate not only singular and plural but also the four cases (nominative, accusative, dative and genitive). Since human beings live within a world of events, both acting and acted upon, personal names are also declined. The basic verb forms, with the appropriate endings, indicate present and past, the other tenses being constructed with the aid of auxiliaries. In addition to the indicative verb forms, familiar from English, the subjunctive is still very much alive, and Icelandic has not only active and passive voice endings but also a middle voice originally formed by suffixing the reflexive pronoun (*meiða*/injure, *meiðast*/be injured; *koma*/come, *komast*/arrive, reach).

Much has been made of the difficulties of learning Icelandic because of the complexity of the inflectional systems. All nouns have grammatical gender, either masculine, feminine or neuter, and occur in singular and plural in the four cases, thus totalling eight forms for each noun (and an additional eight with the suffixed definite article). Adjectives must agree with the gender, number and case of the noun modified, and in addition, as in modern German, come in both strong and weak forms, giving the ordinary adjective a total of 48 potential forms; fortunately for the sake of memorization, a few of these are the same. Like adjectives, the definite article must agree with its referent and is usually suffixed, but can stand alone or occur in an additional set of forms, making a grand total of 72 forms, whereas English has merely *the*! Strong and weak verbs also have their own inflectional peculiarities, and the numbers 1 through 4 are declined. In fact, the word for number 1 occurs in the *plural* as well as the singular, since it is used to mean a) the number 1 with nouns occurring only in the plural, b) "alone," and c) "a pair of" with certain plural nouns: *ein bók*/one book, in the singular; *einir tónleikar*/one concert, plural in Icelandic; *einar buxur*/one pair of pants. Obviously for the foreigner, learning Icelandic involves a good deal of memory work, but any written language requires years to learn; we just usually forget how many years it takes from birth through schooling to learn our own language. The reward in learning Icelandic is to enter an interesting thought world and to enjoy the richness of the numerous idioms.

The earliest Old Norse inscriptions were recorded in runes incised in stones. When Icelandic was first written down, however, the Latin alphabet was used, with the addition of two letters from Old English, *ð* and *þ* (eth and thorn), to express respectively the voiced and unvoiced forms of the sounds that in modern English are written with a *th*. Modern Icelandic continues to use these two letters borrowed from Old English.

The foreigner visiting Iceland is treated to a refrain: "We are all equal" and "Everybody speaks the same language." This view is valid in that the few regional pronunciation differences are usually accepted as equally correct socially. On the other hand, there are modes of expression that are considered substandard, as well as vocabulary differences that depend on education and occupation. Nevertheless, in a 1986 survey, 61.3% felt there was little or no social difference in language use. In contrast, most people refer to certain grammatical and phonetic habits as an "illness," though the same 1986 survey indicated that the higher the speaker's social status, the less likely he or she was to use a nonstandard form. Stemming from the need to preserve identity through the language, a good deal has been written and spoken in an effort to keep Icelandic free of nonstandard errors. Though some Icelanders are not worried, many believe that, without remedial effort, the language will develop in undesirable ways and that it must be carefully nurtured, like a plant, by stressing correct usage and the formation of new words from Icelandic roots.[6]

The Richness of the Language

Though grammar and vocabulary are the building blocks, the character and appeal of a language stem from the way it is actually used. I have often been struck by how easily an Icelander, even after meeting a person for the first time, can turn round and, in five or six well–chosen adjectives, give a perceptive thumbnail sketch of the person. Icelanders also make copious use of intensifiers, the equivalent of English "very," "terribly," "awfully," but do so with no change of facial expression and normally without raising the voice. But the richest store of Icelandic expressions lies in the wealth of proverbs and idioms.

The proverbs, like poetry, often make use of alliteration. Many have parallels in English and other languages:

Neyðin kennir naktri konu að spinna.
Necessity is the mother of invention.
(lit., teaches the naked woman to spin)

Eins dauði er annars brauð.
(lit., one man's death is another's bread, i.e., someone
can benefit from it)
cf. One man's meat is another man's poison.

The Icelandic emphasis on working hard is mirrored in proverbs such as:

Iðjuleysi er rót alls ills.
Idleness is the root of all evil.

Sá árla rís verður margs vís.
He who rises early will be the wiser for it.
cf. Early to bed, early to rise,
Makes a man healthy, wealthy and wise.

Some are more specifically Icelandic:
Glöggt er gests augað.
Clear is the guest's eye
(i.e., the guest will notice clearly or will be critical of what the locals accept)

Gott er að eiga hauk í horni.
It's good to have an ace up one's sleeve.
(lit., a falcon in the corner, as it was a valuable bird to hunt with.)

Betra er berfættum en bókarlausum að vera.
It's better to be barefoot than without books.

Hníflaus er líflaus.
Knifeless means lifeless.
(i.e., as still said at sea, one needs a knife to survive.)

Idiomatic expressions may have roots in ancient customs, or come from sailors' language, or from farm life, the Bible, or chess and other games. They may be as old as the time of the settlement or new, borrowed from English or another language.

Hann fékk ekki rönd við reist.
He could do no more, he couldn't do anything about it
(lit., could no longer raise his shield to ward off blows)

ryðja sér til rúms
make a place for itself/oneself; become common
(lit., sit where one can squeeze in, as on the long benches of earlier times)

galli á gjöf Njarðar
fly in the ointment
(lit., defect in the god Njördur's gift)

kasta perlum fyrir svín
cast pearls before swine (dating from the sixteenth century)

stórlaxinn
the big cheese
(lit., the big salmon)

þungur róður
hard going/uphill battle
(lit., hard rowing)

vera fær í flestan sjó
be able to cope, come what may
(lit., be able in most seas)

leggja árar í bát
stop, quit, give up
(lit., stow your oars in the boat)

það bætti ekki úr skák
It didn't help
(lit., did not prevent a checkmate)

vera af allt öðru sauðahúsi
be cut from a different mold
(lit., come from a different sheep pen)

gera úlfalda úr mýflugu
make a mountain out of a molehill
(lit., a camel out of a gnat)

vera nýr af nálinni
be new
(lit., new from the needle, newly sewn/knit)

Það er allt sama tóbakið.
It's all the same
(lit., the same tobacco)

ástfanginn upp fyrir haus
head over heels in love
(lit., to the top of his head)

Names

The original settlers had to find names for the fields and streams and mountains of their new land. They named some for the places they had left in Norway, used a few Celtic names such as Patreksfjördur, and coined others to fit the characteristics of the new land. For example, they used *reyk*, actually smoke, to name the places where, in this land of volcanoes and geothermal vents, they saw steam rising from the earth, as in Reykholt (smoke hill) and Reykjavík (smoke bay/cove).

The settlers also brought with them their system of naming people. Foreigners faced with Icelandic names for the first time are often confused, but the system is actually quite simple and very logical. A person is normally the son or daughter of his or her father (less commonly of the mother). As was once the norm in other parts of Europe, each Icelander has one, sometimes two, given names followed by the patronymic that indicates the father's name. For example, Sigrídur's father is named Jón; her full name is therefore Sigrídur Jónsdóttir (the daughter of Jón, in the genitive); her brother Einar is Einar Jónsson (the son of Jón). By the same token, if Einar names his son for the boy's grandfather, as is common, the boy will be Jón Einarsson. Furthermore, no matter how many times Sigrídur is married and divorced, she keeps her maiden name.

Icelanders are addressed and referred to by their given names, that is, by their own names and never, for example, as Ms. or Mr. "Jónsdóttir/son" any more than a woman in English would be called "Miss daughter of John." Nicknames usually have two syllables. In our example, Sigrídur Jónsdóttir would be called Sigga by her family and close friends and Sigrídur by all others and would be referred to as Sigrídur Jónsdóttir when necessary to indicate which one of the numerous Sigrídurs she is. By the same token names are listed alphabetically in the telephone directory under the given name, followed by the patronymic, e.g., under *S* in the case of Sigrídur Jónsdóttir.

Despite the custom of naming children for grandparents or relatives, there are fashions in the choice of names, though most of the commonest, like the men's names Sigurdur, Gudmundur, Einar, and Helgi and women's names Helga and Ingibjörg, date from the ninth century. Gudrún has for centuries been the commonest women's name. Magnús, from Latin, dates back at least to 1024, and Gunnar to the mid–twelfth century. Christianity brought Biblical names, including Kristín in the thirteenth century, Jón (John) in the thirteenth century, Anna in the fifteenth century. María was not used until the eighteenth century.[7]

Since names can be formed by combining word elements, not only are a large number of Icelanders named Thor for the god, but the name also appears in combinations like Thorborg, Thórunn, and Thóra for women and Thor-

31

grímur, Thorsteinn, Thórir and Thorvaldur for men. Many women's names end in "rún" (magic, writing): Gudrún, Kristrún, Ástrún. Many other names begin with "sig–" (winner, champion): Sigrídur and Sigurbjörg for women, Sigurdur and Sigurbjörn for men.

Because of the pressure to preserve Icelandic, the Vietnamese refugees who moved to Iceland, for instance, were all given "suitable" Icelandic names, whether they could pronounce them understandably or not.

The law allows a person's "last" name to refer to his or her mother rather than to use the usual patronymic referring to the father, and a wife can legally use her husband's patronymic as a surname, though those who have done so are usually foreign–born wives. The law also legalizes the use of family names as surnames. The earliest known family name, Vídalín, dates from the seventeenth century. Some family names identify the elite during the time of the Danish domination: Thorlacius, Gröndal, Stephensen. Interestingly, the use of surnames is increasing. In 1855 there were 108 in use; by 1994, five percent of Icelanders were known by family names, with a total of 2,227 surnames recorded on the census rolls, though many of these were the names of foreigners residing in Iceland.

Responding to Change

In response to all the technological and social changes since independence, the addition of a huge number of words has been necessary to cope with the material advances and growing sophistication. Some words have been borrowed, such as *hótel* and *bensín* (gasoline) but, in order to preserve Icelandic, most have had to be "found" or "sought" by recycling older words or roots rather than inventing a wholly new term or borrowing from other languages.[8] Whereas English leans heavily on Latin and Greek roots for new words or redefines other words, Icelanders had to embark on a quest through Old Icelandic. For example, the old word *síma*/cord was masculinized to *sími*/telephone, from the lines that carried the message. Radio became *útvarp*/broadcast, and then by analogy television became *sjónvarp*/sight–cast.

The late twentieth century rush to modernize meant, as in other languages, the need for an enormous number of new words and often great difficulty in settling on something suitable. Since the term AIDS does not fit Icelandic grammatical structure, a "native" term had to be found. Over twenty attempts were made to translate AIDS before general agreement settled on two choices: *eyðni* (from *eyða*, destroy), partly because it sounds similar to AIDS, and *alnæmi* (all–sensitivity). "Videotape" also caused quite a problem, with various words bandied through the mass media before *myndband* (picture band) became the accepted translation.

The meaning of new words is often relatively clear to Icelanders because of the recycling of old roots, but in my experience the understanding can be superficial and there is often a tendency to dismiss a new word as just a neologism. Words take time, after all, to become embedded in a language.

One other key aspect of change has been the influence of English. Gone is most of the habit of learning about the world through Danish and of borrowing Danish words; English has become the prime foreign medium of information. Though some borrowed English is simply a passing fad ("cosy" in the 1970s, "yes" rather than the Icelandic *já* in the 1980s), other words present more of a problem. Words have had to be found to translate economics terms, for instance; physicians often use a mixture of Icelandic and amended Latin; and the computer revolution has forced a broader acceptance of English. Some computer terms can be translated directly (*heimsíða*/home page), but others appearing on the computer screen are often borrowed as they stand, regardless of the fact that they do not fit into Icelandic grammar patterns.

The task, now and in the future, is to keep Iceland abreast of world developments while maintaining the language that continues to define identity. Watching the resolution of this tug of war is an interesting game.

Eddas and Sagas

My guide handled the old manuscripts familiarly, as if they were no more than his daily appointment book, whereas I stood in awe of these browning pages covered with careful script. He was giving me a private viewing in the special walk–in safe where the old manuscripts are stored in a building on the grounds of the University of Iceland, the air carefully controlled to preserve them. These old witnesses to a long–gone age are his daily work, their worn vellum leaves testimony of how much they were read and cherished in earlier years.

Iceland is perhaps best known abroad for its rich heritage of literature from the Middle Ages. Despite the loss of manuscripts through the ages a large number of texts still exist, covering a wide range of topics. Some are the source of the last shreds of information left to us about Norse mythology (*Poetic Edda*, *Prose* or *Snorra Edda*), many are religious, and still others record historical events and the events of the day. There are skaldic poems rich in metaphor, and fictional romances, but probably the best known are the sagas which record the history of various leading Icelandic families.

The Manuscripts

With the advent of Christianity in 1000 as Iceland's religion, the church brought the concept of schools, the Latin alphabet, and Gregorian chants as part of the mass. The schools and the monasteries became centers of learning where books were written, records kept, and the priests taught to intone the chants. Literacy and the ability to write became widespread. Chieftains and others were authors, and farmhouses were centers for producing and copying manuscripts.

The books were written with quill pens on vellum made from calfskins. The quills were best taken from a bird's left wing, often from a swan or raven, the better to fit the copyist's hand. The ink was concocted from willow shavings and bearberry. Care had to be taken in preparing the ink; too much willow sap and the ink ran and turned the vellum and, in later copies, the paper, brown. But though it may sound like a witch's brew, the ink has proved durable and is still legible. In the beginning the script used was Carolingian Latin, brought largely from England, with the additional letters, þ (thorn) and ð (eth), both now written in modern English with a *th*. From the twelfth century on the manuscripts were written in Gothic script.

The important thing is that almost all the extant books are written in Icelandic, not Latin. Together, all of these works—history, laws, annals, sagas, and poetry—made, and still make, the statement that Icelanders are a separate people, a distinct nation, practical, capable, striving, imaginative, artistic, defining themselves through their own language and making their own place in the world. The genealogies have given roots and longevity, the annals the events of the time, the law a framework, the sagas and poems a celebration of being an Icelander. The old manuscripts were well handled and much read and, when worn out, were copied to preserve their contents.

The small population of medieval Iceland, sixty or seventy thousand people, managed to provide and process enough calfskins to record the pagan heritage, the lives of bishops and saints and Norwegian kings, the drama of the events in the Saga Age (930–1030), and the later struggles. To produce the manuscript known as *Flateyjarbók*, for instance, required a total of 113 calfskins.[1] Most of these medieval works are available to us through later copies that have been preserved, not least through the efforts of Árni Magnússon in the eighteenth century.

Practicality demanded that the law be recorded, beginning in 1117. Ari the Learned was prompted to write *The Book of Icelanders* (ca. 1130), in part to show that Icelanders were good people with fine pedigrees. A careful historian, he took pains to be as accurate as oral tradition allowed, picking good sources and carefully identifying them. Sturla Thordarson amended the *Book of Settlements*, which lists all the principal original settlers, the lands they held, and various tales about them.

There was a host of other writers, many of them anonymous, but the most famous of these is undoubtedly the crafty politician, Snorri Sturluson. We owe to him the preservation of many pagan myths and of the rules and diction used in the old poetry, written to keep the knowledge of this heritage from dying out; his *Prose Edda* is required reading in Icelandic schools to this day. He also wrote the history of the Norwegian kings, *Heimskringla*, which inspired Norwegians in their later struggle for independence from Sweden, just as the Old Treaty of 1262 and the sagas later justified for Icelanders their claim for independence from Denmark.

At first crucifixes and religious paintings were imported or influenced by foreign styles, but by the twelfth century Icelanders had developed their own artistry.[2] From the thirteenth century on, manuscripts were illuminated, often beautifully. The artists gave free rein to their ideas, painting flowers and foliage, elongated Gothic figures and, in the fourteenth century, monsters and scenes from everyday life, even drunkenness, before the strictures of the Reformation halted such free expression.

Religious Writings and the Role of the Church

The church needed schools to train the priesthood and therefore established centers of learning at the two bishoprics at Skálholt and Hólar and at the Benedictine and Augustinian monasteries. The course of instruction for the priesthood lasted for four winters and covered grammar and rhetoric, singing, mathematics and astronomy. Though some early manuscripts were in Latin, from the twelfth century on most of the books needed for instruction were in Icelandic.

Often trained in England, the clergy brought the Latin alphabet plus

English letters to record Icelandic, and by writing in Icelandic helped promote the native language. They also brought a knowledge of biblical names (*Jón* or John remains the most common man's name today) and Latin words so as to deal with church offices and functions. Many of these remain in modern Icelandic to express concepts connected with schooling and the Lutheran church, for example, *biskup*, *prestur* (priest), *ferming* (confirmation), *stúdent* (a graduate from upper secondary school), *dúx* (the *stúdent* with the highest marks).

A wealth of writings issued from the church centers. There were Icelandic translations of the works of some theologians such as St. Augustine and of other European works. Works on natural science were often based on foreign books, but the scholars also produced their own works: sermons, homilies and hymns of praise; confessions of faith; the lives of the apostles and of the Virgin Mary; biographies of Icelandic bishops; and biographies of various saints to be read aloud on the saint's day.

The churchmen were often poets as well. The most famous of the long religious poems is *Lilja*, written in the fourteenth century by a monk named Eysteinn. Its one hundred stanzas recount the creation and the birth of Christ and are a hymn of praise to the Virgin Mary. The poem is so beautifully written and in Icelandic that is still so contemporary that today it is required reading in Icelandic schools.

The authors of the biographies thought of themselves as historians.[3] They were also historians in another very important sense: the churchmen faithfully kept annals and chronicles of the events of the time, including volcanic eruptions, that today are an invaluable record.

The Poetic Edda

The manuscript known as the Codex Regius contains the *Poetic Edda* ("great–grandmother" poems). The extant manuscript dates to about 1270 but has clearly been copied from an earlier manuscript from about 1200; the question of how old the original poems are, however, remains unanswerable. Since England and Germany were Christianized earlier, the worship of the old Norse gods lasted longer in Iceland than on the continent and the knowledge of the religion did not die out as fast. The eddic poems are therefore among the earliest Germanic poems, an important source of our knowledge about the Norse–Germanic gods and of the exploits of the heroes such as Sigurdur the Dragon Slayer, as well as of rules for living.

The eddic poems are generally constructed with simpler meters and wording than the later court poetry. When the poems are read aloud, the effect is one of great strength. As in Old German and Old English, the lines are compressed, with few syllables, and stress, length of syllable and alliteration are carefully used to convey the meaning. In the six–line stanzas of *Hávamál* (Words of the High One), for example, we find advice on how to welcome a guest, how to live an honorable life, and how to protect oneself from ambush and treachery. It is difficult to find a modern English translation that conveys the same terse strength. The third stanza of the *Völuspá* –*The Sybil's Prophecy* (translated in the chapter "Norse Mythology—The Gods and Creation") begins in Icelandic: *Ár var alda*. The literal meaning "In the beginning of Time" loses the aural and emotional impact of the original terseness and alliteration. The third line in English, "Nor sand nor sea" (*Var–a sandur né sær*), more closely approximates Old Norse style.

It is a moot question how much these early Icelandic writings were influenced by Celtic traditions. Icelanders had ample opportunity to become acquainted with Celtic traditions as they lived, traded and fought in Ireland, the Hebrides and Orkney. In addition, they had Irish slaves who could surely spin a good yarn, even though in Icelandic. The Norse settlers brought their own traditions and beliefs with them from Norway, but Irish motifs may well have enriched the Scandinavian and Germanic tradition and Irish tales been added to the lore. Gísli Sigurdsson[4] presents a goodly list of Norse mythological adventures and story traits that occur in Irish tales, from talking heads to the death of the god Baldur; Mímir was a talking head residing in his well when Ódinn, the All–Father, went to acquire wisdom, and Baldur's death is a parallel of the Irish *Aided Fergusa*. There is no certainty, however, that these traits were imported from Ireland as they occur in other European traditions as well. There is perhaps more agreement on the Celtic influence in the *Rígspula*, wherein the god Heimdallur's prowess in bed with three different women is used to justify the division into the three social classes, peasants, freemen farmers, and the elite.[5]

Celtic influence may be evident in the court poetry and the sagas as well. The meters of court poetry differ from the meters used in the older Germanic eddaic poems, but some of these are to be found in the Irish *filid*, and the handling of dramatic events in the sagas has Irish parallels. The Irish preoccupation with the supernatural is paralleled in accounts in the Icelandic sagas, and still today Ireland and Iceland are among those lands which the inhabitants more often believed to be peopled by elves and other supernatural beings.

But a strong caveat is in order: the similarities between Irish and Icelandic writings could as well have stemmed from the beliefs and tales of a wider shared culture, just as Norse mythology has many parallels in the mythologies of Greece and Rome.

The Eddic Poetry and Sagas as Drama

There has been considerable consensus that both the earliest works and the sagas were presented orally.[6] There is a passage in *Sturlunga Saga* where the guest is asked how he would like to be entertained, by ballad dancing or saga reading. He chooses the latter when he finds they have a copy of the *Saga of Thomas à Becket*. Like Shakespeare reading groups among modern English speakers, medieval Icelanders evidently looked on saga reading as fine entertainment. More to the point, the terse style of the sagas, with much of the work in dialogue form with prose interpolations becomes more meaningful if at least envisioned as dramatic presentation, if not actually performed.

The question of how much the extant versions of the eddaic poems and sagas owe to oral tradition and how much they were the work of very able authors remains unresolved. Icelandic oral tradition certainly preserved a considerable core of knowledge of past events. Building on this core, the authors of the sagas composed tales as dramatic as any to be found. The reader, or a storyteller reading aloud, could easily heighten the dramatic effect with the aid of cues in the text and the margins. The champion who stops in the middle of battle to compose poetry seems to make no sense to us as a fighter. However, spoken, or at least imagined as spoken, the poems, with their change of pace, heighten the tension of the battle scenes just as fluid camera work does for today's cinema audience.

Gunnell[7] analyzes the eddaic poems (concentrating on five: *Lokasenna, Skírnismál, Vafþrúðnismál, Hárbarðsljóð,* and *Fáfnismál*) with a view to unravelling the how, when and where of possible dramatic performances, and in doing so to show that they were in fact performed. Indications, both in the margins and in the body of the text, tell what character is to speak. Gunnell shows by careful analysis of these indicators and of the text that the poems were almost certainly presented by several actors. The performance would have taken place in a defined space, either in the home or out of doors. Though some of the eddaic poems, such as the *Völuspá,* are monologues, others are far more complicated. *Lokasenna (The Binding of Loki),* for instance, would be difficult to comprehend if there were only one narrator, as sixteen speakers are involved with rapid transitions. The difficulties in understanding the poem are resolved if it is envisioned as drama with different actors and movement within a defined area. The margin indicators and prose interpolations may be later additions to help readers who lacked the opportunity to witness an actual performance.

There was ample opportunity for such performances in Iceland: the great feasts the chieftains held, the annual Althing meetings, the later gatherings called *vikivaki* (wake or entertainment; the word is from the fifteenth century), and the *leikmót* or meets for sports and games. In performing the eddaic poems the actors probably wore costumes and masks.[8] The excavations at Stóraborg uncovered a wooden mask that could well have been worn for such a performance.[9]

Early Music

It is impossible to imagine these gatherings without music. The word *ljóðaháttr,* which identifies a type of poem, means "song meter"; such poems were surely chanted or sung in some form. The sagas occasionally record who had a fine singing voice. The *seiður* or incantations to work a charm or foretell the future were probably chanted, a form of recitative.

There were *söngdansar* (sung dances), often historical poems or epics that were sung while the people danced. Though probably brought by the original settlers, they were certainly performed by the thirteenth century.[10]

Perhaps the best evidence for the form and practice of medieval music is the folk songs modern Icelanders still sing. They are often not in the usual major and minor keys of today's western music, but in older modes and with part singing at the intervals of the fourth or fifth (*organum*) that is closest to the music of tenth century Europe.[11] In the fifteenth century the sagas, and even the historical books of the Bible, were turned into epic lays that were "half–sung" as *rímur*, a kind of melodic chanting that fits the Icelandic language. The singing of *rímur* continued into the twentieth century, when the practice began to die out; *rímur* singing has been revived, however, to help preserve Icelandic cultural roots.

The Court Poetry

In addition to the large corpus of eddaic poems, court poetry and other skaldic poems have also come down to us. The eddaic poems are anonymous, growing out of the same misty beginnings that the *Völuspá* sings of, in meters similar to those used by other Germanic peoples. The court poems, in contrast, were written by named poets or skalds to celebrate the deeds of specific kings or events, with an intricate diction and meters not used in other Germanic languages.

Beginning in Norway with Bragi Boddason the Old in the first half of the ninth century (was he named posthumously for Bragi, the god of poetry?) and continuing into the fourteenth century, the names of over 200 court poets or skalds are known. Not all were men, but in the later centuries nearly all were Icelanders and not Norwegians, the most outstanding being the saga hero Egill Skallagrímsson.

Though skaldic verse developed over the centuries, the characteristic *dróttkvætt* stanza consists of a pair of quatrains, the first of which often presents an event that is counterbalanced or contrasted in the second,[12] much as the parts of a sonnet complement each other. Though some characteristics, like the carefully controlled use of alliteration and syllabic length and the compressed style, parallel eddic poetry, the *dróttkvætt* stanza is an intricate marvel of images and thought carefully fitted into precisely 24 syllables per quatrain. The wording is characterized by special vocabulary (for instance, the everyday *maður/mann* for "man" becomes *verr*, cf. Latin *vir*), complex patterns of internal rhyme (*hendingar*), and the richness of the *kenningar* or metaphors. About one hundred concepts, including *ship*, *Óðinn*, *warrior*, *woman*, *sea*, can be expressed in kennings. A ship can be "the bear of the current," "the horse of the sea mountains." "The wave–horse rides the peaks of the whale house" means that the ship sails the sea.

The skaldic poems are rich with vivid impressions and multiple associations, but are compact and deal with action rather than introspection. Like modern Icelanders, the skalds were not verbose. Because of the intricate reliance on metaphor and the complicated, poetic style, today understanding skaldic poetry requires careful study to unravel the meaning; its beauty and ingenuity were more easily understood and greatly appreciated at the time they were written.

39

Skaldic poems deal with heroes and battles, with praise and celebration, but also with other subjects like travel and love and rivalry. The poet might praise his lord or compose a verse about himself. A king or chieftain was obligated to reward the poet for a fine poem of praise, but woe betide the writer of satirical verse. The word had power, thaumaturgy; a laudatory poem was a positive force, an insulting one was punishable by a fine, or worse.

The Sagas

The best known, and also the most accessible, of the medieval writings are the sagas. There are sagas recounting the heroism of Icelanders, and sagas of bishops, kings and saints, as well as knights' tales composed under the influence of the French *chansons de geste*. The old legends, handed down orally, often blended fact and fancy. One of the most entertaining scenes takes place in *Bosi and Heraudur*, where the *bride* comes to her wedding dressed in a battle helmet and coat of mail! Though we are assured they lived happily ever after, the imagination is tantalized by the possible scenarios for disrobing the bride on the nuptial night.

The greatest of these medieval accounts are probably those known as the sagas of Icelanders which recount the histories of the Icelandic chieftains and their families. Based on oral tradition but masterfully expanded, these sagas recount events as they were believed to have taken place in the tenth and eleventh centuries. They were, however, largely written during the civil turmoil of the thirteenth century and recalled an earlier age, though some, such as *Sturlunga Saga*, deal with contemporary events. Both in some earlier and not always adroitly written sagas and in the masterpieces of *Egils Saga*, *Laxdæla Saga*, *Njáls Saga* (from the last quarter of the thirteenth century), and *The Saga of Grettir the Strong* (written in the fourteenth century), the listener/reader is afforded a dramatic insight into the personalities and events that shaped Icelandic history. The style of writing is terse, dramatic, the people introduced as they enter the action. The chapters give short scenes, with the story carried forward largely in dialogue, though some sagas such as *Njáls Saga* rely more on narrative prose than do others. Like Tolstoy's *War and Peace*, each saga is a tapestry of people and events, but each of the key actors has individual characteristics and each of the events furthers the story. The older Norse belief that personality is part of one's fate as much as the events that occur was still important to the thirteenth century writers. To avoid confusion among this multiplicity of characters, we are told not only when someone enters but also when "he is out of the story," not to return.

The sagas give us a vibrant view of medieval life: feasts, fighting, weddings, the settlement of law cases, gift–giving, and above all the preservation of honor. If the canvas seems overly replete at times with limbs hacked off at the knee or shoulder or with heads flying free and torsos sundered, the reader is made aware that the purpose is never wanton murder but rather legal killing carried out in the overriding effort to build and maintain honor, and with honor, of course, the fabric of Icelandic medieval society. The importance of *drengskapur*—respect, fair play, honor—is the driving force behind the feasts and fighting and display of fine clothes and gift–giving. Wealth is acquired to be displayed, not hoarded, to earn and maintain honor. Alliances are cemented in marriages and feasting; sons are exchanged to be raised by the former adversary in order to maintain peace. *Drengskapur*, like the Latin *virtus*, is honor in the fullest sense: being true to family and friends, treating others with respect where respect is due, having courage, and defending one's own and one's family's good name. Skillful mediation of a problem can bring honor. A difference may be settled privately or in the law courts. But if mediation is unsuccessful, then revenge killing may be necessary to preserve one's honor. In a day and age before police and prisons, revenge killing was not wanton violence but the often tragic response, when attempts at conciliation have failed, to restore the balance of the social fabric. Of the 520 feuds recorded in the family sagas, 297 were settled "by private actions of vengeance;" with the exception of 9 that "could not be concluded," the rest were settled by agreement or in court or were arbitrated.[13]

The sagas are not stories of the common people but of the elite, both women and men. The genealogies carefully given as a character enters the story attest the personal worth and high position of each player on the scene. No matter if oral memory was sometimes faulty and the genealogy of the same person given somewhat differently in different sagas. Durrenberger[14] feels that the saga stories unfold in patterns of events rather than with an attempt to build suspense, one reason perhaps being that for the readers this was, after all, their own history and the end was known. Those few of my students who have read some of the sagas both in Icelandic and in English translation have told me that in Icelandic the sagas have depth and historical meaning for them as part of their culture and history, whereas in English they become simply stories. Much of the difference lies in the difficulties of translating and the different tonality of modern English, and some part also lies in the fact that translators tend to omit the genealogies or relegate them to footnotes. Then and still today, in jokes, in stories, in ordinary conversation, Icelanders must establish who the person is through his or her genealogy and thereby accord him or her personal worth and a place in society.

The sagas are replete with vivid scenes, the verve and drama of medieval life. Bets are laid and stallions fight. The wedding feasts are huge; one or two hundred guests stay for several days or longer and dance round dances and recite poems. Great strength is admired. We read of the heroes who catch a spear in flight, turn it round and throw it back to kill their opponent with his own weapon.

The greatest saga characters are individuals we can visualize and understand; the human stage has not changed so much since then. Egill Skallagrímsson recites magnificent poetry in the midst of battle. Ólafur the Peacock rides to the Althing in his scarlet tunic. Gudrún Ósvifsdóttir in *Laxdæla Saga* maintains her magnificent bearing even when her husband's killer wipes his bloody sword on her dress over her pregnant belly. Njáll, the man who so often counselled moderation, still maintains his dignity when he in turn must succumb to fate and be burned alive in his own house. The riddle that Gudrún Ósvifsdóttir gives us at the end of *Laxdæla Saga* still intrigues us: When her grandson Bolli pressed her to tell him which of her four husbands she loved the most, she replied, "I treated worst the one I loved the most." To form your own opinion as to who that was you will have to read *Laxdæla Saga*.

Many of these early Christians still continued to hold beliefs from pagan times. Dreams and prophecies were binding. The dream often served as an effective literary device, foreshadowing the events to follow. A person can be born with luck or, like Grettir the Strong, born unlucky. The supernatural overrides other events; Grettir proved his greatest strength not when he bested opponents or lifted boulders no other man could lift, but when he wrestled Glámur, the undead, and finally put an end to his haunting.

The ferment during the last stages of the Commonwealth entailed jockeying for power and sometimes violent death but also literary achievement of the highest order that has had a lasting influence. Wagner and Tolkien and many others have received inspiration from medieval Icelandic literature. It remains a mine of information and an integral part of Icelandic schooling and Icelandic identification. Ódinn's gift of poetry is still part of Icelandic culture.

Gyrfalcons and Iceland Moss

The gyrfalcon is the national bird of Iceland. Its superior hunting ability made it highly valued by falconers in the Middle Ages, when it was reserved for the nobility and the highest ranking clergy, and gyrfalcons therefore constituted a valuable export item from Commonwealth times until 1806.[1] For the millenary in 1874 Icelanders flew a blue flag with a white falcon. Later the Icelandic shield displayed a falcon on a blue field, a design that was used until Iceland gained sovereignty in 1918.[2]

Since 1940 the gyrfalcon has been protected in Iceland but, as the bird is still highly prized by falconers, thieves have found it well worth their while to try to steal both the eggs and the young birds. There is a market in Europe but the highest prices can be obtained in Saudi Arabia, where a fullygrown Icelandic falcon can fetch as much as $100,000.[3] To protect the bird, Icelanders have learned to report any suspicious behavior and have appointed a falcon warden for the Mývatn area. There have been no thefts of eggs or birds since 1987.

The Flora and Fauna of Iceland

The original settlers in the ninth century found an inviting land, forested with birch and low–growing willow up to an altitude of 400 meters. Birch and some other plants had survived the Ice Ages in unglaciated areas and long before the time of the settlement had spread out and taken root in suitable areas. Cotton grass and sedges grew in the bogs and ferns in the more sheltered spots, and in many places mosses carpeted the older lava flows. Though a large part of the highlands was relatively barren, as were some lava flows and the areas around the glaciers, trout lived in the lakes and rivers, the sea could provide fish and edible seaweed, Atlantic salmon swam upriver to spawn, and in summer the cliffs teemed with nesting seabirds. There were no native grazing mammals and still are no reptiles or amphibians.

The ninth century settlers instituted huge changes. They brought grazing mammals and a variety of plants, cut the forests for fuel, and inadvertently provided the means for mice and various bacteria and parasites to enter the country. Since there were no native grazing mammals, the livestock that the settlers brought changed the face of the land. Grazing and the destruction of the forests reduced the estimated 25,000 km^2 (9700 sq. mi.) of woods to the present 1250 km^2 (480 sq. mi.). Overgrazing, volcanic eruptions, wind and water erosion, and deforestation, which removed stabilizing roots, have resulted in an increase in the area of unvegetated land from the estimated 18,000 km^2 (7,000 sq. mi.) at the time of the settlement to the present 58,000 km^2 (22,400 sq. mi.).[4] Since the key problem is overgrazing, however, in places where grazing has been stopped, as in some areas in the West Fjords, the flowers and other plants have come back quite rapidly.

Icelandic seas are home to gray and harbor seals, which bear their young in Iceland. Five other seal species, walrus, 6 species of baleen and 12 species of toothed whales, and 293 species of fish, including cod, are found in Icelandic waters.[5] The sale of cod, spread flat and salted, was so important in earlier centuries that ca. 1600 the Icelandic shield displayed a flat cod with a gold crown on a red field. However, Icelanders eat more haddock than any other species, and salmon and young halibut are considered culinary delicacies.

Though a good 1245 species of insects have been identified (with others arriving from time to time that do not always survive the winter),[6]

Cotton grass

there are few compared to Europe or North America. Insect larvae provide all–important freshwater fish food. Most of the flora and fauna of Iceland are also found in Scandinavia, especially in Norway. In addition, since Iceland lies south of the true arctic, it is also home to more southerly species not found in Scandinavia.

The only land mammal before the settlement was the arctic fox. Though it will bite sheep, its main food in Iceland is birds, including eider ducks and eggs. Polar bears come only rarely with the pack ice and do not make their home in Iceland. There were no rats until the eighteenth century. Reindeer were imported in the late eighteenth century from Norway; presently there are 3500–4000 animals in the East Fjord region, the herds culled by controlled hunting to keep their numbers within the limits the land will support. Mink were imported in 1931 to be raised for skins but escaped in 1932 to spread everywhere except the barren interior and the sands in the south.[7]

From the beginning Icelanders needed to utilize herbs and other plants for food, medicinal purposes, and sorcery. Angelica, for example, which was raised in home plots, was eaten stripped of the fibre and was also used to flavor distilled liquor or *brennivín*. Families picked crowberries and blueberries in season, as Icelanders still do, and also collected the seaweed dulse, which was usually eaten dried. The herbs and berries provided needed vitamins and minerals. Various herbs were used medicinally, such as stonecrop for congestion in the chest as well as for jaundice and gallstones. And putting either of two orchids, *friggjargras* (*Habernaria hyperborea*), named for the goddess Frigg, or *hjónagras* ("marriage grass" *Leucorchis albida*) under one's bedding was said to encourage desire, help resolve marital difficulties, and ease labor pains.[8]

Other herbs were used for dyeing, to vary the natural palette of flax and horsehair and the off–white, browns and black of Icelandic wool. Birch leaves gave a clear yellow or green, birchbark, gray or brown. Northern dock, bearberry, heather and other plants afforded a full range of colors. In most cases the leaves, bark or herbs were boiled and the tincture used. In the case of buttercups, however- er, only the blossoms were boiled, producing a pale yellow dye.[9]

Perhaps the most important plant was Iceland moss (actually a lichen). The whole family would go out together in late June or early July to gather it, preferably in a mist or light rain as then the leaves expand and it is easy to iden- tify. It was eaten in several ways: chopped and in milk as a thin sauce, or boiled with milk until the milk thickened, or used in making sausage. Iceland moss could also be used for dyeing, giving yellow and light brown shades or, when mixed with cows' urine, red. Today both Iceland moss and other native herbs can easily be purchased in the health food stores.

Gathering Eggs and Snaring Birds

Though about 300 bird species have been spotted, only about 75 or 80 reg- ularly nest in Iceland; some are passage migrants on their way to nesting grounds in Greenland and arctic Canada. Spring is heralded by the call of the Eurasian golden plover in late March, and the arrival of the first arctic tern on the Pond in the center of Reykjavík in early May is usually reported in the newspaper. Other birds, such as certain gull species and the raven, remain all year, the gulls profiting from the quantity of modern society's refuse. Since the croak of the raven so often sounds like human speech, in older times it was thought there were certain individuals who could understand it; today the raven is sometimes thought of as a pest.

Iceland's lack of woodlands and insects has undoubtedly held down the number of passerine and songbird species, though birds such as the wheatear and winter wren, and the redwing, which catches earthworms in urban gardens, have done well. The climate changes over the centuries of Iceland's settlement have also affected the bird population. After the climate warmed in 1920, for instance, shoveler and tufted ducks arrived and began nesting successfully, and starlings came in 1935, but dovekies, who thrive in colder climates, have moved north.

Both eggs and birds have provided valuable food since the time of the set- tlement. The rock ptarmigan, for example, has long been a favorite dish on Christmas Eve. Since the stocks fluctuate over a ten–year cycle, in some years there are not enough to satisfy demand. Today hunting ptarmigan has become more sport than occupation. The birds frequently come close to tourists tenting in the Skaftafell campground.

Beginning in mid–May sea birds nest in tremendous numbers on Iceland's steep sea cliffs. Because they arrived at the end of winter and before the crops were harvested, in earlier times the birds and eggs sometimes meant the differ- ence between starvation and survival. Since auks (murres and puffins) re–lay, the eggs could be collected twice. Men climbed the cliffs, sometimes with the help of a chain or ladder, or were lowered by a rope around waist and thighs to collect the eggs. It was dangerous work as the cliff sometimes collapsed or the collector lost his footing. The eggs were carried in bags or a box strapped to the collector's back and were often padded with grass to keep them from breaking while they were carried home.[10] Some birds were caught with a noose and slipknot on the end of a pole; murres were often caught on a small raft with loops of twine that ensnared any bird that landed. The women plucked the feathers before the men singed the bodies; when not eaten fresh, the birds were salted or stored in whey.[11] Several species of seabirds were eaten, most commonly the puffin. On the Westman Islands young men still perch on the edges of the sea cliffs and snare puffins with a net on the end of a long pole, and, in season, murres' eggs are for sale in the grocery stores, as are the skinned bodies of murres and puffins.

One of Iceland's catastrophes is well known to outsiders: the extinction of the great auk. Flightless, it lived on skerries to the southwest of Iceland and, because it was fairly easy to catch on the rocks and the eggs were so large, it was in demand for food. The great auk population crashed when much of their nesting area was destroyed in a volcanic eruption. The remaining birds were killed by hunters, the last pair on June 3, 1844, when fourteen men rowed out to the island of Eldey, destroyed the eggs, and took the last two birds.

The fate of the other birds nesting in Iceland has been better, and most species are currently protected. The white–tailed sea eagle, for instance, has been protected since 1913, though poison bait used to control foxes and medicine used to cure sheep have been responsible for killing quite a number of eagles.[12] Though their range has been reduced to the west and northwest of Iceland, their numbers are now holding steady.

Ducks are most easily found in the north at Lake Mývatn, where 16 species nest. Since ducks, like chickens, are compulsive layers, local families can safely collect duck eggs without endangering the population. On the other hand, there are often large fluctuations in the duck and fish populations at Mývatn owing to changes in the availability of food.[13]

Eider ducks are raised almost everywhere in Iceland by farmers who provide nest sites and protect them from predation in order to harvest the down. The down is valuable for coverlets or duvets as it is the lightest and warmest material for the weight.

Puffin – Lundi

Protection of the Environment

In earlier times the forces of nature were thought of as something to be endured in order to wrest a living from the land. In time more emphasis was placed on utilization. At the beginning of the twentieth century Tómas Tómasson, the farmer at Brattholt, signed a contract to rent Gullfoss Falls for power development. His daughter Sigrídur was so incensed that she threatened to jump over the falls if anything was done to spoil their natural beauty. Physically strong and very determined, she considered herself the equal of any man and did men's work in addition to the usual housewifely chores. Her father lost the court case to try to invalidate the contract, but his daughter won the battle outside the courtroom; the contract was finally voided in 1928. Sigrídur had awakened public awareness as she argued for the importance of protecting the beauty of nature. A monument to her was erected near the falls in 1978.[14]

The people at Mývatn in the north of Iceland faced a similar problem in 1970 when the town of Akureyri needed more electrical power and the Laxá Power Company intended to add to the height of the existing dam on the Laxá River in preparation for increasing the generating capacity of the hydroelectric plant. Protests by the inhabitants of the area, pointing out that a higher dam would irrevocably flood the Laxá valley and affect trout and salmon fishing and therefore the economy, went unheeded. Finally, in desperation, on August 25 the farmers blew up a weir belonging to the power company. The explosion shook the government and the people throughout Iceland. Once again the point had been made that people were better off if the beauty and the balance of nature were not unduly disturbed.[15] Today Iceland has a national power grid and hydropower is generated in areas that are relatively barren of vegetation, though there are still objections to altering the landscape and arguments as to where best to run high–tension lines so as to least affect the scenery.

The idea of utilization of natural resources is at the forefront but combined with environmental protection. Though the Soil Conservation Service and the Forestry Service were both established in 1907 and a law passed in 1928 to protect the Thingvellir area, it was not until after World War II that the importance of protecting the environment was more fully understood, by politicians and the general public alike. Increased discussion in the 1950s led to the passage of the first Nature Conservation Act in 1956. Wetlands were drained to increase available arable land, though by the late twentieth century it was understood that maintaining habitat diversity, including some wetlands, was an advantage. In 1989 the government established the Ministry for the Environment, based on the policy of environmentally sound utilization of resources and the realization that protection of the enviroment ensures future well–being. By 1990 there were 72 nature reserves, including three national parks. Iceland was a signatory nation at the 1992 U.N. Conference on Environment and Development.[16] The twin goals of utilization and preservation continue to guide decisions concerning use of the land and of fish and whale stocks, though, as in other countries, there are arguments as to how best to define the limits to utilization. Research is carried out at various centers on marine fish stocks, whale stocks, the testing and development of plant stocks, and the feasibility of exploiting newer means of utilizing environmental resources such as the bacteria and algae in geothermal water.

Erosion, largely caused by overgrazing but exacerbated by strong winds, has been a severe problem. Early reforestation has borne fruit and the Norway pine and Sitka spruce and other trees planted near Akureyri and at Hallormsstadir and elsewhere have grown to impressive heights. The importation of foreign plants offers the potential of increasing production, though the varieties chosen must be viable under Icelandic climatic conditions. Lupine imported from North America has taken hold well and, since it is a legume, fixates nitrogen in the soil, thus making the soil suitable for growing other plants; however, although lupine has proved to be an excellent precursor to tree growth, probably partly because its bright purple flowers are so obvious, it has awakened resentment and increased efforts to seed only plants that are considered to be "native."

Though conflicting interests often sway decisions, Icelanders are awake to the need for conservation and pollution reduction. Twelve percent of household and industrial wastes were recycled by 1990, and in the more populated areas paper and beverage containers are collected for recyling.[17] Overfishing is checked through quotas, and overgrazing is at least partially controlled through more careful stocking rates and the fencing of some lands. A 1990 statute is aimed at halting all severe erosion, and the planting of trees and grasses to check erosion has greatly increased. Through volunteer labor Icelanders have marked out and cared for paths so that tourists will not stamp out the vegetation. The awesome sweep of the land, the black sands, glaciers and lava flows are still there. Conservation is aimed at checking erosion and preserving the carpets of summer wildflowers at the same time that the land is economically productive.

Heroic Seafarers

In the dark of night on the 11th of March, 1984, a small fishing boat capsized 3.2 nautical miles southeast of the Westman Islands. Three of the five fishermen aboard were able to save themselves temporarily by hanging onto the upended keel until the boat sank about three–quarters of an hour later. The air temperature was below freezing, −2° C, and the sea a frigid 5°–6° C (41°–43° F).

When the boat went down, the lone survivor, Gudlaugur Fridthórsson, kicked off his seaman's clothes so as not to be hampered by them and, dressed only in jeans, shirt and sweater and with nothing on his feet, set out to swim to land. On the way he actually passed within three hundred feet of a boat, but no–one aboard heard his shout or saw him wave. Though he expected to die, he remained calm and concentrated on where he should try to come ashore.

After nearly 6 hours in the sea he reached land, but as the cliffs were too sheer to scale, he swam back out to sea and came ashore at another place. Once on land, he still had to negotiate rocks, a low cliff, sharp lava from the 1973 eruption, and a dirt road before he could reach the town close to another mile and a half away. He passed a tub of water used for the sheep in summer, broke the inch–thick ice in the tub with his fist, and drank water from his cupped hand. He said that the most beautiful sight of his life was seeing the lights of the town.

No ordinary person could have survived this ordeal. The body loses heat in cold water and wet clothes draw heat from the body 20 times faster than dry ones. Physical effort and constant moving also reduce the body's defenses. Low body heat leads to mental confusion, an irregular heartbeat, and death. Even a heavy man exposed to water as cold as that which Gudlaugur swam through is normally mentally confused after being immersed for only 80 minutes. A rectal temperature of 36° C (96.8° F) is considered the lowest possible for survival if the person must exert himself. Gudlaugur was in wet clothes for 8–9 hours, in near–freezing water and sub–freezing air. His rectal temperature, when he arrived at the hospital, was at least as low as the minimum 34° C (93° F) that the thermometer could register, yet he showed no sign of mental confusion. He should not have been able to remain alive in the sea for more than 20 or 30 minutes. Instead, he survived the ordeal in good health.

How did Gudlaugur survive? True, he stayed calm and did not expend extra energy through emotional stress, but the key factor surprised researchers. Work at the University of Iceland and in other countries has shown that Gudlaugur's fat bears some resemblance to seal fat: it is more solid than the usual human fat, more like that of a seal, and is two to three times thicker than the human average of 7–9 mm.[1]

Gudlaugur's astonishing achievement is celebrated every March when students at the Navigation College on the Westman Islands take turns swimming for 6 hours, usually in the town's warm pool, though sometimes at sea. After the marathon swim they compete in a race and Gudlaugur himself awards the beaker to the winner.

Seafarers

The Importance of Fishing

Iceland has few natural resources other than marine products, hydroelectric power potential, and geothermal heat. Fish and fish products make up the lion's share of Iceland's exports, which are needed to finance the wide variety of raw materials and finished products that the country must import. Television news broadcasts constantly show pictures of trawlers, nets loaded with fish, and fish processing, as well as interviews with fishermen and the women who work in the processing plants.

The emphasis on fishing has left its mark on the language and on the tales that are told. A VIP is known as a *stórfiskur* (big fish) or a *stórlax* (big salmon). One real fisherman who was brave to the point of foolhardiness has passed into legend as Stjáni blái. There is a well–known song about his exploits. He is said to haunt the cliffs where his boat sank, carrying his head under his arm.

Modern day seamen have been recognized since 1938 at the annual Seamen's Day on the first Sunday in June with band music, parades, and awards. Fishermen, merchant seamen and the Coast Guard all continue to play important roles in preserving the Icelandic nation.

Open Rowboats and the Mystery of the Deep

Though Icelanders utilized marine resources, both fish and sea mammals, down through the centuries, fishing was not a separate industry in earlier centuries as it is today. The chieftains of Commonwealth times and in later centuries the big landowners legally owned anything on shore and some distance out to sea. Fishing provided food and exports and in lean years often defined whether survival was possible, but until well into the nineteenth century it remained, for most, a seasonal activity, a part of the "farm" year.

Fishing conditions were primitive. Many walked, often long distances, to live during the winter in a fishing hut with even fewer amenities than the sod farmhouses of the day. The ruins of these huts can be found in different places in Iceland, though usually only the bottom stones of the walls remain. Well into the twentieth century, the fishermen went to sea in open rowboats, usually six–oared, one person to an oar, with a foreman or coxswain to steer and make decisions; with a removable mast, sail could be added for more speed. To this day fishing from a relatively small fishing boat is still known as *róður* (rowing, a rowing trip) even though the boat is propelled by an engine.

The boats were launched from the beaches straight into the sea, often through the surf, there being few places with any kind of dock. Fishing was dangerous work, and even after a successful day the crew sometimes drowned as they returned through the surf to beach their boats.

The crew wore oilskins. A rope around the waist was passed between the legs, ending in a loop in the middle of the waist; if a person fell overboard the others could pull him back by snagging the loop with a boathook. They propelled the boats with long, narrow–bladed sweeps or a sail, and fished with lines and nets, their only food for the day soured milk thinned with water.

The qualities looked for in the *formaður* (foreman, coxswain), besides seamanship and the ability to command the respect of the crew, were diligence and daring. The foreman was rated on the number of fishing trips undertaken, not the size of the catch.[2] A combination of daring and hard work could result in larger catches. The foreman, like the trawler skipper of today, should also have *fiskni*, the innate ability to find fish that fate has given to some and not to others.

The crew most wanted to catch cod and haddock as these fish keep better than fish like herring. Herring were not considered good to eat, except in times of famine, as they spoil easily. The bycatch, fish other than the ones the foreman and boat owner wanted, could be kept by the lucky crew member and added to the value of his share.

The people drew a sharp distinction between the visible and the invisible worlds.[3] The invisible world included the trolls and Hidden People who lived in the rocks and caves on land and the fish and other water beings hidden in the lakes and sea. Though experienced foremen and crews could say to some degree where the fish would be and at what time of year, fishing entailed a great deal of luck mixed with fear and superstition. The crew hauling in hand lines from the invisible depths never knew what had been hooked until it entered the visible world. A long ripple on a calm sea showed where the *huldufólk* or Hidden People had passed in their own boat, as they also fished.

Icelanders believed in sea monsters: sea serpents, mermaids and mermen, and good and evil whales, the evil ones being those that capsized boats. Seals were endowed with human qualities and could shed their sealskins and become humans. Cows were said to run into the sea in response to the call of the sperm whale.

Those who fished took steps to reduce the uncertainties of dealing with wind and sea and the fish and monsters of the deep. Some methods were practical, such as rhymes and sayings to remember where and when to fish, and noting the color of the water and the behavior of birds. Other methods grew out of superstition. Dreams were interpreted to decide whether to put to sea or not. If a man dreamt of kissing the foreman, or of milk, all should be well, but if he dreamt of a boat on land it would be wise to stay home the following day. Singing at sea would bring an evil whale to capsize the boat. The boats themselves were alive and talked together, as did the farm animals, especially on New Year's Eve and Midsummer Night's Eve. The fish caught were a gift that was reciprocated by throwing back into the sea cod roe or a part of the fish that was not used.

Prayers before setting out helped, as did magic charms. There was a strong belief in the power of the word; a poem could tame the elements or call up Satan to bring storms and disaster. The famous eighteenth century magician, Galdra–Loftur, chanted an incantation:[4]

Over all the land
Let storm and terror stand.
Sea spray with sand
Send them, O Arch Fiend!

A tremendous storm followed, cementing the poet's reputation of having the power to control the forces of nature.

Thurídur Formann

Women as well as men fished the high seas, probably from the beginning of colonization. Records from the seventeenth through the nineteenth centuries show that it was fairly common for women to fish.[5] The most famous of these, in fact the most famous of all Iceland's foremen, was Thurídur Einarsdóttir, who became known as Thurídur Formann.[6]

Born in Stokkseyri in the south of Iceland in 1777, she first went "rowing" with her father when she was only 11. After his death she rowed for her brother for six years.

Thurídur was slight but strong, with rather broad shoulders, an able sailor but also a fast walker. One visiting foreigner had to spur her horse to keep up with her. She was alert, observant, and determined. She tried working for a farmer once, but she wasn't good at taking orders from others. She had a hard gaze and was given to quick retorts, evidence of her drive and intelligence, but even when she was slandered she never swore. The men were comfortable rowing with her and enjoyed her company on land as well.

Since women's clothes did not fit well under a fisherman's oilskins, Thurídur, like the other women who fished, learned young to dress like a man. In time she took to wearing men's clothes at home for comfort but, since it was against the law in Iceland, as elsewhere at the time, for anyone to appear publicly dressed like the opposite sex, she wore women's clothes outside her home. One day, after one of Iceland's most famous robberies, *Kambsrán*, she was called to appear before the magistrate without having time to change her clothes.

"I would not have come dressed like this," she excused herself, "only the men insisted."

"Never mind," the magistrate replied. "If you can identify who owns these objects, I'll give you legal permission to wear men's clothes all the time."

So saying, he produced the things the robbers had left behind in their carelessness. By identifying the stitching on a pair of fishskin shoes Thurídur was able to name the woman who had sewn them, thereby leading to the robbers. For a while after giving this information she was worried for her own safety, but eventually the four men guilty of the robbery were brought to justice, punished by whipping and imprisonment, and made to repay the stolen money.

Three times Thurídur was maligned because she wore men's clothes. She sued the offenders for slander and won the lawsuit each time.

Thurídur was engaged more than once and later married, but none of the unions lasted for long. A man named Erlendur proposed to her. However, like everyone else, she was superstitious and, since they lived on a farm that was also "inhabited" by the fetch Sels–Móri, she refused to marry him. In 1808 she was pregnant with Erlendur's child but continued to fish all winter. After the couple left the farm, sure enough, the fetch was seen.

Thurídur bore a daughter and supported them both by fishing, but the little girl sickened during the third winter and died the following summer, a loss that Thurídur felt deeply. Two years later her brother Bjarni went rowing, taking his axe with him. When the boat capsized he managed to sink the head of the axe into the bottom of the boat and hang on, but though he shouted for help, the wind was too strong and the seas too high for anyone to be able to save him. They could only watch while he drowned.

In time Thurídur was made foreman, and people began to call her Thurídur Formann in imitation of the Danish custom of taking a person's occupation as the last name. In good fishing years she did well and at one time even had as many as three servants. In poorer years she helped feed others when she did not have to struggle to keep herself fed. Finally, in 1843 at the age of 66 she retired after 25 years of being foreman. She died in 1848.

The British and the French

The richness of the Icelandic fishing grounds has attracted people from various countries to fish and hunt whales.[7] Beached whales were owned by the landowner and were a valuable commodity. Blubber, meat, bone and baleen were all utilized: the meat and blubber provided food; the oil and blubber, light; the bone, cartilage and baleen, material for fashioning objects such as crochet hooks, containers and crinoline hoops. The value of a beached whale was so high that the *Book of Settlements* and many of the sagas record fights and arguments over ownership of the carcass. The Basques came north to hunt whales in the seventeenth century, joined by the French, English, and Dutch.

As early as the fifteenth century the English and the Germans established bases on land, the Germans to trade, the English principally to fish. The English were so busy fishing in Icelandic waters that the fifteenth century is known in Icelandic history as the English Century. With the English fishing off Iceland so intensively and trading with Icelanders in the fifteenth century it is perhaps not surprising that a clash of interests arose, setting off the first of the ten altercations sometimes called the Cod Wars.[8] Iceland, then under the Danish crown, was caught up in the struggles of the European powers. The first Cod War ended in 1432 with an agreement between England and Denmark, but other Cod Wars followed. The English continued to send ships, but they also turned to exploring North America and to fishing the Grand Banks.

Meanwhile the French were also trying to satisfy the European demand for fish on Friday and during Lent. By the seventeenth century many of them were fishing for herring in the seas around Britain. When they followed the herring north, they discovered the cod off Iceland.[9] In the nineteenth century Paimpol in Brittany was the center of "Icelandic" fishing. In 1880 there were 5000 Bretons fishing around Iceland, from two– and three–masted vessels with a crew of 16–24 men each. They came in February and followed the cod north, fishing until mid–August. The catch was transferred to a freighter in mid–May and transported south.

The French, like others of the day, worked under difficult conditions with no certainty they would survive to return home after the 7–month tour. They stood 12–hour watches, longer if the fish were running, with two men and sometimes three sharing a bunk and with a coal stove for warmth in the colder months. They lacked sanitation and often became ill, and drunkenness was a problem.

When they were able to land, the Bretons learned some Icelandic, picked berries in summer, brought cognac and chocolate as gifts, and have left some dark–haired descendants. Icelanders welcomed them, learned some French, and knit them mittens with two thumbs so that they would last longer. The French had a seaman's home and hospital on land and there is a memorial to them in the Old Cemetery in Reykjavík.

By 1935 the saga of Breton fishing in Iceland came to an end. In the twentieth century their sailing vessels could no longer compete and newer jobs in industry were more lucrative. In 1979 one of the last of these "Icelandic" fishermen visited Iceland as a guest and recalled that when he was young, Bretons felt Iceland was closer than Paris, such was their dependence on catching Icelandic cod.

The nineteenth century saw the increasing importance of British fishing in Icelandic waters. Beginning in 1870 the British used steam vessels and began trawl fishing in 1891.[10] Iceland, in contrast, at that time still part of the kingdom of Denmark, lacked the capital, equipment and experience to utilize her own fisheries effectively.

Icelanders generally profited from trade with the British, as with the French. Since the British fished for haddock, halibut and plaice, they were willing to give Icelanders the by–catch of cod and other species which they did not want. The most important impact of British fishing, however, was not the huge size of their catches but that they introduced Icelanders to modern vessels and fishing gear.[11] The Danish Coast Guard had only sailing ships until 1865 and could not catch the much faster British steam trawlers. Like the French, the British lived under difficult conditions and often sickened or drowned, but their fishing methods were hugely effective. The British used an otter trawl and then perfected a beam trawl that could sweep fish from the sea while Icelanders and Bretons were still using nets and long lines. In the mid–nineteenth century Icelanders fished from three thousand rowboats while the French had a hundred decked ships and caught more than the Icelanders did, and British fishing was even more effective than the French.

The Danish trade monopoly was finally abolished in 1855. New markets in Spain and elsewhere opened up. About 1870 Icelanders began to buy second-hand cutters from the British. The stage was set for change.

The Change to a Market Economy and Improved Technology

The emergence and growth of the market economy entailed fundamental changes in the way fishing was defined.[12] Luck and the struggle against the elements did not disappear as important factors, but the emphasis shifted to a full–time industry with a technological approach toward solving the problems involved. The invisible world was revealed and fish located with equipment such as sonar. The use of decked ships meant the need for proper ports and unloading facilities. By 1906 Icelanders had 169 decked fishing vessels, employing 2000 seamen, and Reykjavík had become the center of marine fishing. The foreman was replaced by a skipper educated for the job. Work specialization followed, as engines demanded mechanics to keep them running. Fishing expanded into offshore waters and called for accurate charts, rather than the old way of using mountains and other landmarks to locate fish and find one's way back to shore. Selling most of the catch to foreign markets meant the need to process a larger quantity of fish; the villages and towns that grew up around the ports provided labor for the processing plants. First icehouses and later in the twentieth century freezing plants were built. The need for capital was expedited by the establishment of, first, Íslands Bank, and then in 1930 the Fisheries Bank of Iceland.

Taste also changed: later in the twentieth century boiled haddock and boiled potatoes, the staples that had nourished Icelanders for several centuries, came to be defined as "ordinary" and were supplemented by the delicacies of herring and Icelandic lobster. Fish and the monsters of the deep no longer controlled the fate of humans; instead, humans began to control the fate of the marine resources.

The change from foreman in a rowboat to ship's captain required training, resulting in the opening of the Marine Academy in 1891. The foreman's success was defined by the number of times the crew went fishing. The skipper's success is defined by the size of the catch. The "catch king" is still thought to know best where to fish, but success is also dependent on the sophistication of the equipment. The competition between skippers to be first with the biggest catch is strong. Seamen sometimes complain that the skipper is too dictatorial, but the modern crew must cooperate if fishing is to be successful.

Though some women still go to sea, usually as maids or cooks, the change from foreman to skipper and the usually longer fishing trips involved have meant that the women's roles have become more sharply separated from the men's. Wives are left alone at home, often for long periods, and more women than men work in the fish processing plants.

The change to a market economy also meant pressure to catch more so as to sell more. Different kinds of nets and lines and trawls make it possible to catch more species and more of each species, but the industry is also prey to price fluctuations and there is the ever–present danger of overfishing the stocks. In the 1960s, when the herring runs were enormous, Icelanders filled their nets. For most of the time Siglufjördur in the north was the center of the "herring adventure" and the women, aided by children, worked day and night without sleep to salt this "silver of the sea." Occasionally, in a lull between landing catches, the people sang and danced in wild abandon in order to stand the pressure of the long hours of work before going back to salting the next batch of herring in wooden casks.

The invention of the harpoon with an exploding head in the middle of the nineteenth century meant that the whale stocks were also jeopardized. The Althing responded by setting a ten–year ban in 1915, extended in 1928 for ten additional years. Iceland became a member of the International Whaling Commission, founded in 1946. The arguments over whaling since then, like most things in Iceland, have been colored by the strong belief in independence, both for the nation and for the individual, as well as by demands for controlled resource utilization consonant with the government's policy to protect the environment.

Increasing pressure on the fish stocks has led to government–imposed fishing quotas in order to insure future catches. Despite marine biological research, how large the quotas should be and how they should best be allocated, or even if quotas are workable, remain bones of contention.

In the years since Iceland gained independence from Denmark in 1918, Iceland has moved from a people who had to learn from others to a nation that has contributed its own inventions and expertise and that now helps other nations learn to utilize their own marine resources.

The Rescue at Látrabjarg

Given Iceland's northern latitude, the storms that often pass over the land, Iceland's dependence on marine fishing, and the recurring volcanic eruptions, organized rescue groups are a must. The Icelandic Civil Defence, the National Lifesaving Association, the Coast Guard and the Scouts all participate in rescue operations.

Coordination of rescue operations is often in the hands of the Civil Defence organization. In January 1995, for instance, they directed the heroic rescue operations in the small fishing village of Súdavík in the West Fjords when avalanches reduced a third of the village to ruins. Force 12 winds in a blinding snowstorm hampered rescue operations, but the loss of life was undoubtedly not as high as it would have been without the efforts of the 300 rescuers, their trained dogs and their equipment.

Iceland's most famous rescue took place in the dark of winter when the British vessel *Dhoon* ran aground at the base of the Látrabjarg Cliff in the West Fjords on December 12, 1947.[13] The National Lifesaving Association alerted people in the area and further phone calls recruited rescuers.

Today a dirt road much used by tourist buses runs out to Látrabjarg. At that time there was no road and in the dark and stormy weather it was so difficult to find their way that everyone who took part in the rescue was lost at some point, either going or returning home. It took three hours for the first 15 rescuers with one pack horse to reach the edge of the cliff, arriving at 8:30 a.m. on December 13 with equipment and food. Twelve men, using a rope, descended the 120 meters (400 ft.) to the sea. The other three held the line fast above.

Once at the bottom, the men still had to climb over the jumble of boulders at the base of the cliff to reach the stranded ship a half kilometer away. Since the ship lay 300 or more feet out, they shot a line to the ship and succeeded in bringing the twelve seamen to land in a breeches buoy. By 4:30 p.m. seven of the shipwrecked crew and one Icelander had been pulled to a narrow, less steep part of the cliff. The others were still below on a small projecting toe of rock. By that time the tide had come in, a heavy sea was running, and it was too dark to do more. The men spent the night where they were.

On December 14 other rescuers managed to reach Látrabjarg in the dark with more food and clothes. It took until 6:00 p.m., working in heavy rain and winds, before everyone had been pulled up to the top of the cliff. Seven of the shipwrecked seamen were taken to farmhouses, but five had to pass a second night with two Icelanders in a tent on top of the cliff. The following day the remaining shipwrecked men walked to the farmhouse as they were too cold to ride the horses that had been brought.

The rescue had taken 75 hours, over difficult terrain and under difficult conditions. The rescued seamen were, of course, deeply grateful, the boatswain praised the Icelanders for their courage and perseverance, and the Icelandic National Lifesaving Association awarded medals to the rescuers.

The Family: Winter Feast –
A Toast to Survival

"We're celebrating Thorrablót," Sigga phoned. "Come join us! Saturday," she added, realizing that in her enthusiasm she had made it sound as though I should drop everything right that moment.

In late January the worst of the winter darkness was beginning to lift after two long months. To enliven the winter, many people go skiing, but I prefer to swim in the outdoor geothermal pools. In the evening a huge number of people sing in choruses; in fact, there are probably more choruses in Reykjavík compared to the population than anywhere else in the world, a wonderful way to combat the long winter. In January and February nearly every club and association has an annual get–together with a fine dinner, short speeches that praise or amuse, and sometimes dancing—and everybody sings together. The invigoration is welcome.

I set off in high spirits to celebrate Thorrablót with Sigga and Gunnar. A short, fat candle burned outside the door to welcome us, the sign of a party. The northern lights were bannered green and red across the sky as Gunnar opened the door with a "*Blessuð*," the feminine form to wish me well, and gave me a hug and a kiss on the cheek. Sigga hugged and kissed me while thanking me for the bouquet of spring blooms I had brought, the usual thank–you gift for dinner. The geothermal heat and greenhouses make flowers easily available all winter long. I took off my boots and set them beside the others in the entryway. In fact, Icelanders slip out of their shoes all year on entering a home so as not to track in dirt. Some of the guests had changed into other shoes and some, both men and women, were in their socks or stockings—with no holes!

In the Icelandic way, I introduced myself to the guests who had already arrived, shaking hands with each one and saying my name to the ones I hadn't met before. We were invited for 8:00, which means that the guests arrive at some comfortable time after eight and we will be fed when the hostess is ready. I settled down in a chair and looked round the room, enjoying the oil paintings on the walls and the many thriving plants.

There were ten of us that night, the women all dressed in the latest fashion and sporting fashionable hairdos. Icelandic women are all stylish with a natural flair for well–cut clothes. If Reykjavík had been farther south, it would have been the fashion capital of Europe.

Gunnar, our host, like most Icelanders, is blond with a broad face, high cheekbones and wide–spaced blue eyes, tall and broad–chested, with thick, strong hands. An importer, he exudes a calm air of authority. He is also a poet, which is not a contradiction in a country that values poetry highly. Like many businessmen, he usually goes for a swim before going to work. His wife Sigga, like most Icelandic women, works outside the home and is a nurse. She, too, is broad–shouldered and blue–eyed, and keeps her hair the blonde it was when she was a child.

The thinner, dark–haired man with the long legs is Sigga's brother Jón, admired for his ability to think up a rhyme on the spot. Jón's wife, Helga, was talking to the other guests, two couples whom Gunnar knows from work and the owner of a fishing vessel.

Thorrablót! In the old Icelandic calendar Thorri was the name of the fourth month of winter, beginning in our calendar in late January. Thorri was evidently a winter or weather god at the outset, and his month came to mean the time when the farmer demonstrated that he had provided enough food to last the household until late spring. The month of Thorri was followed by Góa, when the farmer often left to go fishing and his wife had to see to managing the household. Thorri was still respected in the nineteenth century with an odd rite: in a shirt and barefoot, the farmer put only one leg through his long johns and, thus attired, hopped around his farmhouse! The other custom is more understandable to us: on that day the wife must wait on her husband. If that seems unfair, not to worry: the husband must wait on his wife on the first day of the next month, Góa.

The revival of the ancient feast of Thorri was connected with the Icelandic struggle for independence from Danish rule. The first such rite (*blót*) was held by Icelandic students in Copenhagen in 1873. The custom then spread in fits and starts over the north of Iceland, to be taken up eventually, around 1960, by the country as a whole. Now Thorri's feast is a yearly event, enjoyed by any who wish.

The feast itself may surprise you. The food that was once a necessity for survival has become a celebration of being an Icelander. In the old days food was soured or salted or smoked so it would keep. Icelanders still eat these foods with pleasure, though normally not all in the same meal.

Sigga invited us to help ourselves to the food, which was set out on the "groaning board" in wooden platters or troughs. There was *hangikjöt*, lamb "hung" as it was smoked, rosy–colored and tasty and eaten with well–buttered rye bread. The wool had been been singed off the sheep heads (*svið*) and the skull split lengthwise for easier access to the meat. For most Icelanders the eye is the best part, but I have to admit that I passed on that one. *Hangikjöt, svið* and stockfish (dried cod or other dried fish) are common Icelandic foods year–round. For Thorrablót there are also rams' testicles (known by some in English as Rocky Mountain oysters) soured in whey, special lamb sausages, chunks of whale blubber pickled in whey, and bite–size bits of shark decomposed during burial until there is no ammonium left and the meat is good to eat. There is a strong difference of opinion about rotted shark, however; the number of those who cannot abide it seems to be balanced by the number of those who consider it a delicacy.

59

There was plenty of flatbread and compact rye bread with a delicious, nutty taste. The feast was washed down with beer and *brennivín*, a hard liquor flavored either with angelica root or with caraway seeds and affectionately known as Black Death.

"Please begin," Sigga encouraged us and we set to with enjoyment, using fingers and a sharp knife such as a pocket knife.

"*Skál!*" Gunnar held his glass out toward us, "cheers!" We all drank. Jón, our instant poet, replied with:

> Gunnar serves his guests with beer;
> Fine food is on display.
> Let us one and all take cheer
> In honor of the day!

There were murmurs of approval. The on–the–spot rhyme, with proper alliteration, fits Icelandic ballad rhythm.

"Don't forget Sigga. Thanks to her as well!" This from Helga, and we all toasted Sigga.

While we ate, we thought about what it used to be like in Iceland. The "old days" were not so long ago—in the mid–twentieth century. Two of the guests came from the north and reminisced about what a marvellous excuse Thorrablót used to be for people in the countryside to have a get–together. Some families came by car and some on horseback, but everybody down to the youngest child gathered in the local community center. They brought what they could carry with them, the wooden troughs of food often tied in flour sacking and slung from the horse's saddle or transported by the car, as the case might be. There was home–brewed ale to drink, but with so many children present, drinking was not excessive. There were no cakes or sweets to eat but plenty of coffee, of course. Iceland runs on coffee.

At the end of the meal we all said the polite "thank you for me" and Gunnar and Sigga wished us well. As is sometimes done, we shook Sigga's hand and said how nice it had been before returning to the living room for after–dinner coffee. The couple from the north were still reminiscing. In the countryside the minister would give a short speech, the local men's choir would sing, someone would read poems, and there would be short skits before the dancing began that lasted into the wee hours. Things have changed now that the custom of Thorrablót has moved south to Reykjavík and the grocery stores display the proper food. Nowadays it is even possible to get the meal catered.

The conversation turned to odd occurrences. The trawler owner asked if we had heard of Óskar Thórhallsson, who received a gold watch as a birthday present from his wife in 1964 and then lost it overboard. When his mother–in–law went to the jeweller's to ask about replacing it, the jeweller said he had it! A man had brought it in to have it fixed after having found it in a cod's stomach! Amazingly, it ran perfectly and only needed the strap fixed. Twenty years later, by the way, the watch was still running perfectly. That tale set Jón to looking thoughtful for a few moments, and then he recited:

> Birthday gift of gleaming gold
> Glistened in the ocean.
> Watch encased in codfish bold
> Kept its perfect motion.

When the laughter had died down one of the businessmen asked, "Do you know about Jón Gudmundsson?" This being Iceland, we were first treated to a clear account of which Jón Gudmundsson he was talking about, who his mother and father were, and what his grandparents did. For Icelanders the all–important genealogy that helps define Icelanders as a people is as much fun as the joke. Then we learned that this Jón had back trouble. "So he drove to Reykjavík to see the doctors. They were doomsayers and told him he'd have to have surgery at once. Jón said he was going home first, but he'd be back. So he set out over the long dirt road home." Of course, he drove like most Icelanders, much too fast for dirt road conditions. "All of a sudden he hit a huge pothole and was thrown up so his head bumped the roof. Then he dropped back down onto the seat. And he hasn't had a bit of back trouble since!"

A lot of Icelandic jokes are like that, recounting a sudden turn of events or told with a sharp wit that gives a different interpretation. Helga told us about a grandfather who was baby–sitting his grandson. After we had run through the names and genealogy, we learned that the grandfather had had his usual nip from the bottle. The trouble was that the three year old thought that as long as *afi* drank it, it must be good, so he got hold of the bottle and had a nip, too. The grandfather then became aware that the three year old was walking a bit oddly and finally fell down. He scooped the boy up and drove him to the nearest clinic, where the doctor said there was no need to worry, just let the boy sleep it off. The grandfather, in relief, was speeding homeward when a policeman spied him and had him pull over. The policeman had no trouble smelling liquor, so he asked the old man to take a breathalyzer test. Quick as a wink, the grandfather said to test the boy instead, and sure enough the balloon test on the boy was positive. That time, at least, the grandfather avoided a traffic ticket.

We sang Icelandic songs before the evening got any older, a common thing to do when Icelanders are relaxed and enjoying themselves. For good measure we also sang Laxness's Icelandic words to the tune of "Drink to me only with thine eyes" and a song in English that arrived in Iceland with U.S. soldiers in World War II, "My bonnie lies over the ocean." But mostly we sang Icelandic folk songs and songs about Iceland. The tunes are varied, some catchy, some beautiful, some with a marvellous strength.

Late at night, very late, after all the singing, more coffee and beer, more food to nibble on and more laughter, we decided it was finally time to go home. We donned our boots again and bundled up against the cold. The evening ended with Sigga and Gunnar shaking hands with all the men and giving all the women a hug and kiss, a thank–you from everyone, and our host's heartfelt "Thank you for coming."

Spring—Beginnings

The Family: Birth, Marriage, and Death

At two months she was adorable. She smiled at Sigga, her grandmother, who smiled back, as proud of her as were her parents, Kristín and Hjalti. The little one fell asleep in her baby carriage outdoors, snug under her own tiny duvet, knowing nothing of the excitement that awaited her after her nap.

The baby was born very early in January in the hospital in Reykjavík, delivered by a trained midwife. Her mother, Kristín, had prenatal care provided through the national health scheme, one factor responsible for Iceland's low death rate (in 1989) of only six per thousand children five years of age or younger. At birth she measured the average 50 cm (19 1/2 in.) in length and weighed the average 3.7 kg (15 *mörk* or over 8 lbs.). A nurse visited her mother regularly to keep track of the baby's health and to see that she received the proper immunizations.

Kristín, her mother, now 21, graduated from upper secondary school last year and worked in an office until she took maternity leave. Her father, Hjalti, is a plumber and, since the citizens of the Nordic countries can move freely from one country to another, they have decided to go to Sweden so that Hjalti can earn higher wages. Kristín and Hjalti have been living together, but they have decided to get married before moving to Sweden. This was the day!

The baby was to be christened at their wedding ceremony. The invitations had gone out to quite a few of us, but until the ceremony no one could be told the baby's name. In the old days, when infant death was so common and the power of a name believed to be stronger than it is now, it became the custom not to name the child until the christening ceremony and for the child not to be christened until several months after birth when survival was more assured. Kristín and Hjalti were among the many who adhere to the custom.

Solar Coffee and Winter Weather

In January, after the little one was born, King Winter brought us a succession of storms—"a conveyor belt of lows," one meteorologist called it. Snow was followed by high winds that wailed through any gaps in the windows, despite insulation. Pouring rain then melted the snow, which was followed by a still worse storm one Thursday, with winds gusting to 80 miles per hour, horizontal sleet, and very impressive lightning and thunder. Yes, in winter, lightning and thunder! At one point, within seconds the storm completely covered my living room and kitchen windows with thick sleet and I was shut inside a white wall, unable to see out. But through the weeks of storms the days had lengthened little by little and the light had become brighter.

Sigga's family comes from the West Fjord district in the far north, where successions of lava flows form the ridges that separate the fjords. In the darkest part of the year the sun does not rise above these ridges. There and in the East

65

Fjords, especially, it has been common to celebrate the first return of sunlight over the tops of the ridges with a special family gathering called Solar Coffee. There is no special day, and each family may decide for itself when to meet together. This farm family tradition of coffee and *pönnukökur* (Icelandic crêpes) has been continued in the south of Iceland, where groups of people, especially those whose families came from the West or East Fjords, meet to celebrate. Sigga and her mother and grandmother, who both now live in Reykjavík, met with others in late February to enjoy Solar Coffee and conversation.

The Wedding and the Christening

The church is a modern one, with the altar on a low, broad platform up front and the congregation sitting in wide, high–backed chairs, the red upholstery richly contrasting with the white walls. The high, narrow glass panels behind the altar bear a pleasing design of plant tendrils.

At the wedding Hjalti and his best man sat up front on the right and rose and bowed slightly to each guest in turn as he or she entered, a gesture that in ancient times showed they carried no weapons. Each man who came to the wedding bowed slightly in return; very few women still curtsey. Meanwhile Kristín and her father Gunnar sat on two chairs on the left.

The ensuing service was Lutheran, the state religion supported by our taxes. The minister, dressed in robes and a wide, white ruffled collar, added his own homily to the ritual service, his words of wisdom a good reminder to all who had come. After the wedding ritual, Gunnar moved to sit with Hjalti's father. Hjalti in turn went to sit with Kristín on *her* side of the church, an emphasis on maintaining ties with the wife's family that often carries over into family celebrations throughout the years.

Then Gunnar came forward with the baby, and Sigga and Hjalti's father bore witness to the christening, their only responsibility as godparents. At last we heard the baby's name: Anna Sigrídur. No real surprise after all, as she was named for both grandmothers. Since she is the daughter of her father, Hjalti, her full name is Anna Sigrídur Hjaltadóttir, the name she will keep even after she is married, but she will be known as Anna Sigga to her family.

The Wedding Reception

Though wedding receptions in Reykjavík are often held at the Pearl, the impressive edifice built atop the hot water tanks on Öskjuhlíd Hill, Kristín preferred having the reception at her parents' home. Others in the family helped Sigga with the preparations. As the guests began to arrive, the presents everyone brought, largely books and original art work, were laid on a table.

Sigga's mother Gudrún, now 75, and her husband came, bringing Sigga's grandmother Ingibjörg. Since Ingibjörg's husband, a minister in the West Fjords, died some time ago, she has lived with her daughter Gudrún in Reykjavík. Though Ingibjörg at 93 had shrunk with age, her hearing and sight were still good and her face radiated the interest she felt in her family around her and her quiet patience with what life has dealt her. She sat forward in her chair, taking everything in. Like her granddaughter, she is practical, cheerful, accepting in the face of adversity. She is also a published poet. Of her seven children, she lost three in infancy and a fourth, a sea captain, went down with his small fishing vessel in high seas. One son and a daughter still live in the West Fjords with their families, farming folk all.

Gudrún is a housewife and her husband a semi–retired electrician. Three of their children, Sigga, Jón, the rhymer and salesman whom we met at Thorrablót, and Thorsteinn, who carries on the electrical business his father founded, live in Reykjavík, and the fourth, Inga, lives on a farm on the south coast within easy driving distance of Reykjavík. Inga and her husband and children came to the reception. Gudrún herself prefers the old ways, has second sight, and once saw the Hidden People come out of a cliff on Inga's farm, though she is as addicted to evening television and watching videos as the rest of the nation. She came dressed in the traditional long black skirt, with gilt embroidery decorating both the hem of the skirt and the black bodice worn over a white blouse. On her now gray hair nestled a traditional round black cap with a black tassel.

Sigga and Gunnar's three children, Thórunn, who at 26 is a teacher, Kristín, the bride, and Gudmundur (Gummi), who is only 13, were kept busy greeting the guests and helping serve the food. Gummi (the *u* sounds much like the *oo* in l*oo*k), who is always hungry, had a mischievous look in his eye, but big sister Thórunn cautioned, "Just wait, we'll eat soon."

Gunnar's family was not as well represented at this gathering. His grandfather Magnús, through whom he can trace his descent back to an original Norse settler, as can many Icelanders, did not live to be as old as Ingibjörg. His father, Sigurjón, was in the hospital, so ill it was a question whether he would survive. His mother Kristín, for whom his daughter was named, came, along with his brothers Pétur and Halldór and their families. His bachelor brother Magnús worked abroad for the airline and could not come.

As family and guests all greeted each other we also looked appreciatively at Anna Sigga, the newest member of the family, while we caught up on the news. Jón, who is a condominium manager, recounted an incident that happened in the building where he and Helga live.

"Water was pouring out from under the door of one apartment and running into the basement. The carpet was soaking wet. Nobody home, so we couldn't get in. I called the police, who came, but they don't have lockpicks, so then I had to call a locksmith. When we finally got the door open we could see the apartment was completely flooded. Floors ruined," he added. At this point Jón paused for effect in his recounting and more than one listener said "*Já*" on indrawn breath to encourage him to continue.

"I called the fire department to come and pump out the water," Jón continued. "A bunch of kids gathered outside to see what was up," he added. "They couldn't resist the fire engine." The children weren't the only ones who smiled at that. "What went wrong?" Thorsteinn asked. "The washing machine," Jón replied. "The tub didn't fill and with nobody home to check, it just kept on pumping. The clothes in the machine were absolutely bone dry! About the only things in the apartment that were."

At this point the refreshments were ready. People helped themselves to almond cake and an assortment of other treats and the adults toasted the bride and groom with champagne.

A photographer arrived and the five generations of women posed together: Anna Sigga's great–great–grandmother Ingibjörg, her great–grandmother Gudrún, her grandmother Sigga, and her mother Kristín all said "sheesh" (the Icelandic pronunciation of "cheese") for the benefit of the camera.

Like her relatives and like 75% of the Icelandic nation, Anna Sigga will have blue (or gray) eyes, and like 55%, she will have blonde hair, though it will probably darken with age. She will be attractive, with large, wide–spaced eyes and a pleasant nose. In fact, a British promotion team that came in 1991 found it harder in Iceland than in other nations to choose which little girl was the best likeness of Alice in Wonderland: they all were! She will be tall and, barring accident, she should live a long time: her life expectancy is over 80 years. One other aspect of modern Iceland will help develop her self–confidence. Since Vigdís Finnbogadóttir became Iceland's first woman president in 1980, little girls have been heard to say, "I'm going to be president when I grow up."

There was suddenly a loud wail from the little one in question. She wasn't going to grow up to be any of those things if she wasn't fed *right now*!

A Visit to the Hospital

Either Gunnar or one of his brothers has driven their mother, Kristín, to the hospital every day to visit her husband Sigurjón. Today, when Gunnar and his mother arrived, several friends and other members of the family were already there. Visitors frequently come irrespective of posted visiting hours. Fresh flowers and plants crowded the bed table and lined the window ledge. Several visitors had brought boxes of chocolates, which Sigurjón offered to all who had come. Despite how ill he was with cancer, it was like a daily party, with wry comments on the latest in politics, a joke or two, and everyone taking the time to show how much they care about him. His grandchildren have all visited him regularly, and of course, his granddaughter Kristín has brought Anna Sigga for him to admire.

Nursing care in Iceland is warm and remarkably personal, and hospital care is provided through national health insurance. By the same token, there is no limit beyond the patient's strength on how many visitors may be present at one time, and no hesitation in bringing children to visit a sick member of the family. The women especially took turns holding Anna Sigga.

When Sigurjón's father, Magnús, was ill, he was nursed at home on his farm and died in his bed, his coffin resting in the living room with a candle lit beside it. In the early part of the twentieth century Icelanders died of "senility," pneumonia, and tuberculosis. After World War II, Icelanders came to have one of the best health care systems in the world and to live longer, but the changes that have taken place since World War II have meant, as elsewhere, that the greatest proportion of deaths is from cancer and heart–artery problems and that most Icelanders die, not at home, but in an institution.

On this day it became clear that Sigurjón had become too tired after all this "partying" and the nurses asked that only the immediate family be allowed to visit from then on. Gunnar had already phoned Magnús abroad to tell him to come home while there was still time to see their father before the end.

The Funeral

Within five days after death there is a coffin–closing ceremony, which only the family attends. After Sigurjón's death, his wife insisted that his coffin should rest in her living room rather than in a chapel. She countered her sons' arguments by saying that Magnús was staying with her. Though the family may conduct the ceremony alone, in this case the minister came and spoke the necessary words. The veil was removed from Sigurjón's face and each member of the family then kissed the body and made the sign of the cross over it. There may be tears, if any, at the funeral but not at the closing of the coffin. The coffin was then fastened shut and remained in the house until the day of the funeral, which may take place whenever the family decides, usually a week or ten days after the death.

The day of the funeral the newspaper printed testimonials from friends and associates recounting Sigurjón's life, reiterating the pleasure they had in knowing him and offering their sympathy. Every friend and acquaintance that Kristín has seen since Sigurjón's death, including many of the men, hugged her and warmly expressed their sympathy.

The funeral took place in the old church that is the bishop's seat or Cathedral in the center of Reykjavík. A stone building erected in the eighteenth and enlarged in the nineteenth century, the Cathedral stands near the pond in the center of town, painted an attractive soft cream with green trim. The single bell that tolled for the funeral is in the simple clock tower atop the verdigris copper roof.

As in the eighteenth century when the church was built, the interior walls are white with slender wooden pillars that support the gallery. The wooden pulpit with its roof is carved, the decorations highlighted in gilt. The christening font is of carved marble and the altar–piece is an oil painting of Christ. Though the church seats six hundred, there is a feeling of warmth and closeness, so that all who came to the funeral felt they were in touch with everyone else.

Since Sigurjón was a well known and respected manager of a department of the Agricultural Bank and an active member of the Progressive Party, both positions reflecting his farm roots, the church was packed, both upstairs and down. The family sat downstairs in front on the left, the pallbearers on the right, having taken their seats before anyone else started to enter. The choir stood beside the organ in the rear of the gallery.

The coffin rested in the aisle before the nave. Sigurjón's wife, Kristín, was lost in her thoughts as she looked toward the candles on the altar and the painting of Christ. She seemed frail but steadfast in the face of her grief as the organist began to play.

The funeral followed the Lutheran ritual but was very personal, the minister taking time to trace Sigurjón's life and to praise him quietly for all the good he had accomplished. The soloist and the special music were what Sigurjón himself had chosen before he died. While reciting "ashes to ashes, dust to dust," the minister sprinkled real soil on the coffin with a brass shovel. At the end the pallbearers lifted the white coffin by its brass handles and carried it down the aisle, followed by Kristín, with Gunnar beside her, then the other members of the family, and finally those of us who attended the funeral.

Sigurjón's closest relatives went to the cemetery where, in keeping with the emphasis on the personal, the two undertakers sat in the hearse and the family saw to setting the coffin on the wooden slats over the open grave. Then each one in turn stood by the grave, meditating for a moment before making the sign of the cross over the coffin. A raw wind and rain blew over the mourners, but the weather did not stop them from taking a final farewell.

The family returned to join the other mourners at the reception where all of us were served coffee and cake and where we all drank a toast to Sigurjón. His wife, Kristín, with her sons, will return to place flowers on his grave on his birthday, and candles and pine branches at Christmas. Most of the graves also have electric crosses which bring light during the dark of Christmastime.

Kristín and Gunnar and his brothers said goodbye to all the guests as we left, thanking them for coming. As Magnús was to drive his mother home, Sigga suggested, "Let's go see Anna Sigga," and Gunnar nodded his agreement.

The Myth of Creation

The majority of the original settlers in Iceland brought with them their belief in the Norse gods, the Aesir. Their religion gave them what people everywhere need, an explanation of how things came to be and how they work, and a way to cope with human emotions and the often overpowering forces of nature. The myths were recounted with a verve that still entertains, while they provided answers to universal questions.

These first Icelanders dared to uproot their families and settle in an unknown land. Their myths sustained them with the presentation of a worldview that encouraged an energetic response to the problems of men and nature, coupled with a fatalistic acceptance of what cannot be changed. They valued their honor and achievements and they equally valued wisdom and wise decisions, as the sagas and scaldic poetry attest.

They loved a good story and repeated the tales to each other and to their children. The recounting of events was straightforward, the emotion understood without agonizing, the effect stronger for the minimalist approach. They were clever with words, expressing a great deal in verse and frequently using kennings or allegorical expressions based on the myths to refer to battle, warriors, women.

Icelanders of today still adhere to much of the worldview of the past—the acceptance of the forces of nature, the importance of the individual vis–à–vis other individuals, personal honor, and, for many, the existence of elves and especially of ghosts. The reminders of the old gods still exist in numerous personal and place names. References crop up in speech and writing—Aegir as the ocean and Thor's hammer, the symbol of the god. And for a great many Icelanders the crags and lava are the home of the elves and Hidden People, whose comings and goings sometimes affect the affairs of humans.

The myths themselves have come down to us in fragmentary and often contradictory form. Most have surely been lost and the fragments that remain reflect changes through time, as well as regional differences. Or perhaps we are unjustly asking that the tales recount in a linear progression what is supposed to have taken place, and we should instead accept the underlying meaning and the mood evoked without asking for logical continuity.

Extant sources go back to Caesar and Tacitus. Place names throughout Scandinavia and runic inscriptions carved in stone attest the importance of the gods. The early Christian monks left a record, too, but largely in order to show where paganism went astray. Saxo Grammaticus, writing in Denmark ca. 1200 A.D., recorded the Gesta Danorum. The Prose Edda was written by the Icelander Snorri Sturluson in 1220 A.D. so that knowledge of the past beliefs and the poetic forms and metaphors would not be forgotten; indeed, Icelandic schoolchildren today must study his work. The Poetic Edda was copied in 1270 A.D. from an earlier manuscript, now lost. But all these manuscripts postdate the conversion of Iceland to Christianity in the year 1000 and reflect an unknown degree of Christian influence.

The similarities in these accounts to European and Asian myths is no accident; we share cultural roots. Taken as a whole, however, the Norse myths constitute the northern response to the need for a religion.

71

The Creation

> In the beginning of Time
> Before anything was
> Nor sand nor sea
> Nor ocean swell
> No earth was there
> Nor sky above.
> The void yawned formless
> And nothing grew.
> (*Völuspá—The Sibyl's Prophecy*, 3)

The yawning abyss of Chaos—Ginnungagap—lay between Niflheimur to the north—land of fog and cold, site of the fountain Hvergelmir, source of glacial rivers—and Muspellsheimur to the south—land of fire and rivers of bitter poison. From the hoarfrost that ran into Ginnungagap, warmed by the air from the south, the melting drops became the body of the first being, Ýmir the Giant. Out of the sweat under his left armpit were a man and a woman formed while he slept. With one leg he begat a son on the other; thus came the Frost Giants into being.

As the ice melted, the cow Audumla emerged. Four rivers of milk ran from her udders and nourished the Giants. The cow licked the salty ice and brought to light first the hair, then the head, and then the body of Búri. Búri had a son named Bor, who married the Giantess Bestla and fathered the first of the gods or Aesir—Ódinn, Vili, and Vé. The three brothers then fought the Giants and killed all but two, who escaped to found a new race of Giants.

In the middle of Ginnungagap, the sons of Bor created Midgardur, the earth, from the body of Ýmir. His flesh became the land, his blood the seas and lakes, his bones the rocks, his hair the trees. Then they lifted his skull to be the heavens and set four dwarfs, the cardinal points of the compass, to support it, and threw up the sparks from Muspellsheimur to be the stars. The maggots in Ýmir's rotting corpse became the Dwarfs and were doomed to remain under-ground. "Then was the land grown with green plants," spoke the Sibyl.

The sons of Bor walked along the shore and found two trees and made of them humans. Ódinn breathed life into them, the second brother gave them wit and movement, the third speech, hearing, and sight. Then they gave the man Askur—Ash—and his wife Embla the land Midgardur as home.

The Norse Cosmogony

The Norse view of the world is energetic, a dynamic of movement. The gods go adventuring and keep young by eating Idunn's apples. The Champions, the chosen who have been slain in battle and brought to Valhalla, fight and are wounded daily and healed overnight to fight again the next day. The very tree whose roots unite the worlds is constantly assailed and regenerated. Difficulties are to be overcome, challenges sought and met.

The search for knowledge is a constant theme. Yet the gods are also entrained by fate; the whole system is itself slated from the beginning to end in cataclysmic destruction—and to be reborn.

"Nine worlds I remember," said the Sibyl, though it is not clear to us now which nine worlds these are. The three roots of the tree Yggdrasill stretch into the three parts of this universe, one root to Niflheimur, abode of the dead, one to Jötunheimur, abode of the Giants, where Mímir's well is located, and the third to Ásgardur, abode of the Aesir. A serpent gnaws at the root of the tree, deer and a goat browse on its leaves, and its trunk is rotting. To nourish it the Norns draw water from the well beneath its third root. At its base the Aesir meet daily to hold court.

The world is flat and stretched out to encompass the various abodes, and is encircled by the ocean where Midgardsormur, the World Serpent, dwells. Or it can be envisaged, as it later was, as tiered, with Ásgardur above, Midgardur between, and Niflheimur, the freezing afterworld, as the lowest tier. In addition there are abodes for the Dwarfs, Elves, and Giants. Between Midgardur and Ásgardur runs the rainbow bridge of Bifröst, the red of which is leaping flames.

Night and Day each drive a horse–drawn chariot across the sky, as do the Sun and Moon. Sól, the Sun, rides her chariot, as does the Moon, Máni, his, fleeing from the pursuing wolves who, at Ragnarök, will overtake and swallow them.

Ásgardur, the abode of the Aesir, is situated on a high crag, fortified by a wall. Here Ódinn has his high seat, and here also is Valhalla—the Hall of the Slain, where the Einherjar—the Champions, live. The Valkyries bring the gods drink and wait on table. They, together with the Norn Skuld and with Ódinn, choose who shall fall in battle and carry them over the rainbow bridge to Valhalla, a hall so vast that 800 men can pass at one time through each of its 540 doors. Yet, however many they now seem, when the final battle comes they will be too few.

The Gods

Ódinn is the chief god, the All–Father, sire of all the gods and of men. Frigg, his wife, is perhaps synonymous with Earth, who is at once his daughter and his wife. Ódinn himself is the trinity—High, Equally High and Third, and is known by a host of other bynames that characterize his powers or his exploits. The Romans equated him with Mercury as god of cargoes and leader of souls to the underworld. His name means furious, wild. As god of war he reflected the interest of the kings of the time and was worshipped by the elite. He remains a complex character, often fickle, yet self–sacrificing. Two ravens, Mind and Memory, sit on his shoulders, and he rides the eight–legged horse Sleipnir, who left a footprint, if legend is to be believed, at Ásbyrgi in the north of Iceland. Ódinn himself takes no food and is sustained on mead or honey wine; as High, he is horrified at the idea of being offered mere water.

Ódinn is the Hanging God because he pierced himself with a spear and hung himself ritually in the tree Yggdrasill—Ódinn's Horse or Gallows—for nine days and nights in order to acquire wisdom and the secrets of the runes, the old letters that were both writing and magic symbols. In thus dying he learned nine songs and acquired eighteen runes from his mother's brother and was set free, invigorated. His followers in Scandinavia often practiced human and animal sacrifice in recognition of his hanging.

In the first war of all time, waged between the two sets of gods, the Aesir and the *Vanir*—the Wanes, the latter sent back the head of one hostage, Mímir. Ódinn embalmed Mímir's head and put it in a well, where it became a fount of wisdom. Ódinn went to the well in search of wisdom, but Mímir refused to impart any secrets unless Ódinn should pawn his eye in exchange. Thus Ódinn became the One–Eyed God and often roams the world in a dark cloak and a wide–brimmed hat. Oddly, almost no one he meets in his travels seems to realize at first that the hat and the missing eye are a dead giveaway as to who this is.

So Ódinn is a shape changer, One–Eyed and All–Knowing, the Wanderer as well as the God of Victory. He is warrior and poet, as were the aristocratic Norsemen of the time. But Ódinn, too, is at the mercy of fate and is destined to be consumed by the Wolf at Ragnarök.

There are, in all, twelve important Aesir, Snorri Sturluson wrote, and others who serve Ódinn as children serve their father. Ódinn and Týr together, perhaps, represent law and world order and were commonly worshipped by the elite. On the other hand, Ódinn's first–born son Thór, with his immense physical strength, was the one who appealed to most people and was the god most often worshipped by Icelanders. Njördur, originally a Wane, governs the winds and calms the seas and fire. He had two children, Freyr and his wife Freyja. Freyr is the god of fecundity and peace and provides rain and sunshine and was often worshipped by those who worked the land. Together, Ódinn, Thór, and Freyr are the three most important of the gods.

Heimdallur stands guard at the end of the rainbow bridge to blow his horn to warn the Aesir of an attack by the Giants. Little is known about him, but the poem *Rígspula* recounts his travels when, as Rígur, he visited in turn three different families. In each visit he lay three nights between the husband and wife, and thereafter each wife bore a son. He thereby gave rise first to thralls or slaves, then freemen farmers, and lastly the elite, the three social strata of ancient Nordic society.

There are at least fourteen goddesses, wrote Snorri, and he listed them with their attributes. They are equal to the gods, but there are fewer surviving stories about them. Frigg, as Ódinn's wife, was highest, but Freyja, the sister of Freyr, was equally highborn. Together they seem to complement each other: Frigg, the mother, who mourned the death of her son Baldur, who is called on by women in labor, and who knows the future; Freyja, the lover, goddess of fertility, renowned for magic and witchcraft, who rides into battle and indeed receives half of those slain in battle into her hall.

Giants emerged from chaos even before the Norse gods, and in fact the gods were descended from Giants. Some of the Giants seem to have also been regarded as gods or goddesses, like the wise Mímir, Aegir, the lord of the sea, and Aegir's wife Rán. Aegir's hall is a submarine palace that needs no lamps as it is lit by pure gold. But the Giants are only sometimes benevolent. At other times they are fearful creatures, the personification of violent natural phenomena such as hurricanes, and hostile to humans. Rán's nine daughters are the waves. Rán herself throws a net to capture the drowned so she can greet them in her hall. There are thus four abodes of the dead: the warrior heroes, chosen by Ódinn or the Valkyries, go to Valhalla or, chosen by Freyja, to her hall, while drowned sailors go to Rán's palace under the sea and others to Hel's abode in Niflheimur.

Finally but not least, there are the three Norns, the Weird Sisters Urdur (Fate), Verdandi (Being), and Skuld (Obligation or Necessity), who spin humans' lifelines. But there are also other norns, the bad ones, among the Elves and Dwarfs. Free will operates in the long moments between what Fate decrees, but in the end even the gods are bound by Fate and must face Ragnarök.

Iceland's History: The Settlement

It was inevitable that a European would eventually dare to sail far enough out to sea or be blown off course and discover the island now known as Iceland. After all, since the Earth is a sphere, in the far north the latitude lines are closer to converging than they are further south, with the result that the distances between the islands and the continents are not as great as appears on many maps. With spring easterlies, for example, sailing from Bergen to the Shetlands takes 48 hours at most, and other distances are comparable.[1]

The first sighting of Iceland may be lost to history, but the *Book of Settlements* (sect. 1–5) traces the known attempts to explore this new land. Pytheas from Marseille wrote in 300 B.C. of a land called Ultima Thule, which may have been Norway or possibly Iceland, that was 6 days' sail north of Britain; in Ultima Thule there was no darkness in summer and the sea ice lay only another day's sail to the north. Later, in the early ninth century A.D., the Irish monk Dicuil wrote of Iceland as Thule or Thile.[2]

In the mid–ninth century a man named Naddoddur was blown off course as he sailed from Norway to his home in the Faroes and sighted the east coast of Iceland, which he named Snowland, as he saw snow fall on the mountains. He was followed in the 860s by the Swede Gardar Svavarsson, who went looking for Naddoddur's Snowland.[3] He circumnavigated the island and then passed a winter in the north where the modern town is still named for the houses he built: Húsavík. The slave Náttfari and a girl broke away from the others and settled there. Following the custom of the day, the land was named Gardar's Island after its discoverer.

Again in the 860s, the Norwegian Flóki Vilgerdarson set sail with his household and animals, his friends and three ravens.[4] When he thought he'd gone far enough, he released one raven, but it flew back home. Later he tried again, but the second raven returned to the ship. When it came the turn of the third raven, the bird continued on and the ship followed it to land. Raven–Flóki and his companions stayed, fishing and gathering eggs, but they neglected to make any real provision for winter and their animals died. Flóki is said to have climbed a mountain, seen ice in a fjord to the north, and therefore named the land Iceland. After two winters he left in some disgust, though a man with him actually claimed later, perhaps sarcastically, that butter dripped from every blade of grass! Flóki apparently changed his mind, as he later returned to settle, probably in the West Fjords. Icelanders in the north therefore count Raven–Flóki, and not Ingólfur Arnarson, as the first settler.

Earlier Irish Settlement of Iceland

The monk Dicuil recorded that Irish monks had arrived in Iceland at least as early as 795, a century before the Norse.[5] They came in mid–winter, undoubtedly to avoid fog and take advantage of the winds, and remained until August. The light in summer impressed Dicuil: the monks could see well enough at midnight to pick the lice out of their shirts! An unknown number of monks followed, in keeping with their belief in finding a far–off island where they could contemplate God and Christ, usually alone and in solitude. Nobody knows how permanent these settlements were, nor how many, but it is clear that there were monks in Iceland when the settlers from Norway arrived.

The Norse called the Irish *papar* or fathers. The Icelandic settlers seem to have driven them away rather roughly, at least in some cases, as the *Book of Settlements* records that one group fled, leaving behind "bell, book and crozier." To what extent the Irish simply withdrew from Iceland in the same way they had previously withdrawn from the Faroes, and to what extent some may have remained, is not known.

The Norse had raided and settled in Ireland for some time before the settlement of Iceland. Since Ireland lay west of Norway, the slaves they took there were called Westmen. At the time of the colonization of Iceland an unknown percentage of the settlers were Irish (slaves, wives, and freemen), or the children or grandchildren of Norse settlers in Ireland, most of them probably Christian. These Irish, or the monks who came to Iceland before them, gave rise to Celtic place names, such as Patreksfjördur in the northwest and the island of Papey off the east coast. Not only are Celtic names fairly common in the western part of Iceland, but only 12 pagan burial sites are known from this area (of over 300 known pagan burial sites for Iceland as a whole).[6] Though the Irish monks had no influence on the development of Icelandic culture, the same may not be true of other Irish settlers. The *Book of Settlements* records that Christianity died out in Iceland for a hundred years before it was re–introduced. But although adherence to their religion did not last, the Irish settlers and the contacts the Norse and Icelanders had in Ireland may have had some impact; arguably, the poetry and the storytelling style of the sagas were partly influenced by Irish traditions. The western part of Iceland, where the Christians outnumbered the pagans, was the site of many of the sagas and the area from which the Norse Greenlanders came. Research shows a distinct difference in the genetic inheritance between western and eastern Icelanders.[7] Danish archaeologists have been impressed by the huge Celtic influence on the artifacts and ruins of the two Icelandic settlements in Greenland.[8] Other cultural traits seem logically to be Celtic in origin, such as the practice of eating the seaweed called dulse and a particular type of ball game described in the sagas.[9] Unlike Greco–Roman wrestling, the holds in *glíma*, or Icelandic wrestling, are the same as or related to the holds used in Celtic areas, including Brittany and Cornwall, as well as in Switzerland.

The Age of Settlement, 870–930

News spread among the Norse about this land to the west that was available for the taking. When Ingólfur Arnarson and Hjörleifur Hródmarsson, who was both Ingólfur's brother–in–law and also his close friend and sworn blood brother, had to forfeit their lands in Norway in retribution for having killed the sons of a powerful earl, they set sail from Norway to explore the southeast coast of this new land and then returned to Norway to collect their families, slaves, other freemen, livestock, food, and implements. Traditionally in 874 (though more probably in 870) their ships landed on the coast of Iceland.

Partly because the account was handed down orally until the twelfth century before being written down, and partly because of the literary style of the time, no mention is made in the written record of the excitement that must have prevailed as the settlers first spied the land they sought rising from the sea and growing larger as they neared it. A panorama of contrasting colors grew before their eyes: long, black lava sands, basalt cliffs, snowcapped mountains and lush, green birch forests.

Like the other chieftains, Ingólfur grabbed his high–seat pillars, the carved wooden columns set at the corners of his chieftain's chair, and threw them into the sea off the southeast coast. Where they washed ashore he would build his homestead. While he waited until they were found, he wintered, first at Ingólfshöfdi in the southeast, then at Hjörleifshöfdi, and during the third winter at Ingólfsfjall, a mountain near Selfoss. He sent out slaves to hunt for his high–seat pillars and when they found them at the site of modern Reykjavík, he rewarded them with land. The gods had shown him favor; he moved to Reykjavík and laid claim to a huge tract of land in the southwest.

Statue of Ingólfur Arnarson, Reykjavík

Meanwhile, his blood brother Hjörleifur settled at Hjörleifshöfdi, a headland that was green at the time of the settlement but is now largely surrounded by black sand. Hjörleifur rejected the old religion. When he ordered his slaves to plough and sow grain, they revolted, killed him and the freemen who accompanied him, and sought refuge on the islands to the southwest. Ingólfur found the dead bodies of Hjörleifur and the freemen, proclaimed that the ill deed was what came from rejecting the Norse gods, and pursued and killed the slaves who were responsible. The place where the slaves, or Westmen, had sought refuge has been known ever since as the Westman Islands.

The chieftains, both men and women, as in the case of the Christian, Audur the Deep–Minded, laid claim to huge tracts and then rewarded their followers with gifts of land. The south of Iceland was quickly settled. These early settlers were followed by a stream of people, perhaps 60,000 in all, until about 930, when the land was fully settled. Most of the settlements were below an altitude of 200 m, though some reached an altitude of 460 m (650–1500 ft.). Soon after 900 the settled areas reached far up the valleys and even onto the highlands, where conditions were not as favorable for agriculture. By 1095 the population probably numbered about 70,000.[10] Since the vegetative cover in the highlands was minimal and the climate harsher than at lower altitudes, those who tried living on the rim of the highlands denuded the landscape, with the result that they or their descendants later had to retreat to lower elevations.

The settlement was remarkably peaceful; the *Book of Settlements* records only six cases out of the almost 400 estates listed, where land was taken by force from other Norse. A man could claim the amount of land he could light fires around in one day, a common method to appease the guardian spirits and hallow the land. A woman could have the land she could lead a heifer around between sunrise and sunset on a spring day, in other words, at a time of year when the day was long enough for her to claim a fair–sized tract of land. As time passed, these large claims were subdivided until about 1100 A.D. When quarrels did arise between the original settlers, with their huge tracts of land, and those who came later, the Norwegian king, Harald, was asked to mediate.

The settlement of Iceland cannot really be understood without seeing it in the context of the great Viking outreach of the period and of conditions in Norway at that time. Moving one's entire household to Iceland in the ninth century took a certain daring, but it must be remembered that the Norse had been sacking and settling in the British Isles since the attack on the abbey at Lindisfarne in 793. They sacked Dublin in 795, the same year Irish monks first settled in Iceland. In 845 Ragnar Lodbrók took 120 ships up the Seine, and in 851 a full 350 Norse ships sailed up the Thames. The Norse travelled to Kiev and Constantinople in 865, sailed into the Mediterranean and landed in north Africa. The known world was theirs to roam around in and undiscovered worlds theirs to find: Jan Mayen, Greenland, and North America.

The Norse left Norway for a variety of reasons.[11] A population explosion drove many to seek new lands. The longing for adventure, and ambition and greed, drew others. The Norse were forced to leave Ireland about 900 A.D., thus closing that avenue to Norse raiding and settlement. Others who came to settle in Iceland felt the need to flee the growing power of Harald the Fair–Hair, the king who first united Norway. Harald encouraged others to go, undoubtedly hoping, through them, to obtain power over the new land. All were seeking a new place to build their lives. For all, the move was expedited because the Norse had the most advanced ships of the time.[12]

For the majority of the settlers, who believed in the gods of the old Norse pantheon, the land was a living entity, full of guardian spirits that they, as settlers, expected to share the land with. We do not know when or how they first gave thanks to Thór, and to the gods of the sea, for safe passage, but surely they did. The omens for the settlement were auspicious.

The *Book of Settlements*

In order to record information about the original settlers for posterity, and also to demonstrate that Icelanders came from good stock and were not irresponsible ruffians, Ari the Learned (1068–1148) compiled the *Book of Icelanders* and perhaps had a hand in writing an early compilation of the *Book of Settlements* in the twelfth century. There are still-extant copies of the shorter version of the *Book of Icelanders*. One of the five extant manuscripts of the *Book of Settlements* is the version expanded by Sturla Thordarson in the thirteenth century.

The *Book of Settlements* is far more than a directory of the most important settlers and the land they claimed. There is information about horses, pigs, and boars, called by name. There are references to sorcerers and tales about many of the settlers, as well as their genealogies. And if few seemed to die in bed, remember that they went from death on the battlefield to Valhalla or, if not killed fighting, their spirits joined others in a cliff or a mountain after death.

Many of the men, and some of the women, have wonderful bynames or epithets. They were called the Strong, the Tall, the Stout, the White. There were Chicken–Thórir—named for the hens he once sold, Hrafn Who–Never –Left–Home, Ketill Trout, and Eysteinn Fart, and women like Hlif the Horse–Gelder and Thorbjörg Ship–Breast.

These people took possession of huge tracts of land, bred offspring, fought and killed, defended their rights and their honor, and composed poetry in the midst of battle. They were giants on earth. They were also the real ancestors of living Icelanders.

Helgi the Lean[13] was a Christian, but to play it safe, he invoked Thór, too, when the going got rough.

Hallgerdur Oddsdóttir had hair so long it touched the floor.[14] In the end it led to her undoing. When she refused to accompany her husband, he grabbed her hair, sliced off her head, and rode away.

Then there was the man who lost both a duel and his life when his opponent cut the cord that held up his breeches and they fell down around his ankles!

Who Were the Settlers?

The manuscripts that have come down to us record the "origin myth" of Icelanders: that the Irish fled, that the majority of the settlers came from Norway, and that others came from the other Nordic countries, Britain and Ireland. How accurate are the records?

The comprehensive study of blood alleles by Cavalli–Sforza *et al.* has shown that Icelanders are more closely related to western Norwegians than any other group, and somewhat less closely related to the English, a conclusion that reinforces the historical tradition of settlement from Norway.[15] However, ABO blood grouping of modern Icelanders shows a preponderance of type O not found in Norway. Stefán Adalsteinsson points out, however, that the high rate of type O characterizes "geographically isolated" groups like Scots, Sardinians, and Corsicans, and probably resulted from smallpox epidemics, as happened in Iceland in later centuries, rather than the genetic inheritance of the original settlers; those with type O were more likely to survive. This phenomenon was observed in India in 1965 and 1966, where people with type B or O were more likely to remain alive, and the percentage of type O increased. Analyses of other blood factors, Adalsteinsson feels, indicate that Icelanders are 86% Norwegian and 14% Irish.

Skull measurements of eleventh and twelfth century males show they were medium to longheaded (dolicocephalic). Measurements of living Icelandic males in 1953 defined them as medium headed, but closer to shortheaded (brachicephalic) than at the time of the settlement. In other words, modern Icelanders do not have faces as long as the Norwegian average in the ninth century.[16]

Blood analyses show that the animals the settlers brought with them were definitely Norwegian in origin.[17] Icelandic cattle and goats most closely resemble old Norwegian stock. The sheep and the Icelandic sheepdog are both from northwestern Europe, Icelandic sheep being unlike the Faroese sheep, which came from Ireland. The Icelandic horse is from stock that no longer exists on the mainland, but is related to the Shetland pony; both originated in Norway. The cats in the countryside are Norwegian and unlike British cats. Even the field mice that stowed away on the ships are definitely Norwegian in origin.

There is one other vital and irrefutable piece of evidence: Modern Icelanders still speak the language spoken at the time of the settlement, though, of course, with a vocabulary input to cope with the changing times.

There were surely landfalls and settlements that escaped being recorded. The six Roman coins that have been found in the southern part of Iceland, from the Westman Islands east to the island of Papey, remain an enigma: they may have been acquired in trade. The earlier settlements, aside from the few that sheltered Irish monks, were Norse in origin. The archaeologist Margrét Hermannsdóttir,[18] in excavating an old farm in Herjólfsdalur in the Westman Islands, found artifacts dating to the Merovingian period in the seventh century, considerably earlier than the traditional date of 874 for the first Norse settlements. Though there are arguments over the validity of ^{14}C dating in Iceland, because of a possible confounding effect of volcanic eruptions, there is increasing evidence that some settlement did occur in Iceland, and also in the Faroes, before the traditional date. In any case, the inhabitants of this early Westman Island settlement were definitely Norse and not Irish. The farm remained occupied until the tenth or eleventh century.

Undoubtedly there were events and ideas that escaped being recorded. The name Iceland—*Ísland* in Icelandic—may celebrate a god named *Ís* rather than Flóki's spying an ice–choked fjord. The word was used in Germanic languages and Sanskrit to denote chief god, lord. It is found, for example, in place–names in Germany beginning with Eisen, in the name of the river Isis in Oxford, and in the Icelandic man's name Ísleifur.[19]

The extant manuscripts, written three centuries and more after the event, hardly record every person or every act of settlement, but the picture they give is in the main correct, and in a great many cases modern Icelanders can trace their lineages directly to the people named. Though they came from Norway, as Sigurdur Líndal[20] has pointed out, these people soon came to think of themselves as Icelanders and of the Norsemen as foreigners. Whether or not Norse settlement actually began in 874 A.D. under the leadership of a man named Ingólfur Arnarson (the Son of Eagle) is largely immaterial. Icelanders thereby have their tale of origin and hence testimony of their ethnicity.

Ships and Sailing

A major reason why the Viking Age was such a period of discovery and expansion was the ships the Norse possessed.[21] They were the most seaworthy ships in the world at that time. The Norwegians had ample timber and relatively advanced iron industry and with their ships dared the open sea more readily than others. In fact, in the late eighth and early ninth centuries only Scandinavians and the Irish dared sail across open ocean out of sight of land; others hugged the coasts.

Scandinavians had learned the value of using geometric proportions in designing buildings and other objects to make them practical as well as beautiful. They borrowed the geometric proportions used by the Graeco–Roman world and applied the same formulas to the development of their own stave churches, forts, and ships and even their jewelry.[22] The modern Norwegian wooden Oselver boat is still made in conformity with the same geometric proportions.

The Norse had more than one type of boat. The famous Viking longboat was used for speed and surprise in attack. It was good for river and coastal sailing but was not an ocean–going vessel. Instead, the settlers came to Iceland in the seagoing *knörr*.[23] This ship was clinker–built, i.e., the edge of each strake overlapped and was fastened to the strake below it. The Viking *knörr* had the advantage over the Irish curragh of the time, as it could sail much closer–hauled into the wind. At the time of the settlement, the *knörr* weighed about 40 tons.

Gaia, reconstruction of a Norse ship

The ship was decked fore and aft, with an open hold amidships where livestock and goods could be stored; the weight amidships helped to keep the ship from hogging (arching up in the middle) as she took the swells. Shorter than the longship, the *knörr* had a broader beam, a higher freeboard (to keep out the waves), drew more water, was faster in strong winds, and could carry 20–30 people with their belongings and some livestock.

Conditions in the *knörr* were hardly ideal. An awning or tent was rigged at night, but the people were often wet and cold. The homespun sail was weak when wet, even though reinforced with a cross–pattern of leather straps; the reinforcing straps are clearly portrayed in numerous stone carvings in Scandinavia. The livestock carried amidships were certainly fairly young animals and many probably already pregnant to insure an increase in stocks after landing.

There were several ways to navigate. The *Hauksbók* manuscript gives the oldest example of the use of the lodestone; it floated in a stone bowl marked with the 32 points of the compass. In addition, the color of the water and ocean currents are readily obvious in a small sailing boat. The behavior of birds and different species of whales give clues as to position, and the Norse used a weight to sound the bottom and a kind of stone or stave to keep track of the height of the sun. They measured distances over the sea: one *vika* (probably one "distance across a bay") equalled 4–5 nautical miles; one full day's sail equalled two dozen *vikur*. This has been reckoned as nearly 100 km (60 miles), or a very fast day's sail.[24] The term *dœgr* signified a 12–hour period as distinguished from the *dagr* or 24–hour day.[25] The difficulties in understanding these nautical terms for time and distance have often led to speculation as to where the Norse actually explored.

Nevertheless, steering and navigating were somewhat approximate and the ships could be blown off course in a gale, thus sometimes serendipitously leading to the discovery of new lands. Landing could also be difficult. The ships were beached, not docked, and the sailors sometimes had no choice in a heavy sea but to let the wind drive them onto shore to save both ship and those aboard. In winter the ships were housed in a boathouse or *naust* for protection and not refloated until the following spring.

The early Icelanders needed their ships to be in good repair so as to trade and to keep in contact with other parts of Iceland, but they had to cope with the fact that there was a shortage of trees in Iceland large enough for major repairs. Only Norway had an ample supply of suitable timber. This point was to prove critical as time passed.

Iceland at the Time of the Settlement

The settlers found an inviting land of black lava rock with fertile valleys and ample birch woods to provide fuel. There were fish in the sea and salmon and trout in the rivers, whales and seals for meat and oil for lamps, and walrus for meat and tusks. Seabirds nested on the cliffs in rich abundance and provided eggs, as they still do. Ptarmigan were netted and swans also caught to eat.

The first settlers were farmers; fishing was a sideline, albeit a very important one. The people had settled in a very promising land, but from the beginning the rate of erosion increased. Iceland is almost wholly volcanic, and volcanic soils are friable and crumble easily. The settlers cleared the land and allowed their stock to overgraze. Without the protection of plant and tree roots to hold the soil in place, erosion set in, in some places even at a rate ten times the pre–settlement rate.[26] But on the whole these first Icelanders were fortunate that during the Age of Settlement the climate remained relatively warm and they and their livestock thrived.

The Myth of Thór

Most of the first settlers in Iceland worshipped the god Thór, as indeed did most of the people in Scandinavia at that time. The three principal gods, Ódinn, Thór, and Freyr, were represented together in the same temple in Uppsala in Sweden, with the image of Thór set in the middle. The Romans equated Thór with Jupiter.

Thór was Ódinn's first son, by Earth or Jörd. Snorri Sturluson recorded that he was possessed of incredible physical strength and could therefore best all living things in combat. Ódinn represented the interests of the elite and the monarchy. Thór, on the other hand, with his uncomplicated readiness to rise to any physical challenge and overcome it, better appealed to farmers and freemen and the highly independent chieftains who settled Iceland. He was, in fact, the quintessential Icelander writ large, though he lacked the deep intelligence that so many modern Icelanders display. He was defender of men and gods and Slayer of Giants. As the Thunder God, he also controlled fire and lightning, storms, rain, and fair weather, and therefore the crops. His wife Sif, she of the golden hair, was a fertility goddess, comparable to the Roman Ceres. Thór was the patron, then, of farmers and also of thralls.

Thór was guardian of the worlds of gods and humans, always ready for an adventure, fearless in combating danger. His robustness and simple, rough directness must have made him seem a particularly safe god to rely on in an often violent and uncertain world. He had great vitality and did nothing by halves. He ate and drank with gusto and once consumed at one sitting a whole ox and eight salmon, washed down by three casks of mead. He had a mass of red hair and a red beard and, when roused, a fearsome voice and a penetrating gaze under beetling red eyebrows.

Thór lived in a mansion of no fewer than 540 rooms. He drove a chariot drawn by two billy–goats and owned three invaluable possessions: his hammer, a belt that, when he fastened it round his girth, hugely increased his strength, and a pair of iron gloves with which to wield his hammer. Thór's hammer could produce thunder and lightning and, like a boomerang, came back to him when thrown. People often wore an amulet of his cross–shaped hammer around the neck for protection. In the twentieth century, Sveinbjörn Beinteinsson revived the worship of Thór and was High Priest until his death in 1994.

Icelanders frequently name their children after the god, using either the name Thór, feminine Thóra, or in combinations such as Thorkell and Thórarinn, or the feminine Thórunn.

Quite a few stories about Thór's exploits have come down to us, not least the following, where he travels with the trickster Loki, the most enigmatic of the Aesir, to meet Loki's counterpart among the Giants. The following retelling is based on the Snorra *or* Prose Edda.

Thór's Journey to Útgardar–Loki

Thór, accompanied by Loki, was riding in his chariot pulled by his two billygoats when, at the end of a long day they came to a farmer's cottage and sought lodging. Toward evening Thór skinned and butchered both his goats so he and his companion would have enough to eat, and spread the skins on the ground.

"Eat with us," Thór beckoned to the farmer and his wife and their two children, Thjálfi and Röskva. "Mind that you throw all of the bones on the skins," he warned. But Thjálfi was starved and split one thighbone with his knife to get at the marrow.

Thór slept the night. On awakening the next day, he took his hammer Mjöllnir and passed it over the bones, and the goats rose up whole, but he saw at once that one was lame in the hind leg. In his rage Thór's knuckles turned white as he grasped his hammer. "Who broke this one's thighbone?" he roared. The farmer quailed before Thór's blazing eyes and drawn brows. "Take anything, take everything we have," he pleaded.

When Thór saw their fear, his rage subsided, and in recompense for their hospitality he spared them but took both the farmer's children with him.

The four travellers left the goats and chariot behind and continued on foot until they came to the sea, where they crossed in a boat. Once on the other side they were forced to make their way through a large forest with no end in sight. At nightfall they sought shelter in a lodge they came upon, but oddly the only door was as wide as the house itself. In the middle of the night there was a terrific earthquake and the house shook. The four hastily retreated to a side room. While the others slept, Thór sat in the doorway, keeping guard, his hammer in his hand.

At daybreak Thór went outside and found a Giant lying on the ground, snoring, and now he understood what had shaken the house they sheltered in. Thór girded on his belt and prepared to strike the Giant, but the Giant leapt up and grabbed his glove, the same glove Thór and his companions had called a house and sought shelter in. The side room turned out to be the thumb of the Giant's glove!

"Well," asked Skrýmir, for that was the Giant's name, "shall we travel together?" Thór agreed. "Just let me carry your things, too," the Giant offered, taking the pack, and Thór agreed. So the five proceeded onward that day and as night fell Skrýmir guided them to a huge oak. "I must rest," he said. "Here, you take your bag of provisions."

But the Giant had tied such a clever knot that, try as they might, they could not undo it. Then Thór was angry and grabbed his hammer with both hands and struck Skrýmir on the head.

"It seemed to me a leaf fell on my head," Skrýmir murmured, barely stirring.

When Skrýmir was once more asleep and snoring lustily, Thór struck him again on the crown of the head. And this time Skrýmir woke and asked, "What now? Did a nut fall on my head?"

Finally, just before daybreak, Skrýmir was again fast asleep and Thór, thoroughly aroused, grabbed his hammer and struck Skrýmir such a mighty blow that the hammer sank in up to the shaft. But Skrýmir only sat up and asked, "Have some birds been up in the tree above me? Their droppings seem to have landed on my cheek."

"You haven't much farther to go," added Skrýmir, as he arose, ready for the day. "From here I go north and you should keep on eastward if you still want to go to Útgardar–Loki's."

Thór and his companions walked on until midday, when they came to a hall so huge that they had to crane their necks to see the top of it. They found no way to open the barred gate so they squeezed through the bars. The door to the main hall was open, so they went in. Útgardar–Loki greeted them sarcastically. "Well, if it isn't Thór of the Aesir! What skill do you and your fellows think you can show us? For no man may be here unless he prove himself against one of the Giants here assembled."

"Very well, " said Loki, "I am ready to prove that I can eat faster than anyone." Útgardar–Loki immediately took him up on it and called out for the one named Logi to come forward. Huge troughs of meat were then placed between the two contestants. Loki ate quickly, but in the time that Loki took to clean all the meat off the bones, Logi had consumed not only the meat but the bones and the trough as well!

Then Útgardar–Loki turned to young Thjálfi and asked how he wanted to prove himself. Thjálfi said he would run a race against anyone the Giant named. "That's a good skill," said Útgardar–Loki and stood up and went outside to where there was a smooth field with a good track for running. He called to a lad named Hugi and Thjálfi ran a lap against him, but Hugi outdistanced him. "You'll have to try harder than that, Thjálfi, if you want to win," taunted Útgardar–Loki. Thjálfi ran another lap against Hugi, and yet a third, but Hugi had already reached the end of the track and turned back while Thjálfi had come only halfway.

Now it was Thór's turn. "I can outdrink any man," boasted Thór. "Well then," said Útgardar–Loki, "here is a drinking horn that most empty in one draft or possibly two. No real drinker ever needs more than three drafts," and so saying, he handed Thór the horn. Thór didn't think the horn looked very large though it was a bit long. He was thirsty and took a good draft, but when he ran out of breath and looked he saw that the level of the liquid had hardly gone down at all. "Well done, but you didn't drink very much," said Útgardar–Loki. "I can't believe that Thór of the Aesir can't drink more than that." Without replying Thór took an even longer swig from the horn, but with even less result than before. Again Útgardar–Loki taunted him. Now Thór was truly angry and grabbed the horn and drank long and deep. This time the level of the drink in the horn dropped slightly.

"Obviously you're not the man we thought," said Útgardar–Loki. "Do you want to try another skill?"

"I'd think it strange if such a draft were considered small at home among the Aesir. What sport do you want to offer me now?" Thór replied. With that a large, gray cat jumped onto the floor in front of Thór. "Here the young men think nothing of lifting my cat up," said Útgardar–Loki. Thór grabbed the cat under the belly and lifted it up, but its body only stretched in an arc over Thór's head. When Thór pushed upward as high and as hard as he could, the cat bare-ly lifted one paw from the floor.

"Well, so the cat is large and Thór rather short and small compared with the big men here," said Útgardar–Loki. Now Thór was truly angry: "However little you think me, get me someone to wrestle with me." Útgardar–Loki had his old nurse Elli brought in. The old woman agreed to take up Thór's chal-lenge, but the more that Thór struggled against her, the more the old woman held her ground, and before long Thór lost his balance and fell on one knee.

Útgardar–Loki called a halt to the trials and gave them lodging for the night. Early the next morning, as Thór and his companions were ready to leave, he fed them well and followed them through the hall gate. "Now that you are outside my hall, I shall tell you the truth. I would never have admitted you if I had known how strong you really are. I have tricked you with illusions. I was Skrýmir and bound your bag of provisions with iron fetters. You'd have slain me with your hammer if I had not protected myself with layers of stone. The valleys you see before you are the result of your hammer blows in the rock.

"Loki competed with Logi, or fire, and no one can consume as much or as quickly as can flame. Thjálfi ran against Hugi, my own thought, which outdis-tanced him. As for your efforts, I could hardly believe my eyes when you downed so much from the drinking horn, since the other end lay in the sea. Indeed, you have caused the ocean to ebb and flood with tides. As to the cat, that was the World Serpent and you stretched it upwards so far that you almost made it touch the Sky. The old woman was Elli, or old age, and no man can van-quish her.

"Now, do not return or I will again guard my hall with tricks." When Thór heard this he grabbed his hammer, but as he prepared to strike Útgardar–Loki, the Giant, the hall and all around disappeared, and Thór and his companions were left standing on a wide empty plain. There was nothing left to do but to go home.

Iceland's History:
The Commonwealth and the
Conversion to Christianity

The image of the Viking has mistakenly come down to us as only fierce and warlike. In reality, equally important aspects of Viking–age culture included a productive home life, the exploration and settling of other lands, and the structuring of a viable system of law. The original Norse settlers in Iceland therefore went about setting up a system of law and government that would suit them in their new land.

Those who stood out among the original settlers as the natural leaders were usually wealthier, of higher birth, had a following, or had organized the expedition to Iceland. These people, both men and women, laid claim to large tracts of land and became the chieftains in a new country that as yet had no law or organization. The emptiness of the land was matched by the nonexistence of any military hierarchy or royal elite. There was no need for a military organization—the distance across the sea was a more effective safeguard than a moat around a castle, and no need to be marshalled under the aegis of a royal standard—geography had already determined the boundaries of Iceland. With no imperative to congregate in communities for protection, the people settled on scattered farmsteads. Chieftains and freemen farmers had a chance to mold a social order that, though it derived from the one they had left in Norway, differed in key respects and was more suited to maintaining their independence and their livelihood in the new land.

Goðar and *goðorð*

The need for defining a legal system soon became apparent. Families were often dispersed and had fewer relatives than in Norway to support each other in a dispute. Furthermore, the increase in population led inevitably to a need to resolve conflicts. The Norse brought with them the concept of the *goði* (*pl. goðar*), a priest–chieftain who had both political and religious responsibilities; the freeman chose the *goði* he was contracted to as liegeman. Such a priest–chieftainship was called a *goðorð*; the term stood for the rights and responsibilities associated with the position and not for an area of land. In Iceland the concepts of *goði* and *goðorð* were expanded in a way unknown elsewhere.

The chieftains, as they took possession of the land, built temples to their gods and were themselves the priests; hence the term *goði*. However, a chieftain's religious duties, other than providing and maintaining the temple, are not known, and, since the *goðar* continued in existence after the conversion to

Christianity, the importance of their political and social functions clearly outweighed their religious functions.[1] The *goði* was the social and political focal point of his *goðorð*. He was frequently an advocate for a freeman or arbitrator in a dispute. He was responsible for convening the regional assemblies called *things*, for serving as a member of the national assembly and, if chosen, as a judge in the court sessions. Together, the *goðar*–chieftains gave themselves both legislative and judicial powers, and were influential in seeing that court judgments were carried out.[2]

Power actually lay in the hands of both the oligarchy of chieftains and the freemen. Each freeman was required to be a "*thing*–man" to a *goði*. He was, however, free to choose his *goði*, and indeed could change his choice, but he had to be prepared to fight for his *goði*, should the need arise. On the one hand, the prestige and ability of the *goði* were critical for the freeman; his safety and status as a freeman were dependent on his ties with an influential *goði*. Although he owned land, the freeman needed the support of a *goði* to win a dispute. As Byock points out,[3] the "law...operated principally on the *goði* level." On the other hand, the prestige of the *goði* was enhanced by the number of freemen contracted to him. The structure and continuity of the social order were thus based on the "mutual dependency between chieftain and farmer".[4]

The *goðorð* could be inherited, bought or sold, shared or given as a gift. By law, it was defined as power and not as property. The *goði* acquired income principally from his own lands, including rentals, and additionally from the tax paid by each of his freemen eligible to attend a *thing* or assembly (the *thing* tax), from the temple tax (and after 1097, the tithe), for setting prices on foreign goods, and for several other services such as settling an inheritance. When he spoke at an assembly on behalf of someone or acted as arbitrator, the *goði* was rewarded with land or other gifts.

There were constraints on the power of the *goðar* so that they would not exploit the freemen farmers. There was a high valuation on manliness, defined as high–mindedness, having honor (*drengskapur*); the *goðar* wished to command respect and preserve their own honor. Bonds of friendship (*vinfengi*) often included contractual relations to insure agreement or resolve a former dispute, frequently cemented by agreeing to raise the other man's son. Both the chieftains and the freemen farmers valued decision making by consensus and the containment of violence. The chieftains were also constrained by the power of the freemen. The freemen farmers outnumbered the chieftains, chose which *goðar* should have their allegiance, and themselves had income from renting land, trading and, after 1097, the tithe.

But though the power of the *goðar* seemed to be based more on prestige than on wealth, in the twelfth century, if not before, political control passed into the hands of a few wealthy families.

The Althing

Two assemblies, or *things,* were established to deal with legal matters, one at Kjalarnes, not far from Reykjavík, and the other at Thórsnes in Breidafjördur.[5] The *things* met outdoors, the *thing*–men sitting within an area marked off with stones. Decision–making was by consensus.

The chieftains soon had the foresight to realize that the country as a whole needed a centralized body to set laws and resolve disputes. It was therefore agreed that a national assembly and law court should be established, where the *goðar* from all parts of the country would have voting power. This concept of a national assembly (now referred to as the Althing) was a radical change from the small chieftaincies of Norway at the time, which could be conquered and ruled by a king such as Harald the Fair–Hair. The establishment of the Althing realized the ideal of governing the whole country through representation of the people and was Iceland's major innovation in national government.

Preparations for establishing the Althing probably began about 920. A man named Úlfljótur was sent to western Norway to learn about the law in force there. He returned three years later with laws amended to be suitable for Icelandic conditions. However, the Gulathing law, which Úlfljótur presumably studied, differs considerably from the Icelandic law as it was later recorded.

Meanwhile a site had been found and the name Thingvellir—Assembly

Thingvellir

Fields—came to be used. The traditional date of the establishment of the Althing is 930. The site chosen is impressive, with dark lava cliffs flanking a wide, flat depression and a view of snow–capped mountains in the distance. The lava cliffs are split by long fissures. Grass and low flowers soften the texture of the rock surface and blueberries grow in some abundance. Lake Thingvallavatn fills most of the wide basin. The lake and the falls and stream feeding it were sources of water for the Althing meetings and for the farm later situated at this spot.

The Althing consisted of a Law Court (*lögrétta*), where the *goðar* had the vote and laws were passed or amended, and a Judicial Court, where cases were tried. Thus legislative and judicial powers were separated to some extent, though not completely, as the 36 judges serving in the Judicial Court were each nominated by a *goði*. On the other hand, there was no central executive. District government remained in the hands of the local *goðar*; their independence was thus preserved at the same time that the country as a whole obtained a workable method for co–ordinating laws and adjudicating disputes.

In addition to the Althing there were regional *things* or Spring Assemblies where a case could be brought for trial. If a case was not settled at a Spring Assembly, it could be brought to the Althing on appeal. Autumn Assemblies were added, but to pass on news of what was decided at the Althing rather than to try cases.

The Althing met yearly at the end of June and beginning of July, convening on a Thursday evening. On Friday the judges were appointed, and on Saturday these appointments could be challenged. The meetings were held in the open air, with the representatives sitting within an area marked off with a low stone wall. In the Law Court, the *goðar* sat on benches set in a circle, with advisers on benches in two circles behind and in front of them. The people listened outside the circle and probably made comments. The consensus achieved could therefore have had a wide base.[6]

In 962 the nation was divided into quarters, each with a local assembly, and with Quarter Courts at the Althing. People came to feel they could receive a fairer trial at the Althing than at the local *things*, and increasingly made use of these Quarter Courts. Because of a case brought in 1005, when consensus proved impossible and the court was deadlocked, the Fifth Court, a higher court of appeals, was added. The Fifth Court decided issues by simple majority vote.

The number of *goðar* was increased from 36 to 39. Eventually, with church members and others added, the number of voting representatives at the Law Court reached 147.

The most important man at the Althing was the Law Speaker. Before the law was written down, the Law Speaker had the task of reciting one–third of the laws each year and of stating the law on any given point as needed. He stood on the Law Rock (*Lögberg*) to recite the laws. If he had a lapse of memory or the point of law was difficult, he had to consult five or more "lawmen." He was also consulted when the Althing was not in session, and he could take sides in a dispute. He was a powerful man and well respected, the only public official for the whole country. The names of all the Law Speakers are still known.

The meeting of the Althing was the great political and social event of the year, a two–week festival of young and old, buyers and sellers, poets, jugglers, and just plain adventurers. People came from all over Iceland and others from abroad. They exchanged news and gossip, cemented friendships, made deals, settled disputes, celebrated their gods, and planned marriages. Some undoubtedly tried to steal away, hiding behind lava outcroppings or in the huge lava rifts, looking for privacy during the 24–hour summer daylight. They stayed in "booths," huts with a permanent base of stone walls topped by a cloth roof brought for the purpose. They even diverted the Öxará River to provide a more convenient supply of water.

Commonwealth Law

We know about the law at the time of the Commonwealth from copies of the version originally written down beginning in 1117 and amended in the thirteenth century. This collection of laws and commentary is called, for no known reason, *Grágás* or Gray Goose. It is bulky, three and a half times the size of the Danish East Zealand law of the time.[7] Its size reflects a need to resolve conflict, and clarifying the law was a logical means to do so, but events in the sagas indicate that disagreements persisted.

The law defined a legal person as free, a member of a family, and having a residence. The law carefully protected the rights of this free individual. In case of a dispute, a freeman could seek compromise, and presumably most did, either directly or with arbitration by a neutral party. Duelling was prohibited soon after 1000. The literature preserves the record of family feuds to settle disputes, but the emphasis was on preserving honor, not feuding per se. Justice was often a matter of reputation rather than the question of who was at fault; judgment was often rendered to preserve peace rather than to try to ascertain who was guilty.[8] Getting people to speak for one, and fight outside of court as necessary, determined the outcome. Prestige rested on personal and family ties and behavior, rather than control of sources of income. The freeman could fight and take revenge, but under conditions clearly circumscribed in the law. The law, in other words, supported the values of personal independence and honor, but also promoted arbitration to contain the violence that could ensue from preserving one's honor.

If the case came to court and a person lost, there were three possible judgments: 1) restitution of property or a fine, 2) lesser outlawry, and 3) full outlawry. Fame came to Eiríkur the Red as a result of his receiving the judgment of lesser outlawry, being banished for three years. Full outlawry meant permanent banishment from Iceland, with all property and rights forfeited. Death and physical punishment were not imposed.

What seems odd to us today is that the system made no provision for carrying out the judgment of the courts. A sense of honor seems to have been the main impetus in determining whether a man actually paid the fine imposed or left the country if outlawed. The man who won his case at the Althing could still "lose" his case in a sword fight on the way home; he typically rode home protected by his supporters.

Class and Status

Iceland at the time of the Commonwealth (and indeed into the twentieth century) was a society of farmers. Jakob Benediktsson[9] lists the social classes in post–settlement times as: 1) large and small landowners, who were required to attend the Althing; 2) small farmers, many of whom were tenants; 3) laborers and other landless people, some of whom agreed to work for six months or a year on a farm in return for their keep; 4) slaves or thralls. The farming society had no need to specify occupations such as warrior, poet, or priest. The chieftains and the freemen farmers fulfilled those roles as needed. Being a priest, lawman or doctor was a part–time service. Despite reliance on overseas trade for timber and grain, there was no merchant class.

In the beginning, the slaves were the main labor force. A man could volunteer to be a slave temporarily to pay off a debt. Slavery died out in the eleventh century since plantation agriculture, which profited most from slavery, was nonexistent and renting land to freemen was more profitable than having to support slaves.

A man had the responsibility of seeing to his mother's, father's, and children's maintenance. The father had complete authority over the children.[10] The mother took care of the children and saw to household duties, including dairying. In Iceland the women could be poets and go to school and learn Latin. They were respected, and were sometimes as aggressive as the men, urging them into battle; however, they had no political rights, though they could bear witness and be outlawed.

Preserving status and looking after certain tasks, such as taking care of the indigent, required district organization. Along with population growth, the increasing pressure for land, and a labor surplus, the number of poor had increased by ca. 1200 A.D. The land was accordingly divided into *hreppur* (districts), probably the same number, 164, that existed in 1700.[11] Each hreppur had to include at least 20 farmers of high enough status that they were required to attend the Althing. They were jointly responsible for mutual problems, such as poor relief, and organized joint action, such as the autumn sheep roundup.

Pagan Worship and the Viking Spirit

Very little is known about the actual rites of the pagan Norse religion. The people worshipped out of doors, though in bad weather they probably made use of their houses. More is known about the stories and beliefs that formed the core of the Norse religion than about the rites practiced, though it is clear that they celebrated with sacrificial feasts at which they drank ale and ate lamb and horsemeat. The famous thirteenth century Icelandic writer and historian Snorri Sturluson wrote that they splashed blood over the walls, inside and out, as well as over the guests, but how much the accounts that have come down to us are colored by the exaggerated reactions of the Christians who wrote the manuscripts is not known.[12] The pagan worshippers did drink toasts to the gods and danced, and they surely sang.

Burials were in mounds or on ships that were burnt. Over 300 pagan burials have been found in Iceland but no large mounds such as are known in other Scandinavian countries. The dead were buried in a rectangular excavation, the man sometimes with his bridled horse (never a mare) and weapons, usually a spear.

Icelanders of the time faced life with a combination of equanimity and robust vitality. The belief in fate was strong—gods as well as men had to submit to fate—and they took life as it came. Luck, they believed, ran in families. They admired the man who, above all, upheld his own and his family's honor, who was proud, strong, daring, and who could be trusted to keep his word. The hero was a generous host and might also be a poet.

Despite the tales of a good feast with generous quantities of ale and of preserving honor with the sword, if necessary, personal pride was also enhanced through moderation. The good arbitrator was a man of restraint and highly respected. There was, Brøndsted writes,[13] a "pervasive prudence." Family ties were valued, as was friendship, both implying bonds of honor, including hospitality.

Brøndsted[14] faults Vikings in general for being "more responsive to an opportunity for quick action rather than one for long–term perseverance." Though this may have been generally true, the settling of Iceland and the lands to the west involved a great deal more than "quick action."

As Brøndsted also points out,[15] "The word seems to have meant much to the Vikings." Words had a potency and permanency that could be admired in a poem or chosen carefully to emphasize a man's good qualities. The Norwegian kings generously rewarded poems of praise composed by the Icelandic scalds. Scathing verse that demeaned a man, on the other hand, was considered libelous and the law recorded in *Grágás* provided for outlawry in punishment.

Modern Icelanders have much in common with their long–ago ancestors. Fatalism is still a part of Icelandic beliefs; there is a strong tendency to accept what happens with outward equanimity. "He's always in a good humor," is a strong compliment. Almost all Icelanders maintain a quiet bearing and are pleasant to talk to. Tension is held inside, perhaps the reason that depression is also fairly common, as it is in other inward–turning societies. On the other hand, if a slight is felt, many Icelanders are quick to say, in a normal tone of voice, "I've been insulted" or "That bothers me." The problem is usually resolved on the spot. The few times when Icelanders feel they must criticize someone personally, they do so, but afterwards they offer a handshake to heal any ill feelings. Not all are appeased, of course, but the handshake helps to maintain a workable atmosphere in a society so small that so many constantly rub shoulders with each other. The power of the word, too, is still strong; a person is admired for composing a rhyme on the spot or publishing a book of poems or a novel. And Icelanders have been known for their warm hospitality through the centuries.

The Farmstead and the Economy

The farmstead was the center of Icelandic social and family life and the principal economic unit. In the latter half of the tenth century there were about 4000 independent farms. The larger farms, or manors, were inherited through

Lamb

the father. Each of these was the size of three or more average farms, with out-lying holdings, and usually a shed on mountain pasture.

The frame of the communal home or longhouse was of timber, mostly constructed of imported wood or driftwood, and the walls were panelled inside. To save on scarce wood, however, the outer walls were thick layers of sod with some stone. The single door gave onto an entranceway with a food storage compartment. The main room had wide wooden benches against the walls on both sides, where people worked, entertained, and slept. The benches were covered with soft, warm hides and down comforters for sleeping. Belongings were hung on walls or stored in chests. The floors were of stamped earth. If this was the home of a chieftain, his carved high–seat pillars flanked his wooden seat of honor. The master and his wife usually slept in a large, enclosed, wooden box set on one bench, to afford them some privacy. Imagine the conversation, given the fact that all the family and laborers openly worked and slept together on those wooden benches!

The women worked in an adjoining room with a fireplace in the center and narrower benches around the wall, cooking, spinning and weaving. With no windows, the fires and oil lamps of imported soapstone provided the only light. The building offered good protection from the weather, but the interior was dark and often smoky. The privy was a separate ell with troughs on either side and floor–level drains to the outside. There was another ell for food storage, where Icelandic *skyr* (a delicious soured milk product) was kept in large wooden vats, and separate buildings for the livestock, a smithy, a shed for storage, and a woodpile. Near the sea there was also a boat shed, as the ships were drawn up on land in the winter.

The farm at Stöng in the south of Iceland, which was occupied until the fourteenth century, has been duplicated at a comparable spot. The reconstruction is based on the farmstead at Stöng, as well as on excavations elsewhere in Iceland and in Greenland, and represents construction methods up to about 1250. Later, in the fourteenth century, passage houses were built, where all the rooms opened off a central corridor. The farm at Stöng had 20 head of cattle, but elsewhere a manor might have over a hundred head.

There was always a great deal of work to be done. The women had spindles and upright looms and used chunks of lava rock to weight the warp threads. They wove wadmal, a homespun woolen cloth, for export, though the farmstead was nearly self–sufficient. The fields were fertilized with manure. There were quern stones to grind grain and the men made bog iron and charcoal. Wood was used for fuel in the beginning, peat and manure later after the forests had been depleted. The men had carpenter's and blacksmith's tools. They also had weapons—spear, sword, axe and a round shield. The shield was of wood, thin and flat, with a central boss of metal that covered the hand–grip.

Kristján Eldjárn[16] makes the point that nineteenth century Icelandic farmers were still Iron Age people and would have understood the farmers of the Commonwealth well. The labor–intensive farming techniques were similar; both made charcoal, and the tools for haying were the same. The buildings were still of sod and undressed stone, though the style had changed considerably. Today most of the sheep still run free in the highlands in summer. The settlers, however, used a simpler wooden plough (a colter plough or ord) that cut a furrow but did not turn the earth.

Icelandic sheep grow wool in various shades of off–white, brown, reddish brown, gray and black. Most Icelandic clothes during the Commonwealth were of these natural colors, but several plants were used for dye and those who could afford it wore dyed clothes for more important occasions. Horsehair and flax were also spun. The women wore a long gown or chemise, covered by an over–gown or straight cloth panels that were open on the sides and attached at the shoulder with straps and large brooches. The men wore a long tunic, sometimes belted, and trousers. For warmth the men wore a long cloak, the women a shawl. Intricate designs were used on the armbands and brooches. These designs had Scandinavian roots, as they included intertwined serpents as well as plants, despite the fact there have never been any snakes in Iceland.

The horses and other livestock were vital to the people's livelihood. People frequently walked, even across the highlands, and continued to do so into the twentieth century, though horses, both for riding and as pack animals, remained the main transportation into the twentieth century. In pagan times horses also provided valuable meat.

There were various forms of entertainment. Horses were bred to fight and bets laid on the outcome. Fighting stallions were also exported. The people liked to prove their strength. Wrestling matches were common; until the early twentieth century, when a special leather belt was introduced, they grabbed each other's breeches and, with fancy footwork and special holds, tried to send the other man tumbling. Or several grabbed the corners of a horsehide and tried to hang on, while getting the others to let go by pulling hard or tripping them. Chess remains an Icelandic national sport. There were also the tales of Norse mythology to retell, word games, poems, and songs to sing. One popular game continued well into the twentieth century: the first person recited a verse and the next person had to recite a verse that began with the last letter of the preceding verse.

Goods were bartered within Iceland, but there was a standard of legal exchange. Silver was in short supply, so commodities served as the medium of exchange. The value was agreed at the local Spring Assemblies, and thus varied in different parts of Iceland, but basically the monetary unit was six ells of homespun wadmal cloth. One cow–equivalent equalled six ewes or 120 ells of cloth. Both ounces and marks were originally measures of weight (one mark was ca. 215 grams) but became monetary units in the eleventh century.[17]

Though each farmstead was largely self–sufficient, some goods had to be imported: timber and tar for ships and for houses; better iron implements such as weapons and kettles; and grain, especially after the climate worsened. The chieftains imported their more expensive clothes and honey for making mead. After the conversion to Christianity, candle wax and wine were needed for church services and sacraments.

In exchange, Iceland exported wadmal, skins, wool, sulphur and gyrfalcons. Sulphur is found in the hot spring areas. The gyrfalcon is now the national bird, still greatly prized for its hunting ability but now protected. Wadmal was the most valuable export. Exporting it meant that the women worked long hours to spin and weave it. Assuming a population of 50,000, it took the women a total of one million working days to weave the cloth necessary for home use, and perhaps another half million days to weave cloth for export. Between 8,000 and 11,000 women worked steadily from October to April to spin, card and weave the wool.[18] When the value of wadmal dropped in the twelfth century, raw wool was exported. The conversion to Christianity also meant that the need for fish on Friday increased. However, the exportation of fish could not become important until after 1400 when the ban on exporting food was lifted.

Food and Health

Eating habits were influenced by what had been known in Norway but adapted to Icelandic circumstances.[19] Overall, the people had a healthy diet, composed mostly of animal products, but with sufficient vitamins. They consumed a large quantity of milk products, beef and some mutton (the sheep were more valuable for wool than for meat), fish, geese, chickens, and pork, a high–protein, high–fat diet that sustained them well. Most of what they ate was either not overcooked or was raw, as, for example, dried fish or *harðfiskur*. They ate twice a day, the main meal after the initial farm work was done and supper in the evening before going to bed.

Meat was roasted on a spit or, more often, boiled in a cauldron in a pit heated by hot stones, a method not practiced in Norway. Meat was also pickled in sour milk or whey, like the food for the feast of Thorrablót. Blood pudding was also made, but unlike today, with no or very little grain. Boiling remained the commonest way of preparing meat and fish until foreign eating habits, like fish amandine and pizza, became popular in the later twentieth century.

As today, milk, especially the whey, was drunk and was also preserved as cheese and whey cheese or soured as *skyr,* and dried cod was often eaten with butter.

Salt was obtained from boiling seawater, but there was very little until it began to be imported in the twelfth century. Fish and meat were dried and sometimes salted, processes that do not destroy the vitamins; however, the use of salt for cooking remained minimal.

Grain is the food most mentioned in the records as being in short supply. Before the climate turned colder, barley ripened, especially in the south. Grain was imported to some extent, both wheat and malt. The people made a coarse, black bread and also porridge, usually of barley. Grain was used to make ale, and the chieftains also drank mead made from honey.

For vegetables, there were cabbage—usually boiled, onions—often eaten raw, and angelica. Stripped of the outer skin and fibre, angelica was considered a delicacy when young and fresh. In addition the people used wild herbs and the seaweed called dulse, which was dried or preserved in whey.

Vitamin A was obtained from fats and the B vitamins from meat and fish. Their diet included sufficient vitamin C, for instance from raw onions, raw angelica, and crowberries and blueberries. There was also some vitamin C in liver and in the dried meat and fish. Vitamin D came from fish, milk and butter, and the sun. It is not known when Icelanders first starting consuming fish liver oil.

Skeletal remains and detailed descriptions in the annals and sagas make it possible to know a good deal about what diseases and difficulties the people had to cope with. There was famine in some years, when they must have had to eat spoiled food, though the years of famine were not as numerous as later after the climate turned colder. There was leprosy and some tuberculosis, but rickets and scurvy were exceedingly rare in the early years, and tuberculosis was not common until late in the nineteenth century. Teeth, even in the young, were much worn from eating coarse foods, but there was no dental caries. The people also suffered from lice, as did other Europeans of the time.

Standards of cleanliness were relatively high. The people washed or bathed in the entranceway of their houses or inside where they slept and washed their hands before a meal and before attending an assembly meeting. There were outdoor privies as well as the special ell in the longhouse, and relieving oneself at assembly sites was forbidden. Sometimes the edge of a cliff was the favored place. The walls of the longhouse were hung with wadmal and these cloths and the furs would have been hard to keep clean. The most important factors for maintaining health, however, may have been that the people spent so much time outdoors, exercising, and had a source of clean, fresh water in a stream or spring right by the farmhouse.

Wounds, broken bones and bruises were treated by a person who, in addition to farming, also functioned as a doctor. Sword and knife cuts were the commonest wounds, and were washed and bound, the patient being given sour milk to drink. The law was precise over the amount of damages required to be paid for each type and severity of wound inflicted.

The level of health was lower after the early eleventh century, when people stopped having outdoor privies. Scurvy did not become common until the fourteenth century. The increasing cold from 1250 on took its toll and the average height of adults began to decline.

The Conversion to Christianity

Though some of the original settlers were clearly Christian, Christianity seems to have died out before being re–introduced. Many Icelanders in the tenth century had travelled abroad and learned of Christianity and some were converted. Belief in the pagan religion was on the decline. The Norwegian king Ólafur Tryggvason Christianized Norway and sent missionaries abroad, including to Iceland. Not all the missionaries were completely comfortable with the new religion of brotherly love, however, as is evidenced by the fact that some of them got rid of the people they did not like by killing them off. The most influential missionary in Iceland, a man named Thangbrandur, carried the message to the king in Norway that all Icelanders were bad. King Ólafur thereupon threatened to kill the heathen Icelanders who were in Norway at the time and took hostages. Two Christianized Icelandic chieftains, Gissur the White and Hjalti Skeggjason, visited Norway and promised the king that Iceland would be converted.

Gissur and Hjalti returned to Iceland. As they made their way to the Althing meeting in the year 1000 (or perhaps 999), they were met by the Christian chieftains from the south of Iceland and rode with them to the assembly. Hjalti had previously been judged guilty of a crime and had paid the required fine, but he had also been required to remain within a prescribed area. His leaving this area to come to the Althing was therefore a breach of the law and of the judgment against him, itself enough to cause trouble. The heathen faction prepared to challenge the Christians, but moderates prevented a clash. It was clear to many that they needed the freedom of trade that the Norwegian king could assure them. The highly respected Law Speaker, Thorgeir Thorkelsson, himself a heathen and a moderate, was asked to make the decision as to whether the nation should be converted to Christianity.

Thorgeir retired to his booth, put his cloak over his head, and meditated for a day and a night. The next day he delivered his answer from the Law Rock. Iceland needed one law and one state, he began, and therefore compromise was necessary. Everyone was to be baptized Christian, but worship of the old gods was allowed in private, including the eating of horsemeat and exposure of children. Exposing an infant to the elements until dead, if done right after birth and before suckling, was allowed under the old law and was the only means of population control. The people were to be baptized either at Thingvellir or, since the waters at Thingvellir are icy cold, on the way home in nice, warm geothermal springs.

Thus the conversion to Christianity was accomplished peacefully. There was no opposition afterwards; the large farmers and chieftains wanted peace. Thorgeir himself tossed his images of the old gods over the beautiful falls in the north still called Godafoss, waterfall of the gods. In 1016 the worship of the old gods was forbidden, along with eating horsemeat and exposing children. Horsemeat was not eaten again until the eighteenth century, when more rational thinking prevailed in those times of widespread starvation. Horsemeat remains a part of the Icelandic diet today, but even in the twentieth century there have been ministers who would not touch it because it was once used in pagan rites.

The *goðar* had a new role to play. They built churches and hired priests, in the beginning foreigners, and then sent their sons to school to become priests. But, as Sigurdur Líndal points out,[20] it took another century before Iceland was really Christianized.

The Time of the First Bishops

Though the great Icelandic sagas were not written down until the twelfth and thirteenth centuries, many of the heroes they deal with lived in the Saga Age, from 930–1030, bracketing the conversion to Christianity in the year 1000. During this period, the nation developed and the colonies in Greenland and North America were established.

After 1030, when the Christians controlled the country, the political situation remained stable until the death of Bishop Gissur Ísleifsson in 1118.[21] The large landholdings were subdivided and there were fewer feuds. People went abroad to study to enter the church rather than to be poets and warriors.

The first bishop, Ísleifur, the son of Gissur the White, was consecrated in 1056. He and his son Gissur, who became bishop in 1082, strengthened the church. Their farmstead at Skálholt became the bishop's seat.

In 1106 a second diocese was added in the north at Hólar, which was maintained until 1801. The first of the northern bishops, Jón Ögmundsson, was a puritan at heart; he forbade dancing and continued the pagan ban on composing love songs. In fact, *Grágás* sets outlawry as the punishment for composing a song about a woman! Despite his Puritanism, however, he was known to have sung and played the harp well. A French choirmaster taught in the Hólar school. Many of the choirmasters of the times could compose and a great number of the chants are still preserved. Most were monodic, having one voice or a single line of melody, and were in the old church modes.[22]

Jón Ögmundsson also changed the names of the days of the week to get rid of all traces of paganism. Modern Icelandic thus has no Tuesday, and so on, but instead "third day, mid–week day, fifth day, fast day, and bath day" (*þriðjudagur, miðvikudagur, fimmtudagur, laugadagur*). The bishop seems not to have realized

101

that the sun and moon of the first two days of the week were also pagan deities; he left *sunnudagur* and *mánudagur* untouched.

Bishop Gissur at Skálholt in the south did a great deal for the church and the country during his term of office from 1082–1118. Since the church was severely lacking in funds, he introduced the tithe, assessed at 1% of the property value or 1/10 of the possible income. The tithe law was passed by the Althing in 1097. The tithe was undoubtedly supported by the chieftains as they, too, stood to gain: it was divided equally among the bishop, the local priest, the local church, and the poor. The tithe law was written down even before the compilation of *Grágás*.

Other improvements also ensued. The church brought writing and the Latin alphabet. From about 1100 the nation began not to have to rely solely on memorized accounts to keep track of religious and secular matters. The taxpayers were censused in 1106; the total population is estimated to have numbered 75,000–80,000 people. The law code preserved in *Grágás* was first written down, beginning in 1117, and expanded to include ecclesiastical law when it was recognized by the Althing in 1130. The church prospered, the weather was good for farming, and Bishop Gissur was virtually king until his death in 1118.[23]

The church was important as a center of learning. In 1130 Ari the Learned, at the request of the bishop at Skálholt, wrote the *Book of Icelanders*. The *Book of Settlements* was compiled, largely by Sturla Thordarson in ca. 1275–1280. The first monastery was established in 1133. Eventually there were nine monasteries, both Benedictine and Augustinian, and two convents. All were cultural centers with libraries and facilities for teaching and copying manuscripts.

The social structure was changing. In the beginning the *goðar* established schools, and some trained as clerics and were themselves consecrated as priests. The chieftains owned the local churches and collected the church share of the tithe. The church gained wealth, relative to property values in Iceland, and some *goðar* amassed more wealth and power by owning several *goðorð*. They could donate their land to the church as a fief, thus evading all taxes, yet keep the right to administer the land. With church fiefdoms, the chieftains became independent of the *goðorð*, the Althing and the old law.

In 1152 the church in Iceland came under the jurisdiction of the Archbishop in Nidaros, Norway. In 1190 the archbishop took a major step to keep clerical and secular power separate by banning the consecration of *goðar* as priests. The *goðorð* were concentrated in fewer hands, the chieftains opposed the bishops, and the stage was set for conflict.

Relations with Norway

Icelanders had a surprising amount of contact with other nations in the early centuries, given the distances that had to be traversed.[24] They went abroad for business and for sheer adventure, to trade, to be court poets, or to go on pilgrimages. They joined the First Crusade in 1096. In the twelfth century many went on pilgrimages to Rome. The law, as stated in *Grágás*, required that the tithe must be paid, even if the landholder was in Russia. But for all this contact, in the beginning there was no formal agreement with a foreign nation. Unlike European principalities, Icelanders had no border disputes, and, though the country developed, there were no riches comparable to the riches held by the church and princes in Europe and therefore no treasures to steal. In the twelfth century, few of the powerful families had a yearly income of more than 100 cow–equivalents.[25]

Despite the fact that Icelanders soon came to think of themselves as a separate people, both Norwegians and many Icelanders thought the land should properly be a piece of Norway.[26] It seemed unnatural to the kings and clergy of the time that a country should have a democratic independence. Since Norway had been the home of most of the original settlers, overlordship should be in Norway's hands. The Icelandic church therefore became a part of the archbishopric at Nidaros in 1152.

Harald the Fair–Hair united Norway at the end of the ninth century and extended his suzerainty to cover the islands off the Scottish coast. Though he never mounted a campaign to conquer Iceland, he coveted it. He sent Uni, the son of the explorer Gardar, to secure Iceland for the Norwegian throne, but Uni was badly received and returned home empty–handed. When emigration to Iceland peaked, Harald imposed a tax on anyone voyaging to Iceland. Norway had a population of 250,000, high for the time, but the king felt the loss of the tens of thousands who left for Iceland.

Icelanders looked toward Norway in time of need. During the settlement, they sought advice on how to settle property boundaries. They used Norwegian law as a model, albeit with important modifications. The conversion to Christianity was accomplished in part because they needed trade with Norway.

Ólafur Haraldsson, later St. Olaf, who became king of Norway in 1014, established Christianity in Norway and sent missionaries to Iceland. He, too, coveted Iceland. When Icelanders refused his demand for sovereignty, he asked to be given the island of Grímsey in the north. Again, the king's demand was refused at a meeting of the Althing. A treaty was signed in ca. 1022, Iceland's first pact with a foreign nation, specifying the rights of both Icelanders and Norwegians. Norwegians in Iceland were to have the same rights as Icelanders themselves. Icelanders, in turn, were guaranteed certain rights in Norway, but each Icelandic freeman was required to pay a tax of 2 cow–equivalents on arriving in Norway, and was also subject to military duty.

Nevertheless, in 1179 the Icelandic Commonwealth was still a viable form of government and Icelandic fortunes still strong enough that the time had not yet come when the country must succumb to Norwegian overlordship.

Sorcery and Superstition

On a clear day Snaefellsjökull (Snow Mountain Glacier) can easily be seen from Reykjavík, a perfect volcanic cone rising majestically from the sea to the northwest, capped by a glacier, pristine white in winter or glowing red in the sunset. Driving around the peninsula of Snaefellsnes on a sunny day, with the imposing spectacle of the mountain dominating the western end of the land, is to experience the magnetism of nature at its best. Many people, both foreigners and Icelanders, have felt not only the beauty of mountain and peninsula, but are also convinced that this area is magically electrified. In the summer, people of various faiths often meet here to commune with nature and to practice their religion.

Here "under the glacier" is the home of Thórdur Halldórsson, the "last" Icelandic sorcerer. In 1992 the Icelandic State Television visited Thórdur to interview him. They found an elderly man with white hair and a white mustache, who stands straight and is remarkably spry, very aware of everything happening and obviously very much at ease with life and the natural forces around him. Kittiwakes nesting in the sea cliffs call in the background as he is interviewed. "Sorcery," he says, "is based on living with nature." He has a broad face and wide–set clear eyes that are alight as he talks. Yes, he can protect a boat from danger as it goes to sea. "Power comes from nature that goes straight to a boat with a prayer on it."

Thórdur learned meteorology at the Seamen's School and, untroubled by rheumatism despite his age, still goes to sea to fish. He has a detailed knowledge of the area he lives in and goes foxhunting, too, with a gun. He is also a poet and a painter; in fact he learned painting from the great Icelandic painter Jóhannes Kjarval, among others. "Poetry and painting are the same," he says. "They have the same strength." Thórdur has a quick sense of humor and can recite a poem to fit almost any occasion.

He hops around on stone slabs to show how some spells are carried out or he takes a wishing stone from his pocket and explains that you can carry one to have your wish come true. His mother, he says, made him promise not to do harm with his spells. His conjuring is benevolent and the man himself the ideal sorcerer whose life is an inspiration to all.

Heathen Times and the Period of Catholicism

All humans need to have both an explanation for why and how things work and a feeling of control over events. From pagan times sorcery and superstition have filled the gaps in the known and to some extent provided control, not perhaps of ultimate destiny as decreed by the Norns, but at least of intervening events. Ghosts and other frightening powers can be kept at bay with the use of a countervailing power such as invoking the white magic of the church or carrying a stick carved with the appropriate runes.

There were two words for sorcery in Old Icelandic, *seiður* and *galdur*, both from roots meaning song or chant. The former were spells or incantations intoned at night by sorcerers seated on a platform and performed either to work

Helm of Aegir, for good luck

good or evil or to foretell the future. The old manuscripts relate that the goddess Freyja first taught the old Norse gods *seidur* magic, but elsewhere we learn that this was also Óðinn's contribution. Stephen Flowers[1] has written that the *seidur* techniques were relatively intuitive, employing trance states and relying on animal and plant materials, whereas the practice of *galdur* depended more on the will of the sorcerer, aided by the use of runes and symbols and chanted text. Flowers points out that Icelandic sorcery does not draw as wide distinctions between the evilness of the bad or the benevolence of the good forces as elsewhere and that the Icelandic sorcerer is rarely concerned with protection from the powers conjured up. In fact, the sorcerer's power resides most often within himself.

Unlike many tales of magic from other lands, early Icelandic tales of sorcery from the thirteenth and fourteenth centuries present the sorcerers as popular heroes. These early tales are "optimistic" and "free of fear."[2] God and devil each have their own place; there is no compact with the devil and the sorcerer retains the upper hand. This emphasis on the individual's own power fits well with the continuing emphasis on the importance of the individual in Icelandic culture and is probably in part responsible for the fact that the *galdur* techniques outlasted *seidur* techniques and perhaps survived better in Iceland than elsewhere. *Galdur* techniques also better fit the Icelandic emphasis on the importance of words and knowledge, nor did the use of herbs and potions play as important a part in Iceland as elsewhere.

Different methods were used in practicing sorcery. One was to carve runes or symbols into a stave or wand. The runes were then accentuated with dye or blood and a formula spoken over them to empower them. The rune stick could then be carried for protection.

Frequently the sorcerer awoke the dead, in the early days to foretell the future, but in later times more often to acquire a familiar or an emissary to send elsewhere to harm or kill someone else. These familiars often took the form of birds or dogs or other animals. As Haraldur Ólafsson points out,[3] the folktales rest on a belief that the inner nature of animals and humans is the same and unchangeable, a view that was common in other parts of the world as well. Humans can, therefore, as a matter of course change into animals and animals into humans. Indeed, the fetches that followed a person or family were usually in animal form. Birds were the harbingers of future events. The plague of 1495, for example, came with merchants, but birds were said to have spread it throughout the country.

Some sorcerers employed curses. Under the influence of the Christian church, later sorcerers seem to have employed Latin words in some spells and when performing black magic to have recited the Lord's Prayer and Holy Writ backwards. In a day and age when relatively few could write, the mere use of runes or letters, even for normal communication, was magical, and the Latin of the church was similarly a magical code to the uninitiated. Thus many of those reputed to be sorcerers in Icelandic history were churchmen.

The *Galdrabók* and Other Manuscripts

Until the late seventeenth century, possession of a book that dealt with sorcery was punishable by death. It is therefore not surprising that few such books are still in existence. The most important is the *Galdrabók* or "Book of Sorcery," compiled by four authors from 1550–1680.[4] There are also a few other shorter parchment manuscripts as well as a leechbook or physician's manual from the late fifteenth century that includes magical symbols and prayers for protection. Two other major manuscripts apparently once existed, the *Grayskin* and the *Redskin*, the latter written by a famous Icelandic bishop named Gottskálk and said to have been buried with him.

The *Galdrabók* lists 47 spells, 21 of which do not contain Christian elements. Of the old gods, Ódinn and Thór are called on most often, but the two may be named among a string of gods and names for the devil. The 43rd spell, for example, invokes: Thór, Ódinn, Frigg, Freyja, Satan, Beelzebub—but then it may take all those to "make a woman quiet"!

Despite the fact that the extant manuscripts were written at so late a time, there is evidence that the spells they contain date at least in part from the period of Catholicism from the year 1000 to the Reformation in 1550. The coming of Christianity brought about an amalgamation of former beliefs with Christian ones, and the practice of sorcery, like other folk beliefs, was not altered as drastically as on the Continent as there was no formal Inquisition in Iceland.

The Period of the Reformation and Protestantism

With the coming of Protestantism in 1550, beliefs changed. The view that all sorcery stemmed from the devil reached Iceland via a small number of

well–educated influential individuals, the fear of Satan increased, and the root-
ing out of sorcery began. These were difficult times when the king appropriated church property and a generous share of church income and the people were
suddenly without the crutch the Catholic saints had afforded them. Superstition
and the practice of sorcery spread, not least among the learned.

The seventeenth century was the peak of accusations of sorcery and burning
at the stake. There were 120 court cases, including 10 where women were
charged. Most, but not all, of those accused, were poor workers. Between 1625
and 1685 twenty–five lost their lives: twenty–one men were burned at the
stake, one was hanged, one beheaded; one woman was burned, one drowned.[5]
Some were acquitted, some whipped, some outlawed, and others fled before the
law could reach them. But there was less persecution for sorcery in Iceland than
in some other countries and men, not women, were the usual culprits.[6]

The accusers were not always guiltless either. A Rev. Jón Magnússon
blamed his mental troubles on a father and son, who were then burned at the
stake in Skutulsfjördur on April 10, 1656.[7] However, after the burning the Rev.
Jón was still subject to mental problems. He dreamed that a part of the son's
consciousness was still intact; the ashes were therefore raked over and a piece of
unburned brain was found. A new bonfire was lit to get rid of this last remnant
of the bodies. The people were then relieved, but the Reverend Jón still suffered
emotional problems.

In 1686 the Danish king forbade the death penalty unless upheld by the
Danish Supreme Court. The executions came to an end in 1685, but belief in
sorcery died more slowly—the last person was indicted in 1719.[8] In the public
mind, clerics still possessed the inscrutable power of Latin and knowledge of
dark rites, and tales of several clergymen–sorcerers are well known to this day.
One such was about Galdra–Loftur, Loftur the Sorcerer (1700–1722) who,
while a student at Hólar, is said to have raised Bishop Gottskálk from the dead
and actually touched a corner of the *Redskin* parchment before the bishop slid
back down in his grave, of course taking the forbidden book with him. Loftur
responded by reciting the Lord's Prayer backwards, but in the end he lost his
soul to the devil. As he was fishing one day a gray, furry hand reached up from
the sea and dragged him and his boat to oblivion.

Nevertheless, in the eighteenth century there was less emphasis on the
magical power of clerics than in earlier times. In this period of difficulties—
famine, eruptions, sickness, and economic troubles—people sought help from
"ordinary" Icelanders who, like Thórdur Halldórsson in the twentieth century,
knew how to use spells to protect against catastrophe.

Superstition

The belief in sorcery was accompanied by a host of superstitious beliefs
regarding the prediction of the future or protection from harm.[9] Most of these
have now disappeared from the everyday world of Icelanders. Some herbs and
grasses were good for love potions or solving crimes of theft. The person who

stood so that the end of the rainbow touched the top of his or her head would get a wish fulfilled.

Sorcerers understood the language of the raven. Ravens were known to predict the weather and to bode death, though, like trolls, they amply repaid anyone who did them a favor. If a raven is heard in the night, it is a bad spirit or a fetch, and if it croaks during mass a death will follow.

The number three was lucky in Norse mythology. A visitor was supposed to knock three times on the door to show he or she was not a ghost or an evil spirit. Nine, three times three, could be an even luckier number, though sometimes nine meant bad luck. Like the cat with its nine lives, the raven has nine natures, in a strange mixture ranging from the ability to impart wisdom to the ability to cause insomnia. Though since increased to thirteen, originally there were nine Christmas elves, and prayers and incantations were to be recited nine times to be effective.

The Hidden People were ubiquitous and might obstruct the world of humans at unexpected times. In earlier times the sign of the cross was made over and under a baby as it was laid in its cradle so the Hidden People would not exchange it for one of their own, or a pair of scissors, a charm since the blades form a cross, was put next to the baby for protection. Incidentally, the use of a cross as a good luck charm goes back to Norse mythology and the symbol of Thór's hammer.

Given the importance of fishing it is not surprising that there were careful restrictions on what people could do at sea. Whistling and even reading at sea could bring strong winds and a storm. On the other hand, in a dead calm the captain or the mate could whistle to bring favorable winds.

Some folk sayings are not so much grounded in superstition as based on experience. All beasts fear the shark; it follows ships and waits for someone to fall overboard. If snow buntings and ptarmigan come into a settlement early in the autumn, it will be a hard winter.

Some beliefs that are common elsewhere were not present in Iceland in the old days. Friday, for example, was a lucky day, whether the 13th or not: "Friday to make money," runs the old saying. Though modern Icelanders frequently ask what sign you are born under, astrology came late to Iceland.

Superstition can also be dispelled. Mt. Hekla was thought to be literally the gate to Hell, probably the source of the English expression "Go to heck." In 1750 two Icelandic students came back from Copenhagen and climbed to the top without incident. After that, people were not so afraid of the mountain.

What may have begun as superstition can become symbolic, whether or not retaining an element of superstitious belief. It is very unusual in Iceland to be told the name of a baby before it is christened; the name is kept secret to protect the baby from harm. When quadruplets were born in 1988, for example, they were officially identified in the hospital as A, B, C, and D until they could be named!

The Family: Confirmation and Easter

Confirmation is a great family event in Iceland, an important rite of passage Nearly every 14–year–old child is confirmed, usually in church, though a few choose a civil ceremony.

Sigga and Gunnar's youngest child, Gummi, turned 14 a short while ago and had a birthday party in celebration. At 14 he was "big," grown up, though Sigga didn't think he was nearly as grown up as he himself did. Nevertheless, research has shown that Icelandic children mature sexually earlier than Scandinavian children in general, and the majority have been given responsibility from an early age.

No child's birthday party with cake and candles would do for Gummi. He invited his friends to a proper *party* at his house, with pizzas and hot dogs washed down with plenty of coke. They sang "Happy Birthday" to the internationally popular Irving Berlin tune, a practice that has become widespread in Iceland since about 1970, and they all danced to popular music, played loud enough for the whole neighborhood to "enjoy," until midnight or so. His friends brought him not too expensive presents, like cassettes of popular music ("Great! Thanks!"), and his family gave him books (not so great) and new soccer shoes (just what he wanted).

Like his friends, Gummi plays soccer (European football) and follows the week's scores for British and European teams. Many Icelanders bet on the British and European soccer pools and even more watch the games on television. Gummi is also exuberant about playing computer games, something he tells Sigga about, and thinking about girls and what a certain classmate would look like undressed, something he does not talk to Sigga about.

Bun Day and Ash Wednesday

On Shrove Monday all the restaurants and business canteens serve round buns filled with whipped cream for coffee breaks and lunch. At home, there are homemade buns to tempt the palate. The custom is now entrenched but apparently was introduced into Iceland in the latter part of the nineteenth century and stems from an earlier Scandinavian habit of "eating white," that is, of fasting during Lent by eating only white foods like milk and flour. In Iceland the day is known as *bolludagur* or Bun Day.

Ash Wednesday, on the other hand, is a day for children's pranks. Though apparently originally an extension of the idea of carnival time—never really celebrated in Iceland, on Ash Wednesday children pin small bags of ashes on the back of some unsuspecting person. Nowadays, rather than containing ashes, the bag is decorated in some way, just to show it is a gift. If you walk downtown on Ash Wednesday you can see a lot of people with these little bags hanging from their coats. Most of the children dress in costumes and go downtown to listen to the organized entertainment, singing and short comments over the loudspeakers.

Confirmation

Most Icelandic children are confirmed at Easter time, though they may choose to be confirmed in the autumn instead. In preparation for confirmation, Gummi and his age–mates attended a class taught by their minister once a week starting in early October. In addition to class, they were required to attend Sunday service at least eight times and to participate in the service in some way, for example, by lighting the altar candles. Like most Icelanders, they usually attended the afternoon service. Though some of the children enjoyed the attention and liked taking part, others, like Gummi, were bored stiff with the lessons and would have done anything rather than go to church.

Confirmation requires new clothes. The shops advertise the latest fashions for young teens: suits and jackets, dresses, shoes. The boy usually gets his first real sports coat or suit, so Sigga went shopping with Gummi. Without too much difference of opinion they agreed on a suit, shirt and tie.

As the day of confirmation approached, the list of the names of all the children, with the dates, places and times of confirmation, was published in the newspapers. On the day itself the children assembled in the church and donned white robes. They stood on either side of the altar while the minister performed the special Lutheran service and carefully gave them words of advice.

The church service was followed by a party at home. Like most of the guests, I elected not to attend the church service but joined the family and other well–wishers for the reception afterwards. All the family came, including Gummi's great–grandmother Ingibjörg, as well as close friends who were invited. There was a stack of telegrams congratulating him; in fact the phone lines to the telephone company are always so busy at this time of year that it's hard to get through to get your telegram sent. Some of the telegrams to Gummi came from family members who were not in town, but most were from friends of the family who were living in Reykjavík. Gummi was the star of the day!

His grandmother Gudrún and her husband, Gudmundur, for whom he was named, together with his great–grandmother Ingibjörg gave him an eiderdown duvet. If he goes abroad to study or work when he is older, he will take the duvet with him, as no true Icelander is comfortable sleeping under a sheet and blankets. An eiderdown duvet is lighter than swansdown or synthetic fibre and keeps the sleeper warm without weight. His grandmother Kristín, Gunnar's mother, presented him with the traditional book of *Passion Psalms* by Hallgrímur Pétursson, Iceland's famous poet–minister of the seventeenth century. His parents, Sigga and Gunnar, gave him a portable radio and cassette and CD player, and from others he received CDs and quite a few books. Though some families go into debt for confirmation, deferring the day of judgment with a credit card, Gummi's family had been sensible and held costs within reason.

The party was a cheerful affair with plenty of coffee, coke for the children, and a variety of cakes and good things to eat. Gummi, in his new suit and tie, stood straight and beamed because of all the attention.

Easter

Easter in Iceland is a welcome break from the long winter. Even when Easter comes early the days are markedly longer and brighter by the time it arrives. The *Passion Psalms* by Hallgrímur Pétursson, once read in every home, are now read over the radio during Lent. Almost everyone has five days off, teachers and school children a full week, as Holy Thursday, Good Friday (called Long Friday in Icelandic), Easter Sunday, and Easter Monday (the Second Day of Easter in Icelandic) are all national holidays. Some families take the opportunity to go north to visit their relatives; others, like Sigga and Gunnar, have been too involved with confirmation.

Easter Sunday is one of those few days when Icelanders really go to church; the others are Christmas and the personal rites of passage like confirmation and marriage.

Chocolate Easter eggs have taken over in Iceland, but it is interesting to note that the idea did not come to Iceland until about 1920 when a bakery in Reykjavík introduced first an oval box filled with candies and then chocolate eggs. Icelanders have never really decorated hens' eggs for Easter, but the chocolate egg has caught on. Thousands are made in Iceland, and more still imported to satisfy the demand. During the Easter holiday Gummi and all his family and friends ate their fill of chocolate eggs.

Summer

The Family: The First Day of Summer

The day was stunning, with sunshine, blue sky, warmth and no wind, though there had been frost last night. This was the First Day of Summer according to the old Icelandic calendar, the Thursday that falls between the 19th and 25th of April, and a national holiday. In the old days Icelanders celebrated the First Day of Summer with whatever food was left, often carefully keeping some in reserve for the occasion. From the sixteenth century on they gave presents, usually homemade, a custom that has continued with presents to children on this day. From the seventeenth century the month ushered in by the First Day of Summer has been called *Harpa*, seeding time. Because they were released from work, children played games, a custom that has led to the modern parades of Scouts and to speeches supporting the youth movement. The city of Reykjavík and other towns in Iceland have a full program of concerts, parades and family entertainment. But Sigga and Gunnar have decided to spend the day on the farm in the south of Iceland where Sigga's sister Inga and her husband Kalli live, and they have invited me to come along.

Gunnar's and Sigga's daughter Kristín, with her husband Hjalti and the baby Anna Sigga, had already moved to Sweden. A phone call (Icelanders much prefer personal contact to a letter) had confirmed that Hjalti had obtained a good job as a plumber and that he and Kristín were learning Swedish (not so difficult after the years of Danish and "Scandinavian" in school). Their other daughter Thórunn, together with her fiancé Sveinn and their four–year–old son Thórir, had decided to remain in Reykjavík and enjoy the parade. Their son Gummi, on the other hand, was looking forward to getting back down to the farm.

Traditionally Icelandic children have worked on the farm in the summer; in fact the school year in the twentieth century was shorter than elsewhere in the western world, originally to accommodate farming needs. Today many municipalities hire teenagers to see to the gardening for the town. Some parents now even pay to send their children out to a farm to work. Gummi, on the other hand, has been fortunate in being able to help Kalli in the summer.

The redwings had long since begun their chirping to show that the days had become longer, and flocks of golden plovers, the harbingers of spring, had landed on the larger patches of lawn in the city before they established their nesting territories in the countryside.

The drive to the farm took us east over the pass over Hellisheidi, past lava fields and mountains and the winter ski run. Moss covers much of the lower reaches of the lava here, gray when it is dry, yellow when wet. The snow remained in patches, but where it had melted it had turned the moss gleaming gold against the black of the lava.

We dropped down the switchbacks to the farmland in the south of Iceland where most of Iceland's potatoes are grown. At Hveragerdi, where geothermal water has made hothouse tomatoes and flowers possible, we stopped to buy tomatoes and the delicious rye bread that is cooked by letting it steam for a day in a covered tin buried in the hot ground, before we crossed the river to Selfoss.

Icelanders don't like to sit in a car for long, though—as with many other things—they endure it quietly. "Tell you what," I suggested to Gummi, "I'll play you a game. You name an object in English beginning with each letter of the alphabet and I'll do the same in Icelandic." Like all Icelandic schoolchildren, Gummi has studied English in school and learned still more from pop songs and the movies, which in Iceland have the original soundtrack with subtitles. Gummi agreed and I began with *appelsína* (orange).

My alphabet was different from his, beginning with A, Á, B, D, E, É, and ending with Þ, Æ and Ö. With a good deal of laughter and prompting from everybody we continued the game on the drive toward rolling grassland and Kalli's farm.

Inga and Kalli came out to meet us, Inga a somewhat thinner version of her sister and Kalli brown–haired, wiry, with strong hands. "Happy summer!" we all greeted each other, as we gave Inga the tomatoes from Hveragerdi and the apples we brought from Reykjavík, food they could not raise themselves. The two dogs and the children swarmed out to greet us, their daughter Magga, who was 16, their son Siggi, who was Gummi's age and also newly confirmed, and four–year–old Elín. "Gudrún's gone into Reykjavík with her friends," Inga explained. At twenty, their eldest daughter Gudrún found the big city more attractive than country life.

Sigga reached into the car for the cakes and *kleinur* or twisted doughnuts she had made and we followed Inga into her house, slipping out of our shoes as we entered. The house was built of concrete, one–story, roomy and pleasant. Inga's plants basked in the sunlight pouring through the double–glazed windows. The older wooden farmhouse was close by; Kalli's parents still lived there and Kalli's father continued to farm with him, but they had gone on a "sun" trip to the Canary Islands and were not here that day. "Better to be in the sun in Iceland today than in the Canaries," we all agreed.

Inga and Sigga both went into the kitchen, looking very much the sisters they were despite the difference in age, exuding competence and cheerfulness. Kalli folded his wiry body onto a chair, and he and Gunnar settled down to their favorite topic: what's wrong with government policy. Gunnar expressed his worry about the duties and taxes he has to pay just to get imported goods into the country and Kalli worried about the pricing policy for farm goods. Since this was not a political meeting, in typical Icelandic style they exchanged wry rather than bitter comments, and though neither laughed out loud they each appreciated the other's apt sense of humor.

Soon the nine of us were sitting round the table enjoying food and conversation. We helped ourselves from the platter of hot omelettes and a plate of *flatbrauð* or "flatbread," made of wheat flour or wheat and rye, rolled fairly thin and fried brown, each piece round and served cut in half– or quarter–circles. It is good buttered and topped either with thin slices of pale yellow Icelandic cheese or of *hangikjöt* ("hung" lamb), pink from the curing process, or spread with pâté made from lamb meat or sheep's liver. The *hverabrauð* (hot springs bread) that we brought is still warm and delicious buttered, plain or with cheese. There were tasty slices of black pudding and sausage, home–made in the autumn by stuffing sheep's stomachs with a mixture of meat and milk. To top it off we each had a bowl of *skyr*, a delicious milk product with the consistency of yogurt but fermented with rennet and served with sugar and cream. Most of us drank coke or another soft drink with the meal and the children had milk or coke.

At the end of the meal Inga of course offered us coffee, that staple of the Icelandic diet and Icelandic hospitality for the last three centuries.

"*Takk fyrir mig* (Thank you for me)," we each said appreciatively as we got up from the table.

"Magga will help us wash the dishes. Elín, why don't you take our guest out to see the new lamb," Inga suggested. Siggi and Gummi were already on their way to the barn with an apple each for the horses and a doughnut each for themselves. There was a nicker as Gummi's favorite horse, Faxi, recognized him and stuck his head out for the apple. The boys, joined by Magga, saddled the horses and went for a ride.

Times have changed and the Icelandic horse that in earlier times made colonization and survival possible is now a prime source of enjoyment. The original settlers brought their horses from Norway and the breed has remained unchanged except as it has adapted to Icelandic conditions. Related to the Fjord pony of Norway, and ultimately to the Tundra pony of Alaska, the Icelandic horse (or pony) is adapted to being outdoors all year in rough weather and surviving on coarse grasses. It thrives by growing a thick coat of fur over a heavy undercoat in winter and by having a large head with small nostrils for safe breathing in cold weather. To cope with the coarse fodder the teeth continue to grow from the root and the intestines are unusually large. Mane and tail are thick, the tail tucked close to the body, and the limbs and neck short, all characteristics that have helped ensure survival in a relatively harsh climate. The Icelandic horse is also characterized by a special gait, the toelt, or single–foot as it is sometimes called; in effect, the horse's body absorbs all the movement of locomotion and the rider sits comfortably, carried smoothly forward.

Horses furnished transportation for people and goods well into the twentieth century in Iceland. In pagan times they were used for food, and are again today; horsemeat is both healthy and delicious. In saga times horses were often goaded to fight and bets placed on the outcome. Sometimes a stallion was buried with its owner. Today they are ridden for enjoyment and shown and raced at numerous horse meets throughout the country. They have also been exported for breeding and racing to countries such as Denmark, Germany, and the United States.

The dogs barked excitedly as Elín took me out to see the new lamb. They

Sheep roundup

were Icelandic dogs, a breed that once almost became extinct. Small sheepdogs with upright ears and curled tails, they, too, were originally brought from Norway. An outbreak of hydatid disease caused the Danish king in 1923 to order that the dogs be put down. Fortunately, some were saved and Sigrídur Pétursdóttir, the "Dog Lady," was able to breed them successfully.

"I like them," Kalli said as we approached the barn. "They drive the sheep in front of them to wherever we're going. They'll also bark at a stray ewe, no matter where it is, and get it back with the flock." The Scottish dogs that many Icelandic farmers now own drive the sheep toward the farmer rather than forward. But whatever the breed, the dogs must of course be trained.

Elín picked up the lamb to show me. It was far whiter than its dam. "The TV people came yesterday to film it," she said with excitement. The backbone of the Icelandic economy and of Icelandic life has been the twin pursuits of raising sheep and fishing. Television news coverage therefore takes us through the year with sheep raising and fishing, starting with lambing and trawlers at sea and ending with meat and fish for the table.

The original settlers brought their sheep from Norway, a northwest European short–tailed breed. Most Icelandic sheep are off–white, though many are cinnamon or gray or patterned black and white. Traditional clothing, like most Icelandic sweaters today, made use of the natural colors. Icelandic sheep have a long, relatively coarse coat of wool over a soft undercoat for maximum protection in the winter cold and dampness.

The sheep are kept in barns or on the *tún*, the fertilized home fields, for five to six months of the year. Lambing may continue into mid–June. The sheep are usually sheared in the early part of June and then in July they are turned loose

Icelandic horses

on the upland meadows to graze until mid–September. In the old days some were also taken out to islands to graze. Foxes and sea eagles may take young lambs, but otherwise there are no predators in Iceland and the sheep are free to roam with no herder watching over them. Just how wild they are becomes evident at autumn roundup when it can be difficult to convince them to come back "home," and for this the Icelandic sheepdog has been invaluable.

Kalli led us to a small cave in a lava hillside. A few steps down and we were in a fair–sized "room" where the temperature stays relatively cool all year. The floor was rather flat as the lava had crumbled under generations of trampling feet. There was plenty of headroom, though not in the small extension that went off from the main cave. "They used to live here in the old days," Kalli explained, "when the temperature went below freezing and they lacked firewood. A little cramped but they kept warm. The last time anyone lived here was after an earthquake in the 1890s." "And now?" I asked. "We store potatoes here now." Kalli caught the glint in Elín's eye and added, "The kids play here, too. Their special hideaway."

We went for a walk round the fields. Kalli, with some help from his father, farms 30 hectares (74 acres) and has 15 cows and 100 ewes. Like most Icelandic farms, his land for the most part is either in pasture or mowed for hay, augmented by using the highlands for summer grazing for the sheep. Inga and the children help with a small plot for potatoes and other root vegetables like carrots and parsnips.

As we walked over to see the cows, Elín pointed to a lava mound. "The Hidden People live there." "Have you seen them?" I asked. "Not yet, but Grandpa has."

First Day of Summer

The cows, like the other livestock, are of Norwegian origin and come in interesting shades of brown. They were considered so important in the days of the Commonwealth that land and other assets, as elsewhere in Indo–European languages, were often valued in terms of the number of cows they were worth. Since then cattle, along with other aspects of farming, have been managed to improve productivity. Kalli does not keep a bull; artificial insemination is carried out by a government expert who sees to maintaining cattle bloodlines and preserving the necessary semen samples. Consumption of dairy products remains high, but the government has had to set severe limits on the number of cows and sheep in order to keep meat and milk production more or less in line with market demand.

While we waited for dinner, Magga pointed out the photographs of the family on a table by the sofa and on the wall between colorful pictures that Inga has cross–stitched. Over the centuries the family has been the focal point of Icelandic life. Today, though some families are not as close knit as others, most stay in frequent contact; usually a person knows his or her first cousins very well. The extended family meets on holidays and birthdays all through the year. In the countryside they often talk together in the kitchen in the evening over a cup of coffee, and in the towns they telephone each other to keep in touch between special occasions. Grown children in the city often visit their parents on Sunday evenings.

Inga came from the kitchen to be sure I took note of the pictures of the children who have been raised on the farm, Kalli included, and their own four. There were pictures of Kalli's forebears on his mother's side as well as his father's. The men looked weathered but capable and uncomplaining, the look farmers everywhere have after having learned to live in harmony with the elements. In these older pictures the women looked strong, their sturdy bodies held still for the slow cameras of the time, their faces reflecting their quiet determination and ability to surmount the difficulties of survival they faced; they looked strong enough not just to pick up the lambs but to carry the ewes around as well!

We sat down to an early dinner of leg of lamb and home–grown potatoes and sour red cabbage. While the grown–ups lingered over coffee, the boys escaped to a game of chess, that Icelandic national pastime that occupies many office workers during coffee and lunch breaks.

The conversation turned rather naturally to animals. Kalli is a respected fox hunter. The arctic fox is in a special position as it is the only wild land mammal native to Iceland, having been here since the end of the Ice Age. Foxes were evidently quick to exploit opportunities provided by the coming of the settlers, since laws calling for their extermination date to 1295. Today the population numbers about 3000 animals and is doing well, but some hunting is necessary as the foxes take both lambs and the eider ducks that certain farmers protect in order to harvest the down.

The conversation veered to cows. "Remember the farmer who helped his cow in a difficult calving and lost his ring?" Inga asked. Of course, this being Iceland, the farmer was named, as were his forebears, as well as the cow. "He put his hand into the cow to ease the calf out and his wedding band slipped off. In due course the cow gave birth to the calf, and then the afterbirth, but no ring! He had to wait a whole year until the cow was sent to the slaughterhouse before he got his wedding ring back!"

Cows have minds of their own. We next reminisced about one named Harpa, who was being taken to a slaughterhouse in the West Fjords (in 1987) but had other ideas. "She was always intelligent," her owner said, "and probably understood what was up." She escaped, swam two kilometers over Önundar Fjord, and walked out on the other side. After an hour's swim in cold water she was still in good shape, so the farmer on the other side, one Gudmundur, bought her and renamed her *Sæunn*, "Sea–love."

"There was another one up north near Blönduós in '91," Kalli recalled. "She too got away right at the slaughterhouse door. She didn't run out of steam for close to 24 hours. Must have covered 30 kilometers, broke through fences, crossed a bunch of drainage ditches, and swam over a lake. Led them a merry chase. They gave up when it got dark, thinking they'd catch her the next day. Then at midnight she walked right up to the slaughterhouse door! So they started all over again to try to catch her, but she got away in the dark. It took till noon of the next day to find her."

"Did they let her go then?" one of the children asked. "No, her time was up. But another one named Ófeig was luckier. She escaped into the highlands in '92 and roamed around for 12 whole days. They let her live and she had a fine calf the next year."

When it came time to leave, we all thanked each other for the day, and Inga and Kalli sent us off with a gift of sacks of their own home–grown potatoes.

The Sealskin

Tradition holds that on Midsummer Night's Eve the seals may come to shore, shed their sealskins, and dance together. Once a man in Mýrdalur heard the merrymaking and stole forward to catch a glimpse of the dancing seal maidens. Their sealskins were laid neatly outside the cave where they were gathered. He took one of the skins home with him and locked it in a chest. Later, during the day he went back to the entrance to the cave and found a lovely, naked seal maiden, sobbing bitterly. The man gave her clothes, comforted her, and took her home with him. All went well between them and she bore him children. But she often sat looking out to sea.

The man always kept with him the key to the chest that held the sealskin, but one day he went out to fish and left the key under his pillow. The seal woman found the key, opened the chest, and took out her sealskin. She then said good–bye to her children:

> I don't like how it is,
> I have seven children in the sea
> And seven on land.

And with that she donned her sealskin and returned to the sea.

Ever afterwards the man had good luck fishing, and the children often saw a seal swim near them and look at them intently when they walked along the shore. But their seal mother never returned to land.

Iceland's History: The Settlement of Greenland and North America

Eric the Red, or to use his real name, Eiríkur Thorvaldsson, was a man of magnetism and leadership ability, but he was also overly quick to defend his honor through killing. Over–aggressiveness apparently ran in the family, as both his father, Thorvaldur, and he were banished from Norway "because of killings."[1] The two therefore moved to Iceland, where Eiríkur subsequently married, Thorvaldur later died, and where, once again, Eiríkur killed a man. For this he was sentenced to lesser outlawry, a judgment that meant banishment for three years.

Eiríkur therefore went to the Breidafjördur area in west Iceland, where he claimed possession of several islands. During this time he lent a man named Thorgestur his high–seat pillars. The records do not tell us why Eiríkur, or anyone for that matter, would loan another man the carved posts that decorated the chieftain's chair and helped to set him apart from his followers, but we do know that when Thorgestur did not return his high–seat pillars, Eiríkur went with an armed force to retrieve them. The upshot was that two of Thorgestur's sons were killed, along with others, and Eiríkur and his supporters received a sentence of three years of outlawry at the Thorsnes *Thing* or Assembly, about the year 980. Thereupon Eiríkur decided to spend his outlawry in reconnoitering the land to the west known by the name of its discoverer as Gunnbjörn's skerries.

The Discovery of Greenland

Early in the tenth century Gunnbjörn Úlfsson had sailed from Norway to Iceland but had been driven off course to the west, where he sighted land, probably Ammassalik in modern Greenland.[2] Once back in Iceland, he reported what he saw.

That Gunnbjörn sighted land is not surprising, as at the shortest distance Greenland lies only 287 km west of Iceland, but there are other ways to infer the nearness of land from a boat at sea than by being blown off course.[3] Cloud banks rising high over mountains can be seen far out to sea, and the iceblink, the reflection of the ice, both in Greenland and from the south coast of Iceland, gives a bright glow to the sky long before a boat nears the shore. Furthermore, the reflections in the clouds are often the mirror image of the land below, thus extending the mariner's view over the horizon. Other signs, such as ocean currents and the seaweed and flotsam they carry, the migration patterns of birds and whales, and the pounding of surf on a shore, can also be used to infer the nearness of land.

The Settling of Greenland

Eiríkur set sail to explore Gunnbjörn's skerries during the three years of his outlawry.[4] After sailing down the more forbidding east coast of this land, he explored the southwest coast, was attracted by what he saw, and returned to Iceland to organize a group to colonize the new land. He had found a lush area, unspoiled by grazing, as had happened in Iceland,[5] and so he named the land Greenland to attract settlers—an effective use of advertising hype in the tenth century!

Though Eiríkur may seem to us to have been unduly aggressive, he had no lack of followers. His strength and leadership ability and his description of the unpopulated land he had found attracted some three hundred colonizers, who set sail for Greenland in 25 ships in the year 985 or 986.

Judging from the experience of the replica, the *Gaia*, in 1991, the ships they sailed in made 6–7 knots in a breeze, and easily 8 or 9 and even 10 knots in a good wind. From the Snaefellsnes Peninsula in Iceland west to Greenland was a four–day sail.[6] If the wind did not hold, the ship could be rowed, provided the voyagers could still see either the sun or the North Star to reckon their latitude. Since they had no way of measuring longitude, they crossed straight west from Iceland and then hugged the coast of Greenland southward, helped by the south–flowing East Greenland Current.

Despite the fact the colonizers were sailing in the best European ships of the day over a route Eiríkur had already explored, they must have felt a good deal of trepidation. The clinker construction (of overlapping boards) gave their wooden ships the flexibility to ride the seas safely, but constant bailing was necessary. Various sagas record the perils of storms and shipwrecks and the inability to navigate in fog. Despite excellent seamanship, ships were lost. The written accounts tell us that of the original 25 ships that set out for Greenland, 11 were either lost at sea or turned back. The 14 ships that remained rounded the southern tip of Greenland and then sailed north along the western coast, aided by the north–flowing current, until they came to the lands Eiríkur had explored.

The Eastern and Western Settlements

The settlers of both Iceland and Greenland arrived during the Little Optimum, a time when the climate in the North Atlantic area was relatively warm, a fact attested by both written records and cores from the Greenland ice-cap.[7] Though the climate of Greenland today is far harsher than that of Iceland, then as now the west coast, with its sheltered fjords and fine pasture land, was much more attractive for settlement than the east coast. The original colonizers accordingly claimed two areas on Greenland's west coast. Eiríkur himself settled in a large embayed area near modern Qaqortok, known as the Eastern Settlement. The Western Settlement was 450 km further north near modern Nuuk.

Since Greenland is really a part of North America and not of Europe, these people therefore became the first white settlers in the New World.

The Eastern Settlement, with Eiríkur's homestead at Brattahlíd, became the seat of the Law Speaker (who recited the law at the assemblies and was consulted as to what was required by law), the site of the *thing* or assembly which passed laws and settled disputes and, partly because of its more southern latitude, the larger and more enduring of the settlements. In addition, there were widely scattered farms between the two settlements, and the people hunted and explored in the land to the north, as attested by both the written records and the Kingittorssuaq Stone, carved with runes and found 1000 km north of the Western Settlement in 1824.

Both the original colonizers and later immigrants came mostly from Iceland, with a minority from Norway. The population of the Eastern Settlement, according to Keller's estimate,[8] varied from 225–600 in 1000–1100 A.D. to a maximum of 3500–5250 in 1325–1375 A.D. In any case, the number of Norse in Greenland would not have exceeded 5000–6000 at any time.[9] The colonists' reasons for going were varied: population pressure, poverty, and for some a chance to recoup their fortunes and win fame.[10] Political instability in Iceland and the difficulty of finding available land, especially with the increased erosion of pastures from 1050–1125,[11] made Iceland less attractive for immigrants than before. For some, then, colonizing Greenland offered the solution to their need for land.

The archaeologist Thorvaldur Fridriksson has suggested another reason for emigrating to Greenland.[12] In researching Icelandic graves dating to before the conversion to Christianity in the year 1000, he found a preponderance of Christian/Celtic burial sites in the western and Breidafjördur areas, in contrast to the heathen graves found mainly in other parts of Iceland. This finding agrees well with the Celtic place names in the western and West Fjord areas of Iceland (such as Patreksfjördur) as well as the Celtic artifacts found in Greenland. He hypothesizes that there were two groups of Icelanders, a fact borne out by blood groupings, with the western Christian/Celtic group in the minority, having less power and therefore being more eager to move to Greenland.

There are extant records about the colonizing of Greenland, notably the *Grænlendinga saga* and the later *Eiríks saga rauða* (Eric's Saga). Recent archaeological research has helped illuminate a picture of the social organization and culture as a whole that is not necessarily revealed in the sagas.

The Eastern Settlement was comprised of scattered farms, especially in the northern and southern perimeters. The 444 sites date from the year 1000 to the late 1400s.[13] The density of farms was low as compared to Norway at that time, but the population was comparable to Icelandic coastal villages of today.[14] The farms were either coastal, situated in mid–fjord, with sheep raising the main agricultural pursuit or, more commonly, inland or inner–fjord, with relatively more cattle. Since the main factor determining hay production was the shortage of water rather than the cold, an irrigation system was added, probably in the fourteenth century.[15]

The Greenlanders had a subsistence economy based on both marine resources and livestock, with no full–time artisans and only limited trade.[16] Payment was in kind: no coins have been found. Analyses of bones and bone artifacts show the importance of sheep and seals, with some cattle and caribou bones. Keller[17] reports bone and antler copies of what elsewhere were iron implements, for example, padlocks and arrowheads. Cattle yielded meat, milk, butter and cheese, and sheep gave wool. Horses and small rowboats provided transportation. Spring seal hunting provided meat, oil for lamps, and skins for clothing and bedding. The people had spears, bows, and snares for hunting, and they also collected the eggs of wild birds. There was some driftwood but no native timber. For most of the period the Norse settlers seem to have had only sporadic contact with the Inuits (Thule Eskimos) who lived principally to the north of them.[18]

The differing sizes of the groups of ruins and associated storage buildings excavated by archaeologists attest to marked social differentiation.[19] Keller postulates a federation of chiefdoms, probably with tenant farmers, and a proprietary church. The written records show a society not unlike that of Iceland, with its own Greenlandic law, though patterned on Icelandic law, a *thing* for handling legal matters and disputes and, as in Iceland and Norway, some degree of fighting and killing to obtain justice and to preserve honor.

Building construction went through three stages: first the longhouse, then the passage house (with connecting rooms), and last the centralized house with adjoining rooms.[20] Eiríkur's longhouse was originally a single room measuring 50 ft. x 16 ft. with walls 10 ft. thick. Rooms and an irrigation system to provide water were added later. The churches in Greenland were patterned after the stylistic changes in Norway, progressing from turf and wood construction to Romanesque and, about 1300, to Gothic.[21]

In the early years there was little sea ice, and both colonization and trade were possible. Since Bergen and southern Greenland are at the same latitude, by holding to the same latitude the Norse seamen could sail directly from Bergen to Greenland without landing on the way, the earliest transatlantic trade route in history.[22]

Greenlanders lacked timber, iron and grain. To obtain these commodities they offered in exchange furs, hides and wool, rope, walrus and narwhal tusks, seal oil and gyrfalcons.[23] In the eleventh and twelfth centuries several ships might sail to Greenland in the summer, with the merchants wintering over as guests and leaving the following summer when the winds had abated and the winter ice had cleared.

The Church in Greenland

Though there is a tradition that Eiríkur's son Leifur was converted to Christianity and baptized in Norway before sailing home and converting the Greenlanders in the year 1000 A.D., it is more likely that Icelanders converted the Greenlanders or that they were already Celtic/Christian. Interestingly, though some pagan artifacts have been found in Greenland, no pagan graves are known.[24]

In the beginning the chieftains and freemen controlled the churches, with the result that religious, political and economic power resided in the same hands.[25] By the mid–fourteenth century, however, the bishop and not the chieftain at Brattahlíd "owned or controlled about two–thirds of the best land in Greenland," a conclusion supported by written records and the fact that the bishop's manor was far larger than any of the other homesteads.[26] The bishops and church officials all came from Europe, bringing with them canon law and Gregorian church reform.[27] Game management and the control of the caribou may well have been one of the continental innovations brought by these Europeans, a conclusion borne out by bone counts and, in the Western Settlement, the blinds and cairn line drives that have been found.[28] There were 12 parish churches, an Augustinian monastery and a Benedictine nunnery in the Eastern Settlement, plus the cathedral and the bishop's hall. The cathedral was 88 ft. x 52 ft., cruciform in shape and with glass windows. The bishop's hall measured 52 ft. x 23 ft., large enough to accommodate several hundred people.[29] The Western Settlement had 4 parish churches.

With the founding of the bishopric in Greenland, the Norse medieval world stretched from Mikligardur (Constantinople) to Gardar (modern Igaliku), the bishop's seat in Greenland.[30] The first resident bishop arrived in 1125 or 1126, and in 1152 Greenland, along with Iceland and the Faroes, became part of the archdiocese under the archbishop in Nidarós (modern Trondheim, Norway).

Greenlanders paid the tithe and the annual tribute to Norway in goods such as walrus tusks and cattle hides. Walrus ivory and hides were obtained on the long and often hazardous voyages north to Disco Bay and even perhaps as far as Upernavik at 73° N latitude.[31] The Norse Greenlanders would have encountered Thule Eskimos on these northern ventures. Interestingly, Norse accounts tell only of violent contacts with the natives, whereas Thule Eskimo accounts tell both of violence and of trade.[32]

The Decline and Disappearance of the Greenland Settlements

Though the end of the Norse colonization of Greenland has often been attributed solely to the advent of the Little Ice Age, in fact various factors contributed to the dying out or abandonment of the settlements.[33] In the face of the worsening climate after 1200, the Inuit or Eskimos ventured south more frequently, often in pursuit of seals. The importance to the Norse of the annual seal hunts, especially for those who were less well off, is clear from the archaeological record and apparently became much more important as the climate worsened.[34] However, as they never adopted Eskimo harpoons or other hunting gear and as they were tied to farms and livestock, they lacked the Inuit's more effective hunting technology and flexibility to move in pursuit of game. Though Norse settlement of Greenland continued for about five hundred years,

127

they clearly did not copy the lifesaving cultural traits of the Eskimos including harpoons, skin boats, and clothing suited to a cold climate.[35] Nor did the Norse effect any major change in Eskimo culture. The Norse retained their chief-tain–farmer–church society, looking down on Inuit ways; their graves show no sign of racial or cultural mixing.[36]

As the years passed, the pack ice came farther south and remained longer. In 1385 Björn Einarsson *Jorsalafari,* "the Jerusalem–traveller," arrived in the Eastern Settlement, but he was detained by the ice for two years before he could sail away. In 1406 an Icelander was blown off course and had to remain for four years before he could manage to leave.[37]

The lack of timber meant the Greenlanders no longer had their own ships. Finally, in 1261, conditions had become so difficult that the Greenlanders acknowledged Norwegian sovereignty, thus making King Haakon the largest landholder in Europe.[38] Competition from Russian furs, English and Dutch cloth, and African ivory, as well as the worsening weather and the Black Death in Norway meant that trade with Greenland became unprofitable and died out.

In 1341 Ívar Bárdarson, a priest in the Eastern Settlement, sailed north to the site of the Western Settlement, but found no people, only sheep and cattle gone wild. In time the livestock also died out. The Inuit moved south, follow-ing the seals, and in 1379 attacked the Greenlanders, killing 18 and capturing 2 boys. The Greenlanders' graves became shallower as the ground was progres-sively more frozen.[39]

The last written record for Greenland is of a wedding that took place in the Hvalsey Church in 1408.[40] The clothes in graves from 1450–1480, however, are of contemporary European design and attest some continued contact with the continent. By 1500, however, the settlements were completely abandoned. It is not known whether English fishermen marauded in Greenland as well as in Iceland in the fifteenth century, as Marcus suggests,[41] nor what percentage of the remaining inhabitants the Portuguese abducted in 1470 and 1496.

The Discovery of Mainland North America

The Book of Settlements[42] records that Ari Másson was blown off course to White Men's Land or Greater Ireland, six days sail west of Ireland and "near Vínland the Good." Ari was baptized there and then seems to have had trouble getting away. Did Ari meet white–robed Irish monks, who did sail westward, or did he meet, as Jones suggests,[43] Naskaupi Indians in their white buckskin dancing robes?

In 986, a merchant named Bjarni Herjólfsson returned to Iceland from Norway, only to discover that his father had moved to Greenland.[44] He sailed west with his men to join his father, but he got lost in the fog and was blown off course by northerly winds. When the fog had cleared and he could again reckon his latitude, he sighted a wooded land to the west; two days north of that a flat, forested land with white sands; and after sailing three more days with a southwest wind, glacier–covered mountains. Here, at the right latitude, he changed course to sail east to Greenland for four days and then to the settlements.

The Vínland Voyages

Incredibly, Bjarni Herjólfsson sighted North America three times and did not once land. After reaching Greenland, he and his men certainly talked about their adventure, however, so much so that Leifur Eiríksson bought Bjarni's ship and, probably in 992, sailed west with 35 men. Since a good number of the men had sailed with Bjarni, the actual sailing directions were undoubtedly more detailed than those that have come down to us in the sagas. Eiríkur, himself, did not accompany his son Leifur, as he injured his shoulder and broke a rib when he fell from his horse on the way to the ship. With advancing age he accepted this turn of events philosophically; the task of leading an expedition passed to his son.[45]

Leifur retraced Bjarni's route in reverse, first going north with the current up the west coast of Greenland to Disco Bay and the northern hunting grounds. He then crossed Davis Strait at the narrowest part, sailing west with the current over the 320 km (200 mi.) that separate Greenland from the glaciated mountains of Cape Cumberland on Baffin Island.

Leifur and his men then sailed south to Helluland (Slab or Flat Rock Land, now Baffin Island), where, unlike Bjarni, they landed, but they found the land barren and worthless and continued south to Markland (Land of Forests, now Labrador). Two more days brought them to a cape, where they found fine grass, fat salmon in the river, and plenty of trees for timber. They built a house and passed a mild, frost–free winter in the place Leifur considered he owned: *Leifsbúðir*. They returned to Greenland laden with timber and the grapes they had found. On the way home Leifur rescued several people who had been shipwrecked on the coast of Greenland: the ship's captain Thórir, who died the following winter, his wife Gudrídur, and their crew. After that Leifur was known as "the Lucky."

The second Vínland voyage was carried out by Leifur's brother Thorvaldur, who used the same ship and followed the same route, passing Helluland and Markland. The adventurers were awed by the long, white beaches they found, with huge breakers and no landing place (*Furðustrandir*, Wondrous Shores, near Cape Porcupine); the only comparable beaches in the Norse world are in Iceland where, however, the sands are eroded black basalt. The voyagers replaced a keel at *Kjalarnes* (Keel Peninsula, probably Cape Porcupine). They had permission to live at *Leifsbúðir* and remained for two years, exploring the country round about. During the second summer they encountered nine *skrælingar* (natives) and, after killing eight of them, were attacked by a larger group. Thorvaldur himself was hit by an arrow and killed. Since Eskimos at that time did not have arrows, these *skrælingar* were Indians.[46] The Greenlanders sailed home the following summer with a cargo of grapes and timber.

The third attempt to reach Vínland was ill–fated. Leifur's brother

Thorsteinn, newly married to the Gudrídur whom Leifur had rescued, was defeated by fog and wind. He returned to Greenland late in August and died that winter.

The fourth voyage was perhaps the most important one, for Thorfinnur Karlsefni and the people with him made a concerted effort to establish a settlement. Thorfinnur had married the twice–widowed Gudrídur. In four ships with a total of 160 men, 5 women, livestock, and the necessities for colonization, they set off to live at Leifsbúd or Vínland the Good. At one place two Celts with them were sent off to scout; they returned with grapes and self–sown grain. In defense of the identification of grapes and grain, it should be noted that Jacques Cartier found grapes along the St. Lawrence River in the 1530s, and wild grain at Baie de Chaleur and on islands in the Gulf.[47]

Thorfinnur went on to a fjord they named for its strong current, Straumfjördur (Strait of Belle Isle, though one theory postulates the Bay of Fundy). They spent one hungry winter here and, in 1003–1004, Gudrídur gave birth to a son, Snorri.

They continued south until they came to a place where at high tide they could sail up a river into a lake. The stream was full of fish, there were timber and grazing land, and here at *Hóp* (Landlocked Bay) they spent the winter. They constructed a small settlement but in the end encountered too many difficulties to remain. At first they traded peaceably with the natives, but later the natives wanted weapons; Thorfinnur refused, and there was a fight in which a native was killed. Among the settlers, the unmarried men had an eye for the few women and were restless. With personal troubles within the colony and cut off from the trade with other countries that was a lifeline for both Greenland and Iceland, Thorfinnur made the decision to return to Greenland in the spring of 1006.

Thorfinnur did not remain in Greenland, however, but settled in Iceland. After his death, his wife Gudrídur at first ran their farm in Skagafjördur. When her son Snorri was old enough to take over the farm, she became a nun and went on a pilgrimage to Rome. Three Icelandic bishops and many modern Icelanders are descended from Snorri Thorfinsson, the first white child born in North America outside of Greenland.

Leifur's sister Freydís also sailed to Vínland, but her vicious temper stirred up trouble. Two brothers sailed with her, but in their own ship and with their own people. Freydís refused to let these brothers use her longhouse and had them and their men killed. When her own men refused to kill the five women who had accompanied the brothers, she herself axed them to death.

There were other voyages to North America. For a while oral tradition would have perpetuated the knowledge of detailed sailing directions, but the trips by those less highborn than Eiríkur's offspring were not recorded in sagas. There were later voyages to Labrador for timber—the last recorded (in the *Skálholt's Annal*) was in 1347, but the sailing directions to Vínland itself were forgotten. In 1121 Bishop Eiríkur Gnúpsson tried to find Vínland and failed.

Greenland did not have the resources to support a distant colony. The climate worsened, population pressures in Iceland eased, communication lines were too stretched, the natives in North America resisted, and the Greenlanders had neither the backing of kings and states nor the technological capability to provide the ships, labor, and weaponry that later discoverers were equipped with. The Norse attempts to colonize and utilize the resources in North America came to an end.

L'Anse Aux Meadows

By the nineteenth and twentieth centuries the site of Vínland was a matter of much speculation. After World War II, the Norwegian Helge Ingstad set out to find where the Norse Greenlanders had actually lived. Efforts with a small boat at sea did not result in finding a site, but later aerial reconnaissance revealed a promising spot on Épaves Bay in the extreme north of Newfoundland. Excavations were carried out in the 1960s under the direction of Ingstad's wife, the archaeologist Anne Stine Ingstad. The results of the excavations left no doubt that this had been a Norse settlement.[48]

The site at L'Anse aux Meadows (from the French for Jellyfish or Medusa Bay) fits the description in the sagas: a river with good fishing (Black Duck

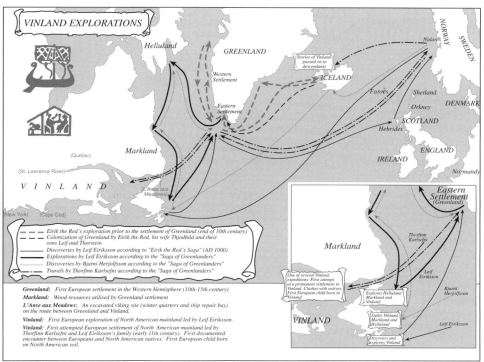

Map: Jean-Pierre Biard

Greenland and the voyage from Iceland

131

Brook) flowing from a lake (Black Duck Pond). The offshore island mentioned in the sagas is Great Sacred Island. Ingstad adds that the site resembles the Greenlandic settlement areas, with grass for grazing and shallow water for landing and beaching the boats, a combination not common on the coast they had sailed past. The irony is that the Canadian inhabitants had known of the site all along, but had thought it an Indian site (as indeed it was after the Norse left), and isolation—there was no road until 1966—had kept it unknown to the outside world.[49]

Excavation revealed a Norse settlement with ^{14}C analysis giving dates around 1000 A.D. There was a large chief's house, 70 ft. in length, that had burned and other buildings with 6–foot–thick walls of sod with a gravel core, as well as boat sheds and a smithy. The iron slag from bog iron could not have been Indian or Eskimo from that period. A Norse spindle whorl and a bronze pin were also found. That no more artifacts were found is not really surprising, as the settlers would have taken their weapons with them when they left and the Indians would have combed the site for usable finds.

Ingstad points out that both weather and fishing in this part of the world are highly variable from year to year, which can explain the very different experiences Leifur and Thorfinnur had in this new land west of Greenland. In the period of comparatively warm weather during the Little Climatic Optimum, the Norse moved freely to expand their world, but the Indians and Eskimos also moved about. The Norse explored from L'Anse aux Meadows, and the Indians went to sea in the summer. It was inevitable that Indians and Norse settlers would meet and trade and that the cultures would at times clash.

There are other indications besides the settlement at L'Anse aux Meadows that the Norse were in North America. A few metal objects at scattered sites, including a balance arm of bronze found on Ellesmere Island, attest to at least trade relations if not actual contact.[50] The Norse would have encountered Indians in Labrador and Newfoundland, Dorset Eskimos in Labrador, and Thule Eskimos, who reached Greenland in the early twelfth century. A Thule Eskimo wooden carving from Baffin Island depicts a man in Norse garb of the times with a cross clearly incised on the front. A piece of anthracite coal from Rhode Island was found in the Western Settlement in Greenland, and a Norwegian coin, minted between 1065 and 1080, was found in a midden on Naskeague Point near Brooklin, Maine.[51]

All these artifacts, with the exception of the wooden carving, could have been acquired in trade; that is, the Norse themselves need not have been at these places, but they surely were in North America.

A very interesting piece of evidence comes from the work of Stefán Adalsteinsson and Blumenberg on cat genes.[52] Research (discriminant analysis) has shown that Iceland has two groups of cats: though the genes of the cats in Reykjavík show some blending with British cats, the country cats have genes like the cats on Yell in the Shetlands, in Skaane in southern Sweden, and on the Faroes, Viking areas all. Furthermore, the cats in Boston and New York (omitting angora and Siamese cats) carry these same "Viking" genes. On the other hand, as no cat bones have been unearthed in archaeological excavations in Greenland, the explanation for these genes in cats in North America remains an open question.

Columbus

Europeans of the fifteenth century were aware of the contemporary Norse settlements in Greenland, itself a part of the New World. It was also well known before the time of Columbus that there was land further west. Furthermore, the existence of such land fit the earlier medieval theory of the world as a flat ring of land surrounded by the ocean. The circle of land that they envisioned as running eastward from the northern coast of Africa, north and then west through Asia, and then down the Scandinavian peninsula was completed by the "islands" of Helluland and Markland in the west, as discovered by the Greenlanders. In this scheme, the ocean was seen as encircling this ring of landmasses.[53]

The story of the new lands spread. The earliest record of the name Vínland is in Adam of Bremen, writing, in 1070–1072, information he had been given by the Danish king. Gudrídur, as we have seen, was one of those who went on a pilgrimage to Rome, and she and others undoubtedly told of the discovery of new lands. Pope Paschal II (1099–1118) appointed Eiríkur Gnúpsson bishop over Greenland and *"the lands to the west."*[54]

In the fifteenth century the English fished in Icelandic waters and carried on a brisk trade with Icelanders. From their contacts with Icelanders the Bristol sailors were well aware of the settlements in Greenland and the earlier Norse voyages to lands in the west.

By the fifteenth century the world was known to be a sphere, and Columbus had easy access to information on lands to the west at the monastery of La Rábida, where the abbot was knowledgeable about sailors' tales and discoveries. By his own account, Columbus went to Bristol, where news of the Norse voyages would have made good conversation over a mug of ale. Icelandic tradition says that Columbus also came to Iceland, and a record in his son Ferdinand's account sets the date at 1477. With royal support, better ships than the Greenlanders had had, and firearms, Columbus's voyages, and subsequent ones, stirred merchants and monarchs to continue to finance expeditions to the lands to the west.

Icelanders in North America

Though Icelanders failed in Viking times to establish a permanent settlement in North America, their nineteenth and twentieth century descendants succeeded in doing so.[55] In the latter part of the nineteenth century conditions in Iceland worsened to the point that many felt impelled to emigrate to North America. The hard winter of 1858–1859 was followed by an epidemic in 1860 that carried off 200,000 sheep. A major volcanic eruption in the Dyngjufjöll Mountains in 1875 meant that pumice blanketed a large area in the northeast.

The pumice fall meant a poor hay crop and worse, that the livestock that survived ingested fluorine when grazing and died, leading to general poverty. The intensified struggle with the elements coincided with the period of increased desire to be independent of Denmark. There was considerable discussion about emigrating, with encouragement from such men as Rev. Páll Thorláksson, who was instrumental in getting the church to supply leadership. The dream of independence was, in part, to take root in the founding of New Iceland.

Beginning in 1855 about 370 Mormon converts emigrated to Spanish Fork, Utah. In the 1860s about 40 people tried Brazil, but though there are people of Icelandic descent in Brazil today, this attempt was not very successful. A small number went to Washington Island in Wisconsin and there was interest in Alaska, but it was the Canadian and not the United States government that offered support, and therefore in Canada that *Nýja Ísland* or New Iceland was founded in 1875 on land by Lake Winnipeg. By 1914 fifteen thousand Icelanders had moved to New Iceland or elsewhere in North America,[56] a significant proportion of the total population of Iceland which, in 1901, numbered only 78,470 inhabitants.

The new world presented immediate problems. The Icelanders had no experience of the trains that took them to their destination, nor of machinery in general. They had to adjust to snakes and a plethora of insects unknown in Iceland. The midcontinent summer heat was greater than they had ever known and in winter they discovered what real cold means. Many had to build their own wooden houses but, as Iceland had very few real trees, they did not know how to fell one or which way it would fall when they did cut it down. They viewed the new vegetables and fruits they found "with suspicion."[57] Unsure of how to manage in this new environment, they suffered from scurvy.[58]

However, they were determined to succeed and, like Icelanders before and since, were optimistic and self–reliant: they set about learning. From the Indians they learned to fish through the ice in winter, from the Germans they learned to eat carrots and cabbage, but the Norwegians were the greatest help, providing farm jobs, loans and encouragement.

They were successful in a search for land to establish New Iceland largely because Lord Dufferin was governor general from 1872–1878, the same Lord Dufferin who had sailed to Iceland in 1856 and been thoroughly taken with the country and its inhabitants. When delegates asked for the west shore of Lake Winnipeg in 1875, he saw to it that they were granted a strip of land about 12 miles wide by 48 miles long, where they could preserve their customs, language, and literature. At that time the land lay north of the "pocket province" of Manitoba but, when that province was enlarged, was later incorporated into it.

When smallpox struck in September 1876, apparently contracted from the Indians, over a hundred died, many of them infants. The stricken settlers were quarantined. Minimal supplies and mail were dumped in the snow at the quarantine line. The quarantine was not lifted for 228 days, four months after the epidemic was over, during which time the settlers barely had enough to survive and were unemployable because of the mistaken fear that they were still contagious and could infect others with smallpox. But survive they did.

Attending school was a new custom; Icelandic children were taught at home to read well. The settlers encouraged their children to learn and closely questioned them about what they read to make sure they had learned it. They had to adjust to the English alphabet and the use of family surnames rather than the Icelandic patronymics (whereby every Icelander is named the son or daughter of his or her father), but they recognized the importance of learning English to succeed on the job and acquired a blend of English and Icelandic words. They retained their cultural values of individualism and education, self–reliance, and a near equality of the sexes. They strove for identification with the Anglo–Saxon majority, but they remained proud of their Icelandic roots.[59] Many "West Icelanders" today can still trace their genealogies in perfect Icelandic but when they talk about things they know about only through English they usually resort to English words. The strange blend of vocabulary, if you understand it, can be great fun to listen to.

The church assumed a central role as helper and center of discussion that it had not had in Iceland. In fact, there were two religions, Lutheran and Unitarian, with a good deal of rivalry between them. The discussion groups and their newspapers in Icelandic were ways of defining the settlers' ethnic roots, of maintaining their culture, and of affording an outlet for their individual ideas. This mixture of survival and cultural attainment furnished a fertile ground for the success of these West Icelanders and their dependents. One of Iceland's greatest poets, Stephan G. Stephansson, moved to Wisconsin in 1873 at the age of 20, then to North Dakota and finally, in 1889, to Canada. Though he never attended school, he was gifted, read a great deal, and wrote some of Iceland's finest poetry. The explorer Vilhjalmur Stefansson discovered many of Canada's northern islands; the arctic research institute in Akureyri, Iceland, is named for him. Some of the settlers returned home to Iceland, bringing new ideas and technology, and others helped finance Icelandic companies.

The number of Icelanders emigrating to North America was swelled after World War II by the brides that U.S. servicemen married when they were stationed in Iceland. Thousands have since gone west to study subjects not taught in Iceland, and some of these have remained for a shorter or longer time, taking advantage of the job opportunities and higher salaries.

The ties between Iceland and North America are still maintained. The descendants in North America come to visit Iceland in the summer. In Gimli, Manitoba, the annual summer Icelanders' Day is an excuse for family reunions and visits from relatives in Iceland, and in October the United States celebrates Leif Ericsson Day. Though the Norse attempt to colonize North America in the eleventh century failed, there are descendants of Snorri Thorfinsson, the first white child to be born in North America outside of Greenland, living in Iceland and, indeed, many of them now live in North America.

The Myth of Loki

Loki was the trickster, the sly one, helpful and destructive to the Aesir by turns. The son of the Giant Farbauti (Ship–Beater), his name perhaps meaning Light–Bearer, he seems originally to have been benevolent, so much so that Loki and Óðinn became blood brothers and Loki became one of the Aesir, or gods. He was good–looking and highly attractive to women but inconstant, a self–centered coward who, when caught in a scrape, kept betraying the Aesir to save his own skin. In time his treachery and finally his vituperation, recorded in the poem Lokasenna, *turned the gods completely against him, and for their own safety they bound and fettered him.*

The scalds and tellers of tales found his complex personality and his escapades so interesting that there are many references to him. He once helped Thór regain his lost hammer, only to turn around and betray Thór into a Giant's hands, defenseless without his hammer. Thór survived that scrape with the help of a Giantess. Loki approached Thor's wife, Sif, and cut off her long blonde tresses, and then, after being caught, persuaded the Dwarfs to fashion new tresses for her of pure gold that would grow like real hair. He was clever at talking his way out of danger. When his head was forfeit for his misdemeanors he reluctantly agreed to losing it, provided not a single smidgen of his neck was chopped off. But where does the head end and the neck begin? As a compromise, the Aesir had his lips sewn together, but he easily broke the stitches and thus escaped fatal punishment. He was a shape–changer par excellence and hermaphroditic, and became a bird, a mare, a fly, a salmon.

In the end it was he who brought about the downfall of the gods at Ragnarök.

Building the Wall at Ásgardur

A smith appeared at Ásgardur, the home of the gods, shortly after it had been built, offering to construct a wall to protect the Aesir against any onslaught by the Giants. He would build the wall in eighteen months, the smith said, but he must be given the goddess Freyja and also the Sun and the Moon as wages for his labor.

The gods hesitated about accepting such an offer—the price seemed dangerously high, but Loki pointed out the value of having the wall. To protect themselves the gods set their terms: "The work must be completed in one winter," they said, "and with no help." Surely the smith could not meet those terms and they would be safe. "If the wall is finished by the first day of summer you shall have Freyja and the Sun and the Moon."

The smith agreed, provided he could use his stallion to help him. The gods hesitated, but again Loki encouraged them to enter into the bargain, and so it was agreed.

The smith began work on the first day of winter, letting his horse haul the stones at night and doing the masonry work by day. The gods were amazed at the size and quantity of stones the horse was able to pull; the horse did half again as much work as the smith. Finally, with three days to go before the first day of summer, there was only the gate left to finish. It was obvious the smith could fulfill his contract after all.

In desperation the Aesir now assembled to decide what to do. Who had advised that this man be allowed to take Freyja and that air and sky be depleted of the Sun and the Moon? They turned on the culprit, Loki, who swore that, whatever the cost, he would find a way so that the smith would fail to keep his end of the bargain and the Aesir would be saved.

That same evening, as the smith drove out with his stallion, there dashed out of the forest a beautiful mare. When the stallion got wind of her, he tore loose from the reins and chased after the mare, which ran back into the forest. The smith gave chase, but to no avail, and the next day little was accomplished on the wall.

When the smith saw that he could not finish the wall, he changed into the Giant he really was. The Aesir saw him coming and called for Thór, who raised his hammer high over his head and struck the Giant, who was then banished to Niflheimur.

Sometime later the changeling Loki appeared, no longer as the mare that had enticed the Giant's stallion, but leading the gray colt that he had given birth to. The colt had eight legs and became Ódinn's steed Sleipnir, the best of all horses known to gods or men.

Loki's Monster Offspring

Loki sired three monsters, with a Giantess as mother: his daughter Hel, the Midgardsormur or World Serpent, and the wolf Fenrir. These monsters were raised in the Land of the Giants until the Aesir learned of them. Then Ódinn cast Hel down and gave her power over the nine worlds in Niflheimur. The World Serpent he threw into the sea, where it grew to encircle the land until it grasped its own tail in its jaws.

The wolf Fenrir presented a different problem. When the frightened gods saw how rapidly he grew, they knew they must fetter him. They tried twice to bind him, but twice Fenrir broke the fetters with ease. In desperation the Aesir approached a Black Dwarf, who forged a bond of the thundering of a cat's step, the beard of a woman, the roots of a mountain, the sinews of a bear, the breath of a fish, and a bird's spittle. You know, of course, that a cat's step is soundless, that a woman has no beard. But I tell you truly. The fetter was forged, thin and smooth as silk.

The Aesir enticed the wolf to come out to a small island. "See, the fetter is so thin. You'll break this one as easily as you broke the others." The wolf was not so sure. "I will gain no honor if I do not break it." Then he considered the fact that it might truly bind him. "Very well, let one of you put his hand in my mouth as surety." The Aesir looked at each other. Then Týr stepped forward and put his right hand between the jaws of the wolf. The Aesir bound Fenrir, who struggled and kicked to no avail; the fetter hardened the more he fought against it. The gods laughed—all but Týr, as the wolf bit off his hand in retribution. When they saw the wolf was truly bound, the gods grasped one end of the fetter and fastened him to a rock deep within the earth and wedged a sword between his jaws so he could not bite. Then they left him alive on the island to await Ragnarök, when he would bring about Ódinn's death.

Lokasenna—Loki's Gibing

Aegir, the god–giant of the sea, held a huge feast to which he invited the Aesir and the Elves, though at a time when Thór was away killing in the Land of the Giants. The gods praised Aegir's two servants, but Loki disagreed and killed one of them, whereupon he was thrown out of the party. Now truly angered, Loki crashed Aegir's feast.

When the gods saw who had entered the hall, they were silent. "I am thirsty," said Loki, "and have come a long way. Can you not offer me a drink of mead?" But Bragi, the god of poetry, who was host, refused to offer him either a seat or drink.

Each of the Aesir in turn berated him, and Loki replied, "Hold your tongue," and recounted what each had done that was humiliating and disgraceful. Bragi offered gifts of a sword, horse and ring in conciliation, to no avail. Sif tried to restore harmony by offering Loki a cup of mead. He drank the mead but called her a whore. He knew, after all, because he had slept with each goddess in turn—chastity not being a strong point among the Aesir.

At this point the very mountains shook as Thór came riding in from the Land of the Giants. He threatened Loki with his hammer, but before fleeing Thór's wrath, Loki reminded Thór of his humiliating defeat at Útgardar–Loki's. In the end, Loki had the last word: at Ragnarök Aegir's hall would be destroyed by fire, as indeed would all the worlds of gods and men.

Iceland's History: The End of the Commonwealth

The Icelandic Commonwealth lasted four centuries. The period of the settlement began, using the traditional date, in 874 and ended in 930, when the Althing was established as the central assembly with legislative and judicial power. This period saw the development of the *goðorð*, the priest–chieftainships that served, with attendant rights and responsibilities, as focal points for the loyalties of the freemen farmers. The Saga Age that followed, lasting from 930 until 1030, is known for its violence, but moderation and wise counsel were deeply respected and, with power shared between the *goðar*–chieftains and the freemen, a certain balance was maintained.

With the formal adoption of Christianity as the country's religion in 1000 A.D., the church became a participant in the struggle to obtain power. Enactment of the tithe law in 1097 provided much–needed money for church coffers, but the chieftains were not slow to recognize the monetary advantages of having churches on their own land; as *kirkjugoðar*, they built up their holdings and exercised considerable control over the country at the same time that the church increased its wealth and its power. Iceland passed through a peaceful period (1030–1118) when the first generation of Christians was in power, especially when Bishop Gissur Ísleifsson (1082–1118) exercised religious, and also some executive, control over the country.

Several factors, however, many of them already inherent in the distribution of power and the social structure in the earlier Commonwealth, upset the workable balance that had been achieved. The result was a period of civil war and then finally accession to the demands of the Norwegian king that Iceland become a part of the kingdom of Norway. The end of the Commonwealth came about through a combination of multiple, interwoven factors: the increasing cold, overgrazing, and the destruction of the forests for fuel and therefore the lack of ships; the changing social structure and patterns of land ownership, particularly after the imposition of the tithe; the internationalization and growing power of the church; the lack of an executive branch of government to check internal conflict and to counteract the power of the international church and the king in Norway; and the increasing intervention of the Norwegian kings and their control over Icelandic trade (though trade was undoubtedly less important at that time than in later centuries). The definition and goals of chieftainship changed from, among other things, an emphasis on vying for honor, backed by a band of supporters, to internecine conflict, fought with large armies and aiming at achieving domination over as much territory as possible. In the Age of

139

the Sturlungs (ca. 1220–1262) power became concentrated in the hands of six families who fought out their differences: the Haukdaelir, Sturlungar, Oddaverjar, Svínfellingar, Ásbirningar and Vatnsfirdingar. In the end, the country was tired of civil war. The experiment in country–wide democracy that had begun in 874 ended with the signing of the Old Treaty in 1262, yielding suzerainty to the Norwegian king.

With all the difficulties and fighting, however, the last century of the Commonwealth was an exciting and productive time to have lived, the period that produced some of the world's greatest works of literature.

Farming and the Changing Climate

From the time of the settlement and continuing well into the twentieth century the main unit of production was the family farm. Written records, pollen analyses, tephrochronology (dating by volcanic ash layers), analyses of ice cores from Greenland, and archaeological excavations have all yielded information about past climates and farm management and abandonment in Iceland.[1] The country was settled during the period of the Little Climatic Optimum, the Medieval Warm Period (500–1100). In the mid–twelfth century the weather worsened and, though there were occasionally warmer periods, the climate generally turned colder through the thirteenth century, often bringing harsh winters and cold summers. Mere survival became more difficult. In 1192, for example, 2400 people starved to death.[2] The worst years were given names, such as the Great Glacier Winter of 1233.

Several factors were responsible for farm abandonment: climate change, eruptions, sheep epidemics, and overgrazing, but chief among these was erosion, for the most part brought on by a disregard for the environment. Gudrún Sveinbjarnardóttir[3] points to the "tremendous escalation" in erosion that followed the settlement of Iceland. The marginal land at higher altitudes was overgrazed to the point of being unproductive, and therefore uninhabitable, even before the climate deteriorated. For each 100 m (330 ft.) rise in altitude, the average yearly temperature drops 0.6°–0.7° C (ca. 1° F). With overgrazing and erosion, and later the increasing cold, the farms at the highest altitudes (300–400 meters above sea level) were no longer productive.

Originally there were extensive forests, but pollen analyses have shown a sharp decrease in birch pollen in the early tenth century. With few tree roots to hold the soil in place, erosion escalated. The problem was recognized at the time, as the law recorded in *Grágás* in the thirteenth century stipulated the cutting of turf or peat, not trees, for fuel. The erosion was exacerbated by the high stocking rates of sheep, which crop close to the ground and prevent regrowth. The increasing cold would have made it that much more difficult for the forest or brush cover to regenerate or for the rangeland to be more productive. The need for wool for export continued, while the drop in temperature meant less hay for sheep and horses and therefore a higher grazing intensity; the result was increased erosion.

Natural factors added to human actions to increase erosion. Rivers like the Markarfljót did, and still do, erode their banks. The sea encroached on many coastal farms in the south, causing the farmers to relocate farther inland. The farm at Stóraborg seems to have been an exception because the houses were built on a somewhat higher mound and escaped flooding. Other farms were abandoned, at least temporarily, because of pumice and ashfall from volcanic eruptions such as the eruption of Hekla in 1104.

The farmers were chiefly animal husbandmen, tending their cattle and sheep and horses and pigs. The quality and amount of grazing land and hay meadows for cutting hay set the limits to productive capacity. The farmers relied largely on winter grazing for their stock, supplemented with hay[4] and they made cheese, which can be stored. Subsistence for one person required 6 ewes and 1/2 cow grazing on 52.5 hectares (130 acres) of land.[5]

About 1200, as the climate worsened, the proportion of sheep to cattle increased. Sheep provided wool for export and required fewer people to tend them than did cattle. Cow byres were built near the farmhouse; sheep, on the other hand, made use of communal mountain pasture in the summer months. Of the cattle and sheep bones from the fifteenth century recovered during the excavations at Stóraborg, one–third are from cattle and two thirds from sheep.[6] With the increasing cold, proximity to the sea and the opportunity to exploit marine resources made the difference between survival and farm abandonment. A lack of good harbors restricted fishing and the use of larger boats, but fishing and the utilization of sea mammals, including stranded whales, were important subsidiary activities.

The Changing Social Structure

The settlers, like Icelanders today, had a strong sense of family and personal ties. As sons inherited from their fathers, wealth remained within the family. After the tithe law of 1097 both wealth and power began to be redistributed. The chieftains had churches built on their own lands and in the beginning were often themselves the priests. Later they had their sons educated for the priesthood and donated their lands to the church to avoid taxation, while continuing to run the estates as their own. A chieftain who owned a *goðorð* obtained his income principally from farming his landholdings. The new breed of chieftains, on the other hand, who were now *kirkjugoðar* owning one or more churches, collected and distributed the greater part of the tithe monies as well.[7] Through management of the tithe monies and also the election of the bishops the chieftains exercised considerable control over church affairs. As the church grew in wealth and power, bishops and chieftains were therefore bound to clash.

The advent of Christianity resulted in the end of slavery and the availability of a pool of seasonal laborers. In the twelfth century there were many small landholdings farmed by various classes of people, principally the *húsmenn* who belonged to the chieftain's household, and tenants and cottagers, who were freemen. Both tenants and cottagers contracted to rent the land for a year and were free to move during the *fardagar*, the four moving days at the end of May.

The worsening climate led to the failure of many of the freemen farmers to keep their landholdings. A bad year meant that those with smaller holdings suffered more than those with extensive holdings; after a few bad years those with smaller holdings often lost their land. The failure of the smaller landholders gave the chieftains the opportunity to expand their own holdings and increase their power, while the ranks of tenant farmers and seasonal laborers swelled and provided the necessary labor to work the larger estates. Amorosi[8] feels that the "impoverishment of the middle–ranking farmers" was the key to the changes in social structure that took place, ending in Norwegian domination. In 1097 there were about 4,500 independent farms. By 1311 the number had shrunk to 3,800.[9] The church had changed the definition of property ownership from family inheritance to private and institutional ownership. The property owner could privately donate land and chattels to the church, and the church waxed rich on the donations.

The effect of the tithe law, coupled with the increasing cold and lowered productive capacity, thus brought about a changed ownership pattern on the part of both church and chieftains: ever–larger holdings and a constant vying for yet more power. The chieftains obtained income by collecting tolls when ships landed on their property and from the productivity of their estates and their share of the tithe. The church, on the other hand, obtained income from donations made in the names of saints, the productive capacity of the lands they directly controlled, and its share of the tithe. Thus the earlier rough balance of power between the *goðar* and the freemen farmers had given way in the thirteenth century to the concentration of power in the hands of the bishops and the six families named previously.

The Internationalization of the Church

With the establishment of the archbishopric in Nidarós, Norway, in 1152 the church in both Iceland and Greenland came under increased foreign pressure to realize the ideas of Pope Gregory VII, namely, that the church should have complete control of its own assets and its own affairs, including judiciary power, and that the church should pay no taxes.

The bishops in Iceland exercised considerable power. They had voting rights in the Althing Law Court and thus influenced civil legislation. They set the boundaries of the tithe area for each church and had the power of ordination; they thus controlled who became priests and the amount of the tithe monies the priests could dispense to cover expenses and give aid to the poor. The bishops founded and supervised the church schools and oversaw the interpretation of religious texts. As titular heads of armies that fought the chieftains in battle, the bishops were the equals of the chieftains; in addition, the bishops held the crucial power of excommunication.

The church brought foreign concepts to Iceland, including immensely beneficial ones like the Latin alphabet and church schools. The bishops strove for the implementation of a church modelled on the prevailing European view that it should be a powerful institution with the pope as head and holding power over secular authority. The church in Iceland, as elsewhere in Europe, became a strong, monolithic institution in its own right. In 1253 the Althing decreed that ecclesiastical law should prevail in the case of a discrepancy between secular and church law, though in actuality this law was never put into practice.[10]

The monasteries and the bishops' seats at Skálholt in the south and Hólar in the north were centers of learning where first religious and then historical and other texts were written in Icelandic more often than in Latin. The people buried their dead in cemeteries rather than somewhere on the farm and began to use Christian names, such as Jón (John) and María.

In 1226 a monastery was established on the island of Videy, near the city of Reykjavík. To begin with, the monastery was supported in part by a yearly payment of a specified amount of cheese. Recent excavations on Videy have borne out the written records attesting to the wealth of the monastery. By the time of the Reformation in 1550 it owned 116 farms. The excavations have also turned up very rare wax tablets, dating to about 1500, with still legible texts in Icelandic, Latin and Dutch.

Following the establishment of the bishopric at Skálholt in the eleventh century, several wooden churches were built in succession to accommodate the size of the congregation and also to replace the church that burned in 1309. The largest of these measured 50 meters (165 ft.) in length and 700 m² (7500 sq. ft.) in area and was larger than any wooden building in Europe at the time. It had glass windows and was decorated with statues and lamps. Some of the objects used for the mass, such as a finely wrought chalice, are still in existence despite the fact that this church too was destroyed by fire ca. 1527. All of the ten successive churches at Skálholt have had foundations built on the rock outcropping overlooking a wide expanse of fertile fields with mountains in the background ringing most of the area. Páll Jónsson, bishop from 1195–1211, was the only person in Iceland to have been buried in a stone sarcophagus, now in the crypt of the modern church.

The early bishops at Skálholt supported the *goðar*, but Bishop Thorlákur Thórhallsson (1178–1193) tried instead to enforce the tenets of the international church. He demanded that the church alone be allowed to administer all church property, tax–free. He tried to improve the morals of priests and laity alike and insisted that the chieftains respect their marriage vows and give up the mistresses so many of them had. He held the club of excommunication over the heads of those who refused. The chieftains, on the other hand, expected to retain rights to their own churches. Thorlákur was a pious ascetic who himself followed the moral teachings of the church.

The devout donated gifts in the names of the saints, but donations in the name of Saint Olaf, the former king of Norway, meant that money and valuables enriched Norway, not Iceland.[11] Iceland therefore needed its own saints. Miracles were attributed to Bishop Thorlákur; five years after his death, in

1198, he was invoked in Iceland as a saint. His sainthood meant not only miracles but the influx of considerable sums from Scandinavia and the British Isles, and a mass was composed to celebrate his good works. In recognition of his sainthood, two days in the Icelandic calendar are known as St. Thorlákur's day: July 20 and December 23. Especially before the Reformation, July 20 was an important feast day. Today December 23 is still celebrated as St. Thorlákur's Day. Thorlákur is the patron saint of Iceland and in 1985 was finally canonized by the Catholic church under Pope John Paul.

It would not do to let donations to saints accrue only at Skálholt in the south. Iceland had a second saint in Jón Ögmundsson, the first bishop at Hólar in the north (1106–1121). He, too, was known for the miracles he accomplished, largely posthumously. He was also one of those Icelanders mentioned in the records as having a fine singing voice. He was recognized as a saint at the Althing in 1200. Though twice married, he was childless so that his biographer saw fit to preserve his saintly image by writing that he had never had carnal relations with either of his wives!

To preserve their own power vis–à–vis the church, the chieftains sought to have their own candidates elected as bishops. In 1203 the chieftains, especially Kolbeinn Tumason, had Gudmundur Arason elected bishop at Hólar, expecting him to be a man they would be able to control, but like Bishop Thorlákur in the south, Gudmundur locked horns with the chieftains and insisted on the supremacy of ecclesiastical over civil law. Kolbeinn and Gudmundur ended by opposing each other in court cases. In 1205 they agreed to let the archbishop in Nidarós judge the matter, a landmark step that invited Norwegian intervention in Icelandic affairs. The archbishop directed Páll Jónsson, then bishop at Skálholt, to support Gudmundur, but Bishop Páll bowed to civil law.

The argument between the chieftains and Bishop Gudmundur continued; the chieftains opposed the bishop and Gudmundur retaliated by excommunicating them. In the ensuing battle in 1208 Kolbeinn was vanquished and killed, but though Gudmundur's forces had won the battle he was chased from Hólar and summoned to Norway. He returned from Norway to lead a strange life, founding a school, regaining and losing his bishop's seat, and wandering round the country with an entourage of a hundred poor and unsavory characters. He died in 1237, old and blind and under house arrest. Gudmundur the Good was thought of as a saint because of his virtue and his ability to heal, but his lack of respect for civil law, the division in the Icelandic church, and his opening the way for foreign intervention in Icelandic affairs added to the upheavals of the age and helped hasten the end of the Commonwealth.

Relations with Norway

It was natural for Icelanders to turn to Norway for trade and assistance. Their family ties and cultural roots lay in Norway, their legal system of assemblies and courts had grown from a Norwegian model, their navigational skills were Norwegian, and both Norwegians and Icelanders spoke the same language.

When the archbishopric was established in Nidarós and when Icelanders ceased to own ships suitable for crossing the ocean, Iceland unavoidably became more dependent on Norway. The critical lack of a higher executive authority led Icelanders increasingly to turn to the Norwegian king for help in settling their problems. Many Icelanders desired to be a part of the Norwegian court and, since they simultaneously held onto their Icelandic rights and positions and were inexperienced in foreign affairs, they were unaware that in the long run they were granting power to the Norwegian kings and playing into their hands. The Norwegian kings, for their part, considered that Iceland was properly a part of their kingdom. To the extent that they were able, they controlled the archbishops in Norway and the bishops in Iceland. They welcomed the many Icelanders who became their liegemen, rewarding them with gifts and titles and manipulating their loyalties and their options.

Though coins were first minted in Iceland in the eleventh century, very few have been unearthed from the medieval period; the upper classes sometimes paid with coin, but both upper and lower classes relied on barter.[12] The value of the goods to be exchanged was set at the assemblies and much trading took place there as well. No towns developed in Iceland, though there were seasonal trading centers, reduced to ten in number by the thirteenth century.[13] Social relations largely determined the exchange of goods. The chieftains and farmers who travelled abroad took goods with them to trade and returned with clothes and other objects that were often much admired. Durrenberger[14] points out that the chieftain dubbed Chicken–Thórir was looked down on, as his wealth stemmed from trade—he sometimes sold chickens—rather than from the usual network of social relations that defined trading partners and often lavish gift–giving.

Norwegian merchants moved in to fill the trade vacuum. They sailed to Iceland, wintered over with a chieftain–ally, and returned to Norway the following summer with wool and woolen cloth to sell. In the altercations that arose between Icelanders and the Norwegian merchants, the merchant needed the support of a chieftain to survive. The landholders controlled the landing places and charged a toll per head and per horse. With the collapse of the market in Europe for woolen goods, the burning of Bergen, the chief Norwegian port, in 1198, and increasing unrest and hard times in Norway, the Norwegian merchants eventually stopped coming to Iceland, but not before chieftain–trader alliances had helped increase the concentration of power in fewer hands.

During the reign of King Haakon IV (1223–1263), the pace of Norwegian intervention in Icelandic affairs escalated. The chieftains increasingly turned to the Norwegian king as the only executive power available to them. The king demanded taxes, sent emissaries, and played the chieftains off against each other, holding them hostage or sending them home as he saw fit.

The Struggles of the Chieftains
The legal system of the Althing and the regional assemblies remained in place,

but major changes occurred. In settlement of a court case payments for damages could be huge and the number of supporters for each plaintiff and defendant grew exponentially. In 1120 the two sides to one lawsuit had 1400 and 900 supporters, respectively.[15] The law was bent, if not broken, as the wealthier had the power to define legality and the supporters to back their decisions. Might came to define legal right as the six families controlled all Iceland. Many of these people were scholars, writers, and poets as well as experts at political maneuvering and fighting. The Haukdaelir in the south were scholars and lawyers who controlled the choice of the bishops at Skálholt and supported the school there. The Sturlungar, like the Oddaverjar, were writers and scholars and gave their name to the period 1220–1262: the Age of the Sturlungs.[16] Modern school textbooks include charts of the genealogies of all six families, as the students are often descended from these historical figures.

Snorri Sturluson (1179–1241), the most famous of these chieftains, is known outside of Iceland for his writings, including *Heimskringla*, the lives of the Norwegian kings. Icelanders know him equally well for his greed and cunning and his shrewd political maneuvering. He married twice, acquiring power and wealth from both wives, and married off his daughters for his own advantage. He became, in a short time, the most powerful figure in Iceland and was twice Law Speaker, from 1215–1218 and again, after his return from Norway, from 1222–1231.

Snorri Sturluson first went to Norway to negotiate an end to a dispute between Icelanders and the Norwegian merchants who had killed the brother of Bishop Páll. In Norway Earl Skúli Bárdarson was regent for the then young King Haakon and was preparing to mount a military campaign in Iceland. Snorri swore fealty to the king, recited a poem to the earl, and promised he would promote the king's interests in Iceland; plans for the invasion were called off.

In 1235 King Haakon sent Snorri's nephew Sturla Sighvatsson to be his emissary in Iceland, but Sturla, like the other chieftains, fought to control Iceland for himself and not for the distant king. Sturla won several skirmishes but lost the crucial battle at Örlygsstadir on August 21, 1238. The victors, Gissur Thorvaldsson and Kolbeinn Arnórsson the Younger, both Snorri's former sons–in–law, then became the two most powerful men in Iceland.

In the thirteenth century fighting in Iceland had become more than a way to preserve honor and obtain justice; the battles were now between large numbers of men in an internecine struggle to expand control over ever–larger territories. There was, however, no standing army. Thordur Sighvatsson kept only a 10–man guard with him, the other chieftains normally fewer, though some built low fortifications for added protection. The farmers provided the bulk of the manpower. Since a farmer cannot leave his fields for long, late summer was the best time to fight, when there was less farm work and there would still be forage for the horses along the way. When fighting was necessary, the objective had to be to win in time for the men to return to their farms. The farmers were untrained, often better at robbing and pillaging than at fighting. During the

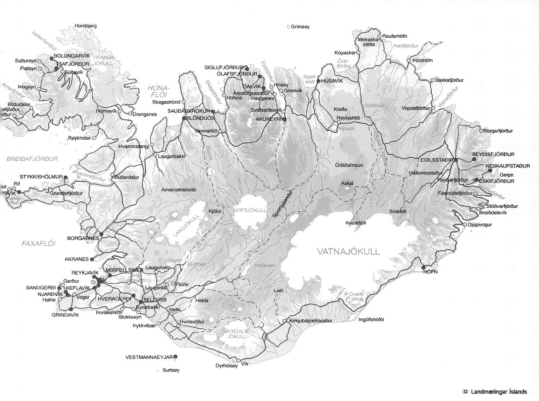

Above: Iceland   *Below: Thingvellir*

Above: Geothermal area, Reykjanes

Below: Almannagjá. Thingvelli

Above: Fissures, Thingvellir

Below: Farm near Vík, South Iceland

Left: Aluminum plant, Straumsvík

Below: Mosfellssveit in winter

Bottom: Hornvík, West Fjords

Opposite page, bottom left: Folk dancing

Opposite page, bottom right: New Year's Eve Bonfi

Above left: Spinning wool, right: Making crêpes. Below left: Picking up the mail, right: Ásmundur Sveinsson Museum

Above: West Fjord region

Below: Leirhnjúkur, lava and sulphur, North Iceland

Above: Hvalfjordur

Below: Breidafjordur

Mýrdalsjökull, South Iceland

Below: Looking toward Mt. Hekla

Above: Autumn sunset, Reykjavík

Below: Reykjane

bove: The Pond, Reykjavík

Below: Lake Mývatn

Above: Dettifoss Waterfall

Below: Seaweed in tidal poo

bove: Skaftafell, South Iceland

Below: Goethermal area, Krísuvík

Left:
Puffins

Left:
Tern colony,
Reykjanes

Kálfas
Lake M

Church,
Farm M

Far
Sleeping qua
Grenjadars

Grenjadar

Far
Stone
Gla

Left: Erup
North Icela

Above: Skagafjörður, North Iceland

Below: Bessastadi

battle of Örlyggstadir in the north in 1238, Sturla and his father and almost 1000 men with them took their stand within and around the low stone walls built to pen the sheep. Gissur and Kolbeinn the Younger beat them with a force of over 1600 men, killing both Sturla and his father.[17]

Snorri Sturluson, once again in Norway, wished to return home in 1239; with Earl Skúli's permission he returned to Iceland. Meanwhile the earl sought to usurp the throne but was defeated in 1240. King Haakon, thinking that Snorri had been part of the conspiracy to dethrone him and displeased that he had not furthered the king's cause in Iceland, sent word to Gissur either to have Snorri return to Norway or to kill him. Gissur proceeded to kill him on the night of September 22, 1241.

What then ensued was a seesawing power struggle between Gissur Thorvaldsson and Thordur Sighvatsson, Snorri's nephew and Sturla's brother, with King Haakon playing an active role. The king sent Thordur, known as *kakali,* perhaps because he had a rasping voice or stuttered, as his emissary to Iceland. Thordur found on his return to Iceland that Kolbeinn Arnórsson the Younger controlled the north and the West Fjords. However, the northerners were dissatisfied with Kolbeinn's iron hand, so Thordur had no trouble assembling followers. On July 25, 1244, Thordur kakali and Kolbeinn the Younger fought Iceland's only sea battle, Flóabardagi, in Húnaflói Bay in the north. Thordur had over 200 men in twelve ships and Kolbeinn 270 men in twenty ships. Kolbeinn was victorious, but in the end his victory did him little good as he lost many men and died the following summer.

On April 12, 1246, Kolbeinn's son Brandur fought Thordur kakali at Haugsnes. Of the nearly 1300 men who fought, a hundred fell, the greatest number of casualties in any battle on Icelandic soil. Though Thordur won, Gissur remained in control in the south, and when the two butted heads again they agreed to go to Norway and let the king decide between them rather than fight. With the archbishop's backing, the king sent Thordur to bring Iceland under the king's rule and detained Gissur in Norway.

Thordur kakali had absolute power over Iceland from 1247–1250. The Althing Law Court still existed, but as a rubber stamp for Thordur's commands, as it had been when Snorri Sturluson was Law Speaker. Once again, an Icelandic chieftain had promised to work in the king's interests and instead promoted his own. When the bishop at Hólar sent word of this to the archbishop, the king recalled Thordur to Norway, where he died in 1256, at only 46 years of age.

King Haakon stepped up his intervention in Icelandic affairs, or as he saw it, control over that part of Iceland that was rightly his, that is, the lands of the various chieftains who had sworn fealty to him. In 1252 he sent Gissur and two others as his emissaries, but Thordur had left his own men in charge in his absence and Gissur was forced to confront them. The Sturlungs treacherously chose the feast to celebrate the wedding of Gissur's and Sturla Thordarson's children as the time to rid themselves of Gissur. Accordingly, on October 22, 1253, they surrounded Gissur's farm at Flugumýri, and burned the house, with all trapped inside. Though he lost his family in the fire, Gissur himself escaped burning to death by hiding in a vat of whey!

Despite continued struggles and the emotional wrench and blow to his honor of losing his mistress and three sons in the fire, Gissur survived to continue to play an important part in Icelandic history. Bishop Henry protected those who had burned the farm and informed the king that Gissur had not promoted the king's cause. Gissur returned to Norway and was detained there until 1258. The king set Thorgils skardi, another of the Sturlungs, over the north of Iceland in 1257, but Thorgils was killed. The king then sent other emissaries to Iceland and some Icelandic farmers paid the tax that they demanded.

With so many of his liegemen dead, the king again turned to Gissur and made him earl over those areas in the north, south, and west that the king felt were rightfully his. However, though Gissur was made earl, Iceland never became an earldom under the king. Gissur returned to Iceland in 1258, but again, he was interested in promoting his own power rather than the king's. Inevitably, more royal emissaries followed, promoting the king's cause and supported by the bishops, but they made little headway.

It had been clear to the farmers for some time that little gain came of having chieftains. One farmer had even killed his chieftain in 1252, his only punishment being the payment of a small fine.[18] The country was tired of fighting; the commonwealth form of government was no longer viable. In 1261 the king sent a man named Hallvardur gullskór to Iceland to bring the matter to an end. Greenland had already become a part of Norway in 1261. Gissur bowed to the inevitable and counselled accepting the sovereignty of the Norwegian king.

The Old Treaty

At the meeting of the Althing in 1262 those present placed their hands on Holy Writ and signed the Old Treaty, *Gamli sáttmáli,* pledging allegiance to King Haakon.[19] By 1264 all those who had boycotted the assembly had also signed. With the death of Haakon in 1263, his son Magnús the Lawgiver became the first king of Norway and of Iceland combined.

By the terms of the treaty, Icelanders promised to pay the king a yearly tax and the king promised to maintain peace. Six ships with grain and other goods were to be sent the first two summers and thereafter as needed. Importantly, the second paragraph gave Icelanders the right to their own law. With the treaty the chieftains bowed to the king who, in return, provided better administration of justice and stronger state control. County officials and governors appointed by the king replaced the *goðar*. Gissur Thorvaldsson, rather incredibly, had survived all the battles and political maneuvering to die in 1269 at the age of 60.

The old order had gone. The young and ambitious sought the king's approval to gain respect. And though the treaty constrained what Iceland could do for the next four centuries, it also formed the legal basis for Iceland's claim to independence in the nineteenth century.

The Family: A Birthday Party

"*Skál*! Cheers for Gunnar!" We lifted our glasses in response to the toast by the master of ceremonies and drank to Gunnar on his fiftieth birthday.

In a nation where adult birthdays are just as much celebrated as children's, the five–year and especially the ten–year ones are considered more important than the others and the celebration is therefore more elaborate. Gunnar was fêted at work on Wednesday, his real birthday, by all the employees in his importing firm. Then, on Saturday afternoon for convenience, he rented a reception room and hired waiters and bartenders. Well over two hundred of us came to his birthday party to help him celebrate.

Gunnar and his wife, Sigga, greeted the guests as they arrived. Their daughter Thórunn, their oldest, took the gifts the guests brought, mostly books and flowers, and arranged them on a side table. Thórunn also saw to it that everybody signed the guest book.

"Did you feel the earthquake this morning?" Sigga asked me after I had greeted Gunnar. We had had a fairly mild quake but strong enough to rattle the dishes in the cupboard and shake the pictures on the wall. "Were you afraid?" she continued.

"Yes, weren't you?"

"Oh, yes. It seemed to hit faster than usual."

"Umm, there's usually a split second beforehand of knowing it's coming. Changes in the air currents, I suppose. I didn't feel any aftershocks, though." Earthquakes strong enough for us to feel are not that common. Sometimes the quakes are so weak that you can only feel them if you are holding still and the geologists with their seismographs are the only ones aware of them.

Gunnar's brothers Pétur and Halldór came to the birthday party with their families. Pétur, a mechanic by trade, is a member of a volunteer rescue squad, as are many Icelanders, and normally spends his Saturdays practicing mountain climbing or hiking or skiing with the other squad members, part of their year–round weekly training to be prepared for an emergency. For Gunnar's birthday, however, Pétur came with their mother, Kristín, who was just beginning to adjust to widowhood.

Gunnar had asked his brother Halldór to be master of ceremonies, a role Halldór enjoys. As an executive for one of Iceland's shipping firms, Halldór regularly does business with many of Gunnar's guests. More importantly, Gunnar is only two years older than he, so that they were together in *menntaskóli*, the upper secondary level of schooling that continues until the students are 20 years old. Graduation from *menntaskóli* is a major rite of passage, when the new graduate, male or female, dons a white peaked cap with a black visor during the graduation ceremony. The family gives a party in honor of the new graduate, who then goes out on the town to celebrate with friends. The friendships made at this time are important for the rest of one's life. The men socialize, often at service club meetings such as Rotary, and meet at work. The girls usually form a group in *menntaskóli* that becomes their "sewing club," though sewing is the last thing they do at one of these meetings; the women usual meet at regular intervals for the rest of their lives. Reunions in Iceland are for fellow *menntaskóli* and not university classmates. In a small society like Iceland, these school contacts play a significant part in keeping the wheels turning.

At intervals as we stood talking, Halldór introduced the next piece of entertainment over the loudspeaker system, this time an Icelandic song everyone knew, and all joined in the singing.

Like the others, I moved among the guests, greeting those I knew and especially those I hadn't seen in quite a while. One friend told me the true story of a man who drove over a rough road in the West Fjord area. The road was so rough that he had to take out his false teeth because they chattered so much!

I joined others in line around the long table laid out with all the refreshments. In keeping with Icelandic tradition, there were not just sweets but other food as well. *Flatbrauð,* fried bread, buttered and topped with slices of pink smoked lamb. White bread sliced horizontally into four layers and filled with smoked salmon, egg, and mayonnaise, the loaf then cut into vertical slices for serving. Cubes of Icelandic cheeses on toothpicks. And round bite–size slices of white bread topped with Icelandic shrimp, mayonnaise, and a thin curl of lemon. To top it off, there were several kinds of cake: Christmas cake, similar to pound cake but with raisins, and four–layer Viennese cake with jam between the layers. And of course plenty of coffee. I sat at a table with others to enjoy the delicacies.

Halldór introduced a longtime friend and business associate of Gunnar's, who gave a very short speech in tribute. His speech was followed by a tribute from another friend. Then we all sang "He has a birthday today" in Icelandic to the tune of "Happy Birthday." On the other hand, we sang "For he's a jolly good fellow" in English!

The woman next to me recounted the true story of a man at a dance who became so angry at another man that he grabbed the other one's hair, but the hair turned out to be a toupee and came off in his hands! It seems the bald man grabbed his "hair" back and fled.

The man across the table countered with the equally true story of the time the neighbors in the east side of Reykjavík called the police because a woman in the next building was screaming so loudly that they were sure she was being beaten to death. The police answered the call, only to find that the woman had merely been singing. This woman was definitely not a choir member.

Next Halldór introduced a group of Gunnar's friends who had composed special words to an Icelandic song, recounting some lighter as well as more serious moments in Gunnar's life. After the laughter and applause we all shouted "HURrah" four times (with the stress on the first syllable).

Like the others, I moved around the room, talking to various people. As at all large gatherings, there were the usual greetings, a chance to catch up on the news, and a few more meaningful conversations. Gunnar himself used the microphone to thank his friends for all they have meant to him over the years.

As I drove home afterwards, I enjoyed the reds and golds of the willow hedges I passed, and the grass was still green. Though autumn was approaching and the nights were dark, the weather was still mild with clear skies.

Autumn

The Family: Afternoon Coffee

A tourist agent friend of mine had just circled Iceland on the ring road with a bus full of tourists. Tall, graceful, with fine features and reddish brown hair, Lisa was charming but also quick to size up a situation, characteristics that made her a good tour agent. Sigga invited us both to afternoon coffee, now that Lisa was back in Reykjavík.

"Welcome," Sigga greeted us, and then to Lisa, extending extreme courtesy, "You don't have to take your shoes off." Since this is a statement guaranteed to astonish any foreign visitor, I had explained in advance that Icelanders take their shoes off indoors so as not to track in dirt. Yes, our hostess was wearing shoes, but she hadn't been outside in them.

"What wonderful plants," Lisa exclaimed, entering the living room with complete aplomb, as if she were always a guest in stocking feet. "And what interesting paintings."

Once, in a conversation in English, I replied with the usual "Thank you" when an Icelander admired an oil painting I have. The Icelander looked at me quizzically for some time and then asked, "Why did you say thank you? Did you paint it or something?" Sigga did not thank Lisa, but instead replied, "Plants are a hobby of mine."

"How do you like Iceland?" Sigga inquired. This is the stock question, asked by reporters, for example, of Pope John Paul as he descended from the plane (had he yet had time to kiss the tarmac?). Fortunately Lisa had been all the way around Iceland and could answer truthfully. "Stunning," she replied, "arresting scenery. The lava rocks come in such variegated forms. Perhaps that's why I find the painting over your sofa so intriguing."

"The painting is by Kjarval, perhaps Iceland's most famous painter," Sigga explained. "He spent hours carefully noticing the lava around us, seeing the spirits of the beings who have lived here. He frequently put those spirits into his paintings."

"How interesting!" Then after a short pause, Lisa added, "But I'm a tour agent and so I'm afraid I don't just admire the country but also think about the service as I travel." Sigga and I were clearly interested in Lisa's opinion. "The guide was warmer than most in other countries but most of the tourists found it hard to accept the fact that a cup of morning coffee wasn't available until 8:30 in some places, however. Tell me, do you eat so late at home?"

"Well, it varies," Sigga replied. "Depends a lot on what job you have." Icelandic living, especially in the countryside, has a relaxed way of going along with the weather and other events.

"And don't forget that the hours of darkness and light are equally divided for only a small part of the year," I reminded Lisa. With twenty–four hours of daylight in summer, there's no need to hurry to get up. "Icelanders are hard workers and get a lot done, but most of them sort of roll with the situation. It's a great way to live."

Sigga brought in an assortment of tempting things to eat, dark rye bread, pale yellow cheese and a knife to slice it thin, homemade *sandkaka* ("sand cake," pound cake), bunches of green grapes, Icelandic crêpes sprinkled with brown sugar and then rolled, and of course, coffee.

The crêpes were still hot, the aroma from the kitchen lingering in the air, mingling with the odor of fresh coffee. Called *pönnukökur* in Icelandic, unlike pancakes they are thin and delicate, served sometimes with jam or brown sugar, sometimes folded in quarters with whipped cream filling. We drank the coffee in small demitasse cups. It is a feast for us, though many older Icelandic women would feel that at least seven different things should be served. Times have changed everywhere.

Lisa exclaimed over how delicious the crêpes were. "I'll give you the recipe, if you like," Sigga offered, "but not everyone makes them quite the same."

Icelandic Crêpes

1–1 1/2 cups flour
1/2 teaspoon baking soda
2 eggs, beaten separately
1 1/2–2 cups milk
2 tablespoons melted butter or margarine

Mix ingredients well. Batter should be rather thin. Pour a small amount on hot griddle and brown lightly on both sides.

Or if you prefer:
250 g flour
1 teaspoon baking powder (or baking soda)
2 tablespoons sugar
1 egg
6–7 dl milk
50 g margarine (or butter)
(a few drops of vanilla, if desired)

Mix the dry ingredients together. Beat the egg with a fork in a cup. Mix half of the milk with the dry ingredients and the other half with the egg. Melt the margarine, cool, and mix all the ingredients together. Fry on a hot pan until lightly browned on both sides. Sprinkle each crêpe with sugar and roll it up.

"Tell me," Lisa said, "what do Icelanders do in the summer? I've discovered the variety offered tourists—bus trips, swimming in geothermal pools, dinner on a glacier, pony trekking, mountain biking, angling." Lisa had also taken a trip into Askja, a volcanic crater in the north, and seen the uninhabited interior. "But what do Icelanders do?"

"I'm afraid many Icelanders go abroad on a *sólarferð*, a sun trip. The Canaries or somewhere. Or fly to Luxembourg with the airline and rent a car and drive around Europe. We like the change and guaranteed sun. But, oh yes, lots of us visit our relatives. In August we go up to the West Fjords to pick blueberries and stay with our relatives. Our daughter in Norway came with us last time, and brought our grandchild, and our older daughter Thórunn came too, with her boyfriend and their four–year–old. A real family reunion! We had a wonderful time."

"You have a younger son, too, I understand?"

"Gummi, yes. He spent the summer on my sister's farm, but he'll come with us, too. My husband sometimes takes him trout fishing. We keep horses on my sister's farm and often go riding on the weekends. The farm's not far from here."

"You weren't here for June 17," I commented. There are things people in Iceland do more or less together, for instance celebrating all the national holidays that mostly come after the worst of winter weather is over, including the traditional May Day march for workers' rights. "Some go to stay in their summer cottages on Ascension Day and during Whitsuntide. But I like June 17 the best."

"Our Independence Day," Sigga explained, "to celebrate when we finally got complete independence from Denmark in 1944. In honor of Jón Sigurdsson, who led the drive to gain independence, the proclamation was signed on his birthday, June 17." Very fittingly, the proclamation was signed where the Althing met in the old days at Thingvellir. A "must" stop for every tourist, Lisa of course went there on her tour around Iceland.

"Thingvellir isn't far from Reykjavík by car, but of course took much longer in the old days on horseback," Sigga commented. "We fly the Icelandic flag to celebrate the day."

In Reykjavík the day's ceremonies begin in the morning when two students from a certain school lay a wreath on Jón Sigurdsson's grave. Everyone then proceeds to the square in front of the parliament building by the statue of Jón Sigurdsson. The band plays, the Scouts line up as a guard of honor, and the president of Iceland and other dignitaries enter and take their places for the ensuing program.

The committee in charge of events chooses the annual Mountain Queen to read a poem. At least in Reykjavík, the queen is always young and attractive. She wears the traditional Icelandic dress called *skautbúningur*, designed by the painter Sigurdur Gudmundsson in the mid–nineteenth century, which is black with a long skirt and long sleeves, and beautifully embroidered with gold around the neck and hem. The dress is set off with a gold–plated filigree belt. She also wears a headdress consisting of a gold band with a white veil that rises from the band in front and is held high above her head with stiffening before falling to her shoulders in back.

After the mountain queen reads the selected poem, the prime minister gives his annual speech. Like the laying of the wreath on Jón Sigurdsson's grave, the prime minister's speech is televised to the nation on the evening news.

The rest of the day throughout Iceland is a time to mill around in a crowd with everybody else in a very relaxed way, swapping comments, buying the little children balloons, and eating Icelandic hot dogs (they are made from lamb) and ice cream cones. The entire family goes to the square or field where the festivities are held. The women all come well dressed, in good shoes. A few women come in traditional clothes, usually in a long black skirt with a bodice over a white blouse. Those others in Icelandic sweaters are tourists! There's always something going on: a demonstration of Icelandic wrestling, live music over loudspeakers, and dancing outdoors way into the night.

"I'm sorry I missed the fun. Haven't I also heard something about a Seamen's Day?" Lisa inquired.

"Oh yes," Sigga replied. "Since we can't live without fishing, we have to have a day for the seamen. My husband of course went to sea to fish in the summer when he was in school, but times are changing. Not all the boys go to sea nowadays."

On the first Sunday in June, or the following week if Whitsunday conflicts, Iceland's all–important seamen are honored. When I played flute in the Reykjavík City Band we started the day by playing in front of the home for retired seamen. The day continues with parades, speeches, and contests of various kinds, and the band often plays between events. If it's wet outside, the bandmembers are issued blue uniform raincoats! Most importantly, since Iceland really earns its living by utilizing marine resources, outstanding seamen are singled out for praise or awarded medals for bravery at sea, but the celebration as a whole honors all seamen. The key events in Reykjavík are televised to the nation.

"Then there's St. John's Eve, Midsummer Night's Eve, I think you say," Sigga continued. "There weren't the beliefs here that there were in Europe. No dangerous creatures abroad, too light for that. The night trolls undoubtedly sleep soundly when it's still daylight at midnight." There was a twinkle in Sigga's eye as she added, "but it was considered healthy to roll naked in the dew."

"In 1989 the police got a call reporting two naked women in Breidholt rolling in the dew," I grinned, "but they never found them."

"Was the report a joke?" Lisa asked.

"Who knows?" Sigga replied. "Later there's Bank Holiday, which is the first Sunday and Monday in August. That weekend *all* Iceland goes to visit relatives or just out into the countryside."

Several places are designated around the country and the people tent there, especially young people, literally thousands in each place, with rock bands and other entertainment. The kids don't bother much with sleep but they have a great time.

"A lot of drinking, I'm afraid, but there are always grown–ups to help in any emergency, and the police as well," Sigga explained. "That's the weekend of the special get–together on the Westman Islands, with entertainment and a huge bonfire. The local people actually leave home and move into large, white tents set out in neat rows in Herjólfsdalur, and several thousand, foreigners and Icelanders alike, come and tent with them."

"It all sounds wonderful." But ever the tour agent, Lisa asked, "Before I go, do you have any advice I should pass on to tourists?"

"*Já–á–á*," Sigga replied, thoughtfully. "Perhaps you should warn them to be prepared for changes in the weather."

"It must be very different in winter."

"Oh, yes, but we have lots of things to do in the winter too—skiing, glacier trips, New Year's. You must come back and find out more."

"I'd love to, and thank you so very much for inviting me today."

"Thank you for coming," Sigga replied. After we had put our shoes on, Sigga shook Lisa's hand and gave me a hug and kiss as I, too, thanked her for a fine afternoon.

Trolls, Elves, and Ghosts

"Do you know who was here today?" a friend asked, her blue eyes alight, as she served me afternoon coffee. "Helga, the fortune–teller."

"Já," I encouraged in Icelandic fashion, with indrawn breath.

"And she saw Bergthóra. She was sitting in that chair there," she informed me with satisfaction. "Bergthóra, the wife of Njáll," she added, which meant that this particular Bergthóra had been dead for several centuries.

My face must have given me away.

"Do you doubt her?" she asked. "Of course Bergthóra was here. How else could the fortune–teller have described the clothes she was wearing?"

Norse mythology entailed much more than the worship of the chief gods, the Aesir. There were lesser gods and goddesses and a host of spirits of various kinds. What has come down to us in writing constitutes a powerful literary tradition of the old religion in which the beliefs and kennings (metaphors) celebrate the principal Aesir. With the official change legislated at the meeting of the parliament at Thingvellir in the year 1000, Christianity became the nation's religion, though worshipping the old gods could be continued in private. What were not touched by this formal change in religion were the folk beliefs in the numerous spirits that abounded in Iceland. These folk beliefs survived the impact of Christianity and, indeed, are in large measure very much alive today.

The original settlers believed in a host of beings: guardian spirits of the land, trolls, the hidden people, elves, mermen and mermaids, fetches, and ghosts that walked. In the early centuries some of the pagan legends gained Christian elements, and trolls and other beings were sometimes equated with the Christian devil, but basically folk beliefs and Christian teaching were two separate and continuing channels. The abolition of saints and holy relics during the Reformation also left a vacuum that was easily filled with the old folk beliefs.[1] The eighteenth century Age of Reason had little effect in Iceland in diminishing the folk beliefs in spirits, and the nineteenth century brought a renewed interest, including an attempt to record beliefs and stories, which continued in the twentieth century.

Erlendur Haraldsson,[2] in surveys in 1974–75 and again as part of a cross–national survey in 1981–84, found that 78% of Icelanders consider themselves religious despite the fact they rarely attend church. Furthermore, he found that two–thirds of the respondents had had an occult experience of some kind. The commonest occult experience was dreaming true, where 36% had correctly dreamed the future. Though these figures and most other results from the research are generally comparable to the percentages in other western countries, Icelanders often evince a very open interest in the occult that is not always found elsewhere. The belief that some people have psychic power has ancient roots. Even Óðinn, who could himself foretell the future, sought prophecies from Mímir and also from the dead Sibyl of the Völuspá.

Today, if you ask Icelanders if they believe in any of the traditional spirits, you get varied answers. The majority seem to reject trolls but may accept Hidden People and elves and believe in ghosts. Many believe in and indeed have experienced a haunting and some have seen one of the Hidden People. Many don't dare not believe. A great many Icelanders will refer to the hidden people, albeit sometimes tongue–in–cheek, but often seriously. One of the best replies, when asked as to whether he was a believer, was made by a former prime minister: "My grandmother believed in the Hidden People. Who am I to say she was wrong?" But for believers and non–believers alike, strange experiences and the occult remain a major Icelandic interest. An ordinary conversation frequently runs: "Something strange happened to me," and the experience recounted is then very real, not just for the teller but for the listener as well.

Guardian Spirits

When the first settlers arrived in Iceland from Norway they looked at the land, as indeed at all lands, as having a full complement of guardian spirits. These spirits were regarded as beneficial for any humans living there but inimical to strangers. The gaping dragon heads on their ships were to scare these spirits away in foreign lands. *Hauksbók* records the law of 930 that required removal of the dragon heads before landing in Iceland so as not to disturb these guardian spirits.

The guardian spirits of the land had feminine names in the beginning, but under later influences came to have neuter names in the folktales. The four guardian spirits that are on the Icelandic coat of arms and are the symbols of the four quarters of Iceland were not original guardian spirits, however, but were suggested by Snorri Sturluson in the thirteenth century. They are, clockwise from the southwest: ox, vulture, dragon, and rock giant.

Bishop Gudmundur Consecrates Drangey

The old guardian spirits that were beneficial in the days of paganism became malicious after the coming of Christianity. Therefore Bishop Gudmundur the Good set out to consecrate the island of Drangey in the north to get rid of the old spirits. He moved around the island, consecrating the lava cliffs as he went. When he had come most of the way round, a huge hand suddenly protruded from the black rock, and a deep voice said: "Somewhere there must be a place for bad spirits, sire." And with that the Bishop agreed. Since that time the unconsecrated part has been known as Heathen Cliff.

Trolls

The Giants of the Norse cosmogony evolved into the trolls of later folktales. Their daughters had originally been beautiful, but in the folktales trolls, though still retaining human form, are inhumanly strong, ugly, and threatening, though they can be driven off with the power of Christianity. If you do them ill they will exact vengeance, but if a troll needs a favor and you comply, you can count on his word that he will return the favor. They often row a boat of stone and draw fish from the sea without benefit of line or bait. Some are night trolls and will turn to stone if caught by daylight before they can get back to their cave or cliff home. Particularly dangerous are the trolls in the bird cliffs.

Tales of Trolls

One night two trolls set out over Breidafjördur Bay to move an island that was there. The man went ahead and threw a rope around the island and pulled. The woman followed behind. Thus they went south over the bay and entered Hvammsfjördur, but the dawn caught them and they turned to stone. The island they were pulling is called Lamb Island, and the man is the stone pillar right by the island, the woman the rock that is a little way beyond. To this day the pillars are known as Karl and Kerling—old man and old woman.

In the eighteenth century in spring it was the custom in the north in Skagafjördur, where there were also two stones called Karl and Kerling, to wish a pleasant greeting to the island of Drangey and these two pillars, a custom that had been passed down from the old days when the guardian spirits were still seen as good. Today, only one of the stone pillars remains.

Once an ugly old man was thirsty and begged for a drink. When he was given it, he wished to return the favor. "Once a year you must pour a gallon of whey into this hollow in the stone," he said, pointing to a natural pile of lava rocks that formed a small enclosure, "and you will have good luck." The farmer thanked him and the troll went away and was never seen again. The farmer and his descendants carried out the old man's directions. One year, a long time later, the wife did not bother to pour the whey into the little enclosure. That year the farmhouse burned down. Ever since the family has kept up the custom.

The Hidden People and Elves

The belief in the Hidden People and elves goes back to ancient times, as attested in the sagas and the Eddas. There were both Light Elves and Dark Elves in Norse mythology and rites to worship elves or local guardian spirits. Sigurdur Nordal[3] feels that the Hidden People, and not just the trolls, are the descendants of the ancient guardian spirits.

Tales from the nineteenth century equate elves and Hidden People. Both the Hidden People and the elves may be farmers, as were most Icelanders in earlier times, and look like human beings, living in hills and cliffs. They are dressed like human beings, though the elves may have pointed hats and the Hidden People are man–sized but may still be in rather old–fashioned clothes. Both can be either helpful or malicious and, like trolls, repay a favor with a favor. Elves are smaller than we are, even tiny enough to be *blómaálfar* and live in flower blossoms. Commonly there are *búaálfar*, elves that live on the farm and are helpful, unless those on the farm forget to put food out for them, and then they become mischievous.

Erlendur Haraldsson's research has shown that 5% of Icelanders have seen the Hidden People. Over half (55%) are either sure they exist or believe their existence is likely or possible, with no response difference by age or place of residence; the belief is as strong in the city as in the country. There is an even commoner belief (68%) in the existence of patches of ground where something bad will happen to those who disturb the Hidden People there.

There are a great many tales involving Hidden People or elves. Many modern Icelandic farmers may tell you they live in a certain rocky hill on their farmstead. Have they seen them? Perhaps not, but they are there. There are records of seeing a rock open, revealing the Hidden People, who may or may not entice a human to join them forever before the rock closes. There is the tale of the woman who was brought in to help with childbirth and then allowed to return to the world of humans; she was amply rewarded for her help.

As with other folk beliefs, Christianity has lent a patina to the telling. The Hidden People may hold their own mass, or Christian symbols may drive them off. Icelanders frequently sing the ballad of "Ólafur liljurós," which, according to Vésteinn Ólason,[4] was brought to Iceland from Scandinavia sometime before the Reformation. In the Icelandic version Ólafur rides out and meets four elf maidens who try to tempt him, but he chooses God over the elves, rather than, as in other countries, an elf bride. As he leans down from the saddle to kiss one of the elf maids good–bye, she stabs him. If it seems unduly tragic that he then rides home to his mother, where he, she and his sister all die, the ballad is actually no more fateful than "Lord Randall, My Son," which many English speakers are familiar with.

Eve and the Hidden People

One day when God was coming to visit Eve, she planned to wash all her children so they would look nice, but God arrived sooner than expected, so Eve kept the unwashed children hidden. God admired the scrubbed children, but he knew Eve had hidden the others. "What has been hidden from God shall also be hidden from men," he decreed. And that is how the Hidden People came to be.

Other Tales of the Hidden People

In 1624 the records show that a woman insisted she had been made pregnant by a man of the Hidden People. She could not be dissuaded from her story.[5]

In the nineteenth century Hidden People moved to North America with the Icelandic immigrants, but not the other spirits, which remained behind in Iceland.

In the summer of 1971 construction plans for the town of Kópavogur called for building on a lot where two stones lay, the larger Gray Stone and Little Brother. When a crane lifted the stones, the larger cracked in two. Subsequently three young men who had helped shift the stones met, separately, with accidents. The young men became believers. This was clearly one of the patches of ground where the Hidden People must not be disturbed. To this day the street narrows to avoid the patch and no construction has taken place on this lot. Similar dissension occurred in 1995 when, to avoid accidents, the Highway

Commission decided to move a split rock out of a roadbed in the countryside. After local complaints, the two parts of the rock were lifted very carefully and slowly by crane so as not to disturb the elves or Hidden People.

In the beginning of January 1987, seven horses were lost in the eastern part of Iceland. A search failed to turn them up. Iceland's largest newspaper duly reported that many people were speculating that either trolls or Hidden People had made off with them. In early June, after a more protracted search, the horses were found dead. Whether or not they had been in the hands of the Hidden People, the harshness of the Icelandic winter and the difficulty of finding fodder had been more than the horses could survive.

There are two maps showing where elves and Hidden People live in the Reykjavík area, though the maps are not based wholly on tradition. One is available from the River Farm Museum and the other from the Municipal Planning Office.

Other Beings

There was magic in other beings and objects as well, the beliefs in which also often go back to ancient times. Certain stones ease childbirth or aid healing, and some make your wish come true. There are mermen and mermaids in the sea and sprites in freshwater. Cows talk once a year, some say on Christmas night and others on Midsummer's Eve. The person who can understand bird talk will be prepared for whatever is to happen. It is especially lucky to save an eagle, and ravens can foretell the future. Horses are the most intelligent of animals; they can see a spirit in the path and avoid it and thus bring the rider safely home. The rorqual whale is well–disposed to men and protects a ship from bad whales. And there is a famous bull that some modern Icelanders have seen: he is dragging his own skin behind him, still attached on his rump.

How the Halibut Became a Bottom Fish

There was a young halibut who wished to amuse the Virgin Mary as she walked on the beach, so he made funny faces as he disported himself in the waves. "Oh, what fun," she said, as he screwed both eyes up onto the top of his head, and there they have been ever since.

Ghosts

In Norse mythology, the dead were seen as simultaneously still in the tumulus they were usually buried in as well as in one of the afterworlds. The dead could walk or be called back to life. There were walking corpses who stayed near their place of burial, ghosts raised by a sorcerer to be sent on a mission, fetches that followed a certain person or family, often to bring good luck, and the spirits of infants that had been left to die of exposure, a practice that, before the conversion to Christianity, was legal in times of famine or great need.

A strong belief in ghosts has continued into the present. Erlendur Haraldsson[6] found that 41% of Icelanders reported having had contact with the dead. This figure was considerably higher than for the other countries surveyed; the European average was 25%, the Norwegian figure 9%. Thus 88% of

Icelanders not only believe in life after death but also consider it possible to see those who have died, and 55% believe that hauntings are possible.

Usually the ghost that walks remains near the corpse, though sometimes near the place of death. The ghost may walk to complete business left unfinished in life or to carry off a loved one. Ghost walking can be dangerous for the living, and there are records of having to burn or behead a ghost to stop it from walking.

Ghosts have been looked on with fear for the damage they can cause, but not all are dangerous. The fetches were at one time protective spirits, usually in the guise of an animal, that followed a person or family. In fact, if you left home ground you could instruct your fetch to follow another member of your family to bring him good luck while you were gone. With the coming of Christianity, the fetch was looked on as a mischievous being who was often named for the place it frequented.

The spirit of a family member is precious. Originally a child would be named after a dead person, to keep not only the name alive but also the spirit of the person. There is still the feeling that it is "nice" to name the child for a family member who is gone, and an even stronger tradition of naming the children after the grandparents, living or dead.

Tales of Ghosts

Höfdi, the house in Reykjavík where Reagan and Gorbachev held the summit meeting between the United States and the then U.S.S.R. in the autumn of 1986, is said to be haunted.

A nurse was killed in a car accident on the highway from Reykjavík to Keflavík. There are those who have seen her at the site of the accident, trying to climb onto the hood of a passing car.

The next drunk Icelander you see may not be satisfying his own thirst. Instead, he firmly believes that it is his dead uncle inside of him craving a drink.

An acquaintance of mine was in a tight spot while driving one day, but her father, who had died some years before, was on the seat beside her and steadied her.

In Tálknafjördur in 1696 the ghost of a man named Bjarni Jónsson caused a great deal of trouble.[7] He was exhumed and given a more thorough burial rite, but to no avail. Again he was exhumed and it was found that he was no longer lying down in the grave but was on all fours. There was nothing for it but to behead him, pierce the head with the blade of a scythe, and re–bury him. After that his ghost was no longer heard from.

Iceland's History: The Norwegian and Danish Domination Through the Reformation, 1262–1550

Some events in history are major watersheds and deeply influence what follows. The Old Treaty, signed in 1262, that led to Iceland's being first under the Norwegian and later the Danish kings was such a milestone, as was the Reformation in 1550 whereby Lutheranism became, and remains, Iceland's state religion.

Interestingly, one other potential watershed did not take place. The Danish king, Christian II, had trouble defending his throne and lost it for good in the Feud of the Counts to Frederick I in 1523. On the latter's death in 1533 war again broke out. Hard–pressed for money to finance the fighting, in 1518 and again in 1523, Christian sent agents to Amsterdam and to Henry VIII of England with instructions to sell the rights to free trade in Iceland or to mortgage the country as collateral for a loan. The asking price was 20,000–30,000 guilders from the Dutch, or from King Henry 50,000–100,000 florins.[1] The idea was not new: Christian I offered Shetland and Orkney as collateral to meet his daughter's dowry; since the dowry was never paid Scotland acquired permanent title to these islands. Both the Dutch and Henry VIII refused Christian II's offer. Had Henry accepted, the loan would almost certainly not have been repaid, Iceland would have fallen under the English crown, and English would have become the national language.

New Laws and a New Government

After Icelanders had signed the Old Treaty in 1262, accepting the sovereignty of the Norwegian king, the need for a new law code was immediately obvious. King Magnús the Lawgiver (1263–1280) first sent the code called *Járnsíða* (Ironside). Since the original version of 1271 caused a good deal of argument, it was amended and finally accepted by the Althing in 1273. Modelled on Norwegian law, among other things it abolished the practice of blood revenge that had so unsettled Iceland in the last years of the Commonwealth.

Magnús then provided for a second and more comprehensive law code for Iceland. Known as *Jónsbók* (John's Book) for the main author Jón Einarsson, the new law code was presented to Iceland in 1280, the year King Magnús died, and was accepted by the Althing in 1281. It was subsequently amended several times in response to Icelandic objections but remained little changed between

1314 and the eighteenth and nineteenth centuries (though by that time Danish law also formed the basis for Icelandic court judgments). The best of the law codes produced under the aegis of Magnús the Lawgiver, *Jónsbók* was even used to teach children to read as it was so well written. In 1578 it became the first non–religious work printed in Icelandic. Over forty sections are still in force, including sections on the ownership of flotsam and whales washed ashore.

The king's interests were seen to by the governors (either one or two) and the sheriffs who were responsible for the 12 counties. From the mid–fourteenth century Bessastadir, once owned by the chieftain and writer Snorri Sturluson, was the governor's mansion, just as today it is the home of Iceland's president. The governors rented their office from the king from the mid–fourteenth century on in return for the right to keep their share of the taxes. Each sheriff was to see that the law was upheld in his own district; he was also judge and tax collector, and appointed members to the legal assembly.

The new *lögrétta* or law court was presided over by a "lawman," as in earlier centuries. In 1283 a second law court was instituted, making one for the south and east and a separate one for the north and west. Though the *lögrétta* was a judicial court, it had some legislative power, its laws being termed "judgments." The *lögrétta* remained the highest court until the establishment of a superior court in 1593. As in other countries, the king had final executive and judicial power, however. The sheriffs appointed 84 committee members to the assembly, or Althing, that met at Thingvellir. The lawmen and the sheriffs together named three men from each regional assembly, a total of 36 members.

Tax revenues were divided, the king taking half, with the other half going to the county sheriffs. Taxes were paid in kind, either homespun cloth or other goods. The king's share represented a considerable portion of Icelandic productivity which was, in effect, exported to Norway without giving Iceland any direct payment in return.

The new law brought fundamental changes in the way Iceland was run. From 1262 on Iceland was under a monarch and the king's agents replaced the old *goðar*. Court judgments were no longer based on precedents, as they had been under the old laws recorded in *Grágás*, but on evidence and facts.[2] Physical punishment was introduced: whipping and the death penalty. On the other hand, as in Europe generally before the French Revolution, there was little separation of legislative, judicial, and executive powers. The Icelandic Commonwealth had lacked an executive, but it was an exception in medieval times in that it had attempted a separation of judicial and legislative powers.

The Large Landholders and the Struggle for Icelandic Rights

The terms of the Old Treaty of 1262 whereby Iceland came under the domination of the Norwegian king were largely the work of the large landholders, who had had enough of the fighting that preceded the downfall of the Commonwealth. Iceland was to be allowed to pass its own laws (though the king could veto them), Icelanders were to be appointed lawmen and sheriffs, and they were not to be summoned to the king's court unless they were his liegemen. The Norwegian king promised peace and a specified number of ships carrying grain and supplies, in return for which Icelanders would pay the king taxes. Unrest and trouble followed when the promised ships did not arrive, foreigners were set over Icelanders, and the king demanded that Icelanders appear in his court.

Haakon Longlegs, king of Norway from 1299–1319, tried to get Icelanders to come to his court to swear allegiance but the large landowners refused. In a district assembly in 1303 Icelanders countermanded the king's orders and reduced the number of committeemen from 84 to 42. In 1305 the king's agent Krók–Álfur attended the assembly at Hegranes, where he was surrounded by young men beating their shields and yelling at him. He stumbled from the meeting and died shortly thereafter.[3] In 1306 an agreement was signed, restating that the lawmen and sheriffs were to be Icelanders and that a certain number of ships loaded with necessities be sent to Iceland yearly. In 1319 Icelanders once again demanded that only Icelanders be appointed lawmen and sheriffs and that six ships be dispatched every summer or Icelanders would not remain under the king's rule. The following summer Icelandic leaders went to Norway to present their demands and, despite their strong feelings, paid homage to the king.

Again in 1375, after Haakon Longlegs' grandson Magnús had died, the large landholders and others met at Skálholt to set their terms for paying homage to the new king, Haakon VI. Among other demands, it was agreed that the *lögrétta* should have the final say in who should be appointed lawmen and that the lawmen and sheriffs should be Icelandic. The large landholders banded together to enlist support to fight together for their rights.

Meanwhile the power of the large landholders, or country squires, increased. They owned 300 landholdings, of which 30 were large estates, amounting to 7% of the total landholdings but 21% of the country's best land.[4] Most of the land was held by these squires and the church, with very little owned outright by the crown.

Though Icelanders had always fished, fishing grew in importance, partly because of the stricter rules of fasting imposed by the church; partly as the result of the worsening climate and heavy death tolls from disease, which left fewer workers to tend cattle; and after 1400 because of the huge European demand for dried cod. Accordingly, the most valuable landholdings were those near fishing stations. The large landholders had their workers fish only during seasons when there was less farmwork to tend to; there was therefore no class of fishermen and no merchant class to sell the fish. When fishing, the workers or *búðsetumenn* and the *tómthúsmenn* (cotters who could not legally own property) lived in turf and stone huts, sometimes with a small amount of pasture and some livestock, but their living conditions were poor. In good years more workers than in poor years could afford to be tenant farmers and pay a tithe to the owner for the use of land. The tenants were required to carry out certain obligations, including fishing for the landowner. The landholders needed labor and kept the workers bound by law to a year's contract, leaving them free to move to another farm only on the legally defined moving days, usually in early June.

Small communities grew up around the fishing stations, but it was the large landowners who profited at the expense of the workers. They raked in money from stockfish (dried cod), and butter became a medium of exchange.[5] After 1400, when it became legal to export stockfish, fishing became more important than agriculture as Roman Catholic Europe demanded fish; exporting fish made it possible to pay for necessary imports. Though some barley was raised, it was more profitable to export stockfish and import grain. The number of sheep increased and the number of cattle dropped, as it took relatively fewer people to tend sheep than cattle;[6] it was also more profitable to employ workers to fish than to tend cattle. There were meat and milk, however, and wool and tanned hides for clothes. The people made bog iron, and the woods were depleted for firewood.

Though the majority of the people were laborers, the few country squires were often rich indeed. Björn Einarsson (d. 1415) twice travelled to Rome (in 1391 and 1411) and once to Greenland, where he was detained for two years by pack ice (1385–1387). He was a man of the times, well educated, surrounded by pets and entertainers, and was the first Icelander after 1262 to become wealthy independently of the monarchy, largely from profits from fishing.[7] In the fifteenth century Gudmundur Arason the Rich of Reykhólar owned 6 large estates and 129 other landholdings.[8] He could supply his overnight guests with no fewer than 33 down duvets for their sleeping comfort.

The Church

Three sides vied for power over Iceland in the period 1262–1550: the crown, the church, and the country squires. The bishops worked to increase the power of the church. The church supported the crown but stood firmly for the separation of church and state. In 1275, during the time that Árni Thorláksson was bishop at Skálholt (1269–1298), the church acquired its own canonical law (though it was not ratified at the bishopric of Hólar in the north until 1354). As in Norway at the time, the church had its own courts, where clerics judged church cases.

Many churches and chapels were actually privately owned. Bishop Árni tried to get monies from these holdings, but the landholders objected. At one point, when the king wanted Icelanders to come to Norway to take up arms on his behalf, Árni backed the king but, led by Hrafn Oddsson, most Icelanders refused to answer the Norwegian call to arms, even though the bishop put Hrafn under an interdict. In 1297 the king settled the dispute: the bishop was to hold sway over the lands wholly owned by the church, but the laity were to control all lands of which they owned at least 50%.[9] The bishops were strict about enforcing the church's moral code; for the laity, no divorce, and for the clergy, celibacy.

Both the church and the church officials individually were wealthy. In the fourteenth century the church controlled 12% of the total value of landhold-ings;[10] by 1550 it owned half the landholdings in Iceland. It paid no taxes and had preferential rights to gyrfalcons (for hunting) and sulphur (for gunpowder). The party held to welcome the Danish bishop Vilkin Hinriksson (1395–1405) when he arrived at Skálholt lasted for a full week, with much drinking and cel-ebrating.[11]

Hard Times and Disasters

Meanwhile, the climate had turned colder than at the time of the settle-ment, inevitably affecting agriculture. It became harder to raise grain than it had been, forests were depleted for firewood, erosion increased, and there was little chance of natural reforestation. In 1306 there was pack ice all summer in the north and many died of an unknown illness.[12] The worst years were given names: for example, 1313—The Winter the Horses Died, and 1405—The Great Snow Winter, with its huge loss of livestock.[13] Sea ice encroached on the land in 1274, allowing 22 polar bears to reach Iceland; they were killed and uti-lized, as were 27 the following year.[14] Ships were becalmed in 1392 and many lost. In 1520 there was too little hay and many were left without horses. In 1522 strong westerlies meant catastrophe: 8 ships were wrecked off Álftanes in the southwest. On the other hand, the same winds provided a bonanza of 18 whales washed ashore.[15]

Other disasters also struck. Mt. Hekla erupted in 1300; the winds carried the volcanic ash over a wide swath in the north, leading to deaths in the Skagafjördur area the following year. Hekla erupted again in 1341, 1389, and 1510. The Öraefajökull eruption of 1362 did far more damage, however, as it covered over a third of the country with 10 km^3 (2 1/2 cu. mi.) of volcanic ejec-ta, undoubtedly causing more loss of life and property than any other eruption in Iceland.[16] It was a hundred years before the area near the volcano was rebuilt and today is still relatively barren.

Smallpox epidemics struck three times in the 1300s and again ca 1431. There were other years with a high death rate, but the greatest epidemics were those identified as *plága* in the contemporary annals: the Great Plague of 1402–1404 and the Later Plague of 1494–ca.1495. These are the only two cases where contemporary writers used the word *plága*. The identity of this disease, however, has raised a great deal of speculation as there is no mention of rats in any Icelandic medieval text. There were no rats in Iceland before the eighteenth century.[17] Without rats and rat fleas to spread the disease to humans the pesti-lence could not have been bubonic plague. Furthermore, there is no mention in Icelandic writings of the boils or lymph node swellings that give bubonic plague its name. The epidemic of 1402–1404 was brought by a ship that evi-dently came from England, where there had been a "disastrous pestilence." The Icelandic word *plága* is an indication of the English origin of the disease, as it is derived from English "plague," itself a derivative of the Latin *plaga* meaning "wound"; in fact, only in England at the time was the word "plague" used to denote "pestilence."[18]

Among the first Icelanders to sicken and die were those from Skálholt who met the ship to collect their share of the cargo it carried. By the end of the year, of the 100–200 people who lived at Skálholt, only three were still alive[19] The annals clearly record that the pestilence went on to strike rich and poor alike and that people died within three days or so; there is no mention of anyone's having recovered, though many did not become infected. The historians Gunnar Karlsson and Helgi Skúli Kjartansson document a crippling death rate of 50%–60% of the population in 1402–1404 and 30%–50% in 1494–1495.[20]

Both Jón Steffensen[21] and Karlsson and Kjartansson conclude that the disease was almost certainly the pneumonic form of the plague. The one hundred percent death rate and the fact that many never sickened point to pneumonic plague. The pneumonic form is spread by contact with a sick person in the coughing and vomiting stage, or by germs in the sick person's clothing, and not by rat fleas, and is "extremely virulent."[22] Contagion can be avoided, however, if there is no contact during the coughing stage or with the victim's clothes. Improved ships in the fifteenth century meant a shorter sea voyage than in earlier times. With an incubation period usually of less than a week but up to twelve days, the germs could easily have been brought by ship. Furthermore, in damp, cold air and especially if there is frost, the germs can survive for weeks and even months.[23]

Karlsson and Kjartansson also point out that, despite the high death rate, Icelandic society was not destroyed by the plague, though they suggest that the simplicity of the social organization may have been part of the reason for this. The huge decrease in population did have an effect, however. There were deathbed gifts of land to the church, thus increasing the church's power; the survivors often became bigger landholders than would otherwise have been the case; property dropped in value as it was abandoned and was bought by those who had money; lawlessness increased; and wages rose as labor became in short supply. But good prices for fish were a bonus for the survivors.

The Kalmar Union

Through a number of diplomatic negotiations the kingdoms of Norway, Sweden and Denmark became united under one monarch, with the result that, in time, Iceland passed from Norwegian to Danish control.

Haakon VI of Norway married Margaret of Denmark (1353–1412) in 1363 when she was only 10 years old. On the death of her father in 1375, Margaret became regent of Denmark and had her infant son Olaf elected king. Olaf also ascended the throne of Norway in 1380 on his father's death, with Margaret acting as regent of both Norway and Denmark. Following Olaf's premature death in 1387 and after the Swedes defeated their unpopular king, Albert of Mecklenburg, Margaret's regency was accepted by the Swedes as well. In 1389 Margaret had her infant cousin, Erik of Pomerania, proclaimed king of Norway;

subsequently Sweden and Denmark also accepted the boy as king. Margaret then proposed a plan for the union of the Scandinavian countries, in part to counteract the growing power of the German Hanseatic League. Though Margaret's proposal was never formally accepted, the Kalmar Union of the Scandinavian countries continued, with the Swedes sometimes a member and sometimes not, until Christian II lost the throne of Denmark in the Feud of the Counts in 1523. Known as the "lady king," Margaret ruled with a strong hand. Under her tutelage the seat of power shifted to Denmark.

Iceland paid homage to King Olaf at the meeting of the Althing in 1382, thus formalizing union with Denmark, a relationship that was not completely dissolved until 1944.

Trade and the English Century

By the fourteenth century competition from better Flemish and other foreign cloth meant a poor market for Icelandic homespun wadmal. Instead, Europeans wanted stockfish. By the 1340's stockfish was Iceland's main export, though, since the exportation of food was curtailed in the fourteenth century because of severe food shortages in some areas of Iceland, the volume exported was not great.[24] After the mid–fourteenth century the city of Bergen held a monopoly over Icelandic trade, and the exporting of stockfish became extremely important to Iceland. The fish was sold at small trading centers that grew up around the fishing stations during the fishing season as, unlike Europe, Iceland had no developed ports with piers and no real towns. The county sheriffs set the rate of exchange.

Alcoholic beverages had not been imported in any quantity previously, but in the late fourteenth century there were complaints of Icelanders getting drunk at the trading centers. From that time on wine was considered a necessary import rather than a luxury, the price of 1 barrel being 100 fish.[25]

The fifteenth century is known to Icelanders as the English century. Though Germans and later the Dutch also came, it was principally the English who fished and traded in Icelandic waters during that time. Whereas the English sailors had formerly hugged their own coastline or sailed to Holland or Flanders, in the fifteenth century they had ships and navigating equipment that allowed them to venture out into open water. They had the compass rose (used in Italy from about 1300), together with the sounding lead and line and the hourglass, by at least the second half of the fourteenth century.[26] The English had better ships than before, two– and three–masted merchantmen with a poop and forecastle and equipped with topmasts and spritsails, as well as smaller broad–bowed doggers.[27] The Germans of the Hanseatic League also had the compass rose and ships that could easily sail to Iceland. Though the Hansa cogs and the other ships of the day look to us like tubs, they held far more cargo than the earlier Norse ships and because of more freeboard (the distance the sides rise above the waves) could more easily navigate rough northern seas. Furthermore, the crews were no longer forced to beach their boats and overwinter, as in earlier times. They usually took advantage of better weather, as had the Norse, and sailed to Iceland in the spring, returning in late summer or autumn.

The English and Germans came for dried cod to satisfy the need for fish on fast days and the general demand for food that could be kept without spoiling. Dried, cod could be stored for a year and even kept until prices rose during Lent. The English sailors came from Bristol and other ports, carrying flour, beer and wine, linen and silver buttons, knives, nails and glass to exchange for stockfish, fish liver oil, falcons, and sulphur.[28]

Beginning in 1408, the English came to Iceland in large numbers to fish and to trade, a hundred or more ships a year, so many that some had to return with empty holds.[29] They established bases, the largest on the Westman Islands. They were also known to steal sheep and stockfish, and they raided Bessastadir.[30] After the plague, England needed a larger labor force, so the English sailors, especially those from Lynn and Newcastle, kidnapped Icelandic children.[31] Icelanders also sometimes gave or sold their children to the English in the belief that they would be provided a better life in England and a better education than under the harsh conditions prevailing in Iceland; some of these children subsequently returned to Iceland, either to visit or to remain.

Duties and the fees for permits from the king of England to trade in Iceland enriched English coffers but cheated the Danish king of income. Since the Icelandic fishing grounds were so rich that one good fishing expedition could nearly pay for a ship plus the cost of outfitting it,[32] it is not surprising that the English came north, principally to fish but also to trade. The German Hansa were also important traders in Iceland, buying fish from the Icelanders.

To balance the power of the Englishman John Craxton, who was bishop in the north at Hólar and who traded with the English, the Danish king persuaded the pope in 1426 that Johannes Gerechini should be bishop at Skálholt. In 1431 the Althing complained about the behavior of both bishops and of other officials, as well as about German and English fishing. In 1432 the Danish king Erik of Pomerania and Henry VI of England signed an accord in which, among other things, they agreed to end the kidnapping of Icelandic children. In 1433 Icelanders, with English backing, drowned Gerechini, and two years later Craxton was driven out of Iceland. Thus ended the first of the ten altercations which later came to be called Cod Wars.

A Dutchman, Gozewijn, was bishop at Skálholt from 1435–1437, and the Dutch, too, sailed to Iceland. Christian I (1448–1481), in response to Icelandic complaints, published changes in the law banning, among other things, bribery, thieving, and collecting taxes without a permit. The English and Irish were to be outlawed in Iceland unless they had a permit from the Danish king, and any Icelanders giving or selling their children to foreigners would have to pay a penalty. The Second Cod War or altercation was thus brought to an end.

Ignoring the agreements, the English continued to come to Iceland with or without permits or paying customs, principally to fish but also to trade. In 1467 they killed the governor, Björn Thorleifsson. Christian I retaliated by blocking access to the Baltic through the Oresund Strait and capturing 6 English ships. Though Denmark had previously fought the Hansa, Christian now sought their support and encouraged them to trade in Iceland. A third, short peace was achieved in 1473, but the English continued to come without permits. Icelanders as well as the Danish king sided with the Germans as they brought a greater variety of goods to trade. The German Hansa established trading bases in Iceland and, from their base in England, even sold the English stockfish they had purchased in Iceland.

The Icelandic squires complained to the Danish king about all the foreign buildings that had been erected and the loss of labor to fishing. In 1484 the English arrived, protected by ships armed with cannon, and captured a Hansa ship and 11 Hansa merchants, later selling both ship and men in Galway, Ireland. The Fourth Cod War ended with the peace agreement of 1490, giving the English the right to trade provided they paid all tolls and got permission from the Danish king every seven years.

The Germans had bases on Faxaflói Bay and at Hafnarfjördur in the southwest, whereas the English had a fortified base at Grindavík on the south coast, as well as on the Westman Islands. In 1532 the Grindavík or Fifth Cod War broke out between the Germans and the English, with fighting there, at Bessastadir, and between armed merchant vessels at sea. The Germans and the Danes together captured Grindavík and killed the English leader. A peace agreement was signed in 1533. The English position was considerably weakened, though the English did not leave the Westman Islands until 1558, after they had turned their attention to exploring the New World and the fishing banks off Newfoundland. Meanwhile the Hansa increased their efforts. To keep Danish control, Christian III (1534–1559) therefore awarded the rights to fish and trade in Iceland to the city of Copenhagen. Though in 1548 Copenhagen had only 2 ships in Iceland to the 20 from Hamburg, the Danish king had made his point.[33]

The Reformation

The church was wealthy and powerful. It continued to acquire more landholdings as gifts, owned shares in trading ships, and raked in a profit from fishing and the produce of church lands. When Frederick I died in 1533, the two bishops, Jón Arason at Hólar (1524–1550) and Ögmundur Pálsson in the south at Skálholt (1521–1541), were appointed governors over their sees, giving them the highest power in both worldy and spiritual matters. The Skálholt church alone owned one–eleventh of all the landholdings in Iceland.[34] In 1550 the Hólar see owned a 25 ton "butter mountain," a 70–ton ship, ornaments of gold and silver, and valuable manuscripts, as well as landholdings, livestock, and cannon.[35]

In the sixteenth century new ideas came to challenge the supremacy of Catholicism. With the printing press making possible broader access to written works, and the discovery of the New World, ideas were changing. Various

Hólar

European monarchs found that conversion to Lutheranism and the expropria-tion of church lands offered a convenient solution to their financial problems. Sweden became Lutheran in 1527 and Christian III (1534–1559) established the Lutheran church in Denmark, Norway, and the Faroes. The Hansa built a Lutheran church in Hafnarfjördur in 1534. A few Icelanders went to Germany to study and returned home to found a group of Protestant adherents.

At first the two bishops, Ögmundur and Jón Arason, were enemies but, though they met at Thingvellir in 1527, each at the head of a thousand or more armed men, there was no clash: they joined forces against their common enemy, the Lutheran heresy. In a letter read in the churches in 1539 Ögmundur threat-ened to excommunicate anyone who took up Lutheranism. The magistrate Dietrich van Minden seized the Videy monastery in the name of the king, but he and his men were captured and killed at Skálholt before they could seize any more church property. In the same year, old and blind, Ögmundur named Gissur Einarsson as his successor. Ostensibly a good Catholic, Gissur was actu-ally a Protestant and agreed with the king that Icelanders were not averse to embracing the new religion. Gissur (1542–1548) was accepted by the king as bishop at Skálholt. However, at the Althing in 1540 Gissur agreed to run the church in the old, Catholic way, thus playing a double game, almost certainly to keep the peace. At this point Catholics controlled the Althing and Jón Arason's son Ari was appointed to collect taxes. Jón Arason wrote the king a let-ter, signed also by other northern officials, asking to be allowed to emigrate with their possessions if the king insisted on establishing the Lutheran church in Iceland.

The Lutheran religion was accepted by the Althing in 1541 when Icelanders swore homage to Christian III. All lands held by the church at Skálholt became the property of the crown and the bishopric's gold and silver and coins were sent to the king in Denmark; the Danish king thus expropriated Icelandic treasures as well as church lands. Ögmundur was arrested and died on the way to Denmark. Gissur and Jón Arason came to a workable agreement. Jón Arason thus became the last Catholic bishop in the Nordic countries.

Gissur, faced with the problem of finding clergy trained in the new faith, was forced to ordain untrained men. As an agent of the government, Spectacles–Pétur, the first man in Iceland known to have worn glasses, drove the monks away and took over the management of Videy. In 1548, when Gissur sickened and died after having had a holy cross destroyed, his death was believed to have been God's justice. Gissur was an able man, but because of the changes he stood for he had enemies and went about with an armed guard. Though he played both sides, no Icelander died because of the Reformation while he was still alive.

Marteinn Einarsson (1549–1557) was next appointed bishop of Skálholt. In 1550 Jón Arason's sons captured him, and the Althing, having received a letter from the pope, set Jón over the Skálholt bishopric as well as Hólar. Jón then captured Skálholt and reinstated Videy as a Catholic monastery before returning north, where he wrote the king that he wanted peace and was willing to swear allegiance. The king, on the other hand, sent a letter outlawing Jón Arason and instructing Dadi Gudmundsson to capture him. The following autumn Jón lost a battle to Dadi Gudmundsson and his forces; Dadi captured Jón and two of his sons and took them to Skálholt. They were to be tried in court the following summer, but instead they were beheaded by their guards, without trial, on November 7, 1550, their bodies buried without coffins in back of the church at Skálholt. Later that winter, masked men from the north killed 14 of those responsible for the execution.

In the spring of 1551 there was no opposition to the three naval ships that the Danish king sent. The Althing paid homage to Christian III and to his heir apparent, Frederick II, those in the north also swearing allegiance. A jury in the north judged Jón Arason and his sons traitors and the king confiscated the lands Jón and his sons had held personally. In 1554, after taking possession of all the monasteries and church properties, the crown owned 19% of the total value of all landholdings. The monasteries had owned 15%, Videy alone having had 116 landholdings, yielding an annual fish catch of 9 tons. In 1560 the king claimed one half of the tithe as well, namely the fourth that had previously gone to support the poor and the fourth that the bishops had had at their disposal. The bishops received money from the crown to run the church, and the local landowners and clergy had to see to the poor. The farmers' lifestyle remained unchanged as they had long since lost their lands. In the power struggle between the monarchy, the church and the Icelandic people the monarchy had won.

Literature, Crafts and Church Art

Jón Arason had been an imposing figure, a poet who brought a printing press to Hólar. The beautifully worked chasuble and choir robe that he wore can be seen in the National Museum, with panels depicting scenes from the Gospels and lives of the saints embroidered in silk and gold thread. Though the king expropriated almost all of the church's chalices and ornaments, enough remain to show that the workmanship was often superb. Gothic art replaced Romanesque at the end of the thirteenth century. Fine altar cloths and triptychs were sometimes imported, but Icelanders also carved wood and whalebone crosses and convent seals.

Trade with and travelling to other countries kept Icelanders current with new ideas in thought and fashion, though Icelanders adapted fashions to suit their own taste. When dressed for a party or wedding, the women wore long skirts with a purse hanging low from the belt and a tall, stiff, white headdress with an embroidered headband. As in later centuries, the women wore fine wrought silver or gilded belts. The men wore a tunic and breeches with long stockings, a short cape, and broad–brimmed black hats, sometimes with a feather. In the sixteenth century Icelanders learned to knit and exported socks and mittens.

By 1400 the language spoken in Norway had changed so much that few Norwegians understood Icelandic without studying it.[36] The political importance of the sagas and the market for them therefore died out.[37] The emphasis shifted to adventure tales about trolls and guardian spirits and to recounting events dependent on chance rather than fate, though the old manuscripts continued to be copied and read for enjoyment. The monk Brother Eysteinn wrote the long religious poem *Lilja* in such beautiful Icelandic that it is required reading in school.

The practice of *rímur* singing began in the mid–fourteenth century.[38] Originally dance songs, *rímur* are long series of ballad poems, usually in the Lydian mode but chanted in a way that imparts a special intonation to the Icelandic language. There was, in addition, a style of singing known as *tvísöngur* or duets (organum) where two voices sing at the interval of the perfect fifth or sometimes the fourth, with the parts crossing at times, as had been common in Europe in earlier centuries. Some of these songs are still sung today.

Oddur Gottskálksson translated the New Testament from Latin and German into Icelandic, but before the book could be printed it was necessary to have the king accept it. Theologians at the University of Copenhagen therefore examined it, every one pronouncing it a correct translation even though not one of them understood Icelandic![39] The book was printed in Denmark in 1540, beautifully illuminated, the first surviving book to have been printed in Icelandic.

A Legendary Outlaw: Eyvindur of the Mountains

In the early years of the Icelandic Commonwealth being outlawed meant either a stay in the "woods" or, as with Eiríkur the Red, a three–year exile abroad. In later times an outlaw was no longer someone sentenced to exile but anyone fleeing the law. The original settlers had routes across the interior highlands, but later, at the end of the Commonwealth period and after the climate turned colder in the thirteenth century, there seems to have been less travel across the interior. Therefore those who fled the law could escape into the highlands, or to the West Fjords, and often avoid capture. In the public imagination the numbers of these outcasts grew until Icelanders of the time were convinced there were sizable outlaw communities in the interior and they became part of the folk beliefs. The fact that the uninhabited and inhospitable interior was a dark unknown to most Icelanders and that some outlaws did escape into the mountains fueled the belief. As Thórunn Valdimarsdóttir writes, from the beginning there were two areas: one was inhabited and governed by law, the other, the home of outlaws and trolls, an outlook that, as Jón Hnefill Adalsteinsson reports, lasted at least until 1905.[1]

The most famous outlaw in Icelandic history, after Commonwealth times, was Eyvindur of the Mountains.[2] He was born Eyvindur Jónsson early in the eighteenth century in Árnes County in the southwestern part of Iceland. When he was grown he found work, but he was caught stealing cheese from an old woman's sack. She was so incensed she declared he would be a thief from that time forward. In a day and age when a curse was believed to have power, the woman's words were tantamount to condemning him, but she refused to retract what she had said.

Eyvindur was described at the Öxará Assembly in 1756 as tall and gaunt, long–legged, and with very blonde hair. He was soft–spoken, with a pleasant manner, clever, very capable with his hands, and fleet of foot.

He fled Árnes County in 1746 for the parish of Grunnavík in the West Fjords, in those days an area that was, in parts, barely passable, even on foot. Ships came occasionally, but though the long arm of the church and of the law did reach to the West Fjords, more than one outlaw could find shelter there with few questions asked. Eyvindur came to live with a widow named Halla and her children. Halla was short, sway–backed, dark–haired and of dark complexion with runny eyes and small, thin hands. Like Eyvindur, she chewed tobacco a great deal.

Snorri Björnsson of Húsafell, the same Snorri who wrote the first play in Icelandic, was minister at Adalvík in the West Fjords at this time. There are many folktales about Snorri and outlaws. Legend says that Eyvindur worked for

Snorri for two years and that Snorri married Eyvindur and Halla, even that Snorri taught Eyvindur how to swim and to turn cartwheels. As a minister Snorri was legally bound to advise the authorities, but, as Thórunn Valdimarsdóttir points out, as a lone traveller he could be at the mercy, not only of the weather, but also of the people in the area, and sometimes the less said, the better.

In 1760 Eyvindur and Halla were living in Grunnavík parish without the official authorization then required of the landless and were discovered. They fled, leaving her children, who were rescued by others. They lived a life of out-lawry for twenty years, settling for a while and then fleeing when discovered: to Hveravellir, later to Arnarvatnsheidi near Húsafell (home of Reverend Snorri, who had now returned from his parish in the West Fjords), in 1762 on to Strand County, and in 1764 to Múli County.

One tale recounts how at one point in his wanderings Eyvindur came to a lush, green valley where a man was herding sheep. The herder was friendly, so Eyvindur followed him home. The two tested their strength against each other in an Icelandic arm wrestling match and Eyvindur won. "You can't beat my brother so easily," said the herder. But at this point a girl brought Eyvindur ewe's milk to drink and warned him, "The owner of the farm and the herder's brothers are coming after you." Eyvindur promptly took to his heels and ran towards the mountains, with the others in hot pursuit. When he saw that his pursuers were gaining on him, he stopped running and turned cartwheels and drew ahead. One of the pursuers gave up the chase, but the other two also turned cartwheels and were closing the gap between them. Eyvindur then climbed up the glacier and came to a wide crevasse. There was nothing for it but to leap across the gap. Winded, he lay down on the far side to catch his breath. His two pursuers decided he could not have made it across the crevasse and turned back. That time, at least, Eyvindur escaped capture.

Eyvindur himself said he would not wish his life on anyone. Starvation often plagued the two of them, though he and Halla had an easier time of it when they lived up the Thjórsá River, where there were not only sheep to steal but also swans, geese and trout to catch. Halla was arrested several times, especially when she was pregnant, but later got away or was let go. Halla killed the babies, even one little girl who was over a year old whom they had hoped to keep, because they couldn't escape capture burdened by children. Eyvindur missed the little girl most of all the children.

Eyvindur moved so often and was so famous that the map of Iceland is dotted with places named after him and the ruins of his huts are still to be seen. Those who found him were often impressed with his handiwork. At Hveravellir he used the geothermal spring to cook in. At one place he built his hut so that water ran under the floor and he had only to lift a stone and dip it up. At another place the posse chasing him arrived too late to catch him but found beautifully made household utensils, including a basket so well woven that it was watertight. The posse grabbed what they wanted and burned all the rest.

Eyvindur

Another time Eyvindur dreamed he would be captured so he moved, but unfortunately to a place where he was easily found. He surrendered at once and was bound and taken to Reykjahlíd at Mývatn in the north of Iceland. One Sunday he asked to attend mass. This seemed admirable, so the usual two–man guard was relaxed. The church was a little way from the community. When all were busy praying, he fled. Since it was unthinkable to give chase until the service was over, he had ample time to get away. After the service the men looked for him high and low, riding far in every direction, but they couldn't find him. Later he said he had hidden in the lava near the church. The men just didn't think to look so close. Eyvindur was at Herdabreidalindir after that, where he had freshwater, but it was his worst winter. There were no sheep around to steal, only a few horses.

Then Halla was captured. One Sunday when almost everyone was at church, Eyvindur returned to Mývatn and asked an unsuspecting old woman for food and shoes and news of where Halla was and repaid her kindness by reading scripture for her. He had disappeared again by the time the men had returned from church.

At the end Eyvindur seems to have returned to the West Fjords, where he died and was buried. Halla may also have died there, or else she moved south to a hut in Mosfellssveit, where she said one evening, "How beautiful it would be in the mountains now." The next night she was gone, and the bones of a woman found in the mountains several years later may have been hers.

Snorri's descendants inherited a well–turned wooden ladle and bucket with iron hasps that Eyvindur evidently made on a visit to Húsafell when Snorri was away. These can now be seen in the National Museum of Iceland.

Iceland's History:
The Hardest of Times, 1550–1830

On June 8, 1783, a 25–kilometer long fissure in southern Iceland opened and poured forth the largest flood of lava in historical times anywhere on earth. By the end of the eruption in January 1784 the Laki Crater Row had spewed forth 14.7 km³ (3 1/2 cu. mi.) of lava covering 598 km² (370 sq. mi.) of land. The flow spread from the crater row down two river valleys, the longest flowing down the Skaftá River bed for a full 60 km (34 mi.). Severe earthquakes followed, and the gas and poisonous ash that blanketed Iceland caused a blue haze seen as far away as Africa and Siberia. Even in Alaska the cold summer that followed caused the trees to produce narrower growth rings than usual.[1]

Near the eruption, the grass yellowed, livestock developed footsores, and the sun turned blood red in the haze and imparted no natural warmth. On July 20, with the lava only a little over a mile from the church at Kirkjubaejarklaustur, Jón Steingrímsson preached his famous Fire Sermon: as he preached the lava stopped flowing. Jón himself was convinced that the eruption was punishment for an unrepentant people for sinning, drinking, and using tobacco.[2]

In the annals for Höskuldsstadir in the north the minister recorded strong earthquakes between June 12 and July 21. His church was destroyed and he and his family fled. Sulphur ash turned the grass copper yellow and burned the skin. The sheep died or ran away. The cows died, so starved that they yielded little meat. The minister and others drove their livestock away as there was no hope of hay. And the people themselves, he wrote, fled, "but one goes toward where another flees from." There was worse to follow in the coming winter: frost, storms, the lack of cattle and horses, many farms laid waste, and pack ice which did not melt until June.[3] A second minister in the north also recorded the hardships of the winter of 1784: the horses in particular died and even those who lost least, lost half of what they owned. There was a large number of deaths from illness and hunger, the people reduced to eating anything possible to stave off starvation: hides, shoes, dogs, rotten meat. The main meat was horse, with the bones used for fuel.[4]

The blue haze caused by the ash and gases from the eruption hung over Europe for months but, though Scotland had poor harvests, in Europe it was "more annoying than poisonous."[5] In Iceland, on the other hand, it was catastrophic. The livestock continued to die of fluorine poisoning ingested as they tried to graze. Icelanders lost 50.1% of their cattle, 75.9% of their horses, and 79% of their sheep. The population, already lower than in the years of the Commonwealth, sank from 48,884 in 1783 to 38,363 in 1786, a drop of 23.6%.[6] A strong earthquake struck in 1784, and when smallpox struck in 1786 a further 1500 died. The Danes considered evacuating children, the old, and the poor and resettling them in Denmark, but the plan was abandoned as unrealistic.[7]

New Government and a New Church

After the Reformation in 1550 there were changes in the government as well as in the church. Though at first there were no major changes and the king still could not raise taxes without the consent of the Althing, the power of the king and his governors increased, in part through the expropriation of church lands; these were leased, the renter keeping the income. The sheriffs and lower officials were usually Icelanders, but the top officials, many of whom never even came to Iceland, were foreigners.

There were three judicial levels: the sheriffs' shire courts, the *lögrétta,* or Althing, and the crown. The sheriffs were charged with seeing that the law was upheld. A new penal code in 1564 deprived the church of the right to judge incest and other cases and also imposed physical punishment and the death penalty for various crimes. In 1593 a Superior Court was added and, though it did not meet yearly until the eighteenth century, it meant still less power in the hands of Icelanders. In 1661 the Danish Supreme Court replaced the crown as the highest court of appeal for Icelandic cases.

In 1662 Frederick III (1648–1670) sent the Danish admiral, Governor Hinrik Bjelke, with an armed guard to coerce Icelanders into signing an agreement. Two hundred fifty leading Icelanders met in Kópavogur and reluctantly swore an oath of allegiance to Frederick, acknowledging him as absolute monarch and giving his heir the right of succession. Though until his death in 1683 Bjelke seems to have made good his promise that Icelanders could still have their own laws, the new agreement actually rescinded that right.

In 1683 a governor (*stiftamtmaður*) was set over Iceland, with deputy governors (*amtmenn*) over the districts (*amts*). A bailiff (*landfógeti*) was agent to the king and oversaw the royal treasury in Iceland. The new, foreign officials were Iceland's representatives in the Danish Chancellery and Chamber of Finance.

The *lögrétta* retained judicial power but no longer had any executive authority, and by 1796 the number of judges was reduced to four. The meeting of the *lögrétta,* as then constituted, was unlike the meetings at Thingvellir in the days of the Commonwealth, when people came from all over to talk, arrange marriages, and enjoy themselves, as well as to settle problems. In its new form the Althing met for only three or four days at the end of June, attended only by the few necessary officials. In 1798 it was moved to Reykjavík, and in 1800, with the agreement of both the king and the Icelandic elite, it was disbanded and replaced by a superior court.

With its lands expropriated, the monasteries abolished, and the jurisdiction of its courts curtailed, the church lost both the income and power that it had had before the Reformation. It was placed under the Danish Chancellery, with the governor of Iceland supervising church affairs. The number of churches and prayerhouses dropped from the 300 or so of the Middle Ages to 193 in 1660 and still fewer later.[8] The church produced few real leaders, though Brynjólfur Sveinsson (1639–1674) and Jón Vídalín (1698–1720) were exceptions. Brynjólfur had a new wooden church built at Skálholt (1650–1651), an imposing building even though it was a fourth the size of the old medieval church, which had burned.

The seventeenth century brought a wave of belief in witchcraft and sorcery, influenced by foreign ideas. In Iceland, however, since women were confined to the home and were an important part of the workforce, they were not looked on as threatening, nor was the belief in sorcery supported by the church in Iceland. Therefore it was nearly always men and not women who were charged as sorcerers and killed; of the 120 cases, only 10 were women, and of the 25 who were convicted and killed between 1625 and 1685 there were only 2 women.[9]

The eighteenth century also brought changes in the church. When the episcopal seat was moved from Skálholt to Reykjavík in 1785 after the earthquake that followed the Laki eruption, the school was also relocated in Reykjavík. In 1801 the see at Hólar in the north was abolished, as well as the school.

The Trade Monopoly

Under the mercantile system foreign trade was to be carried out principally by monopolies; the English, for example, set up the Hudson's Bay Company. Accordingly, in 1602 the Danish king imposed a trade monopoly on Iceland. Only Danish subjects had the right to trade and only in designated ports. The king leased the right to trade, at first to individuals in three cities and then, from 1619–1787, only to Copenhagen trading companies. The monopoly placed Iceland in a straitjacket of low prices for exports and high prices for imports. The profit from this trade enriched the royal treasury and helped build the city of Copenhagen. Though the merchants were required to comply with Icelandic law—and in general they did—the monopoly meant that Iceland was reduced to the status of exploited colony. The conservative Icelandic gentry, afraid of disrupting the system by any redistribution of wealth and already short farm labor and tenants, further contributed to the problem by refusing to release workers for fishing during seasons when they were needed on the farm.[10] The weather and other natural disasters added to the burden the Icelandic people had to bear in order to survive, but the most crippling factor was the terms of the trade monopoly. The result was stability at the price of economic stagnation.[11]

Before 1602 Germans from Hamburg controlled the Icelandic trade, sending an average of 17 ships per year to Iceland.[12] The Danish king squeezed out the Hamburg merchants by seizing their ships in 1574 and by leasing sole permits to others.

The Danish monopoly took different forms in different years. In 1620 a single company traded with Iceland, the Faroes and Finnmark, with the prices set in Copenhagen. The company paid Icelanders a higher price for knit goods than it received and charged less for grain, but it coined money from the major export, fish, which it bought for a low price and sold high.

In 1684 Iceland was divided into small trade areas and the ports of trade auctioned off. Imports were higher priced than before while the exports remained priced the same or lower. On pain of loss of property or incarceration, Icelanders were forbidden to trade outside their own area; they had to accept the prices offered. From 1742–1757 the Chandlers' Guild leased the Icelandic trade rights. The grain they brought was so moldy and full of weevils that Skúli Magnússon, then sheriff, complained in his report to the Danish authorities.

The General Trading Company took over the Icelandic trade from 1764–1774 and began processing salted fish using the *terre neuve* method of the French in Newfoundland, with the cod spread flat before drying and salting. The fish not only kept better but brought a higher price. The terms of trade were still worse than before, but this time Icelanders spoke up and complained to the king's officials about their treatment at the hands of the merchants. The company lost money but expanded Danish trade, selling salted fish or bacalao in southern Europe. The crown took over the General Trading Company from 1774–1787. The company was involved in fishing, not just trading, and provided some risk capital to help develop the Icelandic economy.[13] After 1776 Iceland profited from the rise in fish prices but, with the end of the American Revolution, fishing resumed off the North American coast and the boom came to an end. Since trade was restricted to Danish subjects, the British and French were denied permission to land in Iceland and therefore crossed the Atlantic to find the all–important cod. The French in Canada were exporting 10,000–20,000 metric tons of cod yearly, and the British an increasing amount that reached 39,766 metric tons in 1789. Meanwhile, for most of the eighteenth century, Icelanders exported an average of only 1000–1500 tons per annum.[14] In 1783, the year of the Laki volcanic eruption, the General Trading Company's fixed prices for imports had increased, the price for rye rose 43%, the price for stockfish fell 26%, and the Danish merchants contributed to the famine by exporting more food from Iceland than they brought with them.[15]

The trading companies were obligated to bring goods to Iceland. Since European demand and market prices fluctuated, however, the companies tried to ensure a profit by bringing high–priced goods such as spirits, expensive clothes, and tobacco, rather than staples, and the grain they did bring was often of poor quality.[16] Small quantities of sugar and syrup had been imported, starting in the fifteenth century; tobacco was imported in the form of snuff so that it could be easily used while riding or fishing; and coffee was imported from about 1772, though at first used only for special occasions.[17]

The merchants were so eager for fish that often they would not accept money in payment. Barter values were based on the cow equivalent, where one cow equalled 6 ewes or 120 ells of cloth or 240 fish. In the south and west, for example, one barrel of grain was valued at 80 fish. The result of this system was that there was almost no inflation in Iceland for seven hundred years. In 1776 a new price list was imposed that quoted prices in Danish rixdollars.[18]

The most important export was fish. In the seventeenth century fish, mostly dried, constituted over 70% of the total value of exports, from 1743–1746 one third of the value, with salted meat making up another third, and in the late eighteenth century over 50% of the total value of exports.[19] The south and west of Iceland provided most of the fish and therefore profit for the trading companies. Wool and knitted goods were also exported, along with fish liver oil, sulphur, and falcons (about 150 annually, more after 1763).[20]

Since their profit came from selling fish and meat, the merchants pushed Icelanders to provide more meat and fish for sale. Even in times of starvation the merchants restricted credit and demanded fish and meat in exchange for imports, thus exacerbating the food shortage. The country squires, on the other hand, did not see any gain in releasing laborers for year–round fishing. With the high death rate from starvation and disease, there was a shortage of labor. The size of the usual fishing boats had been reduced from ten to twelve oars in the seventeenth century to six oars or fewer in the eighteenth century. The cold weather meant that the cod catches slumped drastically; the average winter catch per person in the south dropped from 500 cod in the seventeenth century to 300 after the mid–eighteenth century. The workers and tenant farmers were not in a position to change the system and for much of the time were engaged in simply trying to stay alive. There was no leeway for experimentation and innovation. The lack of trees meant no timber for boats. Generally, only landowners operated the fishing boats; the laborers were sent to the fishing stations only during the winter, and the landowner took the catch. The building of towns was forbidden and the few trading centers were closed during the winter. The "vigorous foreign trade" that was needed to provide timber and other necessities so as to develop the fisheries simply did not exist.[21]

The "Turkish" Raids

Iceland was virtually defenseless against foreign invaders. The British pirates who attacked the Westman Islands in 1614 were hanged when they returned to England, though Icelanders did kill the thirty Spaniards who were shipwrecked in the West Fjords in 1615, the last battle fought by Icelanders.[22]

Far worse was the raid in 1627 by pirates from Algiers, known as Turks in Iceland as they were subjects of the Turkish sultan. They came in five ships, two of which marauded and kidnapped people in Grindavík in the south; two went to the East Fjords where they killed several and captured over a hundred people, and the fifth went to the Westman Islands, where they took over 240 people, killed many, and burned and pillaged. The ships rendezvoused off of Bessastaðir, where one ship ran aground. Incredibly, during the full twenty–four hours of fine weather that it took to free the ship the Danes made no move to save the Icelandic captives who were aboard.[23]

The captives, about 380 in number, were sold into slavery in Algiers, though many were taken to other areas, including the Near East. Over the years some wrote home to ask that money be sent to buy their freedom. A tax was imposed on farm assets and the fish catch, and money was collected in Denmark, enough to buy the freedom of at least 37. These arrived in Copenhagen late in the summer of 1636 and sailed home the following summer.

One of those freed was a woman named Gudrídur. She had been kidnapped in the Westman Islands with her daughter. When the opportunity came to be able to return to Iceland there was only one berth still available; she accepted the chance to return but had to leave her twelve–year–old daughter behind. The returnees were taken first to Copenhagen, where the young ministerial student Hallgrímur Pétursson (1614–1674) had been appointed to reindoctrinate these former Moslem slaves into Christianity. Despite the fact that Gudrídur was still legally married to her husband in the Westman Islands, Hallgrímur got her pregnant. The two were shipped home to Iceland in punishment as at that time fornication was a serious crime. Meanwhile, it became known that Gudrídur's husband had drowned; Hallgrímur was therefore no longer guilty of fornication and was allowed to practice as a minister. Gudrídur, known rather disrespectfully as Turkish–Gudda, gave birth to a son and she and Hallgrímur married, but their life together was not an easy one.[24] Icelanders still deeply respect Hallgrímur Pétursson for his poetry and especially for his *Passion Psalms*. The large neo–Gothic church in Reykjavík is dedicated to him.

Hardships

The climate turned colder about 1500 and in winter pack ice quite often encroached on the land. Drift ice drove the cod south to warmer water and a greater number of fishermen drowned when the weather was rougher than usual. Farms were abandoned when conditions were too severe, especially in the north and east, but the people who moved strained the meager resources of the areas where they sought shelter. In 1732, for instance, many even left Snaefellsnes Peninsula, the site of one of the best fishing areas. Accompanying the unusually harsh weather in 1756–1758, the crime rate rose and peaked in 1756.[25]

Hekla erupted several times, especially in 1693 and again in 1766–1768, killing livestock and fish in the streams.[26] But the worst was the Laki eruption in 1783–1784, followed by a long–lasting blue haze in the air and an earthquake, estimated as 7.5 on the Richter scale, that destroyed several hundred farms.[27]

Living conditions for most remained difficult. The family or household consisting of parents, children and workers, was the basic unit of Icelandic society and the farm the basic unit of production. Male workers were paid the value of 60–120 ells of cloth and the farmer contributed food and clothes to the value of an additional 600 ells or so. Women workers earned room and board and some clothes. Upkeep for children cost 120–180 ells.[28]

Milk and milk products provided an estimated 60% of the caloric intake before the 1780s, and grain not more than 5%. Though beri–beri (the lack of thiamine or vitamin B) was not a problem, scurvy (the lack of vitamin C) was common in the lean years, together with mumps, colic, and dysentery. In bad years the death of livestock meant a loss both of food and of milk, the main source of vitamin C. In 1803 17.7% of deaths were attributable to hunger, 4.3% to scurvy.[29]

Smallpox struck in various years during the sixteenth and seventeenth centuries. Slightly over one fourth of the nation died in the epidemic of 1707–1709 and when the disease struck again in 1786, another 1500 died.[30] In some years, especially 1755–1760 and 1780–1785, the number of deaths was greater than the number of births.[31] The male death rate was higher than the rate for females, and between 1770 and 1800 the annual infant death rate averaged 37%.[32] The height of males dropped from the average of 172 cm (5 ft. 8 in.) in the year 1000 to 167 cm (5 ft. 5 in.) between 1600 and 1750.[33] The hardships meant low productivity. Land was needed as the basis for marriage, but the landowners, themselves facing a dwindling labor supply, limited the opportunity for others to acquire land. One percent of the heads of households owned 24% of the land.[34] Limited access to land meant a low marriage rate and therefore a low fertility rate,[35] but the principal checks to population growth were the high death rate from disease and the high infant death rate. Of the children born between 1772 and 1781 only 53.5% were still alive at the age of confirmation.[36] During the time of the Commonwealth mothers nursed their babies for two or more years and the infant death rate was much lower. By the mid–eighteenth century very few mothers nursed their babies for any length of time[37] and nineteen of every twenty farmers were renters who were often near starvation and "thanked God for infant deaths."[38]

Agricultural methods had not really changed since the Middle Ages: there were no roads or wagons, packhorses were used for transport, and manure was often used for fuel rather than fertilizer as the woods had been cut down.[39] In the 1760s and '70s a large number of sheep had to be killed to control an outbreak of scab brought by imported breeding stock. Because raising livestock was more profitable, Icelanders stopped raising grain[40] and became dependent on imported grain. The bishops and the gentry, who had studied and lived in Denmark, followed Danish eating habits (which included, among other things, home–ground and therefore rather gritty barley meal), with the result that they suffered from caries and other dental problems.[41] Potatoes were first raised in an area in Saudlauksdalur Valley in the West Fjords and then at Bessastadir in 1758; they became a staple of the Icelandic diet, together with cabbage.

Though Iceland was surrounded by one of the world's richest fishing grounds, the technology used was little adapted to develop the fisheries. Although there were some decked boats in the Breidafjord and West Fjord areas, most were open rowboats, usually manned by six rowers and a coxswain or foreman and equipped with a removable mast and small sail. Both oarsmen and foremen were sometimes women. There were few harbors suitable for decked ships and usually only a small jetty for landing a rowboat, if that, as most of the boats were launched from shore directly through the surf. The Danes tried to introduce decked vessels in 1776–1787, but they had trouble getting enough Icelanders to work aboard them.[42] Trawl lines up to 100 meters long were used, but usually with only one hook.[43] In the northwest in the sixteenth century landowners had allowed two or three hooks, taking the fish caught on one hook and letting the fishermen keep any others, but court decisions in 1567–1616 forbade the use of more than one hook. The small open boats could sail only a short distance to find fish, as spending the night at sea was virtually out of the question. Furthermore, fishing was only permitted off the coast owned or rented by the farmer.[44] As the cod wintered in the warmer waters off the southwest coast and winter was the only time the big landowners would spare the laborers, the main fishing areas were in the southwest. The demoralizing effect of hunger and low fish prices, the conservatism of the large landowners, and the lack of risk capital for development worked to preserve the status quo—in fact, even resulted in a decline in the level of technology.[45]

Efforts to Help Iceland

The eighteenth century, the Age of Reason, brought an increased interest throughout Europe in the natural sciences. There was also a genuine desire in Denmark to understand and improve the Icelandic situation. Accordingly, two men, Árni Magnússon and Páll Vídalín, were commissioned to census Iceland and to propose changes. Their census of 1703 showed a population of 50,358. The census figures also revealed the extent of the hardships: only 25% of those 20–39 years old were married; there were more women than men, partly because infant deaths were higher for boys; and 15.5% of the people were paupers.[46] The Land Register compiled between 1703 and 1714 listed the landholdings, giving the details of ownership and the number of sheep and cattle. The crown owned 16.3% and the church 31.4% of the land; about one–fourth was owned by the richest elite. Most commonly only four people lived on each farm.[47]

In 1741–1745 the Dane Ludvik Harboe was sent with an Icelander to research the state of religion and education. On their recommendation ministers were required to see that all children were taught to read; as a result, virtually all Icelanders were and continued to be literate into the twentieth century.

The three–man Land Commission (1770–1771) was set up to research the economic situation and to propose improvements. Most of the 1% of the nation surveyed complained about the trading companies but were afraid of change and wanted, instead, to go back to the use of regional trading areas.[48] The commission recommended limited free trade, with ten foreign merchants settling in Iceland, and the development of towns in order to keep the profits in Iceland.[49] Their recommendation led to the introduction of the postal service in 1776. A further recommendation to level and enclose the home fields, though not carried out until much later, was the first real suggestion to improve agriculture.[50]

The Danish authorities made several attempts to send aid following the Laki eruption, but communications were slow and they had no real grasp of the situation; the tremendous loss of livestock meant a lack of horses to transport goods and a lack of cattle to purchase. The officials in Iceland were afraid to prohibit the exportation of food without express permission from Copenhagen.

However, 5300 barrels of rye were sent in the early autumn of 1784 and extra cargoes of timber the following year.[51] A second Land Commission in 1784 concluded that the trade monopoly should be ended. The funds raised to help Icelanders after the Laki eruption arrived too late to help the victims directly; the money was used in part to map Iceland and the rest, together with other funds, to build a school in the 1840s.

Several men also came from Britain to explore the Icelandic countryside. The most famous was the botanist and explorer Sir Joseph Banks in 1772.[52] He and John Thomas Stanley, who led his own expedition in 1789, both felt Icelanders were very much the equal of Europeans, well bred and well informed. Both men came with artists who painted an invaluable record of the people and of the rugged, volcanic landscape. Banks developed a deep love of Iceland and a deep concern for the plight of the people, whom he later tried to assist by sending merchants to trade and by coaxing the British government to annex Iceland.

Skúli Magnússon, Bailiff

Trained in Denmark, Skúli Magnússon (1711–1794) subscribed to the progressive ideas held by many Danes of the time rather than to the conservatism of the Icelandic gentry. Skúli wanted to improve the standard of living through free trade, increased fishing, the development of a wool industry, and the building of towns. He felt that rather than forbid merchants to overwinter, some should be allowed to stay to build up the ports of trade. An able, energetic and determined man, in 1749 he became the first Icelander to be appointed bailiff.

With others as shareholders and with the support of monies from the king, Skúli founded a company that set up several workshops in and near Reykjavík in the 1750s to spin and weave wool, tan hides, and manufacture fishing lines. Skúli introduced the spinning wheel and the loom to use in the workshops. The company also bought two decked fishing vessels, in all providing employment for about one hundred workers.

Reykjavík at that time was only a tiny collection of buildings on the narrow strip of land between the shore and the Pond. Under Skúli's urging, a stone building was built for a jail so that prisoners would no longer have to be sent to Copenhagen, a stone church was built, and a fine stone building was erected on the island of Vídey to be the official residence.

For many reasons, the workshops declined and finally closed in 1802–1803. The difficulties included opposition on the part of the merchants and the conservative gentry. The supervisors were themselves craftsmen, not managers. The rams imported for breeding to improve the wool clip brought disease and the ensuing epidemic caused a shortage of wool and hides. Above all, the size of the enterprise was too large for the market and required a level of technical expertise the people simply did not have. On the other hand, Skúli, known as the Father of Reykjavík, exposed Icelanders to a new and different outlook and provided the impetus for developing Reykjavík, even though in 1801 the town's population still numbered only 307.[53]

The Free Trade Charter

To relieve the restrictions inherent in the trade monopoly and to save the Danish government money, a new Free Trade Charter went into effect at the end of 1787. However, "free" was a relative term: only Danish merchants could trade with Icelanders. With the market for Icelandic fish largely outside of Denmark, the Danes became expensive middlemen. Iceland was divided into six trading areas, each with a trading center. The Danish merchants usually came in March through June and left in August or September. The factors who supervised the trade, however, were often Icelandic.[54]

During the Napoleonic Wars (1807–1815) Denmark sided with France. The British navy captured Danish ships, and Iceland became seriously short of supplies. The British constrained the Danish governor, Count Fr. Chr. Trampe, into signing an agreement allowing ships with British permits to trade with Iceland during the war. The British established a consulate and controlled the Icelandic trade from 1807 on. This trade was generally profitable for both the British and Icelanders.[55]

Sir Joseph Banks and others tried to persuade the British government to annex Iceland, but the British cabinet rejected the proposal. With her navy in control of the Atlantic, Britain held the advantage without the expense of manning another garrison or of developing Icelandic resources.[56]

At the end of the Napoleonic Wars Denmark, considered too weak to be a threat, was allowed to keep Iceland, the Faroes, and Greenland. Denmark needed the Icelandic trade to compete with the English and the Dutch. Since the British were no longer making a profit, principally because there was little market for Icelandic fish products in Britain, their trade with Iceland came to an end in 1818.[57]

Meanwhile, Magnús Stephensen had been appointed chief justice of the Superior Court in 1801. The most influential man in Iceland, he controlled the only printing presses in the country. Though conservative, he stood for free trade throughout Iceland and for letting foreign merchants overwinter. After the war he went to Denmark to discuss the issue, but the Danes refused to authorize any changes as they needed the trade with Iceland. In 1816, however, the merchants could sail directly to foreign ports, bypassing Denmark.

After 1800 the king's and the bishop's lands were sold at one–sixth their value, increasing the number of independent farmers and bettering the outlook for the nineteenth century.[58]

Jörundur the Dog Days King

In 1808 the Englishman Thomas Gilpin arrived in Iceland with a letter of marque allowing him to appropriate assets held by the Danish crown. He thereupon appropriated the box containing the king's treasury as well as church and private funds, claiming he was returning to Icelanders that which was theirs. The British Admiralty Court handed down a judgment against him, however, saying that the letter of marque had no validity on land and certainly was not a permit to steal church property. The monies were finally returned in 1812.[59]

Acting on Sir Joseph Banks' desire to help Iceland, the soap maker Samuel Phelps sent a ship in January 1809, to buy tallow and fats. The Dane Jürgen Jürgensen accompanied the ship's crew as interpreter. The Icelandic officials were forced to allow the British to trade, but their mission was unsuccessful as the ship had come in winter rather than during the summer trading season. The following summer Phelps himself came and arrested the governor, Count Trampe, while Jürgensen took over running the country they had thus captured.

On June 26 Jürgensen proclaimed Iceland free of Danish rule and on July 12 awarded himself the title of Protector. The bewildered and terrified citizens of Reykjavík assumed Jürgensen had the backing of the British government. Genuinely concerned about Icelandic conditions, Jürgensen set out to travel over the country to make improvements, promising a supply of grain, freedom of trade, and schools. In a third proclamation he went far beyond the liberalism of the times by promising universal male suffrage, even for those who owned no land.

Born in Denmark in 1780, Jürgensen was a soldier of fortune who sailed the South Seas as a whaler and explorer, spied for the British during the Napoleonic Wars, and served in the British navy for twelve years. He was on friendly terms with Sir Joseph Banks and other great men of the time. While he was Protector of Iceland, Jürgensen held a ball in the Old Club in Reykjavík. As he was dancing with his mistress her wig caught on the chandelier, so that, as he whirled her away, leaving her wig hanging from the chandelier, it became obvious to all that she was actually completely bald! Jürgensen himself even drew a sketch to commemorate the event.[60]

Jürgensen was a visionary whose grand experiment for Iceland was charitable but hardly realistic. When the British captain Alexander Jones arrived later the same summer, Jürgensen was "deposed." Jones, the Stephensen brothers and Phelps came to an agreement on August 22 stating that Denmark owned Iceland but that Count Trampe should be replaced as governor, and that the British had the right to trade. Jürgensen was returned to Britain as a prisoner, his experiment terminated.[61]

In England Jürgensen ran up gambling debts and was in and out of debtors' prison. In the end, the British government deported him to Tasmania with the proviso that he never return to Britain. In Australia he became something of a hero, but after his wife's death he turned increasingly to drink and gambling and died in 1841.[62]

Jürgensen's Icelandic experiment during the dog days of summer had little effect, though it did show Icelanders that Danish rule was not necessarily inevitable. He has been known since to Icelanders as Jörundur, the Dog Days King.

More Than Survival: Literature

Despite all the hardships, Icelanders of the time still had a rich cultural life. Artistic ability found an outlet in woodcarving and silverwork. The people met at set times once or twice a winter to hold a *vikivaka*, when they sang, chanted *rímur*, and played word games. There are about 900 extant *rímur* or chanted ballads composed after 1600 by about 330 poets.[63]

Though Roman Catholic books and relics were destroyed at the time of the Reformation, the church continued to play a leading role in producing books and recording events. The annals from the seventeenth and eighteenth centuries are particularly detailed. Gudbrandur Thorláksson, bishop at Hólar (1571–1627), by insisting that the Bible and hymns be in Icelandic and not Danish, did much to strengthen the use of the Icelandic language. He and his assistants translated and printed the Bible in Icelandic in 1584. About 1600 the bishop also drew a new and more accurate map of Iceland. In the beginning printing was a church monopoly and the church's presses turned out Lutheran hymns and homilies as well as the *Passion Psalms* of Hallgrímur Pétursson.

The Age of Reason brought a quickened interest throughout Europe in natural history and the past. The rector at Hólar, Arngrímur Jónsson, wrote in Latin in 1593 to correct foreign misconceptions about Iceland; Hekla, he said, was not the entrance to hell and Iceland no nearer the devil than any other nation.[64] Jón Ólafsson's account of his journey to India in 1623–1624 continues to be interesting reading.

Rev. Snorri Björnsson of Húsafell (1710–1803), the same minister who was reported to have power against sorcerers, wrote the first play in Icelandic, a short *Komaedia*.

Bishop Brynjólfur Sveinsson and others collected the old manuscripts and had them copied, but the most famous of these individuals was Árni Magnússon (1663–1730). An assiduous collector, he had the manuscripts shipped to Copenhagen, where he was professor of history. Unfortunately, the fire that destroyed much of Copenhagen in 1728 also destroyed a great number of his books.

When the Dane Rasmus Christian Rask visited Iceland in 1813–1815, he discovered that there was no teaching in Icelandic at the school at Bessastadir and that Icelanders looked on Icelandic as a dead language! He published an Icelandic grammar and founded the Icelandic Literary Society to preserve the language.[65] The society is still very active. Despite the hardships, the people persevered and both they and the Icelandic language survived.

The Family: Sausage–Making

By November the winter winds had come. The snow of the preceding two days was fast disappearing under the onslaught of driving rain and strong winds that whipped through the streets, pounded the windows, and strained to lift the corrugated roofing off the houses. My car rocked in the gusts as Sigga and I drove to Gudrún's house. Once we got there we grabbed the food we had brought and dashed into the house. On such a day and throughout all of Iceland's history the warmth and shelter of a house is more than comforting; it is a necessity.

Sigga's mother, Gudrún, greeted us warmly but with an air of no–nonsense practicality. At 75 she is gray–haired and a bit bony, but still very active. She is known for having second sight, but for all her ability to "dream true" and to foretell the future, she also keeps up with the news and, like most Icelanders, frequently makes wry comments about the idiocies of politics and politicians.

"Ghastly weather," we commented as we hung up our wraps in the small hall. "Terrible," Gudrún agreed.

Gudrún lives in a *timburhús*, one of the old frame houses that gives charm to the center of Reykjavík. Though the house is small, its interior walls of painted wood give it a homey feeling often lacking in today's concrete homes and apartment buildings. The house had been modernized, the old sod insulation replaced with plastic foam, bathrooms added, and the old hearth in the kitchen long since replaced with modern fixtures. After hanging up our wraps, we walked through the dining room on our right to the kitchen in back. With a sitting room on the first floor to the left of the entrance hall, a bathroom off the kitchen, four bedrooms upstairs, and a full basement it was easy to see that, despite the small size, there had been plenty of room for Gudrún and Gudmundur to raise their two sons and two daughters.

Like all buildings in Reykjavík and many elsewhere as well, Gudrún's house is heated by geothermal heat, the hot water delivered by the public utility. The hot water pipes and valves are in a corner of the laundry room, taking up almost no space. They provide both heat, via the radiators in the separate rooms, and hot water for washing and bathing.

Gudrún's mother Ingibjörg, now 93, lives with her daughter but must be helped up and down the stairs. Sigga stays in almost daily touch with her mother and comes for a cup of coffee as often as she can, loving to sit in the warmth of her mother's kitchen and talk to her grandmother.

Today was the day the family had decided to make sausage. A vital task when Ingibjörg and Gudrún were young, sausage–making has become a rite that many families continue to carry out at home, even though it is possible to buy the sausages ready–made. In fact, Sigga and I have just come from the supermarket where we bought "kits" with the right amount of the ingredients to make the two kinds of traditional sausage, black pudding and liver sausage.

Sausage–Making

We are all dressed in old clothes as this is not the neatest of jobs, and we have shoes or slippers on our feet.

Gudrún set out two large pots in which she and Sigga mixed the ingredients we had brought. One pot contained the blood, water, oatmeal, rye flour, lamb suet, and salt for black pudding, the other ground liver and kidneys, milk, oatmeal, rye and wheat flour, lamb suet, salt and sugar for liver sausage. Though both are good, the liver sausage, in my opinion, is delicious.

"We used to put raisins in some of the liver sausages as a treat for the children," Gudrún informed me. "It wasn't so easy to get raisins then."

"How good they were!" Sigga remembered.

As Sigga and her mother mixed the ingredients I sat at the table and started to sew small sacks from the sheep's stomachs. Gudrún gave me a large needle and a spool of white thread, the kind used to stitch up a turkey after stuffing it, and with whipstitches I began to sew each of the stomach patches into a small pocket. Ingibjörg sewed for a while, too, showing me how to keep the stitches even. "Just so long as the stitches are close enough together to keep the stuffing from leaking out." Sigga was patient with my having to learn.

Once the ingredients were mixed, Gudrún and Sigga joined us at the table and we all stuffed the sacks and sewed them up, piercing each one several times with the needle so they wouldn't burst when boiled. With the wind still lashing rain at the window as we worked, we talked about various things to pass the time: the family news, the weather, the latest gossip, the rising cost of living. We fell silent and Ingibjörg fell asleep in her chair.

"How's your book coming?" Sigga broke the silence. "Are you going to tell them about Icelandic sausage–making?"

"Why not? Umm, what else do you want them to know about?"

"Forget all the pizzas everybody's eating today, and American–style hamburgers." Gudrún was very definite. "I raised my children mostly on haddock and potatoes, and they were strong and healthy."

"And you still raise potatoes in the backyard along with flowers and I feed my family the same today," Sigga added, "but we had roast lamb sometimes, too, and of course *svið*." *Svið*, sheep's heads with the wool singed off, are a common Icelandic dish.

"The cheeks and lips are very tender, but I have to admit I can't face the eyes."

"The eyes are the best part." This from Ingibjörg, who had awakened and went back to helping us stuff and sew the sausages. "When I was young we caught birds, gulls and murres, on the cliffs at nesting time, and skinned and ate them. There's not so much of that now."

"And cooked with wild birds' eggs," Gudrún added, "duck eggs, plover eggs. Some people in the countryside still do, but not here in the city."

"There are murres' eggs for sale in the supermarkets in the summer, though," I added. They are large and speckled, tapering at one end. "The yolk is rich, but personally I find the white too strong."

"Much more variety of fruits and vegetables now." Sigga, the nurse, is ever mindful of nutrition. "We are healthier now we have easier access to vegetables all year, fresh and frozen."

"There's so much imported now from Asia that I don't really know what all those fruits and vegetables are, let alone how to eat them," Gudrún observed.

"They're a huge change, all right," I agreed, before adding after a moment, "Other people want to know what kind of a day you have." "Day?" All three looked at me questioningly. "Yes. For instance, what you usually have for breakfast."

"Coffee," Gudrún replied. "Buttered rye bread with cheese and of course coffee," Sigga said, "but often breakfast cereals." "And coffee again in midmorning with a sweet roll or cruller," Gudrún added.

"I won't forget that Gunnar and many other businessmen go swimming in the hot pools before they go to work."

"Office workers always have coffee, usually in the company canteen." Sigga, who has traveled abroad more than her mother, has understood the need to explain. "A hot lunch in the hospital and usually at home. Soup and dark bread, or fish and boiled potatoes. Or something similar in the company canteen, or a light lunch of soup and a sandwich or pickled herring. Maybe *súrmjólk*—sour milk, or *skyr*—Icelandic yogurt. Usually a cold supper, in the hospital, too, often with dark bread, *súrmjólk*, cold cuts and cheese. We have supper, sometimes dinner, at 7:00 or so, sometimes as late as 8:00," Sigga added.

"It's time for our midafternoon coffee," Ingibjörg observed. Gudrún and Sigga put the sausages in the pots to boil and we all cleaned up the table before enjoying our coffee. Gudrún produced delicious homemade crullers. Sweets in Iceland, except as served at parties, are usually eaten with coffee between meals rather than as dessert and often, again with coffee, before going to bed at night. The women each tucked a lump of sugar in one cheek before sipping their coffee, which is sweetened as it passes over the sugar.

Dinner that night became a kind of thanksgiving. The wind had let up, and Ingibjörg had had a nap while the rest of us finished boiling the sausages and cleaning up. Gudrún's husband, Gudmundur, returned home and Sigga's husband, Gunnar, joined us shortly afterwards, bringing Gummi, their youngest, with him. We sat at table, all happily chatting, enjoying the sausage we had made along with boiled potatoes and Icelandic rutabagas. Gummi and some of the others drank coke with the meal, and all the adults celebrated with schnapps.

"*Skál!*" Gudmundur lifted his glass and we all joined in the toast: "*Skál! Cheers!*"

Winter –
Independence and
New Beginnings

The Family: Christmas Eve

The excitement of Christmas was building though it was still several weeks before Christmas Eve. The chorus had been practicing for some time for its annual advent concert and the country was already inundated with advertisements for all the new books that had been published.

"Advent lights," a late twentieth century custom, shone in the windows of most homes. First lit on Advent, the fourth Sunday before Christmas, the light is a seven–branched electric candlestick. Ever since an Icelandic businessman named Gunnar Ásgeirsson first imported these lights from Sweden, Icelanders have increasingly set them in their windows to celebrate the Christmas season.

The lights were welcome as the worst of the darkness had come, increasing daily until the winter solstice on December 21. The sun, never really high in the sky this far north, only rises a short way above the horizon in the dead of winter; on the solstice the sun is up for only a little over four hours in Reykjavik, though sunrise and sunset, especially on a clear day, may extend the light for another two hours or so. The crack of dawn comes in mid–morning, with the sun just coming over the Blue Mountains near Reykjavík.

The darkness is not something that most Icelanders like and therefore is often a topic of conversation, though everyone accepts it philosophically. However, the worst only lasts for about two months and, though the darkness bothers some more than others, it never stops Icelanders from staying active. The more critical factor is how often the sky is overcast and not the actual day length.

"Christmas is light in the darkness," Gunnar observed and continued to swim in the open–air hot water pool before he went to work in the morning. Sitting in the hot pool and swimming in the geothermal water imparts a wonderful feeling, but when the thermometer drops too far below freezing and my nose and the top of my head feel too close to freezing I have to give up.

There is no school on December 1, the day when, in 1918, Iceland first became a sovereign state, though at that time still remaining in a personal union with the Danish king.

In preparation for the coming Christmas, Sigga, like all Icelandic women, had been busy cleaning every nook and cranny in her home. When she and her friends, former schoolmates, came to her house for their regular sewing club meeting, they talked about Christmas baking, the new books for sale, and what to get for Christmas presents.

The emphasis on baking cakes and cookies came later to Iceland than elsewhere, having only begun about 1920 when kitchen ovens and imported flour and baking powder became common. Sigga's family, like many others, took up the northern tradition of making *laufabrauð* or lace bread, a very thin sautéed "bread" incised with intricate lacy designs. Common at least by 1800, lace bread is now available commercially but is still often homemade. Sigga shares her recipe with the sewing club, enough for 20 "slices," using an average size frying pan:

Heat to boiling 4 1/2 dl (1 pint) of milk and stir in 40 g (1 1/2 oz.) of butter and 25 g (less than an oz.) of sugar.
Mix with 500 g (4 cups) of flour and knead well.
Roll a small amount until very thin and cut in a circle using the bottom of the frying pan or a plate as a template. With a knife incise lines and cut and fold back small wedges to make an interesting, lacelike pattern.
Fry very lightly in oil (or butter) on both sides.

Giving presents in Iceland began in the early nineteenth century with the gift of a candle, at least to the children, a prize in a day of homemade tallow candles and no electric light. By the late nineteenth century more people gave presents at Christmas than before, often a deck of cards for playing card games on Christmas Day and on Boxing Day, but never on Christmas Eve for fear of turning up a card that might bring bad luck. Probably because of the higher level of income after World War II the custom of giving gifts at Christmas became widespread, in some cases to the point of extravagance.

The custom of sending Christmas cards began in Iceland at the turn of the twentieth century, though it had been known in England since 1843 after the use of postage stamps began.

Iceland does not have one Santa Claus but rather thirteen mischievous and rather ugly imps known as *jólasveinar*, "Yule swains" or Christmas elves or trolls in English. Originally nine in number, they were the ugly offspring of the troll Grýla and her mate Leppalúdi and were used to frighten children into behaving. Now numbering thirteen, they come down from the mountains—in Reykjavik, from Mt. Esja—one each day until Christmas Eve, and return, one each day, beginning on Christmas Day and continuing through January 6. Their commonest names, rendered into English, are: Sheep–Cot Clod, Gully Gawk, Shorty, Spoon Licker, Pot Scraper, Bowl Licker, Hem Blower, Skyr Gobbler (named for the Icelandic milk product made with rennet), Sausage Swiper, Window Peeper, Door Sniffer, Meat Hook, and Candle Beggar. These imps appear at the National Museum, each on the appropriate day, looking suitably ugly and dressed largely in woolen clothes made from the undyed browns, creamy white, and black of native Icelandic wool. On the other hand, they also appear in the shopping malls and elsewhere as thirteen thin and spritely Santas dressed in red.

On the days that these imps come down from the mountains it has become a twentieth century custom, borrowed from Germany, for the children to set out a shoe and hope for something nice from these Christmas elves. The women at Sigga's Sewing Club exchanged ideas on how to find something different and inexpensive for each of the thirteen days.

Meanwhile Gunnar and all the employees of his firm had been planning their annual Christmas office party. Drinking *glögg*, Christmas cheer, a custom borrowed from Sweden, has made its way into Icelandic culture as a welcome addition to lighten the darkness, and Sigga and Gunnar were invited to quite a few *glögg* parties.

Glögg is served in the usual Icelandic way of drinking, that is, always with something to eat, and though not all *glögg* parties last into the wee hours of the night, many do. Furthermore, many Icelanders at a party where alcohol is served have almost a compulsion to finish any bottle of alcohol that has already been opened. Icelanders at least claim to drink more alcohol in the dark of winter than in the long summer light, and yes, as elsewhere, some drink too much, but in my experience, the ones who get really drunk at a party are always the same few. The police are diligent about picking up drunken drivers so that most people go home in a taxi.

December 23rd is the day of commemoration of St. Thorlákur, the pious ascetic who was bishop of Skálholt and died in 1193. Commemorating the date of his death on December 23 adds to the Christmas festivities.

Sigga and her family, since they came from the West Fjords, maintain the custom of eating skate on St. Thorlákur's Day. Skate, either buried and fermented or salted, has been a common, everyday dish, especially near the sea on the western coast of Iceland. Preparation is simple: merely boil it for ten or fifteen minutes. Salted skate may be soaked in water first before boiling. It has a rather strong taste and, like fish in general, is served with melted butter or, especially for St. Thorlákur's Day, with lamb fat or *tolg*. *Tolg* is white in color and is sold in all grocery stores in a solid block, like lard, and is then melted and served hot.

Like most Icelanders, Sigga and Gunnar, with the help of their son Gummi, always decorate their Christmas tree either the evening of the 22nd or on the 23rd itself. Originally imported from Germany, Christmas trees and evergreen boughs are now an Icelandic custom as well, many of them grown in Iceland. As a gesture of friendship and since Iceland has very few large trees, every year the city of Oslo in Norway sends the city of Reykjavík a huge Christmas tree that is erected in the square in front of the parliament building. Other communities in Iceland, such as Akureyri and the Westman Islands, also receive a gift of trees from the Nordic countries. All are lit during a special ceremony with speeches and music.

Finally the three–day celebration of Christmas itself had arrived. The streets were icy and there was snow on the ground, the sky overcast and promising more snow to come, but the gale force winds of the day before had passed over us. Sigga and Gunnar, along with Gummi, took Gunnar's widowed mother, Kristín, to church for evensong before bringing her home for dinner.

Christmas Eve is the time when most families eat at home or with their parents, and all open their presents. Sigga had lit candles on the coffee table in the living room and on the window sills, their golden glow softening the harsher electric light. Christmas is above all a time for the various members of the family to see each other so, after spending Christmas Eve with Sigga and Gunnar, Kristín would spend Christmas day with her son Halldór, who works for the shipping company, and his family; her other son, Pétur, and his family would visit her there. She told us the news from Magnús, her son who works for the airline abroad, and about Magnús' son, whom she often sees. Like many Icelanders, Magnús has a child born out of wedlock, but that night the boy, as is the usual custom, was with his mother and her family.

I have sat so often at table with Sigga and Gunnar, their son Gummi and Kristín, that there was for me the warm feeling of being home; I said little, cosy in savoring the closeness of their friendship.

We were treated to roast ptarmigan, shot on Mt. Esja by their daughter Thórunn's fiancé Sveinn, served in a thin white sauce. On Christmas Eve some Icelanders eat pork loin, many have rack of lamb, and others have adopted the foreign custom of eating turkey, but ptarmigan is traditional. The meat of the bird was delicious, dark, tender, and tasty. Sigga had made "brown potatoes," small boiled potatoes rolled in a frying pan with caramelized sugar and a little butter. They melted in the mouth. As Sigga served the ptarmigan and we passed around the bowls of potatoes, salad, and pickled beets, we caught up on the news of the family.

"Hjalti's happy with his job in Sweden still, though Kristín misses us." Sigga was referring to their daughter and her husband.

"And the baby, Anna Sigga?"

"Growing every day. I'll show you some pictures of her after dinner," Sigga promised.

Sigga's grandmother Ingibjörg, on the other hand, had grown much frailer and had had to be moved to a home for the elderly. When she had her ninety–fourth birthday recently only the family and the other old people in the home celebrated quietly with her. Sigga's mother, Gudrún, sees to it that she or another member of the family goes to see Ingibjörg almost every day.

"Inga and Kalli and the children will drive up from the farm to be with us for dinner tomorrow."

As we progressed through the meal to *laufabrauð* and ice cream and then coffee, it was clear that Gummi really had his mind on the presents under the tree. We took our coffee cups to sit by the tree in the living room and opened the gifts one by one, enjoying each other's surprise and pleasure, while we listened to Christmas music on the radio. Though carol singing is not an Icelandic tradition, the beautiful "Ave Maria" by the Icelandic composer Sigvaldi Kaldalóns is frequently sung in church and on the radio, and everyone knows "Silent Night" in Icelandic.

Later their daughter Thórunn came to visit, with Sveinn and their four year old son Thórir. Sigga greeted her grandson Thórir with a present and his eyes lighted up. Thórunn and Sveinn live together. A schoolteacher, she was as glad for Christmas vacation as were the students, but Sveinn, an avid computer programmer, doesn't normally get very far from his computer unless it's to go fishing. He and Gummi went off to have fun with the computer game Gummi received for Christmas.

On Christmas Day the family will eat together again, the children and grandchildren amusing themselves, growing up together, the adults talking pleasantly, swapping stories and reminiscences. They will dine on *hangikjöt*, or cured lamb, with white sauce and boiled potatoes and the Christmas elves will start to go back to the mountains, one by one. On the Second Day of Christmas, Boxing Day, the family may eat together again, perhaps dividing up differently and usually eating at a different family member's house, or they may visit each other, or simply stay home and relax. One of those books received on Christmas Eve may be too tempting to read for anyone to want to go out again.

For the Thirteen Days of Christmas, counting December 25th through January 6th (and not twelve, as in English) the Christmas lights, indoors and out, stay lit, the trees and the wreaths remain, and the feeling of a comfortable light in the darkness remains. On the Thirteenth Day, January 6th, the children may throw snowballs at your car as you drive by and there are bonfires to celebrate when the elves move their abode, though not as many people attend as take part in the New Year celebrations.

And now we have come to New Year's and the biggest of all bonfires, but that is another story.

My John's Soul

Once an old man and an old woman lived together.[1] The old man was rather wild and not very well liked, except by his cronies, and a lazy good–for–nothing around the house. The old woman, who was outspoken and not slow to find ways to make ends meet, never let him forget how worthless he was. But despite the fact that they did not always get along, the old woman was very fond of her John.

One day the old man fell ill and was near to death. The old woman watched over him, and as she did so the thought occurred to her to make sure that, when her John died, he would get into heaven. Obviously, the best course was for the old woman herself to see to it that he got there. She therefore held a sack over his face to catch his soul as he breathed his last and then tightly bound the opening shut. She then tucked the sack containing his soul in her apron and set off for heaven.

She sat down to rest on the way and stated confidently to the sack that he was going to heaven. She ignored the grumbling she heard from the sack: "But I don't want to go to heaven. That's not where my friends are."

"Nonsense," she said, and she continued on her way.

Once the woman had arrived at the pearly gates St. Peter answered her knock. "Bless you," she said, "I've brought the soul of my John here. You've surely heard of him. Won't you please let him in?"

"Oh, yes, I've heard of him," St. Peter admitted, "but never anything good."

"I didn't think you'd be so hard–hearted as to refuse," said the woman, "or have you forgotten that you thrice denied the Lord?" At that, St. Peter closed the gates.

Nothing daunted, the old woman knocked again and St. Paul came out. But St. Paul also refused. With that she snapped, "And have you forgotten, Paul, that long ago you persecuted God and good men?" And St. Paul also clanged the gates shut.

There were sounds of relief from the sack, but the old woman knocked again and this time the Virgin Mary came out. "Blessed be you," said the woman, "St. Paul and St. Peter have both refused. I wonder if you'd let my John into heaven."

"Unfortunately, I don't dare," replied the Virgin. "He was so impossible."

"Here I thought you realized others can also be weak, or have you forgotten that you had a child and couldn't name the father." Mary hastened to close the gates.

Undaunted, the old woman knocked again and this time Christ himself appeared. "I want to beg you, " she asked humbly, "to let my poor John's soul into heaven."

"No, woman." Christ was emphatic. "He didn't believe in me." But as

Christ took hold of the gates, the old woman, quick as a wink, tossed the sack with John's soul far into heaven before the gates snapped shut.

Nothing more is known of the old woman, nor is it known how the soul of her man John fared once he had entered heaven.

Iceland's History: The Struggle for Independence, 1830–1918

The year 1830 marked the beginning of a new chapter in Icelandic history, the struggle for independence from Denmark. On the positive side, Icelanders entered the period with a high rate of literacy; they learned at home to read the old writings, the Bible, and Hallgrímur Pétursson's *Passion Psalms*.[1] They still "reverence[d]... the sacred rights of hospitality" for which they had long been famous[2] and stood on the edge of the nineteenth century world with a treasure chest of intellectual and spiritual riches. Moreover, living conditions had improved sufficiently over those of the eighteenth century so that the population, instead of continuing to drop, had slightly surpassed the 1703 census figure and in 1835 stood at 56,035.

The country and the people continued to interest foreigners, several of whom mounted expeditions to study and paint Icelanders and the marvels of the landscape, including Lord Dufferin, later governor general of Canada, and the French physician and natural scientist Paul Gaimard, who brought with him the painter Auguste Mayer.

On the other hand, Icelanders were poverty stricken and technologically backward. With trade still handled by the Danes, there were very few Icelandic merchants and almost no towns or villages. Transportation was on foot or on horseback as there were only tracks and paths rather than roads. The fishing crews were still largely dependent on open rowboats with a small sail and hand lines. The farmers raised sheep and some cattle, and spread manure over the home fields, but the ground was not leveled or planted; nature decreed what grew on the grazing lands. Long hours of work were common in other countries as well, but in Iceland other difficulties were added to the burden of living. Though the large landowners continued to live and dress well, the majority of the people struggled with difficult living conditions. The houses were all too often wet inside as the sod roofs leaked. Danish physicians who travelled round Iceland in the nineteenth century to study the health and living conditions were appalled at the lack of cleanliness, the poor food, and the high disease and death rates. Scurvy, respiratory infections, and skin rashes were common. In 1847, about 5% of the population or 3,329 died of measles, and in 1853 a doctor was moved to ask if there was ever a war so bloody that over 10% of the population was killed every three years.[3]

In the early nineteenth century what Icelanders needed was to regain their own legislature and to control their own trade so as to acquire both capital and education to upgrade their living conditions and farming and fishing methods. One of the problems of the times, however, was the widespread political apathy, born of poverty and the lack of experience in regulating their own affairs beyond the farm level.[4] It would take leadership to counteract the political apathy, to gain Danish recognition of Iceland's problems and, when the time came, to institute changes. Furthermore, the struggle for independence and for better living conditions would have to take place both in Iceland and in Denmark.

The Awakening of National Conscience

Icelanders who went to Denmark to continue their studies at the University of Copenhagen were plunged into the ferment of ideas that characterized nineteenth century Europe. The Paris Revolution of 1830 sparked the growth of liberalism and nationalism that, in Denmark, led to the establishment of four provincial diets to act as consultative bodies. Iceland was given representation in one of these diets, though the two representatives, rather than being elected, were appointed by the king, Frederick VI (1806–1839).

Excited by the new thinking and encouraged by liberal Danes, four Icelandic students in Copenhagen founded an annual, which they named *Fjölnir* (one of Óðinn's names) and in which they argued that their language and nationality should be protected and that the Althing should be re–established at the ancient site of Thingvellir.

Poets played a strong part in the awakening of Icelandic nationalist sentiment, not least among them Jónas Hallgrímsson (1807–1845). His beautiful *Ég bið að heilsa* ("I send greetings") was the first sonnet written in Icelandic. Influenced as much by romanticism as nationalism, the poet tames the harshness of the Icelandic climate to "gentle winds" and the ocean to "little waves," but the poem radiates his love of Iceland as well as of the girlfriend he left behind.

Other Icelanders expressed their nationalistic fervor in more practical ways. Baldvin Einarsson (1801–1833), for instance, encouraged Icelandic farmers to read in order to learn how to improve their farming methods. But the most important leader to emerge was Jón Sigurdsson (1811–1879). Though all were agreed on the need to re–establish the Icelandic national assembly and to preserve the Icelandic language, Jón Sigurðsson felt that the *Fjölnir* group was too dependent on the fashion in literature and therefore, with eleven others, published *Ný félagsrit*.

Born the son of a minister in the West Fjords in 1811, Jón Sigurdsson was descended from Snorri Sturluson, the well–known writer and crafty politician of the Commonwealth period, and from Jón Arason, the last Catholic bishop in Iceland. He was tall with brown eyes and dark brown hair, which turned white rather suddenly in his thirties. He is described as a man whose bearing instantly commanded respect, gentle and kindly but resolute. Intelligent and with an excellent memory, he was well read and indefatigable in promoting Iceland's independence.[5]

In a day and age when, because of poor roads, it was easier to sail to Denmark than to travel around Iceland, Jón Sigurdsson went to Copenhagen in

1833, at first to study and then to make his home.[6] Awarded an Arna Magnean fellowship in 1835, he studied northern antiquities and Icelandic history and earned his living as a librarian and by writing and editing publications about northern history. After turning his attention to politics in 1840, he became the spearhead for Icelandic independence, producing literally thousands of letters and articles to promote Iceland's cause. With the full support of his wife, their home in Copenhagen became a center for Icelanders to meet and discuss political issues and the changing times.

Jón Sigurdsson argued for free trade and autonomy from Denmark. Based on his studies, he wrote about how to promote trade and improve the antiquated agricultural and fishing methods still practiced in Iceland. He also had the foresight to see that, despite the historic and symbolic importance of Thingvellir, Reykjavík should be the site of the reconstituted Althing and would become the center of government, culture, and industry.

Reconstitution of the Althing

A petition to King Frederick resulted in the establishment of a committee of ten officials for the purpose of discussing Icelandic problems. The committee met in Reykjavík in 1839 and again in 1841, but following the accession of Christian VIII (1839–1848) to the throne, Icelanders submitted a new petition asking for their own parliament, free trade, better schools, and more doctors.[7] Legally Iceland was, after all, not a Danish colony but a dependency, subject to Danish law only when the chancellery so decided. The new king, with more liberal views than his predecessor, signed a proclamation restoring the Althing in 1843, but as an advisory body only. It was to meet in Reykjavík, biennially, for a one month summer session at which the members could draft petitions but not enact laws. Twenty members of parliament were to be elected by the people and six appointed by the king for six year terms.

Elections were duly held and the reconstituted Althing met in July 1845, in the Latin School in Reykjavík. The vote was restricted, however, to males who were 25 years of age or older and who owned sufficient property to qualify, actually fewer than 5% of the total population. The property requirement specified that males who were old enough had to own at least 10 hundreds of land (half the average landholding) or hold a life tenancy on crown or church land. Elected members had to be at least 30 years of age and speak Icelandic, and the minutes of the Althing meetings were also to be recorded in Icelandic.[8] Since no one in the Westman Islands qualified as a property holder, 25 rather than 26 Icelandic M.P.s attended the first session. Until 1849 the Althing met behind closed doors.

Though the Althing was limited to passing resolutions, it was an important stage for the discussion of Icelandic concerns. Discussion during the first session centered on freedom of trade and the need to provide instruction in Iceland in law, medicine, seamanship, and theology. The king responded with a promise to establish a seminary, which was opened in 1847.[9] Meanwhile the population of Reykjavík had more than tripled from that of 1801 to 961 inhabitants in 1845, though it still amounted to only 1.6% of the total population of Iceland.[10] Despite its small size, however, Reykjavík was emerging as the center of government, supplanting Bessastadir in importance.[11]

Iceland at the time was characterized by a farming population, dispersed around the coasts, each farm an individual center of decision making; there were no agricultural societies and almost no villages. The country lacked an effective communication system and infrastructure. Political power that was not appropriated by Denmark was exercised by an elite group of landholders bound by kinship ties and a common education at the Latin School in Reykjavík and the University of Copenhagen. The administration, the church, and from 1845 on, the Althing, were centers of power, with the church's influence diminishing during the nineteenth century and, after 1845, the importance of the Althing on the ascendancy. The control held by the Stephensen and Finsen families over the government and the church in the early part of the century gave way to control by other families, but the relationships remained close–knit; of the 115 M.P.s between 1845 and 1874, only 16 did not have close kinship ties with any of the others.[12] Because of the general political apathy, the control exercised by the landholding gentry went unchallenged (before 1900 voter participation often fell below 10%), but these people had the political ability and experience, backed by education and the control of printing, to stand up to the Danish authorities and to work to extend Icelandic rights.[13] Jón Sigurdsson was elected to the Althing in 1845. He returned to Iceland in the summers and attended the Althing sessions, remaining the M.P. for the West Fjords until his death in 1879, serving most of the time as Speaker of the Althing.

The End of Absolutism

After the death of the Danish king, Christian VIII, in 1848 there was again a revolution in France which led to marked changes in much of Europe. The Danish people marched through the streets of Copenhagen to demand a liberal constitution, and the Icelandic students shouted their approval.[14] In 1849 the Danes received a new constitution replacing the old absolute monarchy with a constitutional monarchy, with the king, now Frederick VII (1848–1863), and a bicameral legislature.

At the same time, Denmark was caught up in difficulties with the Germans as there were Germans living in the duchies of Schleswig and Holstein, at that time owned by Denmark. The duchies themselves revolted because they wanted the same freedoms now granted to the Danes. Denmark emerged victorious from the war that followed in 1848–1850, but was defeated in 1864 and ceded claims to the disputed duchies.

Iceland's demands were overshadowed as Denmark grappled with the problems nearer at hand, though a special office had been set up in Copenhagen to see to Icelandic concerns, along with those of the Faroes and Greenland, also owned by Denmark. Nor could Denmark afford to give Iceland more control over its own affairs when Danish efforts were concentrated on maintaining the Danish kingdom intact. On the other hand, the end of the absolute monarchy gave Jón Sigurdsson the opportunity to formulate a legal justification of Iceland's claims to independence. Basing his stand on the historic agreements, he pointed out that in the Old Treaty of 1262 Icelanders had declared allegiance to the king of Norway but had retained for themselves the right to make their own laws; Iceland, in other words, thereby entered a personal union with the Norwegian king but did not become a Norwegian colony or county. When the Scandinavian monarchies were united, Iceland had fallen under the control of the Danish king. With the Kópavogur agreement of 1662, on the other hand, Icelanders had been constrained to swear allegiance to the Danish king as absolute monarch, who thereby expropriated legislative power over Iceland: the Kópavogur agreement rescinded Iceland's right to pass its own laws, as guaranteed in the Old Treaty. Jón Sigurdsson argued that, with the end of absolutism and the institution of a constitutional monarchy, Iceland's legal status as set out in the Old Treaty was again valid. He marshalled his views in *Hugvekja til Íslendinga* ("Exhortation to Icelanders"), the most influential article in Icelandic history.[15]

Icelanders met at Thingvellir on August 5, 1848, and set out the terms of a petition to the king, later signed by 2500 Icelanders, asking for their own legislature and for an elected body of representatives to deal with those problems that concerned only Iceland. The king, however, would make no binding decision until Icelanders had held a special meeting in Iceland to discuss the matter.[16]

Icelanders meanwhile were finding a political voice. The first real newspaper, *Þjóðólfur*, was published in Iceland in 1848, advocating independence, and a new publication in Copenhagen demanded free trade. About 60 farmers in the north rode to protest the behavior of one magistrate, shouting "Long live freedom! Down with oppression!" In 1850 students rebelled when the principal banned the use of alcohol, and the newspaper editor rose in church at the end of the service and demanded a more suitable minister.[17] Clearly Icelanders were emerging from their former political apathy.

The National Convention of 1851

Elections were held in 1850 and a national assembly convened on July 4, 1851. The new governor, Count J. D. Trampe (not to be confused with Count Fr. Chr. Trampe, governor earlier in the century), appeared with twenty–five armed soldiers, who remained outside, to present the bill from the king that would have incorporated Iceland into the Danish kingdom. The Icelandic representatives, on the other hand, had their own demands. They still envisioned Iceland as continuing in a personal relationship with the king of Denmark, but wanted the Althing to have legislative and executive powers alongside those of the king and for Iceland to have its own judicial system.

Count Trampe had been instructed not to allow any discussion of the terms of the bill. When Jón Sigurdsson tried to present the majority Icelandic view, Trampe dissolved the meeting, whereupon Jón Sigurdsson raised his voice and firmly stated: "I protest" the illegality of ending the convention in this way and reserve the right to complain to the king. The other representatives then shouted, "We all protest!" Count Trampe and his staff walked out, and the meeting ended with the representatives' heartfelt "Long live our king, Frederick VII!"

In the wake of the National Convention, the king refused to allow Iceland to become independent, several Icelanders lost their official positions, and the Danish newspapers attacked Jón Sigurdsson. The convention ended in a stalemate for Iceland, but Icelanders had clearly formulated their demands, and Jón Sigurdsson was indisputably their leader.

Free Trade and the Economy

The monopoly control of Icelandic trade, first imposed by Denmark in 1602, had led to centuries of economic stagnation and a severe lack of development.[18] The Free Trade Charter of 1787 still restricted the right to trade to Danish merchants. Jón Sigurdsson argued for a lifting of all trade restrictions. Finding it difficult in the nineteenth century to conclude agreements with nations that did not approve of the Danish treatment of Iceland, the Faroes, and Greenland,[19] and with the support of liberal Danes, the Danish government finally acquiesced. In 1854 the monopoly was lifted, officially ending on April 1, 1855.

Progress after the lifting of trade restrictions was slow, however. On the positive side, the end of the monopoly meant that 25 harbors were opened to merchant vessels and that independent merchants bought and sold, often on the ships' decks. The Norwegians and the British, especially, availed themselves of the opportunity to trade, the former to sell timber, the latter to buy live horses and sheep. Wool, meat and tallow, and from the coastal communities, salt fish and fish liver oil, were the chief exports.[20] The farmers no longer ruled the labor market as many of the former hired hands left to fish, but it was not until later in the century that fishing became an industry in its own right. The nonexistence of roads meant that wheeled vehicles were of little use for transport. People could not freely settle in towns as a permit to move was required in order not to swell the rolls of the poor. The lack of capital and of harbor facilities meant that it was difficult for independent fishing boat owners to get started.

There were signs of progress, however. The small church in Reykjavík that was the cathedral or bishop's seat was enlarged and rebuilt, and Reykjavík sported a windmill to provide power to grind grain. In 1830 farmers had learned to attach the blade to a scythe handle with iron sockets rather than binding blade and handle together, and in 1868 Torfi Bjarnarson had steel scythe blades made in Scotland, which held an edge much better than the old iron ones. Some farmers turned more to growing vegetables in addition to the traditional livestock raising. There were eight physicians in the country and some population increase. But on the whole there was very little change in fishing and agricultural methods. The people had awakened sufficiently from political apathy to argue and complain, but little was accomplished.[21]

The Millenary of Iceland's Founding and a Constitution

The Danes also needed a solution to the Icelandic problem. In 1871 Denmark passed an Act of Union whereby Iceland was annexed as an integral part of the Danish kingdom. The Danes agreed to pay Iceland a certain sum of money yearly and gave Iceland the right to handle judicial, church, educational, and some other matters, but reserved control of, among other things, foreign affairs and the currency.[22] Though Icelanders never accepted the clause proclaiming Iceland an integral part of the Danish kingdom, the act paved the way for Iceland to be given a constitution. A well–attended meeting at Thingvellir resulted in a petition for Icelandic freedom and for a constitution investing the Althing with legislative power and control of finances. Meanwhile, the Danes, with singular devotion to the litany of their monarchs' names, had once again replaced a Frederick with a Christian. In 1874 the king, now Christian IX (1863–1906), agreed to grant Iceland a constitution. It was a milestone decision.

The year 1874 marked the millenary of Iceland's settlement. A celebration was held at Thingvellir, the site of the original Althing in Commonwealth times. King Christian himself came to Iceland to attend the celebration, bringing with him Iceland's new constitution. Christian was actually the first king to visit Iceland and, along with the representatives of other nations, was warmly welcomed. Thousands flocked to Thingvellir and others celebrated throughout the country. One of Iceland's first photographers, Sigfús Eymundsson, has left a valuable record of the festivities and of later events.

To commemorate the occasion Sveinbjörn Sveinbjörnsson, then only 27 years old, wrote the beautiful *Ó Guð vors lands* ("O God of our country") to words by the famous Icelandic poet Matthías Jochumsson. Trained in Leipzig by Carl Reinecke and others, Sveinbjörnsson lived and worked in Edinburgh, producing a considerable corpus of vocal and chamber music and setting an example for other Icelanders to compose music. The song he composed for the millenary became Iceland's national anthem.

The new constitution gave the Althing both legislative and financial power, though the Danish Minister for Icelandic Affairs, acting on behalf of the king, had the right to veto Althing decisions. The bicameral legislature consisted of 36 M.P.s in the lower chamber and 12 in the upper, 6 of whom were appointed by the king. Despite the low level of national income, most of their work dealt with appropriations.[23] Only those who could speak Icelandic were allowed to hold public office. Since 1859 the king had been required to sign the Icelandic text of all laws, though they were published in Danish as well. From 1891 on the laws were worded only in Icelandic. In 1881 the Althing moved to its present stone building in the center of Reykjavík.

In 1875 the members of the Althing voted on comparatively high salaries for the various government officials, an action which split the members and much of the populace into two camps, those favoring the high salaries and the farmers who were opposed to such extravagance.[24] At the same time, in recognition of all Jón Sigurdsson had done for the nation, and to ease his financial problems, the Althing awarded him an honorary stipend. Both he and his wife were in poor health at the end of their lives. They died, childless, she a few days after him, in December 1879. The plaque on his coffin read: "Iceland's favorite son, her honor, sword and shield."[25]

From 1874–1904, Icelandic affairs were seen to by a Danish minister. The period was one of great progress: roads were built, and several bridges, so that finally wagons, and therefore the wheel, could be effectively used for transport. The medieval tithe was abolished in 1877, to be replaced by customs duties and an income tax. From 1877 on, there were scheduled coastal sailings to carry freight, passengers, and the mail, and a few years later winter as well as summer sailings were instituted. The cooperative movement was started in 1882 and the Union of Icelandic Cooperatives founded in 1902. Agricultural products accounted for about a third of exports and, when Britain stopped the importation of live sheep for fear of disease, the sale of horses rose until after 1920.[26] The wool industry was begun with the founding of Álafoss in 1896.[27] Schools were built and an agricultural school was established in each of Iceland's four quarters. The first bank opened its doors in 1886, though in the beginning only twice a week for two hours at a time. The increased income meant the building of more wood–frame houses (*timburhús*) and many moved from the countryside into towns. By 1901 Reykjavík had grown to 6,682 people, and, perhaps more importantly, accounted for 8.5% of the total population of 78,470.[28]

Hardships still plagued Iceland, however. Harsh weather in 1858–59 and again in the 1880s, and an epidemic of scapie that carried off 200,000 sheep after 1855, followed by a major eruption in the northeast, caused large numbers of Icelanders to flee the country. The first 17 Mormon converts settled in and around Spanish Fork, Utah, in 1855–1860, later followed by others who brought the total to about 370. Forty to fifty people tried Brazil in the 1860s, though many did not remain. In 1873 the first group from Akureyri emigrated to Winnipeg. Those who followed founded New Iceland in 1875 in what is now Manitoba. Others settled elsewhere in North America, making a total of about 15,000 Icelanders who emigrated before World War I.[29] Despite losing a large number of people to emigration, however, the population of Iceland continued to increase.

The 1874 constitution was to have been in force for six years and then to be reviewed. An 1885 meeting at Thingvellir resulted in the Althing's agreeing to constitutional changes, which the king rejected. There were strong arguments between the Althing and the government, with the Danes themselves split between the conservatives and the left. The Icelander Valtýr Gudmundsson (1860–1928) felt that the minister should be stationed in Copenhagen, while others felt he should be in Iceland itself, in other words, that Iceland should have home rule.[30]

The Commercialization of Fishing

Though some Icelanders continued to use open rowboats to fish well into the twentieth century, the end of the nineteenth century saw a major shift to decked vessels, the training of ships' captains, the rise of a seaman class, and improvement in fishing gear. The first lighthouse was built in 1878, though at first there was little improvement of harbors. Small decked vessels had been used in the West Fjords since about 1800, but in 1868 there were still only 64 decked vessels to about 3000 open boats. By 1906 most vessels were decked, a total of 169 manned by 2000 seamen, and Reykjavík, with 11% of the population, had become the center of marine fishing and the economy.[31]

From the beginning, Iceland had been a farming nation, with fishing an important sideline. The late nineteenth and early twentieth centuries saw the change to a market economy and the industrialization of fishing.[32] By 1901 marine products, rather than agricultural produce, accounted for four–fifths of exports.[33] The shift to a market economy entailed fundamental changes. Seamen were no longer farm laborers but a class of workers, living in towns and fishing villages. Both they and the fishing vessel outfitters established unions. The Marine Academy was opened in 1891 to provide the technical and navigational training required to be a ship's captain. Selling fish more actively on foreign markets meant pressure to catch more and to process the catch with attention to quality control. Catch sizes were increased by the use of more efficient equipment such as trawl nets, and by fishing throughout the year and not just seasonally. With decked vessels rather than open rowboats, the crews remained at sea, often for long stretches. The wives, thus left alone at home, found jobs in the fish processing plants, which in turn laid more emphasis on the quality of the processed fish.

Iceland's rich fishing grounds inevitably attracted crews from other nations.[34] In the 1870s Norwegians fished Icelandic waters for herring, at a time when Icelanders were still using herring for livestock feed and for bait, rather than for human consumption, because herring did not keep well. In the nineteenth century Breton fishermen came from France to fish from February to mid–August, in 1864 with 260 ships and 4,337 seamen.

Most important, however, were the British who, with steam vessels from 1870 on and trawl nets beginning in 1891, fished Icelandic waters far more effectively than either Icelanders or the French and who introduced Icelanders to the advantages of more modern equipment.[35] On the other hand, the aggressiveness of British fishing clashed with Icelandic demands. The British and French both refused to acknowledge the nineteenth century fishing limit of 16 miles, insisting on only 3 miles instead. Furthermore, the British ignored the agreement not to fish in Faxaflói Bay in order to preserve breeding stocks and to let Icelanders utilize their traditional fishing grounds.[36] The result was the

Sixth Cod War in 1896–1897 (the first had taken place in 1433), which ended with an agreement between Denmark and Britain in 1901. The agreement set a 3 mile limit for the next 50 years and left Icelanders feeling robbed of their livelihood.[37]

Home Rule

In the 1890s it was clear to Icelanders that, despite the accomplishments since 1874, further progress was needed. There was a good deal of discussion in the newspapers about what should be done. In 1897, for example, one newspaper wrote that the Althing members lacked conviction and that the country needed a suitable leader and should be independent of Denmark.[38] The discussion gave rise to the first political parties: led by Hannes Hafstein, those who wanted the minister to reside in Iceland founded the Home Rule Party in 1900, and those who sided with Valtýr Gudmundsson established the Progressive Party in 1902.[39] In 1901 Hannes Hafstein was elected to the Althing and went to Denmark to argue Iceland's case. With a liberal government in Denmark at the time, the king and his ministers agreed to grant Iceland home rule. Hannes Hafstein had achieved a victory for Iceland and, in the election that followed, the Home Rule party won. The Althing accepted the king's bill and the new constitution took effect on February 1, 1904, with Hafstein as minister.

To join the celebration of the beginning of home rule, Icelanders streamed into Reykjavík by ship and on horseback. The tempo of life in the town quickened; people walked faster and slept little in their excitement. The Danish flag was flown, but also a few blue flags with a white falcon to represent Iceland. In the evening there was a dinner party for a hundred guests in honor of Hannes Hafstein.

Iceland's first home rule minister came from Ísafjördur in the northwest, as had Jón Sigurdsson before him. In the late nineteenth century the fishing village of Ísafjördur had a population of 900 and was surprisingly busy. The Norwegians had a whaling station in the vicinity and others elsewhere, the British came with decked ships, and there were two hotels, as well as several gaming clubs where people could bet or dance. Survival, on the other hand, was not always easy. In the 1880s pack ice covered the fjords until late in the year; there was a shortage of hay and many sheep died. In 1899 there was a smallpox epidemic. Many fled to North America, and a cousin wrote to Hafstein from Canada that it was hopeless to remain in Iceland, but Hafstein felt it wrong to leave. In 1896 he had taken a job as an official in order to earn his living, but he was known as one of Iceland's best poets of the time, who also drew cartoons and very good portraits. His poems were like "a breath of spring in hard times," and, like those of Einar Benediktsson, presented a romantic view of nationalism and dreams of the future.[40] In fact, people had trouble believing that such a poet could also be a good politician. Hafstein twice lost an election, but an increasing number came to see him as a national leader.

In order for Icelanders to buy and sell abroad more advantageously, Hafstein

River Farm Museum, Reykjavík

wanted the country to be connected with the rest of the world via telephone. Though it seems strange to us now, the idea sparked huge opposition at the time; there were many who felt that radio contact was preferable. Hafstein worked hard to obtain a favorable contract for laying the marine cable from Scotland to bring telephone service to Iceland. A large number of farmers responded in 1905 by holding an outdoor meeting in Reykjavík to protest the idea of the telephone and the proposed contract, but the Althing accepted the agreement. In 1906 both the undersea cable to the East Fjords region and a telephone line across the country were completed: international telephone service for Iceland became a reality. Hafstein had demonstrated his energy and capability, respect for him rose, and a crowd gathered in the street outside his home to sing to him. When a telegraph station was finally built in 1918, there was no longer any interest in domestic use; the telephone had been accepted.[41]

Improvements came slowly. Horse–drawn wagons were used more or less through World War II, but hay was carried on packhorses. Tractors and machines for haying were increasingly used, as well as milking machines. Slaughtering had been carried out outdoors, the meat for export heavily salted for use by ships' crews. After the turn of the century the meat was processed in slaughterhouses and lightly salted for sale in Denmark and Norway.[42] In 1910 ca. 48% of the population was engaged in farming, and ca. 19% in catching and processing fish.[43] The shift to trawlers revolutionized ocean fishing and the first ones quickly repaid the initial cost. However, the seamen were required to work such long hours that they founded a union in 1915. People moved to the towns, business increased, and the first steamship company was founded in 1914. A small freight train was even used between 1913 and 1930, the donkey engine named Bríet for Iceland's most vocal woman suffragist. The line lay wholly within Reykjavík and was used to carry dirt for landfill to build up the area around the harbor. The cars and trucks that followed on the heels of the railway experiment proved to be more economical and the railway was discontinued after the harbor had been built up.[44] Today the engine is on display at the River Farm Museum in Reykjavík.

The Icelandic economy experienced a 3% yearly growth from 1900–1914.[45] Reykjavík grew, the Technical School opened in 1904 to train craftsmen, and the same year the first car was imported. The number of unions and cooperatives increased and women's and youth associations were founded. Women were given the vote in municipal elections in 1908 and four women were elected to the Reykjavík municipal council. Women were also granted equal rights to education and in 1915 they were allowed limited suffrage in parliamentary elections. Iceland tried prohibition beginning in 1915, but the law was partially repealed in 1922, and completely in 1934.[46]

Those who held political power still constituted an elite group, though the membership of this group had greatly changed since the beginning of the previous century. Control remained elitist in the sense that virtually the same people ran the political, economic, and cultural spheres. With the coming of home rule, however, the elite began to be limited by electoral pressures and came to understand the advantage of political parties and of having a majority vote in the Althing. Under home rule there was still an active struggle for independence from Denmark but, with the increase in the number of people living in towns and working as craftsmen or fishermen, unions were established and class consciousness and some pluralistic pressures began to enter the political equation.[47]

Meanwhile the Danes were showing more interest in Icelandic problems, with King Frederick VIII himself sympathetic to the Icelandic cause. Hannes Hafstein's visits to Denmark began to bear fruit. In 1907 the king sailed to Iceland. On August 1st, with a retinue of people, he set out on horseback to ride to Thingvellir, with Hannes Hafstein riding beside him. A small house had been built for him at Thingvellir and a place prepared for a meeting. He and his retinue partied at Thingvellir before going on to Geysir. The king forded rivers on horseback and rode over trails that had been widened for him, sometimes through rather wild country markedly different from what he was used to in Denmark.

The king appointed a committee of 7 Icelanders and 13 Danes which met in 1908 to put forward proposals for defining the relationship between Denmark and Iceland; the first article stated that Iceland should be independent but remain a part of the Danish kingdom.[48] When the committee's proposals were not accepted by the Althing, Hafstein resigned, but became minister again from 1912–1914. In Denmark Christian X succeeded to the throne in 1912.

Meanwhile, the question of a flag for Iceland still hung fire. A white falcon on a blue field had been used for the millenary, and in 1903 Iceland was granted a coat of arms with a falcon. On June 12, 1913, to amuse himself on a calm day, Einar Pétursson rowed out into Reykjavík harbor, flying a blue and white flag. The fact that the Danes confiscated his flag was the spark for all Reykjavík to sport blue and white flags. The M.P.s held an outdoor meeting and a large crowd attended, resulting in the demand for a flag. The flag committee that met that same year compromised on a sky–blue flag with a red cross within a white cross. The Danes were reluctant to accept it, but the king agreed in 1915 to its use within Iceland's territorial waters. Icelandic ships still had to continue to fly the Danish flag until independence in 1918.[49]

Hannes Hafstein lost the election in 1914, but he had already accomplished a great deal to bring Iceland into the twentieth century. Encouraged by economic growth and building construction, during his term of office the population of Reykjavík had grown to 11,600 or 13.6% of the nation.[50] He had succeeded in getting the highest level of government moved from Copenhagen to Reykjavík and in paving the way for the independence that was to come in 1918.

World War I

After the election of 1914 political dissent continued. The ministers who succeeded Hannes Hafstein had to cope with the still unresolved issues between Denmark and Iceland, and several resigned when they lost the support of the Althing. Some stability was achieved, however, with Einar Arnórsson as minister from 1914–1916. With the question of home rule resolved, political differences shifted to class allegiances; in 1916 two political parties were founded: the Social Democrats, representing the working class, and the Progressive Party, representing farmers and the cooperative movement. A coalition government operated until the end of the war.[51]

With Europe embroiled in World War I, the British could not afford to risk having the Germans receive supplies. The Germans blockaded Britain but the British navy controlled the Atlantic, and the British consul in Iceland, Eric Cable, dealt directly with Icelandic politicians, bypassing Danes as middlemen. With the war dragging on longer than had been expected at the start of hostilities, an Icelandic committee began to meet in 1915 to advise on necessary supplies of food and fuel.[52] Freight costs rose, import prices rose as much as 200%, and coal and salt cost 10 times the prewar price. The lack of fuel meant that many ships were unable to fish for a time, but in general Icelanders did not suffer severe shortages. On the positive side, foreigners had left the fishing grounds to Icelanders and fish prices were high.[53]

1918 and Independence

The year began with extreme cold in January; the harbor in Reykjavík and some of the larger fjords were frozen over and fuel prices were sky–high.

In April the Althing members were agreed that Icelanders must manage their own affairs as soon as possible. A Danish committee appointed to initiate talks arrived in Iceland in late June 1918 and agreed to Icelandic demands: Iceland would be "independent" but remain in a personal union under the Danish king, with Denmark seeing to consular service abroad, the coast guard, and the supreme court. Helped by the fact that the Danes were using the same arguments to try to get North Schleswig returned by the Germans, the Danish parliament passed the Act of Union.[54] A referendum was held in Iceland on October 19, with about 60% of the eligible men voting but only 25% of the eligible women. The number voting in the south was reduced by the violent eruption of Katla a week before, accompanied by a glacial surge. Ninety percent of those who voted said "yes" to Icelandic independence.[55]

One other event on October 19 was fateful: two ships arrived from Copenhagen and New York, bringing Spanish influenza. In the cold of winter and with a fuel shortage, about two–thirds of the population of Reykjavík fell ill, with a high death toll of 486 for the country as a whole.

On Sunday, December 1, 1918, a ceremony was held in Reykjavík to mark the change to independence under a personal union with the Danish king. The festivities were cut short, however, because so many were ill. The terms of the Act of Union promised the possibility of revision after 25 years. On the eve of this first phase of Iceland's independence the nation's population stood at 91,000, with 15,328 living in Reykjavík, and both the port of Akureyri in the north and the fishing town on the Westman Islands in the south showing healthy growth. Icelanders owned a total of 645,000 sheep, as well as 58 horses and 26 cows for every 100 inhabitants; and over 60% of the fleet of fishing vessels had been motorized, accounting for 39% of the tonnage. The future looked promising.

Turf Houses and Filigree Belts

The traveller in the nineteenth century usually arrived at a farmhouse on horseback or on foot, there being no roads suitable for a wagon until late in the century. If no one had seen the traveller approach and no dogs barked, the person knocked on the door three times, the third time to indicate he was not a ghost. By the same token, the traveller tried to arrive before dark as the house was locked against ghosts after sunset. When someone answered the traveller's triple knock, he or she was welcomed with a kiss and served coffee and refreshments. [1]

Housing

Because of the shortage of timber, nineteenth–century farmhouses (*torfhús* or turf/sod houses) were built of sod or dry–stone walls and sod roofs, using wood only for the front of the house and a minimal wood frame that included the ridgepole and rafters. In fact, the change from the longhouse of Commonwealth times to the passage house of later centuries, with rooms opening off a central corridor, was probably occasioned by the shortage of timber and the worsening climate. [2] Until wheelbarrows were used in the late nineteenth century the sod, after being cut and rolled, was carried by men or horses. The thick walls rested directly on the ground, as the house had no cellar, and measured just over 1 meter or even 2.5 meters (4 ft.–8 in.), in width at the bottom, narrowing to about 1 meter (3 ft.) higher up. Despite the thickness of the walls, however, the roofs often leaked and water seeped through the walls such that the houses were usually unhealthily damp and cold. For better drainage and added strength, the sod slabs were laid at a slant in an attractive design, capped at intervals with narrow horizontal bands of sod. The designs thus created varied stylistically in different parts of the country. Grass grew from the sod roofs and had to be cut, and it was best to add gravel to the lower parts of sod walls to discourage livestock from gnawing at them.

The front door to the farmhouse opened onto a narrow passage with rooms to either side. Though only a few feet wide, this interior passageway could be rather long; the one at Glaumbaer in the north is 21 meters (69 ft.) in length with eleven rooms opening off it to right and left. The rooms included kitchen, storage space, and living quarters. Though usually separate, the cattle byre was sometimes inside the house or under the living quarters for added warmth. In order to benefit from the warmth, people often did their chores in the byre, and children played there. The floors of the houses were usually of packed earth, though paving stones were sometimes laid in the entranceway and in the byre, as well as in the churches.

In earlier times, to guard against the danger of fire, the kitchen (*eldhús* or "fire house") had been a separate building. By the nineteenth century the *eldhús* was a room in the main house with a raised stone hearth at one end. As with the sod walls, Icelanders had to use the materials that were at hand: the "stove" or "range" was simply large stones stacked on top of the hearth to form side supports for the large iron kettles used for boiling. The fires (usually more than one) burned between the stacked stone "walls" supporting the kettles. Alternatively, the kettles hung from chains and iron pothooks.

The most characteristic room in an Icelandic house was the *baðstofa*. Originally used for a steam bath (*bað*), with the reduced availability of fuel in later times, the room came to be the living quarters where people worked, ate, and slept. The *baðstofa* typically had its own wooden frame to support the sod walls and a raised wooden floor. There was very little furniture in the *baðstofa*, though there might be a carved wooden chair or two and carved bedboards, often made from driftwood, and if the family could afford it, wood panelling on the walls. Perhaps a half dozen beds stood in a row along either wall; at Glaumbaer the girls and women slept on the window side of the aisle, the men and boys across from them, two and three to a bed. On the larger farms the farmer and his wife slept in an adjoining room. The mattresses were filled with hay or moss or dried seaweed, covered with a thick wool blanket and a down or wool duvet.

In the evenings the people sat on the beds to spin and knit and make horsehair rope, while one person, usually the farmer himself, read aloud. The children were taught at home for several years and often practiced reading aloud, very clearly. Though the elite farmers had clocks in the eighteenth century, most were without clocks or watches until well into the nineteenth century and relied on their innate sense of time. Some farms had a grandfather clock, which, for an unknown reason, was always set one hour ahead.

Grenjadarstadur farmhouse

221

There was little light inside these houses. The few roof openings as well as windows in the *baðstofa* were often covered with translucent skin or the peritoneum (abdominal membrane) from animals, rather than glass. The *baðstofa* had more window area and more light than elsewhere in the house, however. Until the nineteenth century fish and seal liver oil in hollowed stone and metal lamps in addition to candles made from sheep tallow provided light in the darkness. Oil lamps were available in the 1870s, but kerosene was expensive and the people were afraid of the danger of fire, so that they were not widely used until the turn of the century. Later oil lamps were larger with a glass chimney for safety, and the light could be magnified by hanging a glass bowl full of water beside the lamp. Matches, which had been invented in the early part of the nineteenth century, reached Iceland in 1874.[3] Gas lighting was used in Reykjavík from the end of the nineteenth century. At the same time a small amount of electricity was also generated in some places, usually by harnessing water power.[4]

The sod houses sagged and had frequently to be repaired and, though not everyone was equally expert at cutting and laying the sod, it was easy to add or remove rooms as needed. The same techniques were used to construct the smithy, byre and storage rooms, often attached to the main building, and shelter for hay storage and the sheep, sometimes using a cliff as the back wall.

Despite the shortage of wood, enough had been imported so that warehouses and some of the houses in Reykjavík and the few villages had been constructed of wood for some centuries.[5] These *timburhús* (timber houses) were often darkened with creosote to preserve the wood, with white trim around the windows and doors. With the coming of free trade in 1855, buying power increased and lumber was imported. The timber houses, since they were not originally well insulated, had the disadvantage of being cold, though the cooking fires and chimney gave off heat. In 1896 the earthquake that destroyed many buildings in the south provided a strong impetus to turning to the use of corrugated metal for siding and roofs, even for finer homes. Given the Icelandic climate, wood siding frequently rotted. The Icelandic use of corrugated metal for siding finally conquered the leaking and damp that had pervaded Icelandic houses and also continues to give parts of Reykjavík and elsewhere a certain charm. In the early twentieth century concrete began to be used for building in Reykjavík and the towns, though not commonly in the countryside until about 1930.

Farming

Farming was the backbone of the economy, consisting 90% of livestock production, supplemented by raising potatoes and a few other root vegetables and some barley.[6] The *tún* or fields around the farmstead were manured and the hay cut; after 1900 drainage greatly increased the total area of the *tún* or home fields.[7] Horses and cows are pastured near the farmstead, whereas the sheep, then as now, continued to be free to roam widely in the summer.

As elsewhere, farming was hard work. In the nineteenth century the farm day began about 6:00 a.m. Chores were finished before eating, including drawing water from the well or stream, with the main meal at about 2:00 p.m. and a supper at 11:00 p.m. just before going to bed. The workday was a long 16–18 hours, especially during haying; the energy drain seems to have often resulted in slower work habits.[8] One young foreman scheduled fewer hours of labor per day during haying and achieved the same results. On the positive side, there was enough exercise for all and the children were an integral part of the working family.

Various materials were burned for fuel: peat, sheep manure, driftwood, brushwood, heather, and moss. One of the first jobs in spring was to clean out the barns. The sheep manure was cut into slabs with a spade where it had compacted in the sheep shelters, and was spread out to dry and then stacked until needed. In addition, birch was burned for fuel, but also used to fill chinks in the houses and even to feed the cows and horses when hay was lacking, though young willow was better feed.

The seasonal round of farm chores began with manuring the home fields in the spring and cutting peat for fuel. The *púfur*, or mounds in the fields caused by frost heave, were levelled so that the fields could be worked, though there was no real blade for this task until 1910. Today machinery is used to level these frost mounds.

In the summer the sheep were sheared and the wool washed outdoors in large wooden vats, first in hot water and then, as elsewhere, in urine that had been allowed to stand to increase the ammonia content. The sheep were driven to summer pasture, where the ewes were milked. The whole family helped with the haying and collecting Iceland moss and other herbs. Charcoal to process bog iron was made from birch. In the north especially, the people collected the driftwood that the ocean currents had brought from Siberia, to use for fuel or timber for building. Summer was also the time to trade; the farmers traveled to the market centers, where they bought meal and grain, iron, timber, tobacco, and spirits in return for fish, fish liver oil, knitwear, and wool. The goods traded were carried in backpacks or, like the hay after cutting, on packhorses; even long boards were secured on either side of the pack saddle with homemade horsehair rope. There were ferries to cross the major rivers, but the smaller ones had to be forded.

As today, autumn meant sheep roundup. In part of Iceland one man, called the "mountain king," organized the roundup and, with the help of the dogs, the sheep were driven into centrally located pens. It often took long hours, day and night without stopping, to round up the sheep if they had wandered far. Roundup time was often the only day of the year when the young men and girls could meet and the women usually dressed up for the occasion. Slaughtering and butchering followed the roundup, and the sheepskins were hung in the kitchen to dry.

In winter the livestock were kept indoors, except for the horses, though the sheep were often let out once daily to eat snow in lieu of giving them water.

Water was carried from the well in 10–12 liter (2 1/2 gal.) buckets hung from a rectangular wooden yoke supported on the shoulders. During winter, with the help of the children, the women also worked the wool and wove and knit, and the men tended the stock and made rope.

Clothing

Clothing was mostly homemade, utilizing the natural cream, browns, gray and black of Icelandic sheep, though some of the wool was herb–dyed. The finer wool was used for underclothes and inner socks. From the 1860s on, the women had sewing machines and from about 1900, knitting machines.[9]

The men usually dressed in knee breeches and high socks, though sometimes in trousers, with a shirt and vest, a jacket as necessary, a neckerchief tied under the chin, and a cap or hat. Wool clothes and two pairs of socks kept them warm in winter. For everyday wear the women wore a long black skirt with an apron and a blouse or a long dress belted at the waist, a kerchief on the head and, for warmth, a shawl with the ends crossed in front and tied in back around the waist. Children were dressed much as the adults. The townspeople and those who were wealthier, the men especially, wore clothes influenced by European fashions.

Unlike the men's dress jacket with brass buttons and knee breeches, the women's dress clothes are still worn to some extent, though only folk dancers still wear the women's tight shirt with embroidered collar and high, starched white headgear. On the other hand, modern women sometimes wear the embroidered black bodice over a long–sleeved white blouse, with a long, full black skirt, on Independence Day and also at parties. In the old days the skirt was made of wool. A small black skullcap with tassel is worn with the bodice dress. At the June 17 Independence Day celebration the Queen of the Mountain

National costumes, National Museum of Iceland

wears a specially designed dress, black with full skirt and fine gold embroidery, with a high, white headdress. The dress is set off by a beautiful gold–plated filigree belt. The women who have inherited these belts and the filigree pins that were also worn, cherish them.

Shoes for men and women were a kind of slipper made by the women. Women's and children's shoes were of sheep– or calfskin, and in the northwest, sometimes of fishskin. For the men and those who walked more, they were made of smoked cowhide for greater durability. To make them last longer, most shoes were dyed black with imported copper sulphate. As they did not last well, shoes were often repaired, or even made, for guests as part of normal Icelandic hospitality. Given the weather, Icelandic shoes all too often meant wet feet. In 1913 when rubbers were first imported, Icelandic farmers used them as shoes rather than wearing them over their shoes. Rubber boots were also worn and, starting in 1930, rubbers were made at home from old inner tubes.

In Reykjavík cold water was obtained from wells, but clothes were often washed in the hot spring in Laugardalur. Washerwomen collected the laundry from the homes of the well–to–do and carried it to the spring, either in wheelbarrows or on their backs, and returned it, heavy and wet, at the end of the day. It was rough work as the women worked a long day and risked being badly burned by the hot water.

Food and Drink

Milk and milk products formed an important part of the diet: sour milk or kefir, delicious *skyr* (made with rennet from the stomach of an unweaned calf or lamb), cheese, and rice porridge made with milk. The most valuable product was butter; in fact, farm rent was often paid in butter. The main drink was sour whey thinned with water.

In addition, fish was a staple; wind–dried outdoors, it was often eaten buttered. Because of the shortage of salt, smoking, drying and storage in vats of sour milk were the main means of preserving food. Given the open hearth fires used for cooking, there was always smoke to cure meat and leather. Sheep's heads, with the wool singed off, were a delicacy. Autumn meant making black pudding and liver sausage by mixing lamb suet, grain meal, sheep's blood and ground liver and kidneys. Vegetables were in shorter supply, but potatoes, some root vegetables, Iceland moss, some herbs, the seaweed dulse, and dandelion and angelica roots were all good eating. Scurvy grass (*cochlearia officinalis*) was gathered to provide vitamin C, and a tisane could be made from several plants such as blueberries and heather. Coffee became a staple.

There were small water mills in many places to grind grain and, when flour was available, bread was cooked at home. For pot bread, the dough was allowed to rise in a covered pot and then set on the fire with coals on top until it had baked. Flatbread, made with rye and rolled and baked, and delicious hot springs bread, also made with rye flour and baked in a covered tin in the ground by a hot spring, are still Icelandic staples.

Most of the kitchen utensils were of wood. On the farms in the nineteenth century each person had his or her own *askur* or wooden container shaped like a mug with a lid to keep the food warm, and often a horn spoon and pocketknife. The people ate while sitting on their beds and stored their eating utensils on a shelf over each bed. The well–to–do, on the other hand, had porcelain and silverware.

Despite the continued importance of milk products in the nineteenth century diet, average per capita consumption dropped from 776 kg per year in 1703 to 597 kg in 1800 and 488 kg in 1852.[10] Meanwhile, with increasing availability, grain consumption rose from an average of 13.1 kg per person per year in 1703 to 51.4 kg in 1852. In 1703 only 3.8% of total caloric consumption came from grain; by 1900 the figure had risen to 30.8%. Protein had dropped from 33% of the diet in the eighteenth century to 28% by 1850. The people got enough calcium and phosphorus and vitamins A and D and, in fact, more vitamin B than in the twentieth century, but the shortage of vitamin C meant that there were cases of scurvy. In 1800 sugar consumption was an infinitesimal 0.2 kg per person per year, rising to 3 kg in 1852 and 7.6 kg in the 1880s.[11]

Health

Infant mortality was high. Between 1750 and 1850, three hundred of every 1000 children born died during the first year, and from 1757–1845 not quite 57% of the children born were still alive to be confirmed at the age of 14. In the last decade of the nineteenth century life expectancy was only 44.4 years for men and 51.4 for women, and the infant mortality rate, though improved, still stood at 100/1000 births.[12] One custom that contributed to this high death rate was the fact that babies were almost never nursed, perhaps partly because the mothers worked hard and their milk dried up, with the result that the babies died of malnutrition from water–thinned cow's milk.[13]

Adverse living conditions and the lack of cleanliness took their toll. The houses were cold and damp. The windows were nailed shut and the smoky peat fire in the kitchen meant little cleanliness in the preparation of food. The dogs often licked the eating utensils clean.

The people almost never bathed. They applied a little water to their faces before going to church, and the women washed their hair in urine, or sometimes in milk, on the weekends. People slept crowded in the small *baðstofa*, with the bedding washed no more often than once or twice a year. Shirts were washed once or twice a month, underwear (often made of wool) even less often.

Conditions were no better in town. In Reykjavík trash was thrown into the central pond, and in other towns it collected behind the houses until it was dumped on the shore for the sea to wash away.[14]

Nineteenth century law specified that a farmhand should receive 4338 calories per day and a woman 3213 or 74% of a man's requirements, but Jón Steffensen[15] points out that farm labor of the day for all ages demanded physi-

Spinning wool

cal exertion with little rest and that there was consequently less than optimum energy left for body growth; height increased later when children worked less.

The people suffered most from leprosy and hydatid disease (dog tapeworm). In 1896 there were 237 leprosy cases; in 1898 a hospital for lepers was established. Since the dogs frequently slept on the beds with the people, the eggs that caused hydatid disease were easily transferred from the dogs' fur to humans. The disease was eventually checked through public information and treatment of the dogs to kill the eggs.[16] Lice were common and believed to originate within the human body, though a certain herb was often put under the bedding to try to get rid of them. On the other hand, travellers in the latter part of the century said they did not pick up any lice.

Other common ailments included rheumatism, backaches, eye diseases, and earaches. A common remedy for backache was a poultice of warm cow manure. Tuberculosis, typhoid fever, and polio did not become problems until after the beginning of the twentieth century.

Measures were taken to improve health conditions, not least the construction of drier housing at the end of the nineteenth century, but help came slowly. There was no doctor in Iceland before 1760 and no permanent posts for physicians in each quarter of the country before 1876. Vaccination for cowpox had been introduced in 1802 and was used successfully to check the smallpox epidemic of 1839–1840.[17] In 1875 the number of medical districts was increased from 8 to 20 and hospitals were built.[18] In 1909 Reykjavík was provided with water and sewage pipes.[19] In the twentieth century Iceland established one of the best public health systems in the world and today has one of the lowest death rates.

Entertainment

The long winter hours working in the *baðstofa* were enlivened by stories, word games, and singing. In the early part of the nineteenth century there were still men who went from farm to farm to chant the *rímur* or old ballads and to tell tales of ghosts and outlaws, but the practice died out after 1880. Word games were common. One was to compose or recite a verse beginning with the last letter of the last verse; many knew two or three hundred verses by heart so as not to be caught with no answer. The women expressed their artistic bent through embroidery and knitting, the men through carving and gold and silver filigree work. Birchwood was excellent for carving the eating mugs or *askar*, bedboards, and boxes to hold the women's knitting needles. Children's toys were largely sheep bones and the shells and other bits the sea washed up along the shore, which the children pretended were sheep and other animals and objects they knew.

Visitors provided news, and weddings were celebrated with parties, a chance to feast and talk to others. At the end of the day the men sometimes played tug–of–war with a hide, trying to wrest the hide from the opposing group. They also wrestled (*glíma*) by grabbing the opponent's trousers and trying to topple him with fancy footwork. Sometimes there were get–togethers where the men could test their wrestling ability against those from other farms. The townspeople could go picnicking in the countryside in summer, and winter snows meant skating and sledding.

Singing, that pastime that had sustained the people through the difficulties of earlier centuries,[20] continued to be important, with mixed choruses as well as all–male choruses in the latter part of the nineteenth century. The singers were often accompanied on a homemade *langspil*, a small dulcimer with one to six strings that were bowed. There had earlier been a *fiðla*, but its use died out in the eighteenth and early nineteenth centuries and it is not clear exactly what it looked like. The cathedral in Reykjavík acquired a small pipe organ in 1840.[21] The modern violin, together with flutes and accordions, became popular in the latter part of the nineteenth century; in one district in the north, for instance, flutes and violins were to be found on half the farms, the players usually men and largely self–taught.[22] Harmoniums were imported in preference to pianos, which were more expensive and heavier to transport, and

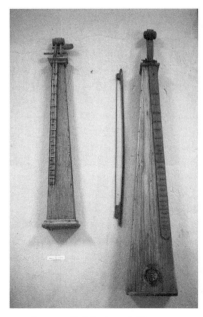

Langspil, National Museum

brass and other wind instruments arrived. Composers went to Europe to study, Icelandic folk songs came to be looked down upon, and the poems of Jónas Hallgrímsson were sung to Danish and German melodies. Though some of the old style of singing has persisted, it largely gave way to an impressive volume of lieder and popular songs written by Icelandic composers.

Attitudes changed in the nineteenth century. The end of the trade monopoly in 1855 brought a greater variety of goods, and nationalism and the struggle for independence brought different interests. Jón Thoroddsen wrote the first Icelandic novel, *Piltur og stúlka* (Boy and Girl), in 1850. The late nineteenth century saw further changes. Even Ísafjördur, with a population of 900, in 1896 sported two hotels, several gaming clubs, and a drama club that had been established in 1891.[23] And by 1900, the awesome landscape, which before had been defined only in terms of struggling with the weather and the hard work of farming, came to be recognized as "scenery" and the worthy subject matter of paintings.

Glíma, Icelandic wrestling

229

The Myth of New Beginnings

Nothing but good was said about Baldur, the radiant, gracious son of Frigg and Óðinn, who was loved by all the gods. His name is still given to the daisy in Icelandic, Baldursbrá—Baldur's brow, whitest of flowers.

The Death of Baldur

One night Baldur dreamt that his life was threatened. Óðinn was sufficiently disturbed to mount his eight–legged horse Sleipnir and descend into the forbidding world of Loki's daughter, Hel, where Óðinn awakened a dead Sibyl to prophesy what was to come. The Sibyl's words foretold of Baldur's death and the destruction of the world in Ragnarök.

On hearing this, Frigg was determined to save Baldur. She went everywhere and talked to everyone, getting each god and each object to swear an oath not to destroy Baldur. They all agreed. But the sly Loki was not satisfied. Dressed as a woman, he visited Frigg and cagily asked if there wasn't one small thing that she had omitted. "Nothing," she said, "only a little mistletoe that was too young and harmless to be a threat."

Now that Baldur was impervious to harm, the gods amused themselves with a new game, which Baldur also delighted in. They each took turns shooting arrows and throwing things at him. Nothing harmed him. One day, while they were playing the game, Loki went up to Óðinn's blind son Höður, and gave him a shaft fashioned from a sprig of mistletoe. "Here is something you can throw at Baldur," said Loki. "But I am blind," said Höður, "how can I take aim?" "No matter," replied Loki, "I'll guide your hand." And with that Höður threw the shaft and Baldur dropped dead.

The gods were grief–stricken. As they prepared the ship that would be Baldur's funeral pyre, Óðinn sent his son Hermóður, riding Sleipnir, down to Hel to try to ransom Baldur. Hermóður found Baldur in a resplendent hall sheathed with plates of gold. "The gods and the world weep for Baldur," Hermóður said, but Hel was unbending. "I will release Baldur only if there is no single living thing that does not weep for him."

Meanwhile the funeral ship was built. When Baldur's body was carried on board, his wife Nanna died of grief and her body was placed beside his. Óðinn laid his gold armband Draupnir on Baldur's chest, the same band the Dwarf had fashioned for him and that dropped eight new gold rings every nine days.

Hermóður returned from Hel with the message that all must weep for Baldur. But one old hag refused: "I will weep dry tears for him," and all the gods knew the hag was really Loki.

The funeral ship, though it rested on wooden rollers, proved too heavy for the gods to launch, so the Giantess Hyrrokkin was called in. She arrived riding a wolf, with serpents for reins. As she launched the ship with a single mighty heave, flames leapt from the rollers that had supported the ship, and the world shook. Then Thór passed his hammer over the ship to consecrate it and the funeral pyre was lit.

The Binding of Loki

Loki, the culprit, the mischief–maker, and now the murderer, would have to be caught. Ódinn from his high seat in Ásgardur saw where Loki had fled. The Aesir raced in pursuit. When Loki saw that the Aesir were close, he threw a net he had fashioned onto the hearth fire and escaped into the river as a salmon. When the Aesir arrived, Kvasir, the wisest, went into the house first, found the ashes of the net, and understood at once where Loki was to be found. Kvasir then wove a net to Loki's pattern. The Aesir waded into the river with the net, Thór in midstream, the others holding the other end of the net. Loki jumped the net and headed toward the falls in an effort to elude capture, but the Aesir brought the net closer. Mighty Thór caught him by the tail and squeezed so hard to keep him from escaping that the salmon ever since has been thin just above its tail fins.

The Aesir had no recourse but to bind Loki, but no ordinary bonds would hold him. They lashed him—now in his ordinary shape—to three stones in a cave, with iron fetters and the entrails of his own son, who had been changed into a wolf and slain. A serpent hangs over him, dripping poison. His wife Sigyn stands beside him, catching the drops of poison in a bowl. But when the bowl is full and she must empty it, the poison falls directly onto Loki, causing him to shudder so violently that the whole earth quakes.

Ragnarök

Roused reluctantly by Ódinn from the sleep of the dead, the Sibyl foretells Ragnarök, the moment when the fatal destiny of the gods must be fulfilled. Three winters of war throughout the worlds, where brother kills brother and father son, will be followed by three winters of intense Fimbul cold, with no summers between. The Earth will be assailed with biting winds and snow from all directions.

The wolf that chases the Sun, now grown stronger, catches up with her and swallows her, and his brother wolf swallows the Moon. The stars disappear from the heavens and the Earth shakes and all bonds are loosed. The Fenris Wolf breaks free, fire flaming from his eyes and nostrils. As he opens his mouth wide, his upper jaw touches heaven, his lower scrapes the earth. The World Serpent, thrown up from the sea, moves by his side, spitting poison, and ocean inundates the land.

The sky cleaves and the Giants, led by Black Surtur, the fire god, thunder toward the battlefield, Loki and the Frost Giants with them. The World Tree Yggdrasill shakes to its roots and the very mountains crumble. Heimdallur, at his post guarding the rainbow bridge, sounds his horn in warning. The Aesir wake and hold council, and Ódinn rides to the wise Mímir at his well to seek advice.

From all points of the compass the Giants and monsters thunder toward the battlefield. As the Fire Giants cross the rainbow bridge, it bursts into flames and collapses. Ódinn girds for battle in his helmet of gold, armed with his sword Gungnir, and heads straight for the Fenris Wolf. Freyr, without his sword, loses to Surtur. Heimdallur and Loki dispatch each other. Týr, the one–handed god, fights the Hel–hound Garmur and both die. Thór, fighting beside Ódinn, engages the World Serpent, the enemy he has fought twice before, as the Midgardsormur and the Giant's cat. Thór kills the Serpent but takes nine steps and falls dead of the poison the Serpent has breathed over him.

Ódinn is swallowed by the wolf Fenrir, but Ódinn's son Vídar slays the wolf and rends his jaws asunder. Gods and Champions, all are slain. Then Surtur raises his flaming sword and the whole world is destroyed in fire.

One circle of time has come to an end, another is about to begin.

Hall sees she stand
Fair in the sunlight,
Roofed with gold.
In Gimlé
There shall good
Men build
For all time
And enjoyment.
(*Völuspá—The Sibyl's Prophecy*, 65)

And so begins a golden age, with better gods and chieftains. Sun has had a daughter yet more beautiful who follows in her footsteps across the sky. The Earth rises from the sea, the fields green with self–sown crops. The sons of Ódinn, Vídar and Váli, live at Idavöllur, where once was Ásgardur, joined by Thór's mighty sons Módi and Magni, who now have Thór's hammer. Baldur returns from Hel's underworld. In the grass they come upon the gods' game board. They sit and talk, remembering the magic of the runes and what has gone before.

Safe from the Fimbul cold and the raging fires of Surtur, a man and a woman, Life and Life–longing, have survived hidden within a wood, nourished only on the morning dew. They have lived to repeople the Earth.

Iceland Since Independence

On June 17, 1944, Icelanders celebrated the founding of the Republic of Iceland. In memory of Jón Sigurdsson, the man who, more than any other, had led the long struggle for Iceland's independence in the nineteenth century, the nation met on his birthday to proclaim independence from Denmark. Icelanders continue to honor Jón Sigurdsson and to celebrate independence every year on June 17.

In 1918, after negotiations, the Danish and Icelandic parliaments passed the Act of Union by which Iceland became a sovereign state but not yet a republic, as the country remained in a personal union under the Danish king, with Denmark continuing to provide some services, including the coast guard. However, the Act of Union also provided for reviewing the agreement after 25 years, by which time World War II had engulfed Europe, and the German invasion left Denmark unable to carry out its responsibilities under the agreement. Britain, meanwhile, had accredited a minister to Iceland, in de facto recognition of Iceland's independence. By April, 1944, initial Icelandic differences of opinion had been resolved and the Althing, the Icelandic parliament, agreed to terminate the union with Denmark. Despite the cable received on May 4th from the Danish king, expressing the hope that Iceland would not change the terms of the union during the current European crisis, a referendum was held on May 20–23. An impressive 97.86% of the electorate voted on the referendum, the turnout reaching as high as 100% in some districts. An overwhelming 97% of those voting cast their ballots for independence.[1] Meanwhile, a constitution had been drawn up, allowing for a parliamentary democracy with a president, a prime minister and cabinet, and a bicameral legislature, with elections required at least every four years. There remained only the official declaration of independence.

On June 17 independence was celebrated throughout the country, but most important were the festivities at Thingvellir, the ancient site where, in the old days of the Commonwealth, the Althing was founded in the year 930. Well over 20,000 people, one–sixth of the nation, congregated at Thingvellir, many staying in tents and others bussed there for the festivities. In pouring rain, the proclamation of independence was broadcast by radio to all the nation, followed by two minutes of silence and then the exultant peal of church bells. Sveinn Björnsson was elected the first president of Iceland, representatives of other nations spoke, and the festivities continued with special music composed for the occasion. A cable from the king of Denmark, expressing his regrets but wishing the country well, calmed the worries some had had. The deluge did nothing to dampen spirits: most of those who recalled the experience fifty years later remembered best not the rain but their elation at achieving independence.

Between the World Wars

The task of the twentieth century was to lift Iceland's standard of living up to a par with the rest of the western world and then to keep pace with the world's emerging standards, even to making Iceland a leader in some fields by the end of the century. To do that, Iceland needed an improved infrastructure, capital to finance development, a more comprehensive educational system, and increased contacts with the rest of the world.

The first task after Iceland became a sovereign state under the Danish king was to elect a government in 1919. At the time all men and women who were at least 25 years of age and not on welfare were eligible to vote, since the voting age limit was not lowered to 21 nor the welfare restriction removed until 1934.[2] The 1919 election resulted in a coalition government, like most administrations since, with Jón Magnússon as Iceland's first prime minister.

The twentieth century brought social changes, including a wider range of jobs, that led to increasing urbanization; by 1920 almost half the population lived in towns.[3] The face of Reykjavík continued to become more cosmopolitan; the National Bank building and the buildings along Bankastraeti were erected in the 1920s so that the street is little changed today. The nation began issuing its own coins after 1918 and other banks were established in 1929 and 1930. First in the city and later in the countryside concrete was used for building and the older wooden houses were faced with corrugated iron siding to provide protection from the damp. In 1926 the Icelandic composer Jón Leifs brought an orchestra from Germany, thus giving Icelanders their first chance to hear a symphony orchestra in their own country.

After World War I, communications were vastly improved and the countryside became less isolated with the building of new and better roads, passable at least in summer. Radio, first privately in 1926 and then government–run from 1930 on, provided national communication. The growth of the Iceland Steamship Company after its founding in 1914, government–operated coastal sailings, and early attempts at establishing an airline expanded domestic communications and the delivery of goods, as well as contact with the outside world.

Meanwhile, the Social Democratic Party and the farmer–backed Progressive Party had both been formed in 1916. A merging of the Conservative and the Liberal Parties led to the establishment of the Independence Party in 1929, which garnered more votes than the other parties and, after a change in the law in 1942, became the largest party. The Communist Party (1930) united with a faction of the Socialists in 1938. Then, as later, various other parties were formed, including a short–lived Nazi party in the 1930s; but in the elections through October 1942 three parties garnered most of the votes: the Independence Party 45% of the vote, the Progressives 25%, and the Social Democrats ca. 20%.

Iceland's post–World War I economy was on a rather shaky footing, however, due in part to the cyclical nature of the size of the fish catches.[4] Britain and Denmark continued as the main source of imports, but for most of the years from 1921–1929 the balance of trade was negative, and in 1924 long–term credits had to be refinanced abroad.[5] The Great Depression translated into a sudden drop in the value of Icelandic exports; as the stocks of some species of fish collapsed, some foreign markets closed and others were protected by customs barriers. Nevertheless, GDP rose an average of 1.8% annually between 1914 and 1939, and between 1914 and 1930 exports increased an average of 4.8% per year, though income from exports was more than offset by a 7.4% annual increase in imports.[6]

Fishing remained the backbone of the export trade, including not only cod but, from 1920 on, herring—"the silver of the sea"—and fishmeal and oil. The modernization of the fishing industry was Iceland's industrial revolution. By 1927 trawlers and smaller coastal fishing boats had completely replaced sailing vessels, and Icelanders acquired the knowledge and the capital to compete with the foreigners who had been exploiting the rich Icelandic fishing grounds.[7] The total fish catch in 1929 was six times that of 1909, with no real increase in the number of fishermen.[8] From 1926 on Iceland had its own coast guard and was no longer dependent on Denmark. Laws, labor unions, and the Union of Icelandic Fish Producers, established in 1932, worked to protect the interests of both fishermen and producers. In 1880, 73.2% of the population was engaged in farming and only 12% in fishing. By 1930 the percentages had changed to 35.8% in farming and 21.5% in fishing.[9] Whereas earlier "fishermen" had usually been farmers and farmhands fishing in the off–season, in the twentieth century fishermen and ships' crews were increasingly trained and experienced, and the term *fisherman* came to signify an occupational status.

Mechanization and improved farming techniques modernized agriculture and raised production levels. Legislation in 1923 and in 1945 provided for public monies and support of cooperatives to finance the joint ownership of heavier equipment, some of which was used to dig drainage ditches, especially from 1942 on. The "home fields" or manured pastures were tilled and enlarged; the average size of the home field in 1920 of 3.6 hectares (9.9 acres) increased to 6.1 hectares (15 acres) in 1940 and to 23 hectares (56.8 acres) in 1974.[10] The use of fertilizer also increased. The principal crop remained hay to feed the livestock, but potatoes and rutabagas were also grown in some quantity.

The number of sheep varied rather widely. A lung disease brought by karakul sheep (introduced in 1933 to improve the breed) killed off a large number, especially in the south. To bring the disease under control it was finally necessary in 1944–1955 to slaughter 290,000 sheep.[11] Since that time the number of sheep, at times over 800,000 head, has had to be controlled to check overgrazing, but the average carcass weight has increased and meat production improved. Fencing and an increased hay supply have also meant less woodland grazing and a chance for regeneration of the woodlands.

Until 1920, butter sold to Britain constituted up to 10% of exports.[12] However, since typhoid fever was common and dairying conditions often unsanitary, Thor Jensen, an entrepreneur who had been immensely successful in the fishing industry, built a huge, model dairy farm at Korpúlfstadir just outside of Reykjavík in the 1920s to demonstrate better dairying techniques. The realization of his dairying dream was a success, but the coalition government of

Progressives and Social Democrats of 1934–1937, representing narrow farming interests and not town dwellers, passed legislation that forced the dairy to close down. The building has been used since for other purposes. On the other hand, dairy associations, beginning in 1917, and stringent laws now assure the sanitary production of milk and milk products.

Food habits changed along with changes in imports. The use of milk products, that in 1703 had accounted for 61.8% of the calories consumed, began to give way to imported grain and sugar. In the eighteenth century animal foods constituted 90%–95% of the diet. In 1703 grain accounted for only 3.8% of calories consumed but 30.8% in 1900. Carbohydrate consumption rose from 24% of the diet in the eighteenth century to over 40% by 1940.[13] Imports of flour and baking powder, as well as kitchen ovens, meant that baked products became more plentiful.

In 1930 the nation held the millennial celebration of the founding of the Althing. As king of Denmark and Iceland, Christian X attended the celebration, as did representatives from many foreign countries, demonstrating that the western world acknowledged Iceland as a sovereign state.[14]

The king's visit was followed by the difficulties of the Great Depression, which struck Iceland in full force in 1931.[15] The drop in prices obtainable, the closing of some foreign markets and the erection of customs barriers meant that Iceland, with its dependence on exports and imports to maintain the standard of living, was hit hard by the Depression. The unemployment level rose in 1932 and was not alleviated until the advent of World War II. Many people moved to town, but all too often, with few jobs to go round, they lived in poverty.

The government acted to ameliorate the situation during the Great Depression by restricting imports, providing loan funds for farmers and fishing vessel owners, supporting the construction of public works, providing loans for generating plants, and enacting the Social Security Act of 1936. Despite the large number of bankruptcies, by 1940 commercial bank deposits had risen and Icelandic ownership of businesses had increased. The National Hospital was founded in 1930; by World War II there were 50 hospitals in Iceland, with 1200 beds.

The fishing industry adjusted to changed market conditions by increasing production of iced and frozen fish. By 1943 Iceland had 62 freezing plants. Fish catches in general dropped, but the drop was offset by good herring runs in 1936–1944.[16] The eruption of the Spanish Civil War in 1936 reduced the market for bacalao or saltfish (made from cod), thus providing impetus to catch other species of fish and to develop other industries.[17] In years with large herring runs, such as the latter half of the 1930s, the value of the herring catch sometimes outstripped the total value of the cod catch.[18] The Icelandic economy experienced zero growth until 1936–1940, when there was some improvement, partly because of much larger herring runs, and GDP increased by 3.2% yearly.[19] Until 1950, herring processing plants remained the largest industrialized plants in Iceland, the people working day and night to process the catches when the fish were running.[20] Though the herring brought in foreign exchange for Iceland, both herring stocks and prices were highly variable.

World War II

As war approached, the majority of Icelanders were agreed that the nation should remain neutral. Both Germany and Britain had been principal trading partners and both wanted continued access to agricultural and marine products. Iceland, on the other hand, wanted to be assured of a supply of needed goods, to improve its financial standing, and to maintain sovereignty.

In September 1939 the British navy blockaded Germany. In October a committee of Icelanders headed by Sveinn Björnsson went to London with the objective of ensuring trade with Britain. After lengthy negotiations, Iceland agreed to supply Britain with food on condition that Britain pay high enough prices and provide needed supplies and financing. The prices obtained for icefish in Britain rose and the Icelandic economy recovered. Iceland turned to the United States to obtain the fuel and goods it needed and the Iceland Steamship Co. began scheduled sailings to the U.S. After the German occupation of Denmark on April 9, the Icelandic government assumed all responsibility for the nation's foreign affairs.

At the outset of World War II there was a contingent of 134 Germans in Reykjavík, plus refugees and the German wives of Icelanders. The German consul general was, of course, a staunch Nazi. In the interests of maintaining neutrality, Iceland acceded to German demands to ban a book and a movie deemed offensive to German interests. Though Iceland accepted some Jews, in a cruel twist of fate, the Icelandic government also extradited other Jews who had escaped from Nazi Germany.[21]

Werner Gerlach's notes include interesting observations on Iceland and Icelanders at the time: "primitive living conditions," "no fruit available," "daily newspapers full of poems, mostly poorly written," "lacking in discipline." In a letter to Heinrich Himmler, the Nazi chief of police, Gerlach wrote that Jews could not succeed in Iceland as Icelanders themselves were so much "tougher."[22]

Geographically, Iceland is strategically situated as a base for monitoring and controlling the sea lanes from Iceland to the Faroes and to Greenland, and to provide a landing and refueling stop for transatlantic ships and aircraft.[23] With the capture of Denmark and the impending fall of Norway, Germany stood to gain increased access to the Atlantic Ocean. It was therefore important for Britain, after occupying the Faroes, to capture Iceland before the Germans did. Accordingly, the British launched Operation Fork by cobbling together at only four days' notice a contingent of marines that departed from Britain on May 8, 1940.[24]

Operation Fork was one of those poorly prepared maneuvers that, incredibly, succeeded. No air cover was provided. No German U–boats threatened the convoy, though they had previously patrolled the north Atlantic. The British marines were only half–trained and had only out–dated rifles and almost no heavier artillery. During the two days it took to sail to Reykjavík most were sea-sick.

Meanwhile, in Reykjavík, it was necessary to maintain secrecy for fear that Gerlach and the Germans would act. The city was rife with rumors, however, and the only real question among the Icelanders was whether it would be the British or the Germans who would come; the majority much preferred the idea of British occupation as the lesser of two evils. A coded cable advised the British consul general of the approaching landing. A cocktail party on May 9, ostensibly to celebrate the birth of a son to a British vice–consul, was the excuse for assembling British personnel—including the baby's father, who was himself a spy for the Germans—and keeping them incommunicado until the British forces arrived. A lone British reconnaissance plane flew over Reykjavík in the middle of the night, waking many of the inhabitants. In the half–dark of the spring night, Icelanders on shore watched the ships sail toward Reykjavík, where, early on the morning of May 10th, they landed. The British military had half–expected resistance by the Germans or the Icelandic police, but met none.[25]

The British at once secured the radio and post office but, out of respect for Icelandic sovereignty, left the Althing building untouched. They did take the German consul general prisoner, however, in contravention of international law (since Iceland was a neutral state), and moved quickly to capture other German males; 113 were interned on the Isle of Man for the duration of the war.[26] The consul general was returned to Germany in 1941 in exchange for British diplomatic internees.

Iceland became a needed supply center for the Allies and a base that extended the range of the Allied planes and warships that protected the Atlantic convoys. It was a major link in the Allied chain of defense that ran from North America through Greenland, Iceland and Britain. The United States at first defined the Monroe Doctrine on nonintervention by foreign powers in the western hemisphere to include Greenland, then owned by Denmark; however, in April the U.S. secured the right to establish air and naval bases in return for agreeing to defend Greenland against attack. The U.S. also refused to take over the defense of Iceland without the consent of the Icelandic government. The issue of the establishment of a foreign military base on Icelandic soil became a divisive factor in Icelandic politics. Nevertheless, recognizing the need for defense, the Althing voted 39 to 3 to allow the United States to establish a military base in Iceland, but only on condition that, among other things, the U.S. would respect Icelandic sovereignty, would leave at the end of hostilities, and would provide a defense force at no cost to Iceland. With Britain hard–pressed for manpower in the Mediterranean, U.S. forces arrived in Iceland on July 7, 1941 to assume the main responsibility for Icelandic defense.[27] On the 16th of August, 1941, Churchill reviewed the British troops in Iceland on his journey home after signing the Atlantic Charter with Roosevelt. Following the Japanese attack on Pearl Harbor on December 7, the United Sates officially entered the war. Allied troops reached a maximum of about 52,000 servicemen, largely American but including several thousand British, plus some Norwegians and a small number of Canadians. The impact of this "invasion" must be judged against the fact that Iceland at the time had a population of only about 130,000.[28]

With the coming of the military, the Icelandic economy rebounded from the Great Depression. World War II brought an end to unemployment and an average growth in GDP of 11.6%.[29] Britain consumed the fish that Iceland exported, and the lend–lease agreement with the U.S. in the autumn of 1941 provided needed foreign exchange and an assured source of imports. Despite export sales, however, the balance of trade in some years was negative.[30] Inflation cut into the buying power of wages, which initiated spiraling wage and price increases.[31] The unions fought for indexation of wages and prices and the initiation of price controls tied to the cost–of–living index.[32]

Beginning in the 1920s generating plants had been built; by 1944 there were 40 generating plants, 19 of them hydroelectric and 21 run with diesel fuel.[33] Two buildings in Reykjavík were heated with geothermal water in 1930, an innovation little known in the western world at the time. Further development of the municipal heating utility was delayed by World War II as Denmark, under German occupation, could not meet its promise to provide development capital and materials. By 1945, however, a total of 2850 buildings in Reykjavík were heated with geothermal water.[34]

Living conditions during the war changed markedly. The military occupation created an instant demand for labor that further encouraged the growth of towns, especially Reykjavík, where the population reached 46,578 in 1945. The military provided foreign exchange, built roads, bridges, and airfields, and improved harbor facilities. Despite the difficulty in obtaining supplies, some new housing units were built during the latter years of the war to relieve the acute shortage. The use of city buses, initiated in 1931, continued and the number of passenger cars rose to 3,479 in 1946.[35] With Denmark and Germany closed as an avenue for advanced study, many Icelanders went to the U.S. and a few to Canada to enroll in technical and university courses not taught at home, including pilot training.[36]

From the point of view of the occupying forces, duty in Iceland often meant living under difficult conditions. In the beginning the British lived in tents and had poor food and only primitive, outdoor cooking facilities. In the late summer of 1940 they brought in 20,000 Nissen huts to alleviate the situation. From 1941 on the Americans came, bringing with them an impressive volume of matériel, including Quonset huts and trucks, but the large number of servicemen continued to strain Icelandic facilities. The servicemen tried to rent apartments but, since they were willing to pay such high rents, the Icelandic government had to impose restraints.[37] On the other hand, a great number of the servicemen made friends with Icelanders and after the war about five hundred went home with Icelandic brides.[38]

From the point of view of Icelanders, Iceland was now a "two–family home-stead," with the locals on the one hand and the influx of foreign servicemen on the other. The arrangement had its advantages as well as its difficulties. The black market flourished despite the law banning trading with soldiers. The incidence of syphilis increased, with the infection treated with the new sulfa drugs; interestingly, most of the Icelandic cases were men and not women, despite the close relations some women had with the military. Coca Cola arrived in 1942 and caught on immediately. Many of the servicemen kept Icelandic friends supplied with gifts of tinned fruit, candy, tobacco, and chewing gum. Because of its rarity, fruit was available only on a doctor's prescription, leading to a marked increase in the number of patients.[39] New words entered the Icelandic language, including *sjoppur, ókei,* and *bæ* (shop, okay, 'bye), and Icelanders learned to sing "Clementine" and "My Bonnie Lies Over the Ocean."

Though some Icelanders tended to ignore air raid warnings and even sat on rooftops to watch what might happen, the real horror of the war came home to them. A blackout was imposed and public places in Reykjavík closed after 10:00 p.m. Some of the fishing grounds were designated danger zones and closed. Shipwrecked sailors arrived in Reykjavík almost daily during the worst of the German U–boat attacks,[40] and Icelandic ships were sunk and quite a few Icelanders died as a result of the war.[41]

The Icelandic Achievement

With the end of the war in 1945, Iceland's task was to fulfill the promise inherent in the proclamation of independence from Denmark in 1944. The degree to which Iceland achieved prosperity within only a few decades of inde-pendence is a triumph and a lesson in what can be accomplished despite limit-ed resources and a small population.

The Base at Keflavík. The end of military occupation meant that Iceland ben-efited from the airports and roads that the military had built. Some of the quon-set huts in Reykjavík that had housed the military became a temporary solution to the acute housing shortage created by the continuing growth of the city.

What to do about the base in Keflavík remained a problem, however, since at that time Icelanders lacked the expertise to run a major airport. After con-siderable argument, the Keflavík or Airport Agreement was ratified by the Althing in 1946, with 32 votes to 19. The agreement provided for joint admin-istration by U.S. and Icelandic civilian personnel, with the United States grant-ed use of the airport for six years.[42] The last U.S. servicemen left on April 8, 1947.

The question of membership in the North Atlantic Treaty Organization (NATO) intensified the political debate. Though most Icelanders would have preferred to be unarmed and not part of the dissension between the larger pow-ers, most also saw the need for the collective security provided by NATO. Antagonism among a small minority was so intense, however, that the crowd that assembled in protest on March 30, 1949, and threw rocks at the Althing building had to be disbanded by police with tear gas. Nevertheless, the NATO defense treaty was signed in Washington on April 4, 1949, with Iceland as one of the founding members.[43]

World events, including the Korean War (1950–1953), brought a change in attitudes and an appreciation of the need for a defense force. After several months of negotiations, Iceland signed the Defense Agreement with the United States in 1951, providing for the U.S. military to operate the base on behalf of NATO.[44] The agreement was revised in 1954 to assure, among other things, that all construction would be carried out by an Icelandic firm.[45] In 1961, with changed military capabilities and objectives, operation of the base was turned over to the U.S. Navy.[46]

In the ensuing decades before the collapse of the U.S.S.R. the presence of the American military base remained a thorn in the side of many Icelanders who felt it infringed on their independence and even jeopardized their safety. A small but vocal minority held yearly demonstrations in protest. The majority of Icelanders, however, declared their support of the presence of U.S. troops on the base in a petition in 1973. In fact, the government used the threat of renegotiating the future of the base as leverage to induce the United States and NATO to put pressure on Britain to bring about a successful resolution of the fishing dispute.[47]

Attitudes in Iceland toward the base and toward NATO membership completely changed, even before the collapse of the Soviet Union. In 1978 even the pro–communist People's Alliance did not demand withdrawal from NATO as a condition of participation in the coalition government.[48]

In 1992 direct payments from the base accounted for 8% of export earnings or the equivalent of 100,000 tons of cod.[49] With jobs for well over 2000 Icelanders at stake, in 1996, when the United States planned a reduction of military personnel, the country fully accepted the continued U.S. military presence and a new agreement guaranteed Iceland that the U.S. would continue to provide a defense force, a helicopter rescue service and, at least for the time being, an international airport. In the event, earlier worries about the possible loss of Icelandic culture and the Icelandic language from exposure to American base personnel and base television have paled before the onslaught of the international mass media and the demands of international relations.

The Economy. After the war the United States offered Marshall Plan aid to the war–torn countries of Europe to help them re–establish themselves economically. The Organization for European Economic Co–operation was founded in 1948 to handle the loans and grants, with Iceland one of the eighteen members. Marshall Plan loans provided Iceland with the needed infusion of capital to finance development. The Althing agreed to loans that were used to build two generating plants and the fertilizer plant, and to build and improve fish processing plants, as well as to purchase agricultural equipment and increase the fleet of trawlers and merchant vessels. After May 1953 Iceland's economy had improved to the point where the government felt no further need of Marshall Plan aid.[50]

Despite the increase in population (to about 270,000 in 1996), the relatively small number of people remains a constraint on the Icelandic economy, as does the lack of more variety of resources. Even with the addition of other sectors, such as the processing of aluminum, initiated in the 1960s, the dependence on fishing means that the economy tends to have too little buffer against cyclical variations in fish stocks and fish prices. The economy is characterized by a large number of small, low–profit firms, paying low wage rates as compared to other OECD countries (Iceland is a member of the Organization for Economic Co–operation and Development), with dependence on a wide variety of imports to maintain the standard of living. Iceland's success has been based on the increasing utilization of scientific and technological knowledge and of developing needed technological innovation, including software marketable abroad. Annual production increased a healthy 4.6% on the average between 1945 and 1980.[51] Taking into account the 1.5% annual population growth, per capita GNP increased 2.4% between 1945 and 1992.[52]

The rapid economic growth in the 1940s yielded foreign reserves and improvements in the trawler fleet, but in the years following World War II the economy continued to improve or decline based in large part on the size of the herring stocks.[53] In the 1970s the economy experienced rapid growth despite the jump in oil prices. To some extent, expansion of the geothermal heating utilities reduced dependence on imported fuel, but petroleum products remain essential for operating the fishing trawlers. The wage–price spiral continued, leading to a plethora of strikes for higher wages, followed by government devaluations of the króna, which in turn reduced buying power. During one strike only small private businesses were allowed to operate, and only with family members; suddenly at one bakery all the clerks looked alike but came in different sizes, including the very young!

In 1986 the government paid out 10.35% of total expenditures to develop hydroelectric power; by 1990 geothermal power produced 31% of energy needs and hydropower 37%.[54] Reykjavík and other areas benefit from the clean, cost–effective use of geothermal water for heating and bathing.

In 1986 the Althing also finally legalized the sale of beer. In 1987 disposable income reached a peak that was reflected, among other things, in the purchase of more motor vehicles; in 1988 Icelanders owned 498 passenger cars per 1000 people. The increased traffic in turn led to noticeable air pollution in Reykjavík, followed by government regulations to require the use of unleaded gasoline. Bankruptcies became common. In 1990 the high inflation that had plagued the Icelandic economy, as high as 48.1% from 1975–1984, was finally brought under control but the unemployment rate, which had only twice exceeded 1% during the preceding decade,[55] rose markedly in the mid–1990s.

Despite the cyclical nature of the economy, changes in job emphases and training reflected changes elsewhere in the western world and the standard of living continued to rise. Both the public sector and industry expanded after World War II and, as elsewhere, the service sector came to account for most jobs; by 1988, 58.5% of workers were employed in service jobs as against 31.1% in industry.[56] On the other hand, the high cost of living and relatively low wages compared to the other OECD countries have meant that a large number of people make ends meet by holding down two jobs, and women have increasingly joined the workforce. In 1990 unskilled male workers worked an average of 50.4 hours per week. In some years, both professionals and workers have emigrated in search of opportunity and higher wage rates abroad;[57] by 1996 slightly over 20,000 Icelanders were living abroad.[58] Nevertheless, the standard of living rose; from 1980 on, 83% of Icelanders owned their own home;[59] and in 1991 the per capita GNP of USD 22,580 was slightly higher than the figure for the United States of USD 22,560.[60]

Mechanization and fertilization of larger areas improved agricultural production, with a reduction in the number of people engaged in farming to 5% of the workforce.[61] Better cultivars and grazing techniques improved plant and livestock yields. Greenhouse growing provides tomatoes, lettuce, and flowers. Fur farming (mink and angora rabbits) and fish farming have extended rural opportunities, but both are subject to market demands and also to the difficulties of keeping the stocks healthy.

Export volume increased after World War II, with seafood products accounting for 71% of export value in 1989.[62] Though cod have accounted for the major share of the export value, other seafood products are also processed. The traditional exports of fish and hides, wool and woollen products are supplemented by processed aluminum (12.9% of export value in 1989)[63] and ferro–silicon. Icelandic horses are in demand in some countries. The Icelandic firm Marel has invented and produces on–board fish weighing scales that have been installed in over half the world's trawlers. Oz, the software firm founded by two school dropouts, provides software for Microsoft and others. Iceland's main trading partners are the European Union, the United States, and Japan.

Communications improved with the construction of better roads and the use of long–haul trucks to deliver goods. In 1974 the road over the sands in the south was made passable for passenger cars, thus making it possible for the first time for all vehicles to drive completely round Iceland. That summer the only real vacation question was whether a family would drive around Iceland clockwise or counterclockwise. Ships, planes, and satellite communication keep Iceland in touch with the rest of the world every day of the year and tourism has zoomed; by 1995 the number of tourists arriving annually from North America, Germany, Britain, Scandinavia, and other areas had risen to 100,000, plus a large number of businessmen, scientists and diplomats.

In the 1980s Iceland finally acquired a fully functioning stock exchange, broadening the base of share ownership. In January 1994, after the króna had become fully exchangeable for other currencies, Icelanders could legally invest abroad. The catchword in business and in banking became "rationalization," with mergers and other effective steps to establish more cost–efficient means of operating. Some government services were also privatized to enhance efficiency. In assessing the Icelandic economy, it should be borne in mind, however, that, though Iceland operates a coast guard, the country has no expenditures for military forces and that government borrowing abroad has been necessary to maintain the level of imports and construction that support the high standard of living. However, Iceland also maintains a high bond rating, and in 1994 the public debt of 58% of GDP was lower, for example, than that of the United States or Denmark.[64]

Politics. Elections from 1959–1991 were marked by an average voter participation of almost 90%.[65] The Independence Party has been a part of most of the coalition governments since World War II. From 1945–1980 the Independence Party received an average of 38.9% of votes in national elections, the Progressive Party 25%, after its formation in 1956 the communist People's Alliance 17%, and the Social Democrats 16%.[66] Various smaller parties have also competed for votes and been partners in forming governments.

In 1942, Ólafur Thors, the head of the Independence Party, became prime minister. In all, Ólafur Thors was prime minister during five administrations, though his terms of office alternated with those of the Progressive Party head Hermann Jónasson (prime minister from 1956–1958) and others. Following the redrawing of voting district boundaries in 1959, Thors formed a coalition government with the Social Democrats, thus setting in motion the Reconstruction Government that was to last through three administrations until 1971. With increased emphasis on a free market, the króna was devalued 57% to facilitate sale of exports,[67] customs duties were lowered, the Central Bank was established, the fishing fleets increased, and Iceland became a member of the European Free Trade Association in 1970. Inflation averaged only 10.5%, with virtually no unemployment, and per capita disposable income increased 55%. Currency reserves rose to 8%–12% of GNP.[68] At the same time, both the United States and the Soviet Union attempted to influence post–war Icelandic politics.[69] Since the demise of the U.S.S.R. the fact that the People's Alliance was clearly supported and directed by the Soviet government has become well documented.

The period of the Reconstruction Government coincided with rapid social change, not all attributable to government measures. Fewer workers were engaged in primary production than before, and more in services. The welfare system was expanded. The importance of longer–term schooling was recognized, with an increase in the proportion of specialists, and the population in the southwest grew at the expense of rural areas.[70]

Political organization underwent change after 1971. According to one view, the parties no longer represented class divisions so much as individual differences of opinion or "umbrella associations of independent leaders",[71] with the emphasis on wielding power rather than formulating or carrying out policy. In addition, the expansion of the mass media in the latter part of the twentieth century created a very different kind of podium, giving Icelandic politicians the opportunity, as elsewhere, to promise a great deal, and to explain publicly, usually very carefully, what is wrong with an opponent's reasoning, even when that other person belongs to the same party.

Other changes also occurred. The M.P.s came to represent a wider range of backgrounds and interests and were more broadly educated than before, a higher percentage having a university degree in a field other than law.[72] In order to reduce expenses, in 1991 the Althing was changed from a bicameral to a unicameral legislature, and throughout the 1990s many of the smaller municipalities voted for amalgamation into single more efficient units. In the smaller municipalities legislative and judicial powers were not completely separated until July, 1992, when judicial power was transferred to the district courts.

As elsewhere, emphasis shifted to include opportunities for women. Vigdís Finnbogadóttir was elected president in 1980 (serving until retirement in 1996), and from 1983–1991 as many as 23.8% of the members of the Althing were women.[73] The breakup of old political parties and the establishment of new ones included the formation of the Women's List in 1983, and a woman was elected mayor of Reykjavík in 1994.

Foreign Relations. After independence one matter still remained to be settled with the Danes: the return of the old manuscripts that had been taken to Copenhagen in the eighteenth century in order to preserve them. With good cause, both Icelanders and Danes claimed legal ownership. It was not until 1971, after the matter had been settled in court, that a Danish naval vessel finally arrived with the first manuscripts to be returned, *Flateyjarbók* and the *Codex Regius of the Poetic Edda*.[74]

Iceland faced an urgent need after World War II to protect fish stocks. Increased fishing and better equipment led to a 32% plunge in haddock stocks. In 1945 U.S. President Harry Truman had proclaimed that the United States had rights over all resources out to the limits of the continental shelf, and Mexico and Britain followed suit. In 1949 Iceland declared that, beginning in 1951, it would cease to respect the three mile limit imposed by the 1901 treaty, and proposed that a U.N. committee review the rights of coastal states.[75]

In 1952 a Hague court decision granted Norway a four mile limit. Britain at first refused to accept the World Court's decision and Icelanders were unable to land their fish catches in Britain. The difference of opinion reopened the altercations with Britain over fishing rights that had begun in the fifteenth century and that have come to be known as the Cod Wars. The Seventh Cod War (some call it the first)[76] ended without fighting when Britain accepted the four–mile limit in 1956. The Eighth Cod War began when Iceland declared a twelve–mile limit in 1958, and the British responded by sending a naval vessel to protect its trawlers, but the two countries reached an agreement in 1961.

Since Independence

In 1972 the Althing set the limit at 50 miles, thus precipitating the Ninth Cod War. In order to stop British fishing, the Icelandic Coast Guard cut the trawl cables of 82 British ships. The affair ended after fourteen and a half months with a treaty allowing the British limited fishing between 12 and 50 miles.

In 1975 Iceland declared a 200–mile limit. This time the two countries broke off diplomatic relations and British naval vessels rammed Icelandic Coast Guard vessels 54 times; one such "duel" on April 1, 1976, lasted for nine hours. After six and a half months the Tenth Cod War ended in a truce. By then Iceland had cut a total of 117 British and 30 German trawl cables. In 1985 the problem was resolved when the international Law of the Sea granted a 200–mile exclusive economic zone to all the signatory states.

Pope John Paul II visited Iceland in 1989 and, together with the Icelandic bishop, officiated at mass at Thingvellir; the beauty queen known to the world as Hófi was elected Miss Universe in 1986; and Jón Páll Sigmarsson won the Strongest Man in the World competition. But the event that made Iceland finally well known to the world was the Summit Meeting in October 1986, between U.S. President Ronald Reagan and U.S.S.R. General Secretary Mikhael Gorbachev. Icelanders organized the meeting with only ten days' notice, partly using Scouts as guards along the route to Höfdi House, where the meeting was held. Though no disarmament treaty resulted from the meeting, it marked the beginning of the end of the arms race between the United States and the U.S.S.R., and indeed the beginning of the end of the Soviet Union. Iceland was first to recognize the independence of the Baltic States in 1991.

The People. Icelanders responded to the improved living conditions after World War II—an ample supply of food, heated houses, and better health care—by growing taller and living longer. In 1994 life expectancy at birth had reached 80 years for females and almost 76 years for males, the second highest, after Japan, of any country in the world.[77] Diet improved, especially in the 1980s, with ready availability of vegetables, both fresh and frozen, ample vitamin C, and a wider variety of foods than before. On the other hand, sedentary jobs meant lower energy requirements at the same time that more calories were consumed, amounting in 1989 to 3,611 per person per day,[78] and unfortunately resulting in the fact that more people became overweight. Icelanders have been consuming a high–protein, high–fat diet, including more fish than most other European nations, but less than the recommended amount of carbohydrates.[79] Icelanders have consumed more Prince Polo candy bars from Poland than any other country except Kuwait. As elsewhere in the western world, cancer and heart–artery diseases are the main causes of death. While Icelanders consume the least amount of alcohol per capita of all the European countries, drinking habits have been such that the country has needed three times as many hospital beds for alcoholics as any other European country.[80]

The size of families has shrunk; in 1989 the fertility rate was just over 2.2

per female and most parents had 2 children. The first child was more apt to be born out of wedlock, a fact that is entirely acceptable in Iceland, with the child bearing no stigma. In earlier years the parents often waited to marry until they could afford their own home, but urbanization has provided rental opportunities and the couple may marry younger or simply live together. In 1992 the groom was usually 25–29 years old and the bride 20–24.[81]

Not all those who live in Iceland are of Icelandic descent. Many Icelanders have married Danes, Britons, and other foreigners. Acceptance of some racial stocks has not always come willingly, however. During World War II, Prime Minister Hermann Jónasson specifically requested that the U.S. not station blacks on the base, only "select" troops. The U.S. acceded to Icelandic demands in 1941 and in 1951, but by 1964 U.S. human rights legislation meant that the American government could no longer treat blacks differently from whites. Nevertheless, some blacks sent to the base were still reassigned as late as 1972. Since then, blacks, Filipinos, and others have served with their units on the base without Icelandic protest, though some have felt the sting of prejudice.[82] Those American blacks who have come to Iceland to help develop an Icelandic basketball program have been appreciated. Since World War II Iceland has welcomed its share of refugees, including Hungarians and Poles. Accepting Iceland's share of Vietnamese, however, was not without opposition, though the results have been positive. The Red Cross helped 34 Vietnamese refugees in 1979 and a further 60 in 1990–1991 to find jobs and housing and to learn the language.[83] In addition, a considerable number of foreigners have become citizens, usually because they are married to Icelanders, and others, principally from the Nordic countries but also from as far away as Asia and Africa, live in Iceland for varying lengths of time.

Living with Change. Iceland leapt into the modern world. The bank tellers in the 1970s were still using hand–cranked adding machines; "fresh" vegetables usually meant small potatoes still covered with the soil they grew in, and limp, misshapen carrots; almost no roads were paved; there was no television on Thursday; and few businesses bothered to answer the telephone promptly, if at all. The rapid changes that followed are tribute to the inherent ability of the majority of Icelanders. The rising standard of living has meant that supermarkets carry fresh and frozen vegetables all year, including Asian and other foods previously unknown in Iceland. With the change in the law permitting private television channels, competition forced the state channel to televise every day of the week. As soon as computers were programmed for the Icelandic alphabet, Icelanders grabbed them, and bank tellers jumped from hand–cranked to computerized teller machines. At one point Icelanders had more VCRs per capita than anywhere else in the world, in the 1990s had more e–mail addresses per capita than any nation except Australia, and in 1996 more Internet users per capita than anywhere else including the U.S.[84] E–mail and advertising on the World Wide Web are ideal ways for a small country like Iceland to be in close touch with the wider world and to market local products and inventions at minimal cost. As the population in Reykjavík approached and passed the 100,000 mark in 1992, businesspeople had come to understand that what worked well in a small village where everyone knew everyone else was no longer viable in a city; they had learned to advertise more effectively, to develop customer goodwill, and yes, to hire someone to answer the telephone promptly and politely.

Educational opportunities have expanded as people are interested in learning a greater variety of subjects and skills. University students now come from all social strata and those who go abroad to finish their training are no longer principally the elite. The school system has had to grow beyond outmoded definitions of education, however, which led to a much shorter school day and school year than in other OECD countries, a deficit in the amount of material covered in Icelandic schools, and, since their importance has not been generally recognized, low teacher salaries.[85] Many more Icelanders than previously have become cosmopolitan and more accepting of the results of scientific research, and the need for professional training has been recognized and the opportunities expanded. Nowadays English, rather than Danish, affords access to information and communication with the rest of the world. Icelanders have made their name abroad in various fields. The Icelandic nation includes a full complement of computer experts, has taught the United Nations University Geothermal Training Programme (beginning in 1979) and more recently the Marine Fishing Programme, and has advised other countries such as Namibia, Chile, Kenya, and Rumania, on fishing and the utilization of geothermal potential.

A relatively large number of Icelandic artists, authors, and musicians are among those who have made a name for themselves abroad. Probably the best–known artist is Jóhannes Kjarval (1885–1972), with his depiction of Icelanders against the intricacies of the lava–strewn landscape. Rev. Jón Sveinsson's "Nonni" books for children have been widely read in parts of Europe. Halldór Laxness won the Nobel Prize for Literature in 1955. Helgi Tómasson became well known for his dancing with the New York City Ballet and then, as director, made the San Francisco Ballet into one of the top companies in North America. Despite the low level of financing, an impressive film industry has developed, utilizing both the landscape and Icelandic themes to produce a special film genre. Of the many composers in the twentieth century, Jón Leifs (1899–1968) stands out, though his works were not widely recognized before the 1990s. A spate of singers emerged in the latter part of the twentieth century, most of them performing in the opera houses of Europe, including the tenor Krístján Jóhannsson and the bass–baritone Kristinn Sigmundsson. Many Icelandic bands have performed jazz and rock, and the pop singer Bjoerk soared to the top of world charts in the 1990s.

There have been, as elsewhere, negative aspects to the rapid social changes, and stress has become a modern health problem. The high cost of living has meant long working hours away from home, usually for both parents, with the result that they are often not available to give young children the support they need. The crime rate has risen, illegal drugs are all too readily available, and Iceland had its first bank robbery in 1995. Better and more rapid communication with the rest of the world also means that AIDS reached Iceland; one spin–off of the worry about AIDS, however, was the willingness to discuss sexual problems publicly, even incest and child abuse, and to begin to deal with them.

Social and technological change has been the main characteristic of modern Icelandic life. The one certainty is that the next year will bring something different from the previous one. In the midst of all this change there is an emphasis on holding on to some core of what is Icelandic—language, history, beliefs, and customs—while still being open to innovation. Iceland will continue to have a relatively small population where family and schoolmates will be important throughout life and where, to a marked extent, traditional customs and beliefs will be upheld alongside Icelandic innovation and imported technology and ideas. In 1995 Iceland was ranked as one of the top twenty nations in the world in terms of per capita wealth: USD 486,000 in comparison to USD 421,000 for the U.S.[86] Iceland's continuing aspiration is to realize the potential of that wealth, in terms of well–being, financial income, and self–realization. If the past is a guide, Iceland will continue to meet that challenge.

The Family: New Year's Eve

New Year's Eve! The best night to be in Iceland. Despite the winter darkness, the night is one of the lightest nights of the year!

Sigga's parents had come to eat dinner with Sigga and Gunnar, joined by their daughter Thórunn with Sveinn and their son, Thórir. With their son, Gummi, and me there were nine of us round the table. Over roast lamb and potatoes the conversation flowed.

"A friend of ours on the Westman Islands turned the water on to fill the bathtub and nothing came out."

Sveinn took up the story from Thórunn. "The water was off for the whole area, something wrong with the pipes."

"And it came back on while she and her husband were asleep. When she got up later, her feet landed in a flood of water. They'd forgotten to turn the faucet off!"

"Remember the time the police saw a small fishing boat just going round and round in circles?"

"What was the matter with it?" Gummi asked as he helped himself to more of everything to eat.

"When the police got there they found the man sound asleep and the boat running on its own. Fellow never stirred while they towed him into harbor!"

"He'd had a good nip out of the bottle," we all agreed.

"The police saw a man recently carrying a safe out of a building at 6 o'clock Monday morning. The man claimed to have been out for a walk before delivering the paper and, when he found a broken window, decided to go off with the safe so no robbers would find it!"

We laughed, but there's more: "Got caught in his own lie: there's no paper on Monday morning."

"Funny things happen to foreigners, too," I added. "An English lady came to visit her daughter when she was teaching here, and the daughter of course took her mother swimming. You always see someone you know at the swimming pool, including while you're undressing and showering. So the daughter introduced her mother to her friends. Afterwards this nice English lady said she'd never before in her life met so many people naked!"

As Thórunn helped her mother clear the dishes, Gudrún commented, "Sheep have their personalities too. There was a ewe when I was young that often came to visit. She'd walk in the door if she found it open and go in the living room and stare at an oil painting that hung on the wall!"

"Did you read about the ewe that had triplets?" Sigga's father, Gudmundur, asked.

"The farmer was lucky if the ewe bore triplets," Sigga observed as she brought in the ice cream.

"That ewe had a mind of her own, too. Took her three lambs down to the seashore with her and the lambs went in the ocean and headed for the open sea. The farmer saw it from a distance and started down to try to save them, but he didn't have to. Three seals appeared, raised their heads above the water, and the three lambs turned back toward shore."

"The farmer was right when he said in the old days that would have been retold as a folktale," Gunnar commented. "Three shepherds in sealskins who could not be released from a witch's spell until they had rescued three lambs."

"And maybe that is what happened," Gudrún said with some conviction.

Gummi, too, had a story to tell. "Remember the time the alarm sounded in a branch post office right in the worst of the Christmas rush?"

"Did the police answer the alarm?" I asked as Gummi spooned in a huge mouthful of ice cream.

"Oh, sure," Gummi continued, "but when they got there the postal clerks were so busy that they told the policemen that it didn't make any difference that they were in uniform, they'd have to get in line and wait their turn like everybody else!"

After the laughter died down, Sigga added, "Don't worry. There was a happy ending. Turned out to be a false alarm."

"Now for the bonfire!" Gunnar got up from table.

"You can have more ice cream when we get back," Sigga promised her grandson, Thórir, as we all put on our boots and bundled up well.

There were snow and ice underfoot as we walked a short way to the bonfire, the air sharp with cold but no strong wind. The fire had already been lit, the people silhouetted against the flames as we approached.

The New Year's bonfire has to be seen to be believed. For some time before New Year's all the wood, cartons, and old tires that need to be gotten rid of are piled high in one of the several places designated by the city (or elsewhere in Iceland by the community) as safe for such a fire. Lit, the enormous pile becomes a mountain of orange flame, too hot to approach closely and clearly visible from a long distance away. The fire is so huge that it will burn for hours, the coals sometimes still smoldering the next morning.

The custom of lighting a bonfire on New Year's Eve dates back to the late eighteenth century, when Icelanders first began to have enough firewood for something other than cooking. Now bonfires are a yearly New Year's event, provided the wind is not dangerously strong.

There is an age–old belief that the elves move to another home on New Year's Eve or in the beginning of January, and another *álfabrenna* (elf fire) may also be lit, often on the thirteenth day of Christmas or January 6th, with people dressed as elves or santas dancing around the flames, but the people around the New Year's blaze are bundled up in ordinary clothes.

Friends greet us as we arrive. Watching the fire together is a yearly rite. A few produce hip flasks and share them. A group forms to sing Icelandic songs, their voices undoubtedly warmed both by the fire and the contents of the flasks.

We move around, talking to others. Gummi goes off with his friends and the rest of us return home in time to watch the yearly television spoof of what has happened during the year.

The aurora borealis puts on a spectacular display as we walk home, gossamer bands moving rapidly across the sky: long green streamers, sometimes edged with red, the patterns constantly shifting.

Once home, Sigga's brother Jón and his wife, Helga, come to join us and we all have cake and coffee. Friends drop in for a while before going on to visit other homes.

When midnight draws closer the fireworks begin, set off by private individuals. Sveinn has brought a sack of rockets and fountains sold by the Scouts and the rescue units to finance their rescue work. Thórir hands the rest of us sparklers as Sveinn and Gummi set off the rockets on the lawn behind the house. Shortly before midnight the barrage of fireworks intensifies until the sky becomes an incredible mass of exploding lights, the whistles and bangs and brightness pushing back the darkness, defying nature.

While Sveinn and Gummi set off more rockets, the rest of us gather round the television, watching the fireworks through the open door, each with a glass of schnapps in hand. At midnight we toast the year together and sing, along with the TV, *Nú árið er liðið* (Now the year has passed), and each of us, including Thórir and Sveinn and Gummi, go round to hug and kiss or greet every other person and thank each one for the past year.

The ring of seasons has begun again.

Common Words Found on a Map of Iceland

The place names on a map of Iceland need not seem intimidating. There are not really so many of them and the names are very graphic, saying exactly what is to be seen. The following list will make the map more meaningful.

á – river
bakki – bank
berg – rock; cliff
bjarg – cliff
bruni – lava
bær – community; farm
dalur – valley
dyngja – shield volcano
ey (pl. *eyjar*)– island
eyri – spit of land, point
fell – mountain, fell
fjall (pl. *fjöll*) – mountain
fjörður – fjord
fljót – (large) river
flói – (large) bay
foss – waterfall
gnúpur – steep mountain, promontory
heiði – heath, moor
hólmur – islet, holm
hraun – lava, lava flow
hver – geyser
höfði – headland

höfn – harbor
jökull – glacier
klettur (pl. *klettar*) – crag, cliff
kvísl – braided river channel
laug (pl. *laugar*) – hot spring
nes – ness, peninsula, point
ós – river mouth
sandur – sands; beach
skagi – cape, peninsula, headland, point of land
skarð – mountain pass
sker – skerry
staður (pl. *staðir*) – place, stead
tangi – spit/tongue of land, point
tindur – peak
tjarn – pond, small lake
tunga – tongue/spit of land
vatn (pl. *vötn*) – lake (also water)
vegur – road
vík – bay, cove
vogur – cove, inlet
völlur (pl. *vellir*) – field

Key Dates

874	Beginning of Norse settlement of Iceland
930	Founding of the Althing
930–1030	The Saga Age
985/986	Eiríkur the Red settles in Greenland
999 ?	Leifur Eiríksson sails from Greenland to North America
1000	Christianity made Iceland's religion
1030–1118	The Age of Peace
1117–18	Icelandic law written down
ca 1130	*Íslendingabók* written by Ari Thorgilsson
1179–1241	Snorri Sturluson, leading chieftain and author
1220–1262	Age of the Sturlungs
1262–64	End of the Commonwealth: the Old Treaty gives Norway sovereignty over Iceland
1387–1520	The Kalmar Union with Denmark
1400–	The English century; the English finally leave the Westman Islands in 1558
1402–1404	The Great Plague
ca 1500	End of settlements in Greenland
1550	The Reformation; Bishop Jón Arason beheaded
1602	Danish trade monopoly imposed
1614	Attack by British pirates on the Westman Islands repulsed
1615	Spanish attack in north repulsed
1627	Marauding "Turks" (Algerian pirates)
1703	First census
1749	Skúli Magnússon the first Icelandic bailiff
1783–1784	The Laki eruption
1783–1785	The Haze Hard Times
1798	The site of the Althing moved to Reykjavík
1800	The Althing disbanded
1809	Jörundur, the Dog Days king of Iceland
1841	Beginning of Jón Sigurdsson's struggle for Iceland's independence
1845	The Althing re–established as an advisory body, meeting in Reykjavík
1855	The Danish trade monopoly abolished
1870–1900	Peak migration to North America
1874	The Althing given executive power and control of finances
1904–1918	Home rule
1914–1918	World War I

Key Dates

1918	The Union Treaty with Denmark, Iceland granted independence under the Danish king
1940	The British take Iceland in World War II
1944	Establishment of the Republic of Iceland
1949	Iceland joins NATO
1952	Iceland becomes a member of the Nordic Council
1955	Halldór Laxness wins the Nobel Prize in literature
1970	Iceland becomes a member of EFTA
1986	Reykjavík the site of the Reagan–Gorbachev Summit Conference

Notes

What Is an Icelander?

1) Roy A. Rauschenberg, "The Journals of Joseph Banks's Voyage up Great Britain's West Coast to Iceland and to the Orkney Isles,, *Proc. Am. Phil. Soc.* June 1973; Urður Gunnarsdóttir, "Íslands vinurinn," *Morgunblaðið* 25 July 1993: B2–B3.
2) Anna Agnarsdóttir, *Great Britain and Iceland 1800–1820*, 10.
3) Lord Dufferin, *Letters from High Latitudes* 36, 44.
4) Stefán Ólafsson, "Hvernig eru Íslendingar? Nokkrar vísbendingar um gildi í menningu Íslendinga."
5) *Morgunblaðið*, "Lífsskoðanir Íslendinga" 17 Sept. 1991: Section B.
6) Stefán Ólafsson 91.
7) Stefán Ólafsson 56, 57, 59.
8) Erlendur Haraldsson, "Representative National Surveys of Psychic Phenomena: Iceland, Great Britain, Sweden, USA and Gallup's Multinational Survey," *Jr. Soc. for Psychical Res.,* Oct 1985: 145–158.
9) Agnes Bragadóttir, "Íslensk stjórnmál hafa heillað mig gjörsamlega." Interview with Ambassador Charles Cobb, *Morgunblaðið*, 9 Jan. 1992: 25.
10) Stefán Ólafsson 24.
11) Kristín Marja Baldursdóttir, "Hraustir menn eða hvað?" *Morgunblaðið* 17 Jan. 1993: 1B–2B, 4B.
12) *The Economist*, n.d.
13) Stefán Ólafsson 92.
14) *Morgunblaðið*, "Ný rannsókn á skammdegisþunglyndi" 8 Dec 1992: 63.
15) Stefán Ólafsson 77, 81.
16) Stefán Ólafsson 62.
17) Guðmundur I. Sverrison and Helgi Kristbjarnarson, "Könnun á svefnháttum íslenkra barna," *Læknablaðið* 76 (1990): 360.
18) Stefán Ólaffson 39.
19) E. Paul Durrenberger and Gísli Pálsson xvii.
20) Cf. Sigurður A. Magnússon, *The Northern Sphinx* 171–172.
21) Ólafur Ragnar Grímsson, "The Icelandic Power Structure," *Scand. Pol. Studies* 11 (1976): 14.

The Formation of the Land

1) Árni Johnsen, *Eldar í Heimaey*.
2) Árni Johnsen 158, 165.
3) Grímur Gíslason, "Engan mann sakaði en 400 hús eyðilögðust," *Morgunblaðið* 23 Jan. 1993: 14–16.
4) Þorleifur Einarsson, *Geology of Iceland* 236; "Jarðsaga Íslands" 6–7.
5) Don L. Anderson *et al.*, "Plate Tectonics and Hotspots: The Third Dimension," *Science* 19 June 1992: 1654–1650; R.S. White, "A hot–spot model for early Tertiary volcanism in the N Atlantic;" R.S. White and Dan P. McKenzie, "Volcanism at Rifts;" Millard F. Coffin and Olav Eldholm, "Large Igneous Provinces;" M.H.P. Bott, "A new look at the causes and consequences of the Icelandic hot–spot;" R.I. Hill *et al.*, "Mantle Plumes and Continental Tectonics" *Science* 10 Apr. 1992: 186-192.
6) Robert Decker and Barbara Decker, *Volcanoes*; H.W. Menard, *Islands*; R.S. White.
7) Þorleifur Einarsson, *Geology of Iceland* 245.
8) Þorleifur Einarsson, *Geology of Iceland* 254; "Jarðsaga Íslands" 6–7; Jóhannes Nordal and Valdimar Kristinsson, eds. *Iceland 874–1974*, 4.

Notes

9) Sigurður Þórarinsson, "Sambúð lands og lýðs í ellefu aldir," *Saga Íslands I* 43.
10) Kristján Sæmundsson 21.
11) Sigurdur Thorarinsson, *On the Geology and Geophysics of Iceland* 55–60.
12) Arna Schram, "Jarðhræringar á Þingvöllum," *Morgunblaðið* 3 Sept. 1995: 22.
13) Sigurður Þórarinsson, "Sambúð lands og lýðs" 84; Björn Hróarsson.
14) Sigurður Þórarinsson, "Sambúð lands og lýðs" 59–60; Einar H. Einarsson, *et al.*, "The Sólheimar tephra layer and the Katla eruption of ca 1357" *Acta Naturalia Islandica 28:* 20–21.
15) Sigurður Þórarinsson, "Sambúð lands og lýðs" 64.
16) Th. Thordarson and S. Self; Guðmundur Pétursson in Gísli Ágúst Gunnlaugsson, *Skaftáreldar 1783–1784*, 81–97; Gísli Ágúst Gunnlaugsson, *Skaftáreldar 1783–1784* 119–128.
17) Sigurður Þórarinsson, "Sambúð lands og lýðs" 69.
18) Decker and Decker 18–29; Sturla Friðriksson, *Surtsey* 20–28; Sveinn Jakobsson, "Rof Surtseyjar."
19) Páll Einarsson and Sveinbjörn Björnsson, "Earthquakes in Iceland *Jökull* 29 (1979): 41.
20) Th. Thordarson and S. Self 26; Decker and Decker 46.
21) Árný E. Sveinbjörnsdóttir and Sigfús J. Johnsen, "Nýr ískjarni frá Grænlandsjökli," *Náttúrufræðingurinn* 64.2 (1994): 83; Gerard C. Bond and Rusty Lotti, "Iceberg Discharges into the North Atlantic on Millennial Time Scales During the Last Glaciation," *Science* Feb. 1995: 1005–1010.
22) Þorleifur Einarsson, *Geology* 264; "Jarðsaga Íslands" 17.
23) Þorleifur Einarsson, *Geology* 264, 251; Decker and Decker 145.
24) Þorleifur Einarsson, *Geology* 249, 277–278; Þorleifur Einarsson, "Jarðsaga Íslands" 20–21; Sturla Friðriksson, "Þróun lífríkisins og nytjar af því," *Íslensk þjóðmenning I* 159.
25) Sigurður Þórarinsson, "Sambúð lands og lýðs" 43.
26) *Morgunblaðið* 10 Feb. 1994: 6 Mar. 1994.
27) *Morgunblaðið* 27 Oct. 1995: 13.
28) Tómas Tryggvason and Freysteinn Sigurðsson, "Hagnýt jarðefni," *Náttúra Íslands*.
29) Ministry for the Environment, *Iceland: National Report to UNCED* 58; Hitaveita Reykjavíkur, *Almennur Bæklingur*; Árni Gunnarsson, *et al. Nesjavellir Geothermal Co-Generation Power Plant*; State Electric Power Works, *Krafla Power Plant*.

Living with the Weather

1) Páll Bergþórsson, *The Weather in Iceland*, 2nd ed.
2) Árný E. Sveinbjörnsdóttir and Sigfús J. Johnsen, "Nýr ískjarni frá Grænlandsjökli," *Náttúrufræðingurinn* 64.2 (1994): 83–96.
3) Sigurður Þórarinsson "Sambúð lands og lýðs í ellefu aldir," in Sigurður Líndal, *Saga Íslands I* 51–52.
4) Sigurður Þórarinsson 94.

The Icelandic Language

1) Stefán Karlsson, "Tungan," in *Íslensk þjóðmenning VI* 52–54, 440.
2) Stefán Karlsson 26–27.
3) Gísli Pálsson, "Language and Society," in Durrenberger and Pálsson, eds., *The Anthropology of Iceland* 122.
4) Björn Þorsteinsson and Bergsteinn Jónsson, *Íslands saga til okkar daga* 276.
5) Stefán Karlsson, "Tungan" 439.
6) Gísli Pálsson, "Language and Society" 121–134.
7) For Icelandic names see Guðrún Kvaran and Sigurður Jónsson, *Nöfn Íslendinga*.
8) Cf. Þorsteinn Gylfason, "Að hugsa á íslensku," *Skírnir* (1973): 135.

Ring of Seasons

Eddas and Sagas
1) Jónas Kristjánsson, *Handritin og fornsögurnar* 36.
2) Björn Th. Björnsson in *Icelandic Sagas, Eddas and Art.*
3) Guðrún Nordal, *et al.*, *Íslensk bókmenntasaga I* 422.
4) Gísli Sigurðsson, *Gaelic Influence in Iceland: Historical and Literary Contacts.*
5) Cf. Guðrún Nordal, *et al.* 112.
6) Magnus Magnusson and Hermann Pálsson, transl., *Njal's Saga*, Introd. 25.
7) Terry Gunnell, *The Concept of Ancient Scandinavian Drama: a Reevaluation.*
8) Gunnell.
9) Cf. Guðrún Sveinbjarnadóttir, *Farm Abandonment in Medieval and Post–Medieval Iceland: An Interdisciplinary Study.*
10) Áskell Snorrason, "Um sönglist á Íslandi."
11) Percy A. Scholes, *The Oxford Companion to Music* 922.
12) Roberta Frank, *Old Norse Court Poetry: The* Dróttkvætt *Stanza*, 39.
13) E. Paul Durrenberger, *The Dynamics of Medieval Iceland: Political Economy and Literature* 56.
14) Durrenberger 14.

Gyrfalcons and Iceland Moss
1) Björn Þórðarson, *Íslenzkir fálkar.*
2) Björn Þorsteinsson and Bergsteinn Jónsson 353.
3) *Morgunblaðið*, "Fálkanir fljúga með þotum til Saudi Arabíu" 5 Apr. 1987: 22B.
4) Ingvi Þorsteinsson, "Landgæði á Íslandi fyrr og nú," *Morgunblaðið* 12 Nov. 1987.
5) Gunnar Jónsson, *Íslenskir fiskar.*
6) Erling Ólafsson, *Íslenskt skordýratal.*
7) Páll Hersteinsson and Guttormur Sigbjarnarson, *Villt íslensk spendýr* 81.
8) Árni Björnsson, *Saga daganna* 169–170.
9) Kristín Þorsteinsdóttir, *Jurtalitum. Forsagnir.*
10) Lúðvík Kristjánsson, *Íslenskir sjávarhættir* V 176, 183, 250.
11) Sigurður Ægisson, "Sjófuglanytjar Íslendinga fyrr á tímum," *Lesbók Morgunblaðsins* 14 May 1994: 4–6.
12) *Morgunblaðið*, "120 hafernir á landinu," 16 Sept. 1991 (Interview with Kristinn H. Skarphéðinsson)
13) Arnþór Garðarsson, "Íslenski húsandastofninn," *Náttúrufræðingurinn* 48. 3–4 (1978): 162–191.
14) Eyrún Ingadóttir, "Sigríður í Brattholti og Gullfoss," *Lesbók Morgunblaðsins* 21 Dec. 1994: 21–23.
15) Haraldur Ólafsson, "A True Environmental Parable: The Laxá–Mývatn Conflict in Iceland, 1965–1973" *Environmental Rev.* 5.2 (1981): 2–38.
16) Ministry for the Environment, *Iceland: National Report to UNCED*, especially 144, 136, 109, 110, 128, 129.
17) Ministry for the Environment 151, 153, 161.

Heroic Seafarers
1) Jóhann Axelsson & Mikael Karlsson, "Furðulegt dæmi um kuldaþol," *Morgunblaðið* 23 June 1985: 22–23.
2) Gísli Pálsson, *Coastal Economies, Cultural Accounts* 91.
3) Gísli Pálsson 96.
4) Lúðvik Kristjánsson, *Íslenskir sjávarhættir* V, my transl.
5) Gísli Pálsson, *Sambúð manns og sjávar* 146.
6) Brynjúlfur Jónsson, *Sagan af Þuríði formanni og Kambsránsmönnum.*
7) Lúðvík Kristjánsson; Jon Th. Thor, *British Trawlers in Icelandic Waters.*
8) Björn Þorsteinsson and Bergsteinn Jónsson; Björn Þorsteinsson, *Tíu þorskastríð.* I have used throughout Björn Þorsteinsson's naming of the Cod Wars.

Notes

9) Jacques Dubois, *Yves frændi. Íslands sjómaður* 199, 202.
10) Jon Th. Thor, *British Trawlers in Icelandic Waters* 16.
11) Jon Th. Thor 244.
12) Cf. Gísli Pálsson, *Sambúðs manns og sjávar* and *Coastal Economies, Cultural Accounts.*
13) "Björgunarafrekið," *Lesbók Morgunblaðsins* 5 Dec. 1987: 11–12.

Iceland's History: The Settlement
1) G.J. Marcus, *The Conquest of the North Atlantic* 41.
2) Marcus 24, 27.
3) *Book of Settlements*, sect. 4.
4) *Book of Settlements*, sect. 5.
5) Marcus 27.
6) "Merkur fundur húsarista og steina á Dagverðarnesi við Breiðafjörð." Interview with archaeologist Þorvaldur Friðriksson, *Morgunblaðið* 16 July 1985.
7) L.L. Cavalli–Sforza *et al.*, *The History and Geography of Human Genes* 271.
8) "Merkur fundur...," interview with Þorvaldur Friðriksson. See also Christian Keller, *The Eastern Settlement Reconsidered: Some Analyses of Norse Medieval Greenland.*
9) Gísli Sigurðsson, *Gaelic Influence in Iceland: Historical and Literary Contacts.*
10) Sigurdur Thórarinsson, "Sambúð lands og lýðs í ellefu aldir" 93.
11) Cf. Marcus 35.
12) Marcus 49.
13) *Book of Settlements*, sect. 218.
14) *Book of Settlements*, sect. 152.
15) Stefán Aðalsteinsson, "Írskir þrælar," *Lesbók Morgunblaðsins,* 18 Jan., 1991, and "Hvar eru rætur okkar?" *Heilbrigðismál* 3 (1995); L.L. Cavalli–Sforza *et al.* 129, 271–272, 277.
16) Kristján Eldjárn in Sigurður Líndal, *Saga Íslands* 104; Björn Þorsteinsson and Bergsteinn Jónsson 17.
17) Björn Þorsteinsson and Bergsteinn Jónsson 16–17.
   K.K. Kidd and L.L. Cavalli–Sforza, "The role of genetic drift in the differentiation of Icelandic and Norwegian cattle"; Stefán Aðalsteinsson, "Um uppruna íslenskra nautgripa,"*Náttúrufræðingurinn* 4 (1976): 238–240.
18) Margrét Hermanns–Auðardóttir, *Islands Tidiga Bosättning* and "The Beginning of Settlement in Iceland in Light of Archaeological Investigations in Herjólfsdalur, Vestmannaeyjar."
29) Interview with Agnar Þórðarson,"Er Ísland kennt við guði en ekki hafís?" *Morgunblaðið* 7 Dec. 1986.
20) Sigurður Líndal 215.
21) Marcus 49.
22) Else Christie Kielland, *Stave Churches and Viking Ships.*
23) Marcus 50, 83–86.
24) E.J. Stardal, *Íslandssaga* 52.
25) Richard Cleasby, *et al.*, *An Icelandic–English Dictionary.*
26) Sigurdur Thórarinsson 53.

Iceland's History: The Commonwealth and the Conversion to Christianity
1) Jakob Benediktsson, "Skipulag þjóðveldisins," in Sigurður Líndal, *Saga Íslands I* 172ff.
2) See, e.g., Björn Þorsteinsson and Bergsteinn Jónsson 31 ff; Jesse L. Byock, *Medieval Iceland, Society, Sagas and Power*; Peter Foote and David M. Wilson, *The Viking Achievement.*
3) Byock 166.
4) Byock 66.
5) Björn Þorsteinsson and Bergsteinn Jónsson 31ff.
6) Byock 61.
7) Byock 26.
8) Foote and Wilson 374.

9) Jakob Benediktsson, "Stéttaskipting," in Sigurður Líndal, *Saga Íslands I* 187ff.
10) Foote & Wilson 116.
11) Björn Þorsteinsson and Bergsteinn Jónsson 41.
12) Jón Hnefill Aðalsteinsson, "Norræn trú," *Íslensk þjóðmenning V*.
13) Johannes Brøndsted, *The Vikings* 257.
14) Brøndsted 318.
15) Brøndsted 250.
16) Kristján Eldjárn, "Fornþjóð og minjar," in Sigurður Líndal, *Saga Íslands I* 101ff.
17) Byock 28.
18) Björn Þorsteinsson and Bergsteinn Jónsson 47.
19) The section on food and health is based on Skúli V. Gudjónsson, *Manneldi og heilsufar í fornöld* and comments by Hallgerður Gísladóttir.
20) Sigurður Líndal 248.
21) Björn Þorsteinsson and Bergsteinn Jónsson 63ff.
22) Áskell Snorrason, "Um sönglist á Íslandi."
23) Jón R. Hjálmarsson, *A Short History of Iceland* 42.
24) Björn Þorsteinsson and Bergsteinn Jónsson 79f.
25) Björn Þorsteinsson and Bergsteinn Jónsson 73.
26) Sigurdur Líndal,"Ísland og umheimurinn" and "Upphaf kristni of kirkju," *Saga Íslands I*.

Sorcery and Superstition
1) Stephen Flowers, *The Galdrabók, an Icelandic Grimoire*.
2) Ólína Þorvarðardóttir, "Galdrasagan – þroskasaga þjóðar," *Lesbók Morgunblaðsins* 24 Dec. 1994.
3) Haraldur Ólafsson, *Dýr og menn*.
4) Stephen Flowers.
5) Björn Þorsteinsson and Bergsteinn Jónsson 218ff.
6) Björn Þorsteinsson and Bergsteinn Jónsson 219.
7) Jón Helgason, *Öldin sautjanda* 120–123.
8) Björn Þorsteinsson and Bergsteinn Jónsson 218–219.
9) Jón Hnefill Aðalsteinsson, "Norræn trú" and "Þjóðtrú" in *Íslensk þjóðmenning V* and *Strandarkirkja. Helgistaður við haf*; Símon Jón Jóhannsson, *Sjö, níu, þrettán. Hjátrú Íslendinga í daglega lífinu*.

Iceland's History: The Settlement of Greenland and North America
1) *Book of Settlements*, sect. 89.
2) G.J. Marcus 55.
3) Marcus 108.
4) See, e.g., Marcus, 55–58; Gwynn Jones, *The Norse Atlantic Saga*.
5) Ingvi Þorsteinsson and Valdimar Jóhannsson, "Brattahlíð og Þingvellir," *Lesbók Morgunblaðsins* 19 Oct. 1996: 6–7.
6) Judy Lomax, *The Viking Voyage* 123, 125.
7) Christian Keller, *The Eastern Settlement Reconsidered: Some Analyses of Norse Medieval Greenland* 28.
8) Keller 163.
9) Thomas H. McGovern, "Climate, Correlation, and Causation in Norse Greenland, *Arctic Anthropology*, 28.2 (1991): 81.
10) Hermann Pálsson, "Minnispunktar 1988: Langskip voru illa fallin til singlinga yfir Atlantshafið," *Lesbók Morgunblaðsins* 26 Nov. 1988: 13–14.
11) Keller 316f.
12) "Merkur fundur húsarústa og steina á Dagverðarnesi við Breiðafjörð," *Morgunblaðið* 16 July 1985. Interview with the archaeologist Þorvaldur Friðriksson.
13) Keller 5.
14) Keller, map 49; 130ff.

Notes

15) Gwynn Jones, *The Norse Atlantic Saga* 66; Ingvi Þorsteinsson and Valdimar Jóhannsson 6.
16) Keller, 303f.
17) Keller 179.
18) Robert McGhee, "Contact between native North Americans and the medieval Norse: A review of evidence," *Am. Antiquity* 49.1 (1984): 4–26.
19) Keller 168; McGovern 81.
20) Keller 175.
21) Keller 177.
22) Marcus 66.
23) Jones 52.
24) Keller 317.
25) Keller 289.
26) McGovern 81.
27) Keller 314.
28) McGovern 92f.
29) Marcus 69f.
30) Keller 21.
31) McGhee 6.
32) McGovern 94; McGhee 20.
33) Keller 32; McGovern 93.
34) McGovern 87.
35) McGovern 94.
36) Helge Ingstad, *Land Under the Pole Star* 23; Jones 73.
37) Jones 69f.
38) cf. Herman Pálsson, "Minnispunktar 1988: Langskip voru illa fallin til singlinga yfir Atlantshafið," *Lesbók Morgunblaðsins* 26 Nov. 1988.
39) Jones 61–64.
40) Keller 23.
41) Marcus 161f.
42) *Book of Settlements,* sect. 122.
43) Jones 93.
44) Jones 77, 147.
45) See Jones; Ingstad 1966, 1969; *Grænlendinga saga; Eiríks saga rauða.*
46) Jones 93.
47) Jones 86.
48) Ingstad (1996, 1969).
49) Ingstad (1969) 114.
50) McGhee 21, 6, 12, 16.
51) Ragnar Borg, "Hvers vegna finnst víkingamynt í Maine?" *Morgunblaðið* 6 June 1987: 20.
52) Bragi Óskarsson, "Staðfestir kattastofninn í Boston landnám Leifs heppna?" *Morgunblaðið* 18 Sept. 1983: 22– 23. Interview with Stefán Aðalsteinsson.
53) See, e.g., Jones 78.
54) Thorstina Walters, *Modern Sagas: The Story of the Icelanders in North America* 24.
55) See, e.g., Walters; Wilhelm Kristjansson, *The Icelandic People in Manitoba*; John S. Matthiason, "Adaptation to an Ethnic Structure: The Urban Icelandic–Canadians of Winnipeg," in Durrenberg & Pálsson, *The Anthropology of Iceland*; Anne Brydon, *Celebrating Ethnicity: The Icelanders of Manitoba.*
56) Björn Þorsteinsson and Bergsteinn Jónsson 317.
57) Walters 70.
58) Brydon 13.
59) Matthiasson in Durrenberger & Pálsson 160.

Iceland's History: The End of the Commonwealth
1) E. Paul Durrenberger 46.
2) See Gudrún Sveinbjarnardóttir, *Farm Abandonment in Medieval and Post–Medieval Iceland: An Interdisciplinary Study*; Sigurdur Thórarinsson in Sigurður Líndal, *Saga Íslands I*; Thomas Amorosi in Durrenberger and Pálsson, *The Anthropology of Iceland*.
3) Guðrún Sveinbjarnardóttir 1.
4) Guðrún Sveinbjarnardóttir 10.
5) Guðrún Sveinbjarnardóttir 161.
6) Amorosi in Durrenberger and Pálsson.
7) See, e.g., Björn Þorsteinsson and Bergsteinn Jónsson 63ff
8) Amorosi, in Durrenberger and Pálsson 217.
9) Gudrún Sveinbjarnardóttir 16.
10) Njörður P. Njarðvík, *Birth of a Nation*, 78.
11) Cf. Njörður P. Njarðvík; Björn Þorsteinsson and Bergsteinn Jónsson 90ff.
12) Christian Keller 301– 304.
13) Keller 304.
14) Durrenberger 13, 71.
15) E.J. Stardal 91.
16) See, e.g., Björn Þorsteinsson and Bergsteinn Jónsson 83ff.
17) Björn Þorsteinsson and Bergsteinn Jónsson 107
18) Björn Þorsteinsson and Bergsteinn Jónsson 113.
19) Björn Þorsteinsson and Bergsteinn Jónsson 115, 119ff.

Trolls, Elves and Ghosts
1) Jón Hnefill Aðalsteinsson, *Íslensk þjóðmenning V*.
2) Erlendur Haraldsson, *Þessa heims og annars*; "Representative National Surveys of Psychic Phenomena: Iceland, Great Britain, Sweden, USA and Gallup's Multinational Survey," *Jr. Soc. for Psychical Res.* 53 Oct. 1985: 145–158; Erlendur Haraldsson and Joop M. Houtkooper, "Psychic Experiences in the Multinational Human Values Study: Who Reports Them?" *Jr. Soc. for Psychical Res.*, 85 Apr. 1991: 145–165.
3) Sigurður Nordal, *Þjóðsagnabókin II, III*.
4) Véstein Ólason, "Kvæði af Ólafi liljurós," in *The Traditional Ballads of Iceland*.
5) Jón Helgason, *Öldin sautjánda* 59.
6) Erlendur Haraldsson, "Representative National Surveys of Psychic Phenomena."
7) Jón Helgason 215.

Iceland's History: The Norwegian and Danish Domination Through the Reformation, 1262–1550
1) Björn Þorsteinsson and Bergsteinn Jónsson 173.
2) Björn Þorsteinsson and Bergsteinn Jónsson 122.
3) Björn Þorsteinsson and Bergsteinn Jónsson 128.
4) Björn Þorsteinsson and Bergsteinn Jónsson 126.
5) Björn Þorsteinsson and Bergsteinn Jónsson 132.
6) Guðrún Sveinbjarnard 9.
7) Björn Þorsteinsson and Bergsteinn Jónsson 146.
8) Björn Þorsteinsson and Bergsteinn Jónsson 160.
9) Björn Þorsteinsson and Bergsteinn Jónsson 125.
10) Björn Þorsteinnson and Bergsteinn Jónsson 126.
11) Björn Þorsteinsson and Bergsteinn Jónsson 141.
12) Björn Þorsteinsson and Bergsteinn Jónsson 128.
13 Gunnar Karlsson and Helgi Skúli Kjartansson, "Plágurnar miklu á Íslandi," in *Saga* (1994): 66.
14) Björn Þorsteinsson and Bergsteinn Jónsson, 131.
15) Jón Helgason, *Öldin sextánda* 63.

Notes

16) Sigurður Þórarinsson, "Sambúð lands og lýðs í ellefu aldir," in *Saga Íslands I* 65, 70–72; Sigurdur Thorarinsson, *On the Geology and Geophysics of Iceland* 59.
17) Páll Hersteinson & Guttormur Sigbjarnarson, *Villt íslensk spendýr* 338.
18) Jón Steffensen, *Menning og meinsemdir* 331, 334.
19) Jón Steffensen 329.
20) Gunnar Karlsson and Helgi Skúli Kjartansson (1994).
21) Jón Steffensen 330, 338.
22) *Blakiston's Gould Medical Dictionary*.
23) Jón Steffensen 324, 70.
24) Björn Þorsteinsson and Bergsteinn Jónsson 135.
25) Björn Þorsteinsson and Bergsteinn Jónsson 136–7.
26) G.J. Marcus 129.
27) Marcus 128–9, 133.
28) Peter Foote and David M. Wilson 61ff; Björn Þorsteinsson and Bergsteinn Jónsson 153.
29) Björn Þorsteinsson and Bergsteinn Jónsson 152; Marcus, 140.
30) Björn Þorsteinsson and Bergsteinn Jónsson 156.
31) Marcus 139.
32) Björn Þorsteinsson and Bergsteinn Jónsson 168.
33) Björn Þorsteinsson and Bergsteinn Jónsson 193.
34) E.J. Stardal 171.
35) Björn Þorsteinsson and Bergsteinn Jónsson 182–194.
36) Gísli Pálsson, "Language and Society: The Ethnolinguistics of Icelanders," in Durrenberger and Pálsson 122.
37) Guðrún Norðdal, *et al.*, *Íslensk Bókmenntasaga I* 401.
38) Percy A. Scholes, *The Oxford Companion to Music* 922; Áskell Snorrason, "Um sönglist á Íslandi."
39) Jón Helgason, *Öldin sextánda* 121.

A Legendary Outlaw: Eyvindur of the Mountains

1) Þórunn Valdimarsdóttir, *Snorri á Húsafelli*; Jón Hnefill Aðalsteinsson, *Íslensk þjóðmenning V*.
2) The account of Eyvindur's life is based on Sigurdur Nordal, *Þjóðsagnabókin III*, and Þórunn Valdimarsdóttir, *Snorri á Húsafelli*.

Iceland's History: The Hardest of Times, 1550–1830

1) Th. Thordarson and S. Self 19; Þorleifur Einarsson, *Geology of Iceland* 40, 49; Sigurður Þórarinsson, *Saga Íslands I* map 63; *Science* 17 Mar. 1995: 267.
2) Jón Steingrímsson in Gísli Ágúst Gunnlaugsson, *et al.*, eds., *Skaftáreldar 1783–1784*; Björn Þorsteinsson and Bergsteinn Jónsson 252.
3) *Annálar 1400–1800 IV* 591–602.
4) *Annálar 1400–1800 IV* 455–462.
5) Robert Decker & Barbara Decker 210.
6) Sigurður Þórarinsson, in Sigurður Líndal, *Saga Íslands I* 61. See also Sveinbjörn Rafnsson 163–178, and Guðrún Larsen and Þorvaldur Þórðarson 59–66, in Gísli Ágúst Gunnlaugsson, *et al.*, *Skaftáreldar 1783– 1784*: 163–178.
7) Gísli Ágúst Gunnlaugsson, *Skaftáreldar 1783–1784*: 187–214.
8) Björn Þorsteinsson and Bergsteinn Jónsson 195.
9) Björn Þorsteinsson and Bergsteinn Jónsson 218–9.
10) Gísli Gunnarsson, *A Study of Causal Relations in Climate and History with an emphasis on the Icelandic experience* 10–13, 16.
11) Gísli Gunnarsson, *Monopoly Trade and Economic Stagnation, Studies in the Foreign Trade of Iceland 1602–1787* 12.
12) Gísli Gunnarsson, *Monopoly Trade* 61.
13) Gísli Gunnarsson, *Monopoly Trade* 119, 138–9.
14) Gísli Gunnarsson, *A Study of Causal Relations in Climate and History* 17.

Ring of Seasons

15) Gísli Gunnarsson, *Monopoly Trade* 144, 146.
16) Gísli Gunnarsson, *Monopoly Trade* 18–20, 171–177.
17) Björn Þorsteinsson and Bergsteinn Jónsson 268.
18) Gísli Gunnarsson, *Monopoly Trade* 18–20, 28, 171–177.
19) Björn Þorsteinsson and Bergsteinn Jónsson 232–233.
20) Gísli Gunnarsson, *Monopoly Trade* 156.
21) Gísli Gunnarsson, 11; Ogilvie, A.E.J. "Climate and Economy in Eighteenth Century Iceland," *Consequences of Climatic Change* 62.
22) Björn Þorsteinsson and Bergsteinn Jónsson 207–208.
23) Björn Þorsteinsson and Bergsteinn Jónsson 208–209.
24) Jón Helgason, *Tyrkjaránið* 150–1, 184, 196–7, 202, 206.
25) Ogilvie 63–67.
26) Sigurður Þórarinsson, *Saga Íslands* 65–68.
27) Sigurður Þórarinsson 84; Sveinbjörn Björnsson and Páll Einarsson, "Jarðskjálftar," in *Náttúra Íslands*, 2nd ed. 136–137.
28) Björn Þorsteinsson and Bergsteinn Jónsson 13–17, 23.
29) Jón Steffensen, *Menning og meinsemdir* 24, 251, 342, 370, 390, 392, 397.
30) Jón Steffensen 295–297; Björn Þorsteinsson and Bergsteinn Jónsson 232, 251.
31) Björn Þorsteinsson and Bergsteinn Jónsson 250.
32) Gísli Gunnarsson, *Monopoly Trade and Economic Stagnation* 15.
33) Sigurður Þórarinsson 94.
34) Gísli Gunnarsson 17.
35) Gísli Gunnarsson 14–16.
36) Jón Steffensen 436–437.
37) Jón Steffensen 437–438.
38) Björn Þorsteinsson and Bergsteinn Jónsson 235.
39) Björn Þorsteinsson and Bergsteinn Jónsson 243, 214, 270.
40) Gísli Gunnarsson, *A Study of Causal Relations in Climate and History* 24.
41) Jón Steffensen, "Líkamsleifar," in *Skálholt* 176f.
42) Gísli Gunnarsson, *A Study of Causal Relations in Climate and History* 15.
43) Gísli Gunnarsson, *Monopoly Trade* 169.
44) Gísli Gunnarsson, *A Study of Causal Relations in Climate and History* 14–16.
45) Gísli Gunnarsson, *Monopoly Trade* 168–170.
46) Björn Þorsteinsson and Bergsteinn Jónsson 228, 230.
47) Björn Þorsteinsson and Bergsteinn Jónsson 230–231.
48) Björn Þorsteinsson and Bergsteinn Jónsson 246.
49) Gísli Gunnarsson, *Monopoly Trade* 132.
50) Guðrún Sveinbjarnardóttir 11.
51) Gísli Ágúst Gunnlaugsson, *Skaftáreldar 1783–1784*: 187–214; Sigfús Haukur Andrésson, in *Skaftáreldar 1783–1784*: 215–233
52) Anna Agnarsdóttir, *Great Britain and Iceland 1800–1820*: 10; Roy A. Rauschenberg, "The Journals of Joseph Banks's Voyage up Britain's West Coast to Iceland and to the Orkney Isles, July to October, 1771," *Proc. Am. Phil. Soc.*1973: 216-7.
53) Gísli Gunnarsson, *Monopoly Trade* 115–6, 134; Björn Þorsteinsson and Bergsteinn Jónsson 239, 243.
54) Anna Agnarsdóttir 9.
55) Anna Agnarsdóttir i–ii, 67, 184, 213.
56) Anna Agnarsdóttir 13–23, 215, 277, 277.
57) Anna Agnarsdóttir 211, 249.
58) Björn Þorsteinsson and Bergsteinn Jónsson 256.
59) F.B. Maggs, *Jorgen Jorgensen, the King of Iceland*. N.B.: He himself wrote his name as Jürgen Jürgensen.
60) Lýður Björnsson, *Frá síðaskiptum til sjálfstæðisbaráttu*.

Notes

61) Anna Agnarsdóttir 85–129, 137–9, 162.
62) F.B. Maggs.
63) Björn Þorsteinsson and Bergsteinn Jónsson 216.
64) Björn Þorsteinsson and Bergsteinn Jónsson 201.
65) Björn Þorsteinsson and Bergsteinn Jónsson 266.

My John's Soul

1) This account of a well–known folk tale is based on the version in Sigurdur Nordal's *Þjóðsagnabókin II*, with an assist from the play *The Golden Gates* by Davíd Stefánsson.

Iceland's History: The Struggle for Independence, 1830–1918

1) Kristján Albertsson, *Hannes Hafstein. Ævisaga I*, Book 1 54.
2) Lord Dufferin, *Letters from High Latitudes,* 3rd ed. 142.
3) Björn Þorsteinsson and Bergsteinn Jónsson 292.
4) Ólafur Ragnar Grímsson 14.
5) *Jón Sigurðsson* 10–11, 48.
6) Björn Þorsteinsson and Bergsteinn Jónsson 286.
7) Björn Þorsteinsson and Bergsteinn Jónsson 273.
8) Björn Þorsteinsson and Bergsteinn Jónsson 274.
9) Björn Þorsteinsson and Bergsteinn Jónsson 275–276.
10) Hagstofa Íslands, *Landshagir 1991*: 21.
11) Björn Þorsteinsson and Bergsteinn Jónsson 276.
12) Ólafur Ragnar Grímsson 27.
13) Cf. Ólafur Ragnar Grímsson 12–19, 25–27.
14) Björn Þorsteinsson and Bergsteinn Jónsson 276.
15) Björn Þorsteinsson and Bergsteinn Jónsson 276.
16) Björn Þorsteinsson and Bergsteinn Jónsson 278.
17) Björn Þorsteinsson and Bergsteinn Jónsson 280–281.
18) Gísli Gunnarsson, *Monopoly Trade* 176.
19) *Jón Sigurðsson* 15.
20) Björn Þorsteinsson and Bergsteinn Jónsson 293.
21) Björn Þorsteinsson and Bergsteinn Jónsson 289–291.
22) Björn Þorsteinsson and bergsteinn Jónsson 297–298.
23) Björn Þorsteinsson and Bergsteinn Jónsson 311.
24) Björn Þorsteinsson and Bergsteinn Jónsson 312.
25) *Jón Sigurðsson* 53.
26) Björn Þorsteinsson and Bergsteinn Jónsson 331, 305.
27) Árni Björnsson, *Gersemar* 242.
28) Björn Þorsteinsson and Bergsteinn Jónsson 306; Hagstofa Íslands, *Landshagir* 21.
29) Björn Þorsteinsson and Bergsteinn Jónsson 316–17.
30) Björn Þorsteinsson and Bergsteinn Jónsson 317–18.
31) Jón R. Hjálmarsson 117; Björn Þorsteinsson and Bergsteinn Jónsson 312, 301.
32) Cf. Gísli Pálsson, *Sambúð manns og sjávar* and *Coastal Economies, Cultural Accounts.*
33) Björn Þorsteinsson and Bergsteinn Jónsson 331.
34) Lúðvík Kristjánsson, *íslenskir sjávarhættir,* V, 1986; Jon Th. Thor, *British Trawlers in Icelandic Waters*; Björn Þorsteinsson and Bergsteinn Jónsson 304, 293; Jacques Dubois, *Yves frændi. Íslandssjómaður.*
35) Jon Th. Thor 16, 244.
36) Jon Th. Thor 59.
37) Björn Þorsteinsson and Bergsteinn Jónsson 308, 310.
38) Kristján Albertsson, *Hannes Hafstein. Ævisaga*, Ia, e.g. 207, 221. For this and other details about Hannes Hafstein and the times, see books Ia and Ib.
39) Björn Þorsteinsson and Bergsteinn Jónsson 346.

Ring of Seasons

40) Björn Þorsteinsson and Bergsteinn Jónsson 325.
41) Björn Þorsteinsson and Bergsteinn Jónsson 533.
42) Björn Þorsteinsson and Bergsteinn Jónsson 330–333.
43) Jóhannes Nordal & Valdimar Kristinsson, eds., *Iceland 874–1974.* 178.
44) Björn Þorsteinsson and Bergsteinn Jónsson 325, 327, 330; Jón R. Hjálmarsson 122–23.
45) Jón Ólafur Ísberg, "Dýrtíð og neysla á árunum 1914–1918," *Lesbók Morgunblaðsins*, 1 Oct 1994: 1–2.
46) Björn Þorsteinsson and Bergsteinn Jónsson 340, 342, 334; Jón R. Hjálmarsson 125.
47) Ólafur Ragnar Grímsson 9, 15–19, 27.
48) Björn Þorsteinsson and Bergsteinn Jónsson 349–350.
49) Ólafur Ásgeirsson, "Íslenska fánann í öndvegi," *Morgunblaðið*, 11 Mar 1994; Björn Þorsteinsson and Bergsteinn Jónsson 353–354.
50) Hagstofa Íslands, *Landshagir* 1991: 21.
51) Jón R. Hjálmarsson 125–26; Björn Þorsteinsson and Bergsteinn Jónsson 354f.
52) Björn Þorsteinsson and Bergsteinn Jónsson 356.
53) Jón Ólafur Ísberg.
54) Jón R. Hjálmarsson 130.
55) Björn Þorsteinsson and Bergsteinn Jónsson 361–362, for these and the facts in the following paragraphs.

Turf Houses and Filigree Belts

1) For this chapter, see especially Guðmundur Þorsteinsson, *Horfnir starfshættir og leiftar frá liðnum öldum*; Hörður Ágústsson, "Íslensk torbærinn," *Íslensk þjóðmenning, I*; and Jónas Jónasson frá Hrafnagili, *Íslenskar þjóðhættir.*
2) Sigurður Þórarinsson, *Saga Íslands I* 40.
3) Guðmundur Ólafsson, *Íslensk þjóðmenning, I* 365.
4) Guðmundur Ólafsson 367–368.
5) Björn Þorsteinsson and Bergsteinn Jónsson 337–339.
6) Páll Bergþórsson, "Sensitivity of Icelandic Agriculture to Climatic Variations," *Climatic Change* 7 (1985): 111.
7) Jóhannes Nordal and Valdimar Kristinsson, *Iceland 874–1974*: 180.
8) Jónas Jónasson 2–3; Guðmundur Þorsteinsson 49, 42–43.
9) Árni Björnsson, *Gersemar*; Guðmundur Þorsteinsson 75.
10) Jón Steffensen, *Menning og meinsemdir* 248–253.
11) Jón Steffensen 249; Hagstofa Íslands, *Tölfræðihandbók* 319.
12) Jóhannes Nordal and Valdimar Kristinsson 298.
13) Jónas Jónasson 311.
14) Kristján Albertsson, *Hannes Hafsteinn. Ævisaga*, Book Ia 171, 34.
15) Jón Steffensen 248, 254–255.
16) Jóhannes Nordal and Validimar Kristinsson 299.
17) Jón Steffensen 313.
18) Björn Þorsteinsson and Bergsteinn Jónsson 314.
19) Jón R. Hjálmarson 124.
20) Áskell Snorrason 5.
21) Goren Bergendal, *New Music in Iceland* 21.
22) Páll H. Jónsson and Garðar Jakobsson in Garðar Jakobsson, *Fiðlur og Tónmannlíf.*
23) Kristján Albertsson, Ia 171.

Iceland Since Independence

1) Björn Þorsteinsson and Bergsteinn Jónsson 412.
2) Svanur Kristjánsson, *Conflict and Consensus in Icelandic Politics 1916–1944*: 30.
3) Björn Þorsteinsson and Bergsteinn Jónsson 377.
4) Guðmundur Gunnarsson, *The Economic Growth in Iceland 1910–1980*: 14.

Notes

5) Chamberlin 71, 67.
6) Guðmundur Gunnarsson 14, 19.
7) Chamberlin, *Economic Development of Iceland Through World War II*: 27.
8) Stefán Ólafsson, *Modernization in Iceland* 91.
9) Chamberlin 26.
10) Jóhannes Nordal & Valdimar Kristinsson 183.
11) Jóhannes Nordal and Valdimar Kristinsson 181.
12) Björn Þorsteinsson and Bergsteinn Jónsson 370.
13) Jón Steffensen, *Menning og meinsemdir* 249–253.
14) Björn Þorsteinsson and Bergsteinn Jónsson 391.
15) Chamberlin, 71; Björn Þorsteinsson and Bergsteinn Jónsson 390; Stefán Ólafsson, *Modernization in Iceland* 120; Jóhannes Nordal and Valdimar Kristinsson 34.
16) Björn Þorsteinsson and Bergsteinn Jónsson 392–394; Hagstofa Íslands, *Tölfræðihandbók*, table 94.
17) Chamberlin 27, 74–75.
18) Hagstofa Íslands, *Tölfræðihandbók*, table 94.
19) Björn Þorsteinsson and Bergsteinn Jónsson 392; Guðmundur Gunnarsson 15.
20) Björn Þorsteinsson and Bergsteinn Jónsson 370, 461.
21) Urður Gunnarsdóttir, "Fangarnir frá Íslandi," *Morgunblaðið*, 11 Feb. 1996.
22) Þór Whitehead, *Milli vonar og ótta* 48.
23) Benedikt Gröndal, *Stormur og stríð* 121–130.
24) For information about Operation Fork, see Þór Whitehead, *Milli vonar og ótta*.
25) See also Þór Whitehead, *Hernám og stríðsár á Íslandi 1940–45*; Tómas Þór Tómasson, I 26, 62, 64; Michael McConville, "Friðsamlegt innrás á Íslandi," *Lesbók Morgunblaðsins*, 19 Nov. 1994.
26) Snorri G. Bergsson, "Fangarnir á Mön" *Ný saga* 1996.
27) Robert Arnason, *Political Parties and Defence: The Case of Iceland 1945–1980*: 17.
28) Björn Þorsteinsson and Bergsteinn Jónsson 401–402; Tómas Þór Tómasson, I 44, 83, 131–132 & II 36–37, 43; Robert Arnason 45.
29) Guðmundur Gunnarsson 16.
30) Tómas Þór Tómasson, II 152.
31) Björn Þorsteinsson and Bergsteinn Jónsson 406; Chamberlin 117.
32) Stefán Ólafsson 21; Chamberlin 105.
33) Chamberlin 38.
34) Tómas Þór Tómasson, II 117.
35) Tómas Þór Tómasson, II 104, 111, 142.
36) Björn Þorsteinsson and Bergsteinn Jónsson 421, 423.
37) Tómas Þór Tómasson, II 63, 49.
38) Þór Whitehead, personal communication.
39) Tómas Þór Tómasson, I 36–37, 46, 50, 71, 78–79; II 135.
40) Tómas Þór Tómasson, I 69, 93; II 38, 44.
41) Gunnar Hersveinn, Tundurdufl í næturkíki," *Morgunblaðið*, 11 June 1995: B 30-31.
42) Björn Þorsteinsson and Bergsteinn Jónsson 449; Robert Arnason 14, 18, 23; Benedikt Gröndal *Stormur og stríð* 65.
43) Björn Þorsteinsson and Bergsteinn Jónsson 427–429.
44) Benedikt Gröndal, *Stormur og stríð* 83, 88; Robert Arnason 19.
45) Robert Arnason 45–46, 49.
46) Benedikt Gröndal *Varnarlið*, 30.
47) Robert Arnason 52, 59.
48) Björn Bjarnason, "Iceland's Security Policy," *Iceland, Nato and Security in the Norwegian Sea Morgunblaðið* 7 May 1993: 85-6, 49.
50) Björn Þorsteinsson and Bergsteinn Jónsson 427, 451; Þórhallur Ásgeirsson, "Efnahagsaðstoðin 1948–1953." *Fjármálatíðindi* II 2 (1955): 61–70.

51) Guðmundur Gunnarsson 2, 93.
52) Hagstofa Íslands, *Þjóðhagsreikningar 1945–1992*: 119.
53) Stefán Ólafsson 100; Guðmundur Gunnarsson 16.
54) *Þjóðhagsreikningar 1945–1992*: 394; Ministry for the Environment, *Iceland: National Report to UNCED* 58.
55) *OECD Economic Surveys: Iceland 1990/1991*: 43, 55.
56) *OECD Economic Surveys: Iceland 1990/1991*, "Basic Statistics."
57) Hagstofa Íslands, *Landshagir 1991*: 39.
58) *Morgunblaðið*, 9 Mar. 1996.
59) *Morgunblaðið*, 16 Feb. 1996.
60) *The World Atlas*, 25th ed.
61) *UNCED Report*, 1992 55.
62) *Landshagir,* 1991 Table 10.10.
63) *Landshagir,* 1991 Table 10.10.
64) Sigurdur B. Stefánsson, "Engin verðbólga, uppbygging eigna, aukin framleiðni" *Morgunblaðið* 8 Sept. 1994.
65) Svanur Kristjánsson, *Frá flokksræði til persónustjórnmála* 233.
66) Robert Arnason 29–31.
67) Guðni Einarsson 16.
68) Gylfi Þ Gíslason, *Viðreisnarárin* 253, 256–257.
69) Þór Whitehead, "Iceland's Foreign Policy, 1946–1956."
70) Svanur Kristjánsson 183.
71) Svanur Kristjánsson 202, 213, 217, 219, 233, 220.
72) Svanur Kristjánsson 19; Ólafur Ragnar Grímsson 13.
73) Svanur Kristjánsson 18.
74) Björn Þorsteinsson and Bergsteinn Jónsson 444; Sigrún Davíðsdóttir, "Handritamálið pg stjórnmálatogstreita," *Morgunblaðið* 17 June 1994.
75) Björn Þorsteinsson and Bergsteinn Jónsson 213–215.
76) For the Cod Wars, see Björn Þorsteinsson, *Tíu þorskastríð*. I have used his system of naming and counting these altercations.
77) *Morgunblaðið*, 17 Jan. 1993: 2B, 4B and 6 Mar. 1994; Stefán Ólafsson 106.
78) Jón Steffensen, *Menning og meinsemdir* 255; *The World Bank Atlas*, 25th ed.
79) Icelandic Nutrition Council, *Nutritional Goals for Icelanders, 1994.*
80) *Morgunblaðið* 17 Jan. 1993: 4B.
81) *Morgunblaðið* 29 Nov. 1992.
82) Þór Whitehead, "Kynþáttastefna Íslands, " *Lesbók Morgunblaðsins* 13 Jan. 1974.
83) *Morgunblaðið* 17 Oct. 1993: B2.
84) *Morgunblaðið* 8 May 1996.
85) OECD Education Committee, *Review of Educational Policy in Iceland* (1986): 1–3.
86) *Time,* 2 Oct. 1995: 35.

Bibliography

(Note: Icelandic authors are listed alphabetically by first name, others by last name. Icelandic names and titles are written with the correct Icelandic spelling.)

Adolf Friðriksson. "Hofminjar." *Lesbók Morgunblaðsins* 8 May 1968: 7.

Aðalgeir Kristjánsson. "Vildi koma Íslandi undir Rússakeisara." *Lesbók Morgunblaðsins* 1 Sept. 1990.

Agnar Klemens Jónsson. "Lýðveldishátíðin." *Morgunblaðið* 17 June 1994: 32–34.

Agnes Bragadóttir. "Íslensk stjórnmál hafa heillað mig gjörsamlega." (Interview with Ambassador Charles Cobb). *Morgunblaðið* 9 Jan. 1992: 25.

Almenna bókafélagið. *Náttúra Íslands*. Reykjavík: Almenna Bókafélagið, 1985.

Althingi, transl. Jón Skaptason. Reykjavík: Alþingi, n.d.

Anderson, Don L., Toshiro Tanimoto, and Yu–shen Zhang. "Plate Tectonics and Hotspots: The Third Dimension." *Science* 19 June 1992: 1654–1650.

Anna Agnarsdóttir. *Great Britain and Iceland 1800–1820*. PhD thesis. London School of Economics and Political Science, 1989.

Annálar 1400–1800, IV. Reykjavík: Hið Íslenzka Bókmenntafélag, 1940–1948.

Ari Páll Kristinsson. "Skvass eða squash. Nýyrði eða slettur." *Málfregnir* Dec. 1990: 26–28.

Arna Schram. "Jarðhræringar á Þingvöllum." (Interview with Freysteinn Sigmundsson). *Morgunblaðið* 3 Sept. 1995: 22.

Arnason, Robert. *Political Parties and Defence: The Case of Iceland 1945–1980*. National Security Series 4/80. Kingston, Canada: Centre for International Relations, Queens University, 1980.

Arnþór Garðarsson. "Íslenski húsandarstofninn." *Náttúrufræðingurinn* 48.3-4 (1978): 162–191.

Árni Björnsson. *Icelandic Feasts and Holidays*. Reykjavík: Iceland Review History Series, 1980.

— . *Saga daganna*. Reykjavík: Mál og Menning, 1993.

— , ed. *Gersemar og þarfaþing*. Reykjavík: Hið Íslenska Bókmenntafélag, 1994.

Árni Böðvarsson. "Foreign Words in Icelandic." *65 Degrees*, n.d.: 31–33, 38.

Árni Gunnarsson, *et al*. *Nesjavellir Geothermal Co–Generation Power Plant*. Reykjavík: Hitaveita Reykjavíkur, 1991.

Árni Johnsen. *Eldar í Heimaey*. Reykjavík: Almenna Bókafélagið, 1973.

Árný E. Sveinbjörnsdóttir and Sigfús J. Johnsen. "Nýr ískjarni frá Grænlandsjökli." *Náttúrufræðingurinn* 64.2 (1994): 83–96.

Ásgeir Ásgeirsson. "Hvað á fjallið að heita?" *Iceland Review*, n.d.

Ásgeir Jakobsson. *Þórður kakali*. Reykjavík: Skuggsjá, 1988.

Bibliography

Ásgeir Sverrison. "Sérstakar reglur um starfsemi KGB á Íslandi." (Interview with Oleg Gordievskij). *Morgunblaðið* 20 Nov. 1990: 30–31.

Áskell Snorrason. "Um sönglist á Íslandi." MS, May 1959.

Áslaug Helgadóttir. "Ræktun erlendra nytjaplantna á Íslandi." *Náttúrufræðingurinn* 65.3-4 (1996): 127–136.

Ásmundur Ólafsson. "Upphaf vélaaldar í íslenskum landbúnaði." *Morgunblaðið* 26 May 1994.

Bæksted, Anders. *Goð og hetjur í heiðnum sið.* Transl. Eysteinn Þorvaldsson. Reykjavík: Örn & Örlygur, 1986.

Baldur Jónsson. "Íslenskt orð fyrir 'telefax'." *Málfregnir* July 1990: 18–22.

Benedikt Gröndal. *Stormur og stríð.* Reykjavík: Almenna Bókafélagið, 1963.

— . *Varnarlið á Íslandi. Viðhorf 6.* Reykjavík: Varðberg og Samtök um vestræna samvinnu, 1983.

Bergendal, Gören. *New Music in Iceland.* Transl. Peter Lynne. Reykjavík: Iceland Music Information Centre, 1991.

Bergsteinn Jónsson. "Mannlíf í Mjóadal um miðja 19. öld." Rpt. in *Saga.* Reykjavik: Sögufélag, 1975.

— . "Frá sauðfjárbúskap í Bárðardal til akuryrkju í Wisconsin." *Saga XV.* Reykjavík: Sögufélag, 1977.

Birgir Sigurðsson. "Korpúlfsstaðir – glæsilegasta stórbýli á Íslandi." *Morgunblaðið* 20 Nov. 1994: 10–11.

Bjarni Vilhjálmsson and Óskar Halldórsson. *Íslenzkir málshættir.* Reykjavík: Almenna Bókafélagið, 1982.

Björn Bjarnason. "Iceland's Security Policy." *Iceland, Nato and Security in the Norwegian Sea.* Reykjavík: The Icelandic Association for Western Co–operation, 1987.

Björn G. Björnsson. "Landnám í Utah." *Morgunblaðið* 17 Sept. 1995: 8–9B.

Björn Hróarsson. "Suðurlandsskjálfti." *Lesbók Morgunblaðsins* 24 Aug. 1996: 4–5.

Björn Þorsteinsson. *Tíu þorskastríð.* Reykjavík: Sögufélagið, 1976.

Björn Þorsteinsson and Bergsteinn Jónsson. *Íslands saga til okkar daga.* Reykjavík: Sögufélag, 1991.

Björn Þórðarson. *Íslenzkir fálkar.* Reykjavík: Hið Íslenzka Bókmenntafélag, 1957.

Blakiston's Gould Medical Dictionary, 4th ed. New York: McGraw–Hill Book Co., 1979.

Bond, Gerard C., and Rusty Lotti. "Iceberg Discharges into the North Atlantic on Millennial Time Scales During the Last Glaciation." *Science* 17 Feb. 1995: 1005–1010.

Bott, M.H.P. "A new look at the causes and consequences of the Icelandic hot–spot." In A.C. Morton and L.M. Parson, eds., *Early Tertiary Volcanism and the Opening of the NE Atlantic.* Oxford: The Geological Society, Blackwell Scientific Publications, 1988.

Boucher, Alan, transl. *Elves, Trolls and Elemental Beings.* Reykjavík: Iceland Review Library, 1981.

— , transl. *Ghosts, Witchcraft and the Other World.* Reykjavík: Iceland Review Library, 1981.

Ring of Seasons

Bragi Óskarsson. "Staðfestir kattastofninn í Boston landnám Leifs heppna?" (Interview with Stefán Aðalsteinsson). *Morgunblaðið* 18 Sept. 1983: 22–23.

— . "Reiknar írablóðið úr Íslendingum" (Interview with Stefán Aðalsteinsson). *Morgunblaðið* 14 July 1985: 6–7B.

Branston, Brian. *Gods of the North.* London: Thames and Hudson, 1955.

Brøndsted, Johannes. *The Vikings,* transl. Kalle Skov. Harmondsworth, Middlesex, UK: Penguin Books, 1965.

Brydon, Anne. *Celebrating Ethnicity: The Icelanders of Manitoba.* Hamilton, Ont.: McMaster Univ., 1987.

Brynjúlfur Jónsson. *Sagan af Þuríði formanni og Kambsránsmönnum.* Ed. Guðni Jónsson. Reykjavík: Eyrbekkingafélagið, 1941.

Byock, Jesse L. *Medieval Iceland, Society, Sagas and Power.* Berkeley: University of Calif. Press, 1988.

Cavalli–Sforza, L. Luca, Paolo Menozzi, and Alberto Piazza. *The History and Geography of Human Genes.* Princeton, NJ: Princeton University Press, 1993.

Chamberlin, William C. *Economic Development of Iceland Through World War II.* Studies in History, Economics and Public Law, no. 531. New York: Columbia University Press, 1947.

Cleasby, Richard, Gudbrand Vigfusson and W.A. Craigie. *An Icelandic–English Dictionary,* 2nd ed. London: Oxford Univ. Press, 1975.

Coffin, Millard F., and Olav Eldholm. "Large Igneous Provinces." *Sci. Am.* Oct. 1993: 26–33.

Crossley–Holland, Kevin. *The Norse Myths.* London: André Deutsch Ltd, 1980.

Davidson, H.R. Ellis. *Gods and Myths of Northern Europe.* London: Penguin Books, 1990.

Decker, Robert, & Barbara Decker. *Volcanoes,* revised and updated ed. New York: W.H. Freeman & Co., 1989.

Dennis, Andrew, Peter Foote and Richard Perkins, transl. *Laws of Early Iceland I: Grágás.* Winnipeg: University of Manitoba Press, 1980.

Dubois, Jacques. *Yves frændi. Íslandssjómaður (Le jardinier des mers lointaines, Tonton Yves pêcheur d'Islande).* Transl. Jón Óskar. Reykjavík: Steinholt/Iðunn, 1981.

Dufferin (Lord Dufferin). *Letters from High Latitudes,* 3rd ed. London: John Murray, Albemarle Street, 1857.

Durrenberger, E. Paul. *The Dynamics of Medieval Iceland: Political Economy and Literature.* Iowa City: Univ. of Iowa Press, 1992.

Durrenberger, E. Paul, and Gísli Pálsson, ed. *The Anthropology of Iceland.* Iowa City: University of Iowa Press., 1989.

E.J. Stardal, *Íslandssaga,* 3rd ed. Reykjavík: Ísafold, 1975.

Einar H. Einarsson, Guðrún Larsen, Sigurður Thorarinsson. "The Sólheimar tephra layer and the Katla eruption of ca 1357." *Acta Naturalia Islandica 28.* Reykjavík: Icelandic Museum of Natural History, 1980.

Elín Pálmadóttir. "Alþing hið nýja." *Morgunblaðið* 7 Mar. 1993: 32–33.

— . "Nýir Skaftáreldar stöðva þotuflug í marga mánuði." *Morgunblaðið* 23 Jan. 1994: 14–15.

Bibliography

— . "Ísland undir jöklum." (Interview with Helgi Björnsson.) *Morgunblaðið* 20 Mar. 1994: 20–21.

Erlendur Haraldsson. *Þessa heims og annars*. Reykjavík: Bókaforlagið Saga, 1978.

— . "Representative National Surveys of Psychic Phenomena: Iceland, Great Britain, Sweden, USA and Gallup's Multinational Survey." *Jr. Soc. for Psychical Res.* Oct. 1985: 145–158.

— and Joop M. Houtkooper. "Psychic Experiences in the Multinational Human Values Study: Who Reports Them?" *Jr. Am. Soc. for Psychical Res.* Apr. 1991: 145–165.

Erling Ólafsson. *Íslensk skordýratal*. Fjölrit Nátturufræðistofnunar 17. Reykjavík: Náttúrufræðistofnun, 1991.

Eyrún Ingadóttir. "Sigríður í Brattholti og Gullfoss." *Lesbók Morgunblaðsins* 21 Dec. 1994: 21–23.

Eyþór Einarsson. "Grös og gróður." In *Náttúra Íslands*, 2nd ed. Reykjavík: Almenna Bókafélagið, 1981.

Flowers, Stephen. *The Galdrabók, an Icelandic Grimoire*. York Beach, ME, USA: Samuel Weiser, Inc., 1989.

Foote, Peter, and David M. Wilson. *The Viking Achievement*. London: Sidgwick & Jackson, 1970.

Frank, Roberta. *Old Norse Court Poetry: The* Dróttkvætt *Stanza*. Islandica XLII. Ithaca & London: Cornell University Press, 1978.

Freysteinn Sigmundsson and Páll Einarsson. "Jarðskjáltabeltið á suðurlandi." *Náttúrufræðingurinn* 66.1 (1996): 37–46.

Garðar Jakobsson and Páll H. Jónsson. *Fiðlur og tónmannlíf í Suður–Þingeyjarsýslu*. Reykjavík: Garðar Jakobsson & Heimir Pálsson, 1990.

Gardarsson, A. "Population trends in diving ducks at Myvatn, Iceland, in relation to food." *Verh. orn. Ges. Bayern* 23 (1978–1979): 191–200.

Gísli Gunnarsson. *A Study of Causal Relations in Climate and History with an emphasis on the Icelandic experience*. Lund: Lunds Universitet, 1980.

— . *Monopoly Trade and Economic Stagnation, Studies in the Foreign Trade of Iceland 1602–1787*. Lund: Ekonomisk–Historiska Föreningen, 1983.

Gísli Ágúst Gunnlaugsson, *et al*. *Skaftáreldar 1783–1784: Ritgerðir og heimildir*. Reykjavík: Mál og Menning, 1984.

Gísli Jónsson. "Ár eindrægni og sundurlyndis." *Morgunblaðið* 17 June 1994: 45

Gísli Pálsson. *Sambúð manns og sjávar*. Reykjavík: Svart á hvítu, 1987.

— . "Language and Society: The Ethnolinguistics of Icelanders." In E.P. Durrenberger and G. Pálsson, eds., *The Anthropology of Iceland*. Iowa City: University of Iowa Press, 1989, 121–139.

— . *Coastal Economies, Cultural Accounts*. Manchester: Manchester University Press, 1991.

Gísli Sigurðsson. *Gaelic Influence in Iceland: Historical and Literary Contacts*. Studia Islandica, 46. Reykjavík: Bókaútgáfa Menningarsjóðs, 1988.

— . "Norrænir menn í Dyflinni." *Lesbók Morgunblaðsins* 17 Nov. 1990: 4–5.

— . "Vík er Paradísu lík." *Lesbók Morgunblaðsins* 13 Nov. 1993: 4–5.

— . "Mótunarár Kjarvals." *Lesbók Morgunblaðsins* 30 Sept. 1995: 1–2.

Green, Roger Lancelyn. *Myths of the Norsemen*. London: Puffin Books, 1988.
Grímur Gíslason. "Engan mann sakaði en 400 hús eyðilögðist." *Morgunblaðið* 23 Jan. 1993: 14–16.
Grímur M. Helgason & Vésteinn Ólason. "Laxdæla Saga." *Íslendingasögur 3*. Reykjavík: Skuggsjá, 1969.
Grossman, Mary Louise, John Hamlet. *Birds of Prey of the World*. New York: Clarke N. Potter, Inc., 1964.
Guðbrandur Gíslason. "Komnir af Keltum ekki síður en norskum skerkóngum." *Lesbók Morgunblaðsins* 20 Aug. 1983: 2–3.
Guðmundur Gunnarsson. *The Economic Growth in Iceland 1910–1980. A Productivity Study*. Acta Univ. Upsaliensis, Uppsala, 1990.
Guðmundur Jónsson. "Forfeðravandi Íslendinga." *Morgunblaðið* 28 May 1993.
Guðmundur Ólafsson. "Ljósfæri og lýsing." *Íslensk þjóðmenning I*. Reykjavík: Bókaútgáfan Þjóðsaga, 1987.
Guðmundur Óli Ólafsson. *Skálholt*. Reykjavík: Kirkjuráð íslensku þjóðkirkjunnar, 1988.
Guðmundur P. Ólafsson. *Fuglar í náttúru Íslands*. Reykjavík: Mál og Menning, 1988.
Guðmundur I. Sverrison & Helgi Kristbjarnarson. "Könnun á svefnháttum íslenskra barna." *Læknablaðið* 76 (1990): 357–61.
Guðmundur Þorsteinsson. *Horfnir starfshættir og leiftar frá liðnum öldum*. 2nd ed. Reykjavík: Örn & Örlygur hf., 1990.
Guðni Einarsson. "Risi deyr" *Morgunblaðið* 18 Oct. 1992: 16–18.
——. "Mesta kjörsókn sem um getur." *Morgunblaðið* 17 June 1994: 57.
Guðrún Bjartmarsdóttir, ed. *Bergmál*. Reykjavík: Mál og Menning, 1988.
Guðrún Guðlaugsdóttir. "Allir voru í sólskinsskapi." *Morgunblaðið* 17 June 1994: 62.
Guðrún Kvaran. "Lög un íslensk mannanöfn." *Málfregnir,* n.d.: 13–17.
Guðrún Kvaran and Sigurður Jónsson. *Nöfn Íslendinga*. Reykjavík: Heimskringla, 1991.
Guðrún Norðdal, Sverrir Tómasson, Vésteinn Ólason. *Íslensk Bókmenntasaga I*. Reykjavík: Mál og Menning, 1992.
Guðrún Sveinbjarnardóttir. *Farm Abandonment in Medieval and Post–Medieval Iceland: An Interdisciplinary Study*. Oxbow Monograph 17. Oxford: Oxbow Books, 1992.
Gunnar Hersveinn. "Tundurdufl í næturkíki." *Morgunblaðið* 11 June 1995: B30–31.
Gunnar Jónsson. *Íslenskir fiskar: lýst 293 tegundum sem fundist hafa í íslensku hafsvæði*, 2nd ed. Reykjavík: Fjölvi, 1992.
Gunnar Karlsson and Helgi Skúli Kjartansson. "Plágurnar miklu á Íslandi." *Saga* XXXII 1994: 11–74.
Gunnell, Terry. *The Concept of Ancient Scandinavian Drama: a Reevaluation*. Unpubl. Ph.D. dissertation, University of Leeds, 1991.
Gylfi Þ. Gíslason. *The Problem of Being an Icelander, Past, Present and Future*. Transl. Pétur Kidson Karlsson. Reykjavík: Almenna Bókafélagið, 1973.
——. *Viðreisnarárin*. Reykjavík: Almenna Bókafélagið, 1993.
Hagstofa Íslands. *Tölfræðihandbók (Statistical Abstract of Iceland)*. Reykjavík: Statistical Bureau of Iceland, 1967.
——. *Mannfjöldaskýrslur, árin 1971–80 (Population and Vital Statistics)*. Reykjavík: Statistical Bureau of Iceland, 1988.

Bibliography

——. *Landshagir 1991 (Statistical Abstract of Iceland)*. Reykjavík: Statistical Bureau of Iceland, 1991.

Halldór Halldórsson. *Íslenzkt orðtakasafn I, II*. 2nd ed. Reykjavík: Almenna Bókafélagið, 1978.

Hallmundsson, May and Hallberg Hallmundsson, transl. *Icelandic Folk and Fairy Tales*. Reykjavík: Iceland Review Library, 1987.

Haraldur Ólafsson. "A True Environmental Parable: The Laxá–Mývatn conflict in Iceland, 1965–1973." *Environmental Rev.* 5.2 (1981): 2–38.

——. *Dýr og menn*. Reykjavík: Félagsvísindastofnun Háskóla Íslands, 1992.

Hastrup, Kirsten. *Culture and History in Medieval Iceland*. Oxford University Press, 1985.

Haukur Halldórsson. *Trolls in Icelandic Folklore*. Reykjavík: Örn & Örlygur, 1982.

Helgi Einarsson. *A Manitoba Fisherman*. Transl. George Houser. Winnipeg, Canada: Queenston House, 1982.

Helgi Kristbjarnarson, *et al.* "Könnun á svefnvenjum Íslendinga." *Læknablaðið* 71 (1985): 193–8.

Helgi Torfason. "Strokkur." In *Eyjar í eldhafi*. Reykjavík: Gott mál hf., 1995 109–116.

Hermann Pálsson. "Minnispunktar 1988: Langskip voru illa fallin til siglinga yfir Atlantshafið." *Lesbók Morgunblaðsins* 26 Nov. 1988: 13–14.

——. Minnispunktar 1988: Höldum ráðstefnu um Vínlandsmálið í heild." *Lesbók Morgunblaðsins* 3 Dec. 1988: 14–15.

Hermann Pálsson and Paul Edwards, transl. *Gautrek's Saga and Other Medieval Tales*. London: University of London Press Ltd, 1968.

Hight, G.H., transl. *The Saga of Grettir the Strong*. London: J.M. Dent & Sons, 1972.

Hill, R.I., I.H. Campbell, G.F. Davies, and R.W. Griffiths. "Mantle Plunes and Continental Tectonics." *Science* 10 Apr. 1992: 186–192.

Hitaveita Reykjavíkur. *Nesjavellir*. Reykjavík: 1992.

——. *Almennur Bæklingur*. Reykjavík: July, 1992.

Hjálmar R. Bárðarson. *Fuglar Íslands*. Reykjavík: Hjálmar R. Bárðarsson, 1986.

Hollander, Lee M. *The Skalds: A Selection of Their Poems with Introduction and Notes*. Ann Arbor Paperbacks: University of Michigan Press, 1968.

Hringur Jóhannesson and Þorsteinn frá Hamri, ed. *Tíu þjóðsögur 3*. Reykjavík: Helgafell, 1973.

——. *Tíu þjóðsögur 6* Reykjavík: Helgafell, 1974.

Hulda Valtýsdóttir and Gísli Sigurðsson. "Geysir og hverasvæðið í Haukadal." *Lesbók Morgunblaðsins* 18 June 1987: 7–10.

Hörður Ágústsson. "Íslenski torfbærinn." *Íslensk þjóðmenning I*. Reykjavík: Bókaútgáfan Þjóðsaga, 1987.

Icelandic Nutrition Council. *Nutritional Goals for Icelanders*. Reykjavík: 1994.

Icelandic Sagas, Eddas, and Art (booklet accompanying the Scandinavia Today art exhibit). New York: The Pierpont Morgan Library, 1982.

Ingimar Einarsson. *Patterns of Societal Development in Iceland*. PhD dissertation. University of Uppsala, 1987.

Ingimar Sveinsson. "The Icelandic Horse, Its History, Development and Use." Lecture, Hvanneyri Agric. Coll., 1995.

Ingstad, Helge. *Land Under the Pole Star.* London: Jonathan Cape Ltd, 1966.

— . *Westward to Vinland: The Discovery of Pre–Columbian Norse House–sites in North America.* London: Jonathan Cape Ltd, 1969.

Ingvar Birgir Friðleifsson. "Geothermal activity in Iceland." *Jökull* 29 (1979): 47–56.

Ingvi Þorsteinsson. "Landgæði á Íslandi fyrr og nú." *Morgunblaðið* 12 Nov. 1987: 24–25.

Ingvi Þorsteinsson and Valdimar Jóhannsson. "Brattahlíð og Þingvellir." *Lesbók Morgunblaðsins* 19 Oct. '96: 6–7.

Jóhann Axelsson and Mikael Karlsson. "Furðulegt dæmi um kuldaþol." *Morgunblaðið* 23 June 1985: 22–23.

Jóhannes Nordal and Valdimar Kristinsson, ed. *Iceland 874–1974.* Reykjavík: The Central Bank of Iceland, 1975.

Jón Hnefill Aðalsteinsson. "Norraen trú" and "Þjóðtrú" in *Íslensk þjóðmenning, V.* Ed. Frosti F. Jóhannsson. Reykjavík: Bókaútgáfan Þjóðsaga, 1988. 27–55, 341–400, 415–418.

— . *Strandarkirkja. Helgistaður við haf.* Reykjavík: Univ. of Icel. Press, 1993.

Jón Helgason. *Öldin sautjánda, minnisverð tíðindi 1601–1700.* Reykjavík: Iðunn, 1966.

— . *Öldin sextánda, minnisverð tíðindi 1501–1550.* Reykjavík: Iðunn, 1980.

— . *Tyrkjaránið.* 2nd ed. Reykjavík: Iðunn, 1983.

Jón R. Hjálmarsson. *A Short History of Iceland.* Reykjavík: Almenna Bókmenntafélagið, 1988.

Jón Ólafur Ísberg. "Dýrtíð og neysla á árunum 1914–1918." *Lesbók Morgunblaðsins* 1 Oct 1994: 1–2.

Jón Sigurðsson, The Icelandic Patriot. [n.a.] Reykjavík: S. Eymundsson & S. Jónsson, 1887.

Jón Steffensen. *Menning og meinsemdir.* Reykjavík: Sögufélagið, 1975.

— . "Líkamsleifar" in *Skálholt. Fornleifarannsóknir 1954–1958.* Reykjavík: Lögberg, 1988.

Jon Th. Thor. *British Trawlers in Icelandic Waters.* Transl. Hilmar Foss. Reykjavík: Fjölva Útgáfa, 1992.

Jónas Jónasson frá Hrafnagili. *Íslenskir þjóðhættir.* Reykjavík: Ísafold, 1934 & 1961.

Jónas Kristjánsson. *Handritin og fornsögurnar.* Reykjavík: Bókaforlagið Saga, 1970.

Jones, Gwynn. *The Norse Atlantic Saga.* London: Oxford Univ. Press, 1964.

Keller, Christian. *The Eastern Settlement Reconsidered: Some Analyses of Norse Medieval Greenland.* Oslo: 1989.

Kidd, K.K. and L.L. Cavalli–Sforza. "The role of genetic drift in the differentiation of Icelandic and Norwegian cattle." *Evolution* 28.3: 381–395.

Kielland, Else Christie. *Stave Churches and Viking Ships.* Oslo: Dreyers Forlag A/S, 1981.

Kristinn H. Skarphéðinsson, *et al.* "Varpútbreiðsla og fjöldi hrafna á Íslandi." *Bliki* Mar. 1992: 1–26.

Kristín Ástgeirsdóttir, ed. *Reykjavík miðstöð þjóðlífs.* 2nd ed. Reykjavík: Sögufélag, 1978.

Bibliography

Kristín María Baldursdóttir. "Átak, erindi sem erfiði?" *Morgunblaðið* 15 July, no year.

Kristín Marja Baldursdóttir. "Hraustir menn...eða hvað?" *Morgunblaðið* 17 Jan. 1993: 1B–2B, 4B.

——. "Lundin eins og landið." *Morgunblaðið* 5 Nov. 1995: 12.

Kristín Þorsteinsdóttir. *Jurtalitun. Forsagnir.* Reykjavík: Skrifstofan íslenzk ull, 1942.

Kristjansson, Wilhelm. *The Icelandic People in Manitoba.* Winnipeg: Wallingford Press, 1965.

Kristján Albertsson. *Hannes Hafstein. Ævisaga.* Reykjavík: Almenna Bókafélagið, 1961.

Kristján Eldjárn, et al. *Skálholt, Fornleifarannsóknir 1954–1958.* Reykjavík: Lögberg, 1988.

Kristján Sæmundsson. "Outline of the geology of Iceland." *Jökull* (29) 1979: 7–28.

Kristján Þórhallsson. "Mývatnseldar 1724–1729." *Morgunblaðið* 11 May 1993: 43.

Landström, Björn. *The Ship.* Transl. Michael Phillips. Garden City, NY: Doubleday & Co., Inc., 1961. 52–65.

Langer, William L., compiler and ed. *An Encyclopedia of World History.* Boston: Houghton Mifflin, 1952.

Laufey Steingrímsdóttir. "Hvað borða Íslendingar?" *Morgunblaðið* 1 May 1991: 14.

Lomax, Judy. *The Viking Voyage.* London: Hutchinson, 1992.

Lúðvík Kristjánsson. *Íslenskir sjávarhættir V.* Reykjavík: Bókaútgáfa Menningarsjóðs, 1986.

Lýður Björnsson. *Frá siðaskiptum til sjálfstæðisbaráttu. Íslandssaga 1550–1830.* Reykjavík: Bókaverslun Sigfúsar Eymundssonar, 1973.

Maggs, F. B. *Jorgen Jorgensen, the King of Iceland.* Typescript. Radlett Literary Society, Oct. 20, 1952.

Magnusson, Magnus. *Viking Hammer of the North.* London: Orbis Publishing, 1976.

Magnusson, Magnus and Herman Pálsson, transl. *Njal's Saga.* Harmondsworth, England: Penguin Books, 1960.

——. *King Harald's Saga.* Harmondsworth: Penguin Books, 1966.

——. *Laxdæla Saga.* Middlesex, England: Penguin Books, 1969.

Marcus, G.J. *The Conquest of the North Atlantic.* Woodbridge, Suffolk: The Boydell Press, 1980.

Margrét Hermanns–Auðardóttir. *Islands Tidiga Bosättning.* Umeå Universitet, Arkeologiska Institutionen, 1989.

——. "The Beginning of Settlement in Iceland in Light of Archaeological Investigations in Herjólfsdalur, Vestmannaeyjar." 1993.

Margrét Þorvaldsdóttir. "Vínlandsfundur og leiðangrarnir fimm." *Morgunblaðið* 17 Dec 91.

Markús Á. Einarsson. *Veðurfar á Íslandi.* Reykjavík: Iðunn, 1976.

——. *Veðurfræði.* Reykjavík: Iðunn, 1981.

Matthiasson, Thorolfur. "Consequences of local government involvement in the Icelandic ITQ market." Manuscript. 6 Jan. 1997.

McConville, Michael. "Friðsamleg innrás í Ísland." *Lesbók Morgunblaðsins* 19 Nov. 1994: 4.

McGhee, Robert. "Contact between native North Americans and the medieval Norse: A review of the evidence." *Am. Antiquity*, 49.1 (1984): 4–26.

McGovern, Thomas H. "Climate, correlation, and causation in Norse Greenland." *Arctic Anthropology*, 28.2 (1991): 77–100.

Menard, H.W. *Islands*. Scientific American Library 17. New York: Scientific American Books, Inc., 1986.

Ministry for the Environment. *Iceland: National Report to UNCED*. Reykjavík: 1992.

Morgunblaðið. "Merkur fundur húsarústa og steina á Dagverðarnesi við Breiðafjörð." (Interview with Þorvaldur Friðriksson). 16 July 1985.

— . "Vestmannaeyjar: Dauf lundaveiði en úteyjalífið hefur sinn gang." 22 July 1986.

— . "Peningaverslun hefði komið Íslendingum vel en kaupmenn voru henni andsnúnir." (Interview with Gísli Gunnarsson). 27 July 1986.

— . "Sagan var skráð við Hagatorg." 24 Oct. 1986: 14–15.

— . "Breytingar á skórdýrafánu Íslands eftir landnám." (Interview with Gísli Már Gíslason). 23 Nov. 1986: 4C–5C.

— . "Er Ísland kennt við guði en ekki hafís?" (Interview with Agnar Þórðarson). 7 Dec. 1986 .

— . "Fálkarnir fljúga með þotum til Saudi Arabíu." 5 Apr. 1987: 22B.

— . "Björgunarafrekið við Látrabjarg fyrir 40 árum." *Lesbók Morgunblaðsins* 5 Dec. 1987: 11–12.

— . "Ísland og umheimurinn. Írsk svik." (Interview with Anna Agnarsdóttir). 13 Mar. 1988.

— . "Almenningur á verði gegn fálkaþjófum." 11 June 1988.

— . "Víkur hann sér í Viðeyjarklaustur. Gömul saga rakin." 14 Aug. 1988: 4B

— . "Höll höfðingja." 14 Aug. 1988.

— . "Sigríður Pétursdóttir, Hundadaman." 30 July 1989: C3.

— . "Hertaka Íslands: 'Ekki stundinni lengur en stríðsnauðsyn krefur.'" 11 May 1940 (Rpt. in *Lesbók Morgunblaðsins* 5 May 1990: 1.

— . "Lífsskoðanir Íslendinga." 17 Sept. 1991: Section B.

— . "Diplómatískur stórsigur Íslendinga." 15 Dec. 1991: 26–27.

— . "Réttarfarið tekur stakkaskiptum." 1 July 1992: 21.

— . "Ný rannsókn á skammdegisþunglyndi." 8 Dec. 1992: 63.

— . "Fálkaþjófar handteknir í Þýskalandi." 25 Mar. 1993.

— . "Greiðslur varnarliðsins jafngilda tekjum af 100 þúsund tonna þorskafla." 7 May 1993: 18.

— . "Surtsey þrítug." 14 Nov. 1993: 1–2B, 4B.

— . "Eins og tíu Esjur væru á ferðinni." 10 Feb. 1994.

— . "Jökulmassinn springur og ryðst fram með braki og brestum." 6 Mar. 1994: 12B–15B.

— . "120 hafernir á landinu." 16 Sept. 1994. (Interview with Kristinn Skarphéðinsson).

— . "Heimaeyjargosið 1973: Stærsta innlenda verkefni RKÍ frá upphafi." 10 Dec. 1994: E7.

— . "Jólasiðakönnun Hagvangs." 24 Dec. 1994: 10.

Bibliography

— . "Eitt stærsta hlaup frá upphafi." 28 July 1995: 6.

— . "Eitt kröftugt nafn í stað tikkatikk." 18 Aug. 1995: 4–5B.

— . "Bölsýnin kvödd." 27 Aug. 1995: 11.

— . "Reykjavíkurfundurinn markaði tímamót." 1 Oct. 1995: 14.

— . "Kenninafn til móður verður sífellt algengara meðal íslenskra kvenna." 13 Oct. 1995: B5.

— . "Miklir mannskaðar í snjóflóðum." 27 Oct. 1995: 13.

— . "Ættarnöfn fleiri en föðurnöfn." 27 Apr. 1996: 64.

Njörður P. Njarðvík. *Birth of a Nation*. Transl. John Porter. Reykjavík: Iceland Review, 1978.

— . *Dauðamenn*. Reykjavík: Iðunn, 1982.

OECD Economic Surveys: Iceland. OECD, 1991.

OECD Education Committee. *Review of Educational Policy in Iceland: Examiners' Report and Questions*. Paris: OECD, 9 May 1986.

Ogilvie, A.E.J. "Climate and Economy in Eighteenth Century Iceland." In Catherine Delano Smith and Martin Parry, eds., *Consequences of Climatic Change*. Nottingham: University of Nottingham, 1981. 54–69.

Ólafur Ásgeirsson. "Íslenska fánann í öndvegi." *Morgunblaðið* 11 Mar. 1994.

Ólafur Briem, ed. *Eddukvæði*. Íslenzk úrvalsrit 5. Skálholt, 1968.

Ólafur Egilsson. "Kólumbus á Íslandi." *Lesbók Morgunblaðsins* 17 Dec. 1991: 44.

Ólafur Ragnar Grímsson. "The Icelandic Power Structure, 1800–2000." *Scand. Pol. Studies* 11 (1976): 9–33.

Ólafur Stephensen. "Viðey. Gömul saga að baki vinsældum nútímans." *List* 3.1 (1991).

Ólína Þorvarðardóttir. "Galdrasagan – þroskasaga þjóðar." *Lesbók Morgunblaðsins* 24 Dec. 1994.

Óperublaðið. "Mikill fjöldi tónlistariðkenda." Mar. 1993.

Óskar Halldórsson. *Hrafnkels Saga, Freysgoða*. Reykjavík: Skálholt, 1971.

— . *Egils saga*. Skálholt hf., 1975.

Páll Bergthorsson. *The Weather in Iceland*. 2nd ed. Reykjavík: Icelandair, n.d.

— . "Sensitivity of Icelandic Agriculture to Climatic Variations." *Climatic Change*, 7 (1985): 11–127.

— . "Jan Mayen er Svalbarði." *Lesbók Morgunblaðsins* 5 June 1993.

— . "Sigling á víkingaskipum." *Lesbók Morgunblaðsins* 26 Aug. 1995.

Páll Einarsson and Sveinbjörn Björnsson. "Earthquakes in Iceland." *Jökull* 29 (1979): 37–43.

Páll Hersteinsson and Guttormur Sigbjarnarson. *Villt íslensk spendýr*. Reykjavík: Náttúrufræðifélag– Landvernd, 1993.

Páll Theodórsson. "Hófst landnám á Íslandi skömmu eftir árið 700?" *Lesbók Morgunblaðsins* 20 Mar. 1993: 8–9.

Pétursson, P.M. "A Résumé of the Story of the Icelandic Unitarian Church." *Lögberg–Heimskringla* 14 Mar. 1968.

Ponzi, Frank. *Ísland á 18. öld*. Reykjavík: Almenna Bókafélagið, 1980.

Ragnar Borg. "Hvers vegna finnst víkingamynt í Maine?" *Morgunblaðið* 6 June 1987: 20.

Ragnhildur Sverrrisdóttir. "Eilífur ófriður um mannanöfn." *Morgunblaðið* 27 Apr. 1996: 32–33.

Rauschenberg, Roy A., ed. "The Journals of Joseph Banks's Voyage up Great Britain's West Coast to Iceland and to the Orkney Isles, July to October, 1771." *Proc. Am. Phil. Soc.* June 1973.

Scholes, Percy A. *The Oxford Companion to Music.* 10th ed. London: Oxford University Press, 1975.

Self, Margaret Cabell. *Horseman's Encyclopedia.* Stanford CT: A.S. Barnes & Co., Oak Tree Publications 1963.

Severin, Tim. *The Brendan Voyage.* New York: Avon, 1979.

Sigrún Davíðsdóttir. "Handritamálið og stjórnmálatogstreita." *Morgunblaðið* 16 June 1994: 50–51.

Sigurður Bjarnason. "Frá slóðum Jóns Indíafara." *Lesbók Morgunblaðsins* 5 Sept. 1992.

Sigurður Líndal, ed. *Saga Íslands I.* Reykjavík: Sögufélagið, 1974.

Sigurður A. Magnússon. *The Northern Sphinx.* London: C. Hurst & Co., Ltd., 1977.

Sigurður Nordal, ed. *Þjóðsagnabókin II, III.* Reykjavík: Almenna Bókafélagið, 1973.

Sigurður B. Stefánsson. "Engin verðbólga, uppbygging eigna, aukin framleiðni." *Morgunblaðið* 8 Sept.1994: 4B.

Sigurður Þórarinsson (S. Thorarinsson), ed. *On the Geology and Geophysics of Iceland.* Reykjavík: Icelandic Government Organizing Committee, 1960.

— . "Sambúð lands og lýðs í ellefu aldir." *Saga Íslands I.* Reykjavík: Sögufélagið, 1974. 29–97.

Sigurður Ægisson. "Sjófuglanytjar Íslendinga fyrr á tímum." *Lesbók Morgunblaðsins* 14 May 1994: 4–6.

Símon Jón Jóhannsson. *Sjö, níu, þrettán. Hjátrú Íslendinga í daglega lífinu.* Reykjavík: Vaka–Helgafell, 1993.

Skarphéðinn Þórisson. "Landnám, útbreiðsla og stofnstærð stara á Íslandi." *Náttúrufræðingurinn* 51.4 (1981): 145–163.

Skúli V. Guðjónsson. *Manneldi og heilsufar í fornöld.* Reykjavík: Ísafold, 1949.

Smiley, Jane. *Grænlendingarnir.* Transl. Sigurlína Davíðsdóttir. Reykjavík: Bókaútgáfan Hildur, 1991.

Snorri G. Bergsson. "Fangarnir á Mön." *Ný saga* 1996: 4–30.

Snorri Sturluson. *Edda.* Ed. Heimir Pálsson. Reykjavík: Mál og Menning, 1984.

State Electric Power Works. *Krafla Power Plant.* n.d.

Stefán Aðalsteinsson. "Um uppruna íslenskra nautgripa." *Náttúrufræðingurinn,* 4 (1976): 238–240.

— . "Írskir þrælar og landnám Íslands." *Lesbók Morgunblaðsins* 18 Jan. 1991: 10–11.

— . "Hvar eru rætur okkar? um írskan uppruna og norskan." *Heilbrigðismál* 3 (1995): 21–24.

Stefán Karlsson. "Tungan." In *Íslensk þjóðmenning VI.* Reykjavík: Bókaútgáfan Þjóðsaga, 1989. 3–54, 439–440.

Stefán Ólafsson. *Modernization in Iceland.* Multilithed copy. Reykjavík: University of Iceland, 1981.

— . *"Hvernig eru Íslendingar? Nokkrar vísbendingar um gildi í menningu Íslendinga."* Multilithed copy. Reykjavík: University of Iceland, 1985.

Sturla Friðriksson. "Grass and grass utilization in Iceland." *Ecology* 535.5 (1972): 785–796.

Bibliography

— . "Þróun lífríkisins og nytjar af því." *Íslensk þjóðmenning I.* Reykjavík: Bókaútgáfan Þjóðsaga, 1987, 149–194.

— . *Surtsey. Lífríki í mótun.* Reykjavík: Náttúrufræðifélag–Sursteyjarfélagið, 1994.

Suðurnes Regional Heating Corp. *Suðurnes Regional Heating.* n.d.

Svanur Kristjánsson. *Conflict and Consensus in Icelandic Politics 1916–44.* Ph.D. dissertaion. Urbana IL: University of Illinois, 1977.

— . *Frá flokksræði til persónustjórnmála. Fjórflokkarnir 1959–1991.* Reykjavík: Félagsvísindastofnun, University of Iceland, 1994.

Sveinbjörn Björnsson, ed. *Iceland and Mid–Ocean Ridges.* Report XXXVIII. Reykjavík: Vísindafélag Íslendinga, 1967.

Sveinn Jakobsson. "Rof Surtseyjar." In *Eyjar í eldhafi.* Reykjavík: Gottmál hf., 1995. 277–282.

Sölvi Sveinsson. *Íslenskir málshættir með skýringum og dæmum.* Reykjavík: Iðunn, 1995.

— . *Íslensk orðtök með skýringum og dæmum.* 2nd ed. Reykjavík: Iðunn, 1995.

Thordarson, Th., and S. Self. "The Laki (Skaftár Fires) and Grímsvötn Eruptions in 1783–1785." *Bull. Volcanol.* 2993.375 (1993): 1–31.

Tómas Þór Tómasson. *Heimsstyrjaldarárin á Íslandi 1939–1945 I, II.* Reykjavík: Örn & Örlygur hf., 1983.

Tómas Tryggvason and Freysteinn Sigurðsson. "Hagnýt jarðefni." In *Náttúra Íslands.* Reykjavík: Almenna Bókafélagið, 1981. 201–235.

Tonnelat, E. "Teutonic Mythology," in *New Larousse Encyclopedia of Mythology.* London: Hamlyn, 1982. 245–280.

Turville–Petre, G. *Origins of Icelandic Literature.* Oxford: Clarendon Press, 1975.

Urður Gunnarsdóttir. "Íslandsvinurinn." (Article on Sir Joseph Banks). *Morgunblaðið* 25 July 1993: B2–B3.

— . "Fangarnir frá Íslandi." (Interview with Snorri G. Bergsson.) *Morgunblaðið* 11 Feb. 1996: 20.

Valþór Hlöðversson. "Hvalveiðar eldri en Íslandsbyggð." *Þjóðviljinn* 16 Nov. 1986: 4–5.

Vésteinn Ólason. "Kvæði af Ólafi liljurós." In *The Traditional Ballads of Iceland.* Reykjavík: Stofnun Árna Magnússonar, 1982.

Vilhjálmur Örn Vilhjálmsson. "Beinaflutningur á Stöng í Þjórsárdal." *Lesbók Morgunblaðsins* 18 Jan. 1997: 4–5.

Walters, Thorstina. *Modern Sagas: The Story of the Icelanders in North America.* Fargo, North Dakota: North Dakota Institute for Regional Studies, 1953.

Wesneski, James. "Success on an International Scale." *Atlantica,* Summer 1992: 59.

White, R.S. "A hot–spot model for early Tertiary volcanism in the N Atlantic." In A.C. Morton and L.M. Parson, eds., *Early Tertiary Volcanism and the Opening of the NE Atlantic.* Oxford: The Geological Society, Blackwell Scientific Publications, 1988.

White, Robert S., and Dan P. McKenzie. "Volcanism at Rifts." *Sci. Am.* July 1989: 44–55.

Wilson, Ian. *Kólumbus í kjölfar Leifs (The Columbus Myth).* Transl. Jón Þ. Þór. Reykjavík: Fjölvaútgáfa, 1992.

Þjóðhagsstofnun. *Þjóðhagsreikningar 1945–1992*. Report #13. Reykjavík: Aug., 1994.

Þorgeir Ibsen. "Landnám sonnettunnar á Íslandi." *Lesbók Morgunblaðsins* 21 Dec. 1994: 32–33.

Þorleifur Einarsson. "Jarðsaga Íslands." In Sigurður Líndal, ed., *Saga Íslands I*. Reykjavík: Sögufélagið, 1974: 3–26.

—— . *Geology of Iceland, Rocks and Landscape*. Transl. Georg Douglas. Reykjavík: Mál og Menning, 1994.

Þorsteinn Einarsson. "Keltnesk fangbrögð." *Lesbók Morgunblaðsins* 21 Dec. 1987: 44–46.

—— . "Íslenskar súlubyggðir or saga þeirra." *Náttúrufræðingurinn* 57.4 (1987): 163–184.

Þorsteinn Gylfason. "Að hugsa á íslensku." *Skírnir* 1973: 129–158.

Þorvaldur Þórðarson. *Skaftáreldar 1783–1785: gjóskan og framvinda gossins*. Reykjavík: Háskólaútgáfan og Raunvísindadeild, 1990.

Þór Whitehead. "Kynþáttastefna Íslands." *Lesbók Morgunblaðsins* 13 Jan. 1974: 4–6, 14–15.

—— . *Hernám og stríðsár á Íslandi 1940–45*. Reykjavík: Norræna Húsið, 1990.

—— . *Milli vonar og ótta*. Reykjavík: Vaka–Helgafell, 1995.

—— . "Iceland's Foreign Policy, 1946–1996." ms.

Þórhallur Ásgeirsson. "Efnahagsaðstoðin 1948–1953." *Fjármálatíðindi II* 2 (1955): 61–70.

Þórunn Valdimarsdóttir. *Snorri á Húsafelli*. Reykjavík: Almenna Bókafélagið, 1989.

Ævar Petersen. "Brot úr sögu geirfuglsins." *Náttúrufræðingurinn* 65.1–2 (1995): 53–66.

Index

Index

Index

Index

Index

Index

About the Author

Photo by: Guðmundur Kr. Jóhannsson

Following a childhood spent in Baltimore and on an island off the Maine coast, Terry G. Lacy earned a B.A. degree from Smith College in music, and was elected to Phi Beta Kappa. College included a year studying at the University of Florence and living with an Italian family. Marriage, three children, teaching flute, and living in various parts of the United States were followed by a return to graduate school and completion of the Ph.D. degree in sociology at Colorado State University, with strong components in anthropology and psychology. A deep interest in cultural differences and in Iceland in particular led her to accept a Fulbright Senior Lectureship in 1973 and subsequently to make her home in Reykjavík.